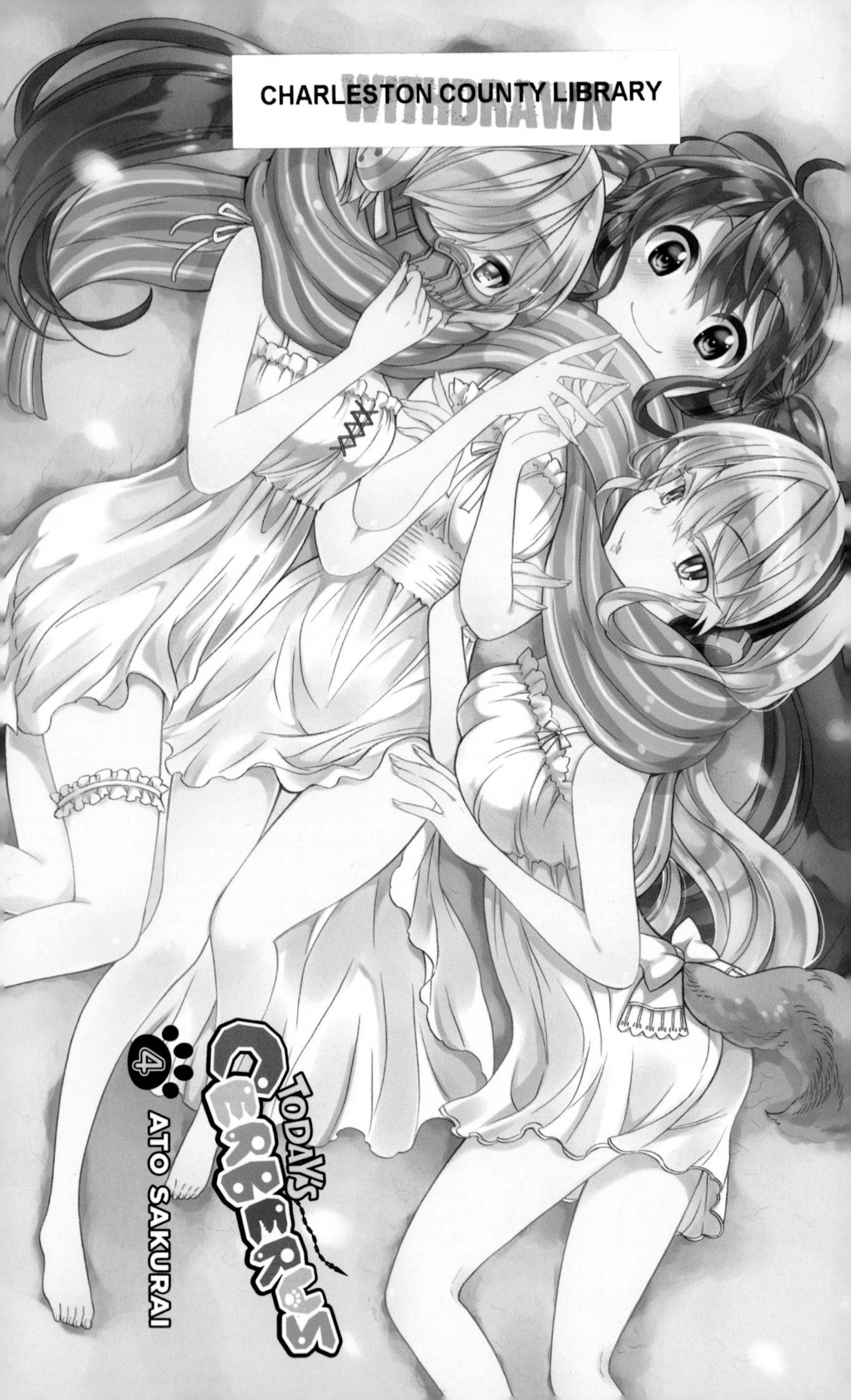
TODAY'S CERBERUS
4
ATO SAKURAI

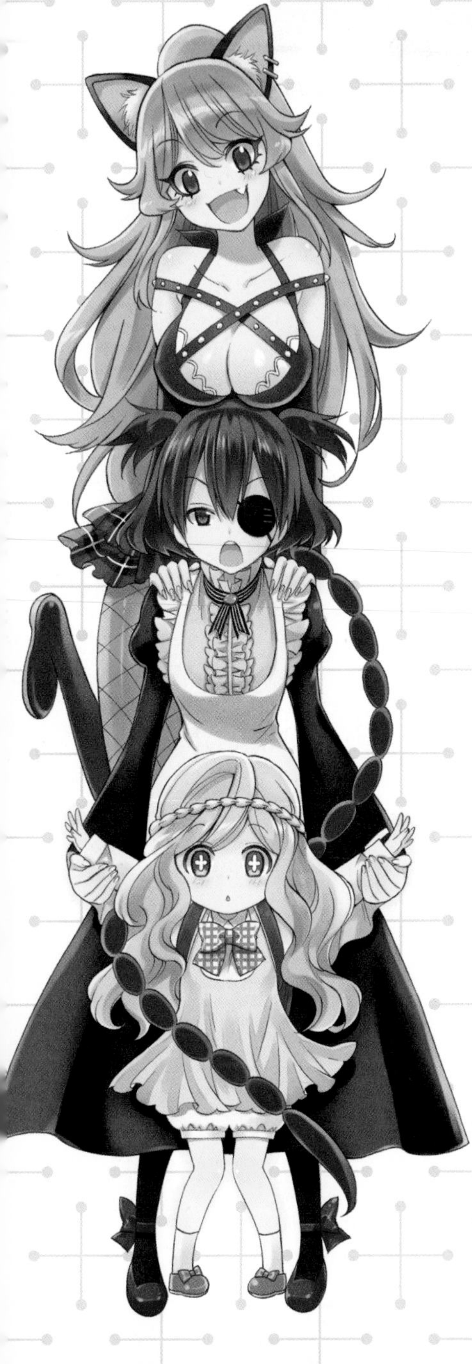

CONTENTS

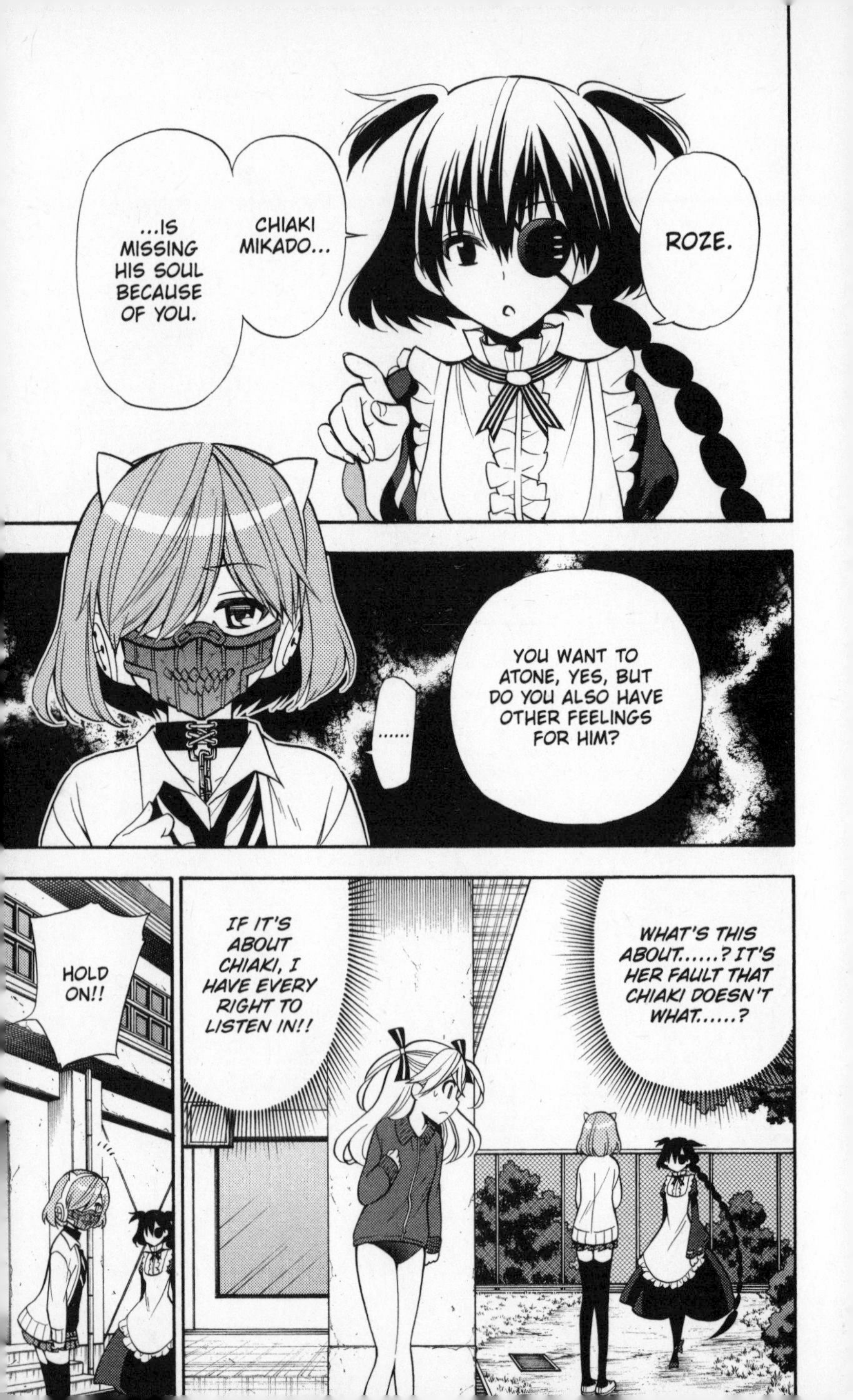
ROZE.
CHIAKI MIKADO...
...IS MISSING HIS SOUL BECAUSE OF YOU.
YOU WANT TO ATONE, YES, BUT DO YOU ALSO HAVE OTHER FEELINGS FOR HIM?
......
WHAT'S THIS ABOUT......? IT'S HER FAULT THAT CHIAKI DOESN'T WHAT......?
IF IT'S ABOUT CHIAKI, I HAVE EVERY RIGHT TO LISTEN IN!!
HOLD ON!!

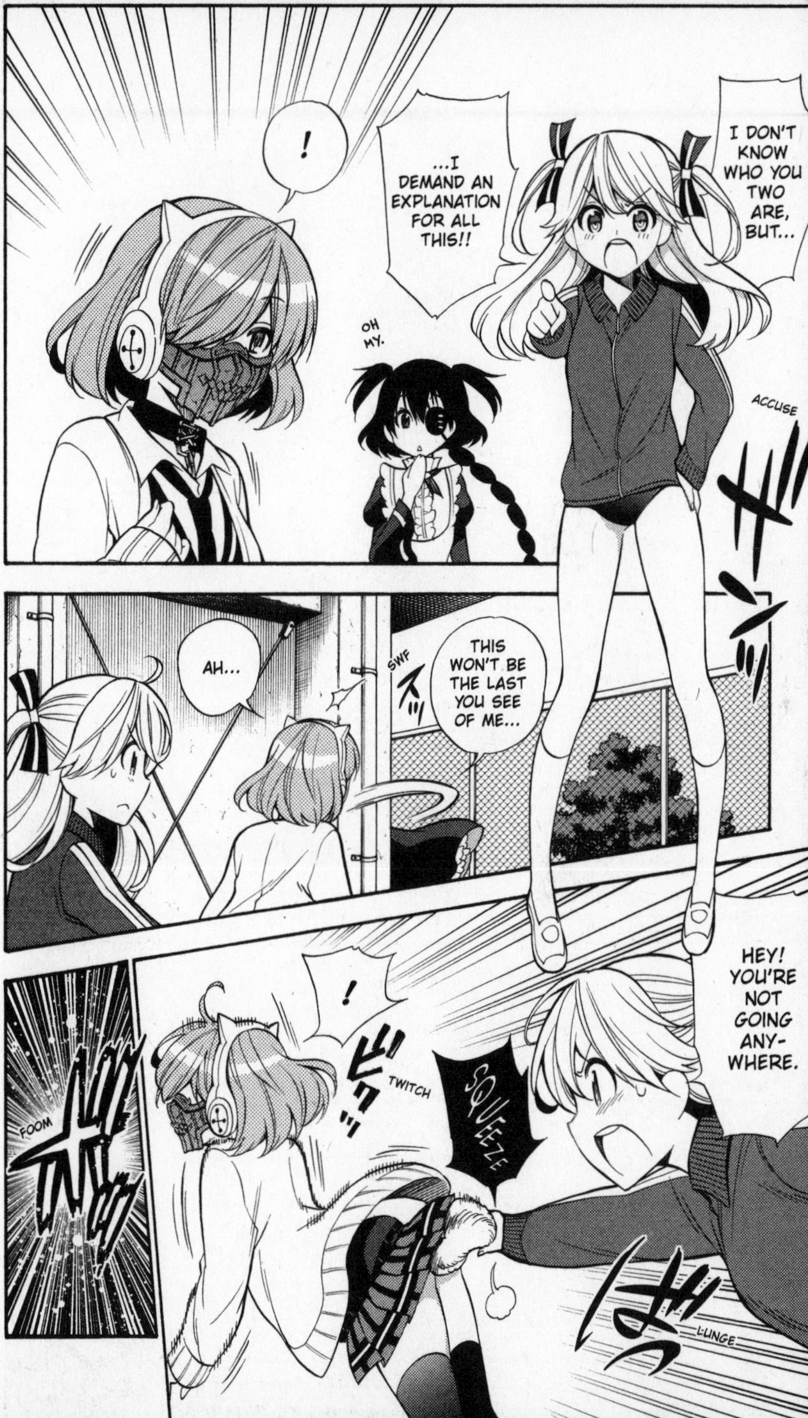
I DON'T KNOW WHO YOU TWO ARE, BUT...
...I DEMAND AN EXPLANATION FOR ALL THIS!!
!
OH MY.
ACCUSE
THIS WON'T BE THE LAST YOU SEE OF ME...
SWF
AH...
HEY! YOU'RE NOT GOING ANY-WHERE.
LUNGE
SQUEEZE
TWITCH
!
FOOM

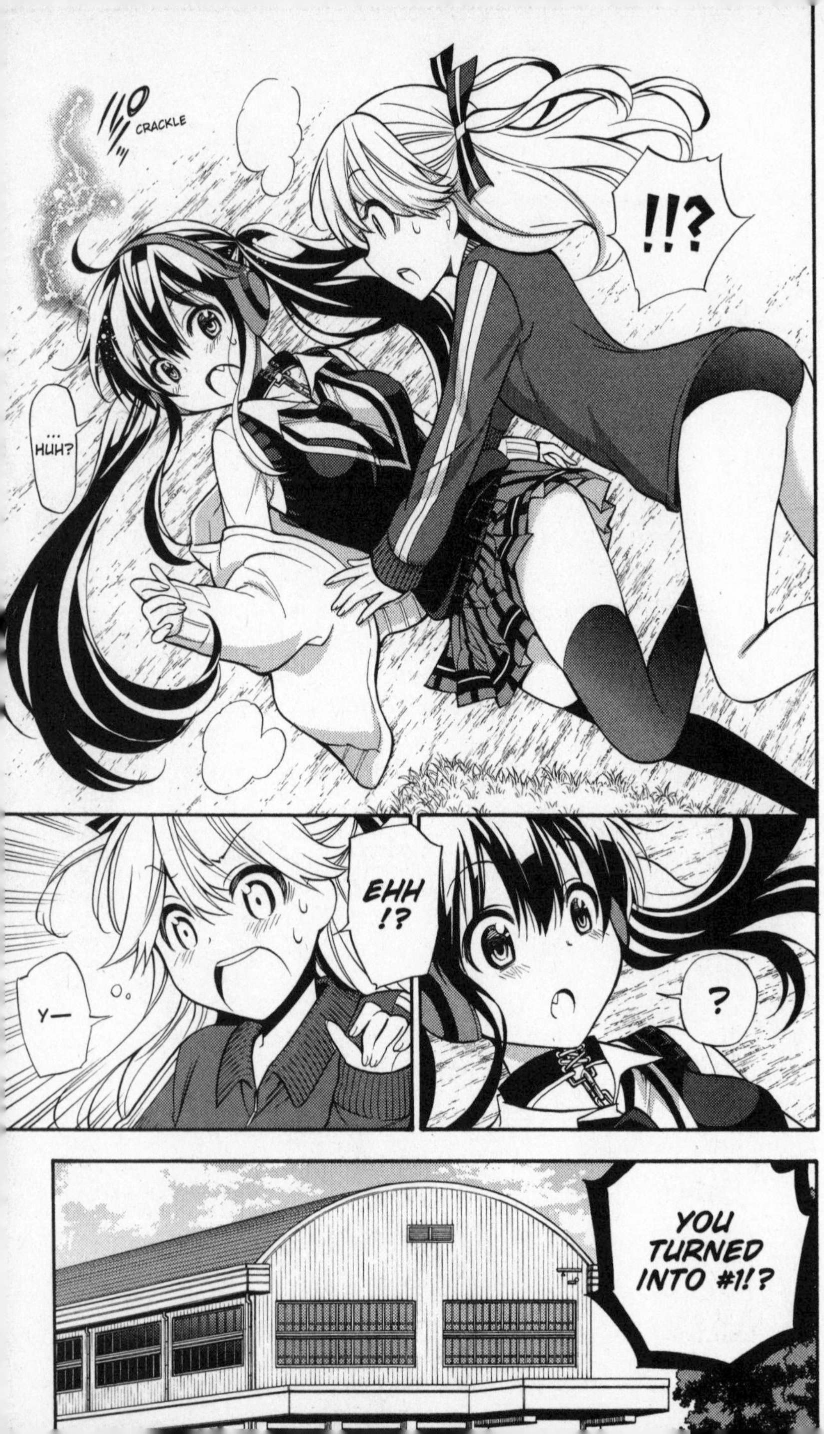
CRACKLE
!!?
...HUH?
?
EHH!?
Y—
YOU TURNED INTO #1!?

CHAPTER 15
ROZE'S HEART

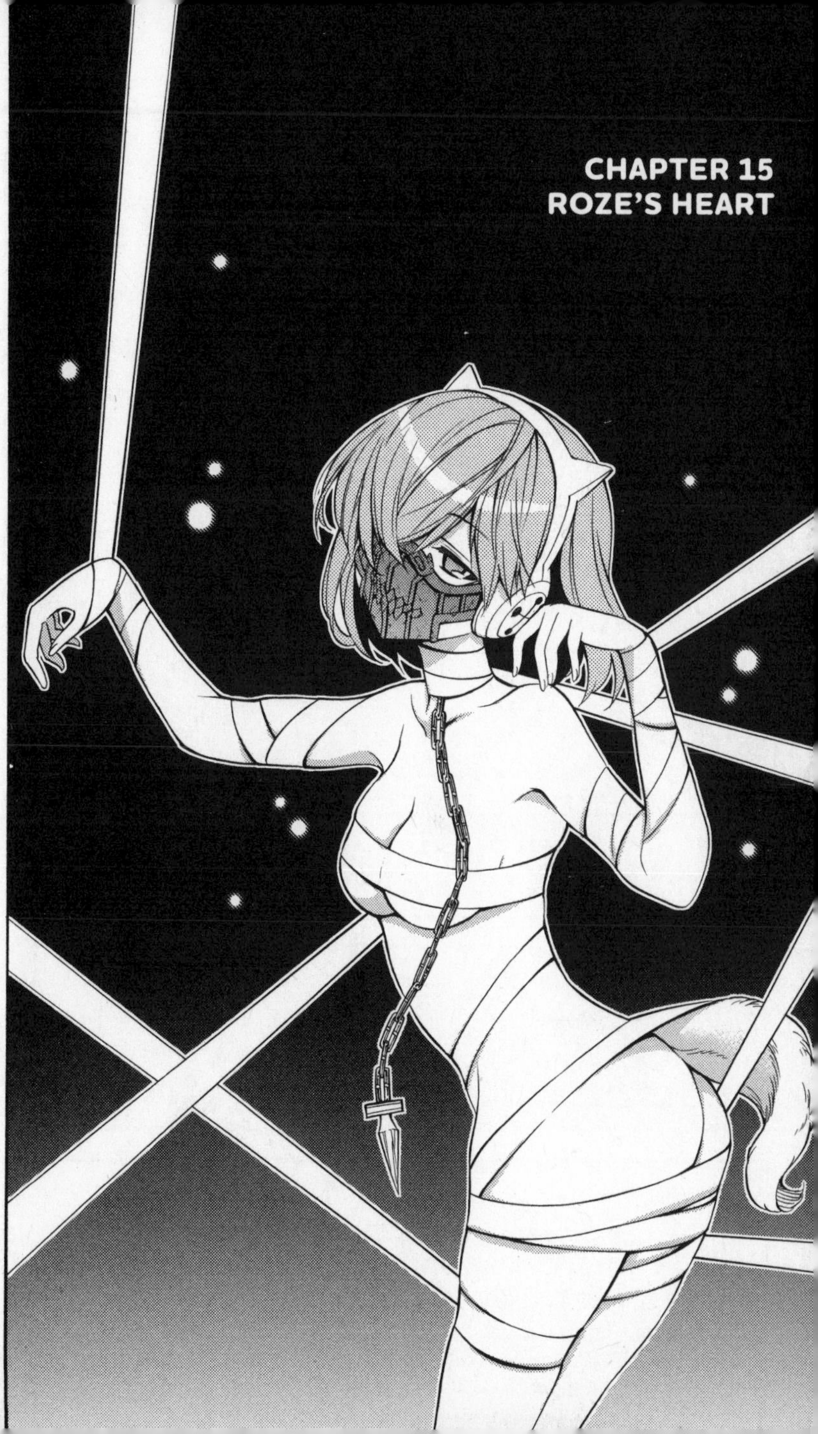

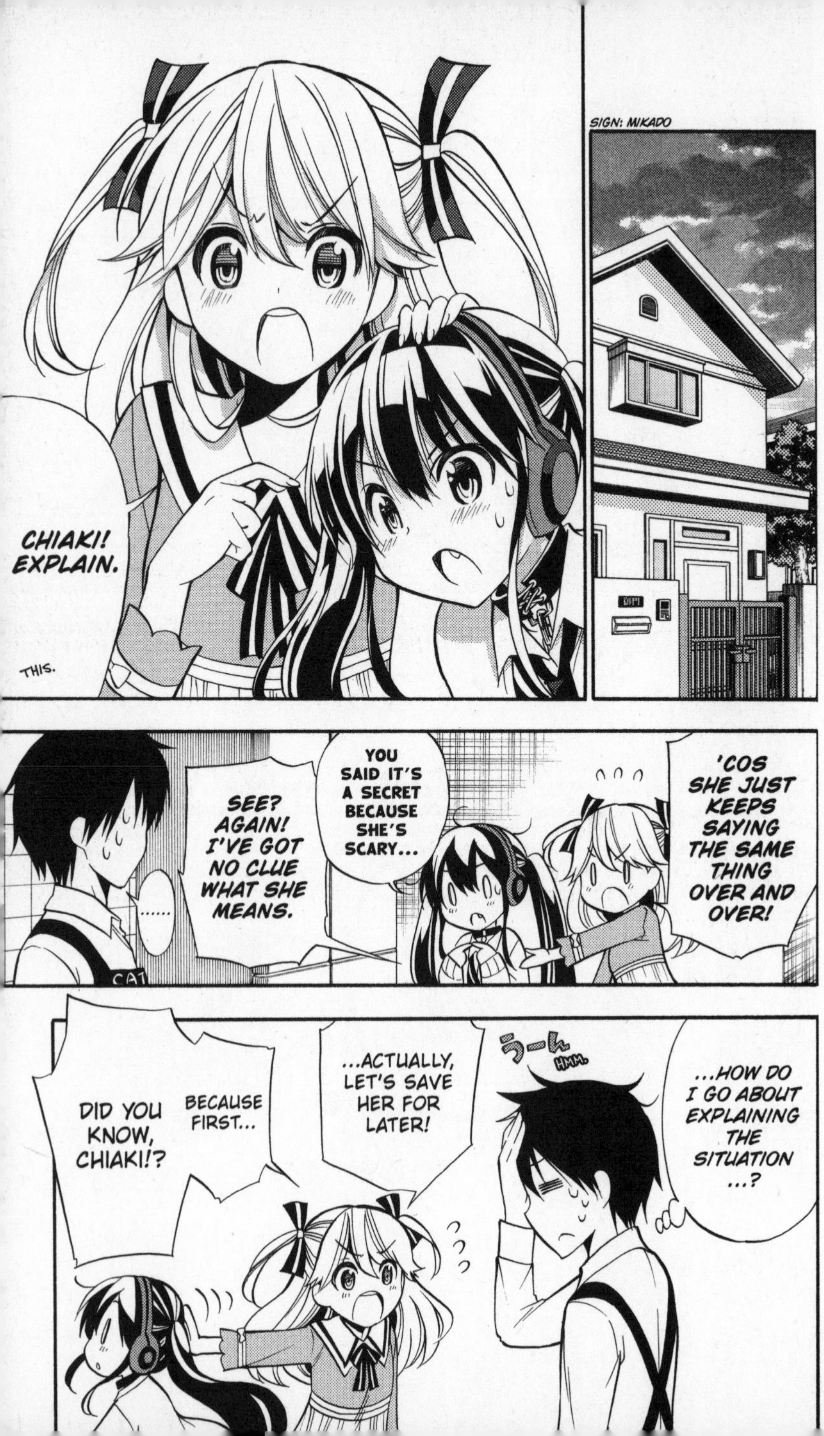
SIGN: MIKADO
CHIAKI! EXPLAIN.
THIS.
'COS SHE JUST KEEPS SAYING THE SAME THING OVER AND OVER!
YOU SAID IT'S A SECRET BECAUSE SHE'S SCARY...
SEE? AGAIN! I'VE GOT NO CLUE WHAT SHE MEANS.
......
...HOW DO I GO ABOUT EXPLAINING THE SITUATION ...?
うーん
HMM.
...ACTUALLY, LET'S SAVE HER FOR LATER!
BECAUSE FIRST...
DID YOU KNOW, CHIAKI!?

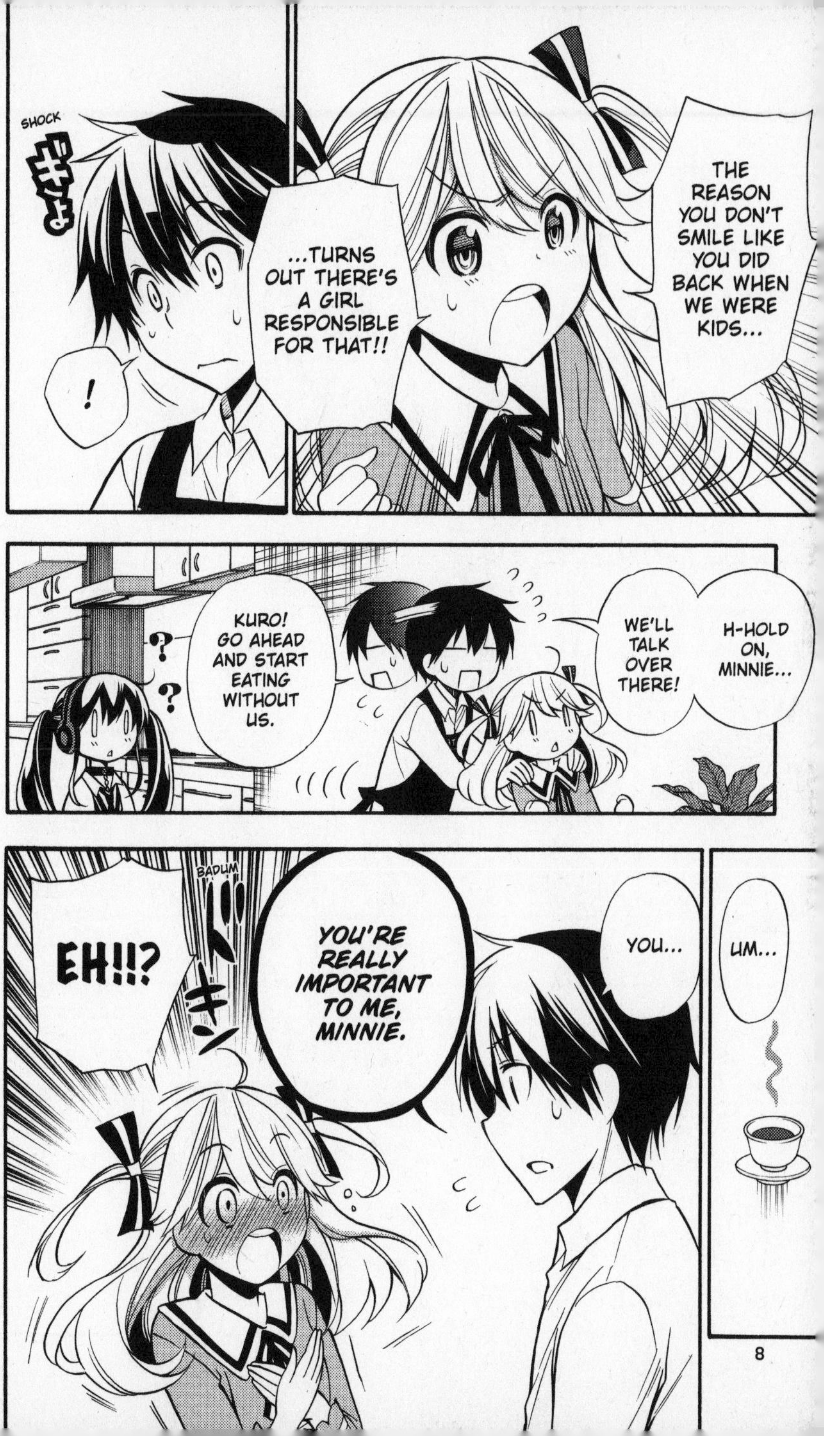
THE REASON YOU DON'T SMILE LIKE YOU DID BACK WHEN WE WERE KIDS...
...TURNS OUT THERE'S A GIRL RESPONSIBLE FOR THAT!!
SHOCK
!
H-HOLD ON, MINNIE...
WE'LL TALK OVER THERE!
KURO! GO AHEAD AND START EATING WITHOUT US.
?
?
UM...
YOU...
YOU'RE REALLY IMPORTANT TO ME, MINNIE.
BADUM
EH!!?

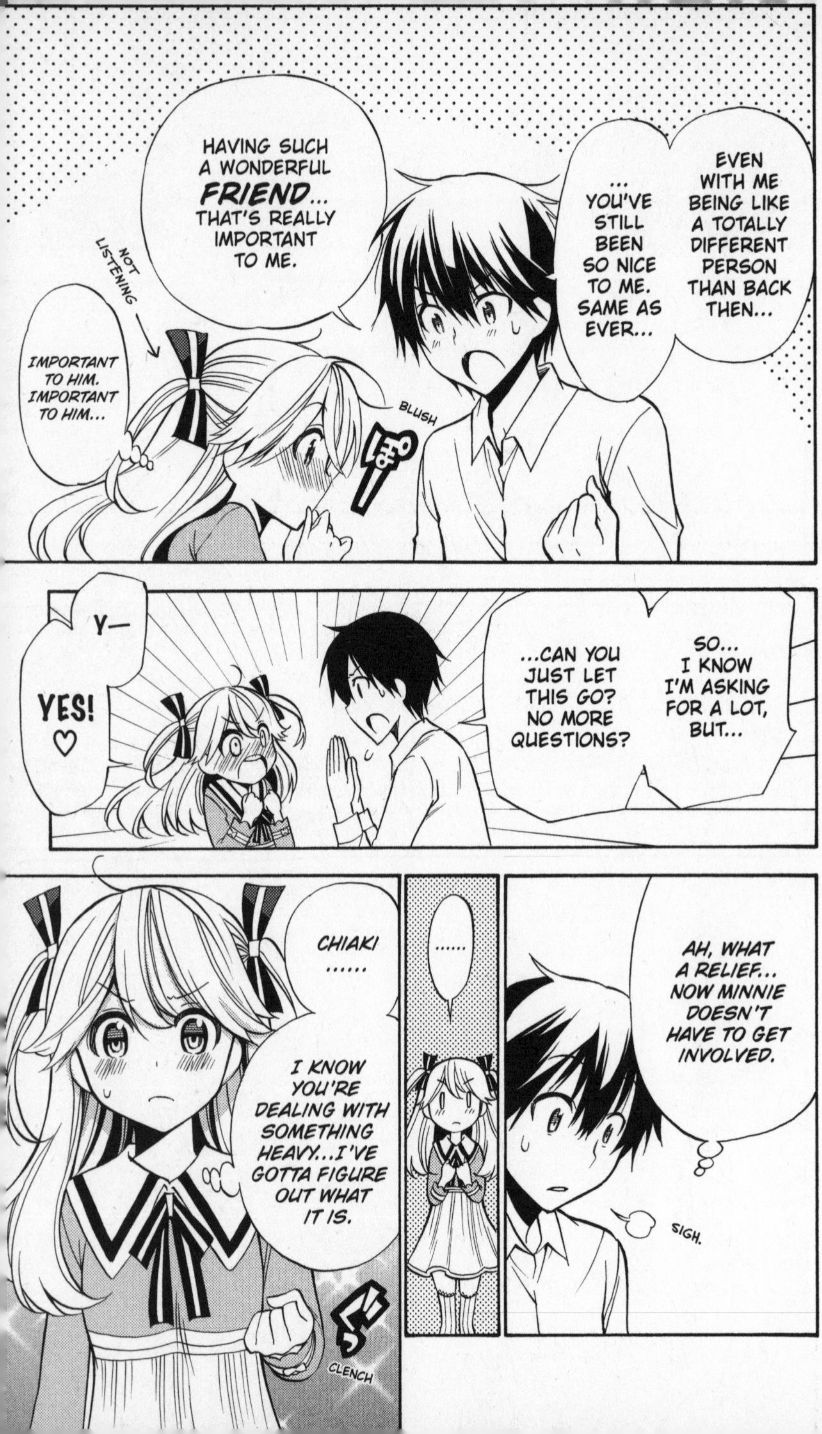

EVEN WITH ME BEING LIKE A TOTALLY DIFFERENT PERSON THAN BACK THEN...
... YOU'VE STILL BEEN SO NICE TO ME. SAME AS EVER...
HAVING SUCH A WONDERFUL FRIEND... THAT'S REALLY IMPORTANT TO ME.
NOT LISTENING
IMPORTANT TO HIM. IMPORTANT TO HIM...
BLUSH
SO... I KNOW I'M ASKING FOR A LOT, BUT...
...CAN YOU JUST LET THIS GO? NO MORE QUESTIONS?
Y— YES! ♡
AH, WHAT A RELIEF... NOW MINNIE DOESN'T HAVE TO GET INVOLVED.
SIGH.
......
CHIAKI ......
I KNOW YOU'RE DEALING WITH SOMETHING HEAVY...I'VE GOTTA FIGURE OUT WHAT IT IS.
CLENCH

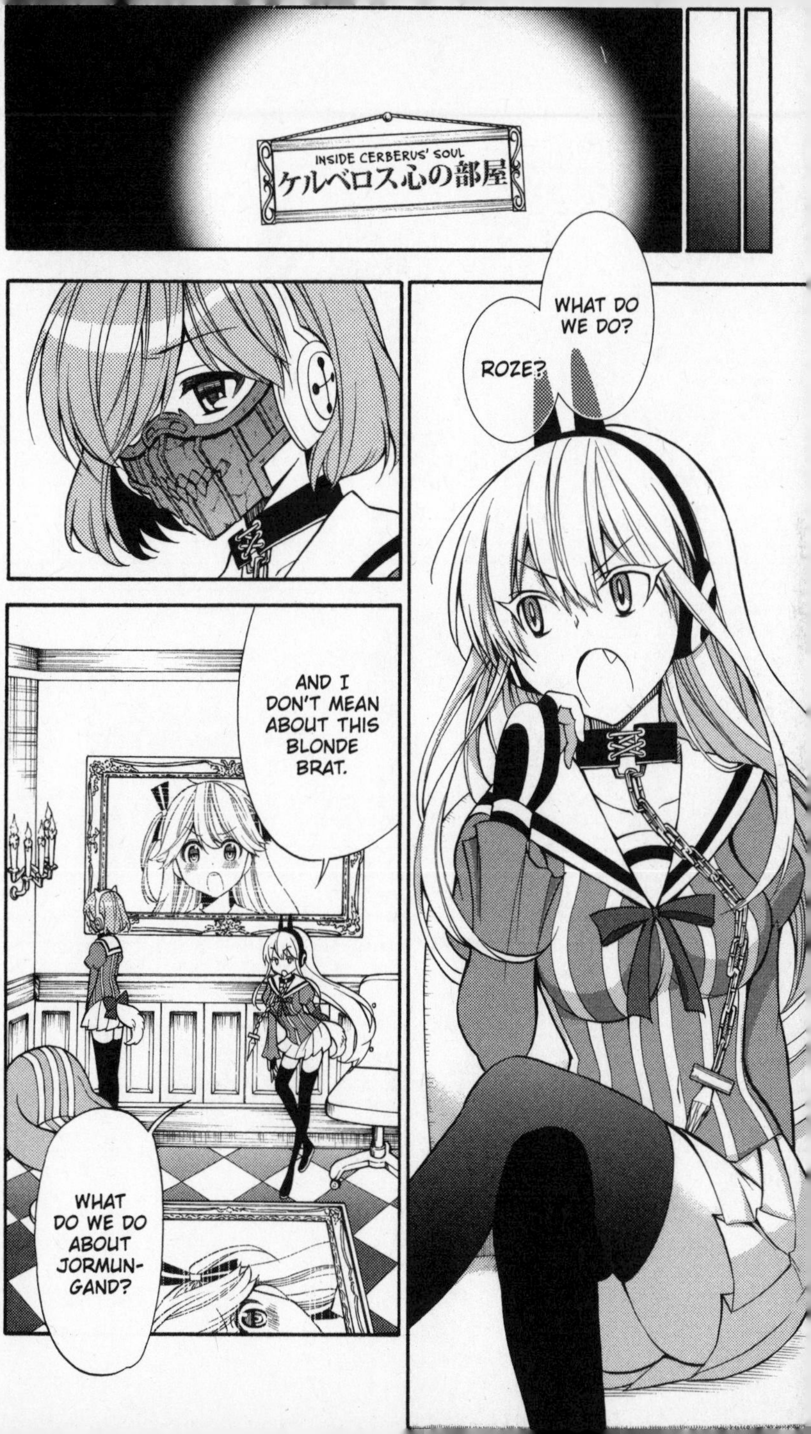
INSIDE CERBERUS' SOUL
ケルベロス心の部屋
WHAT DO WE DO?
ROZE?
AND I DON'T MEAN ABOUT THIS BLONDE BRAT.
WHAT DO WE DO ABOUT JORMUN-GAND?

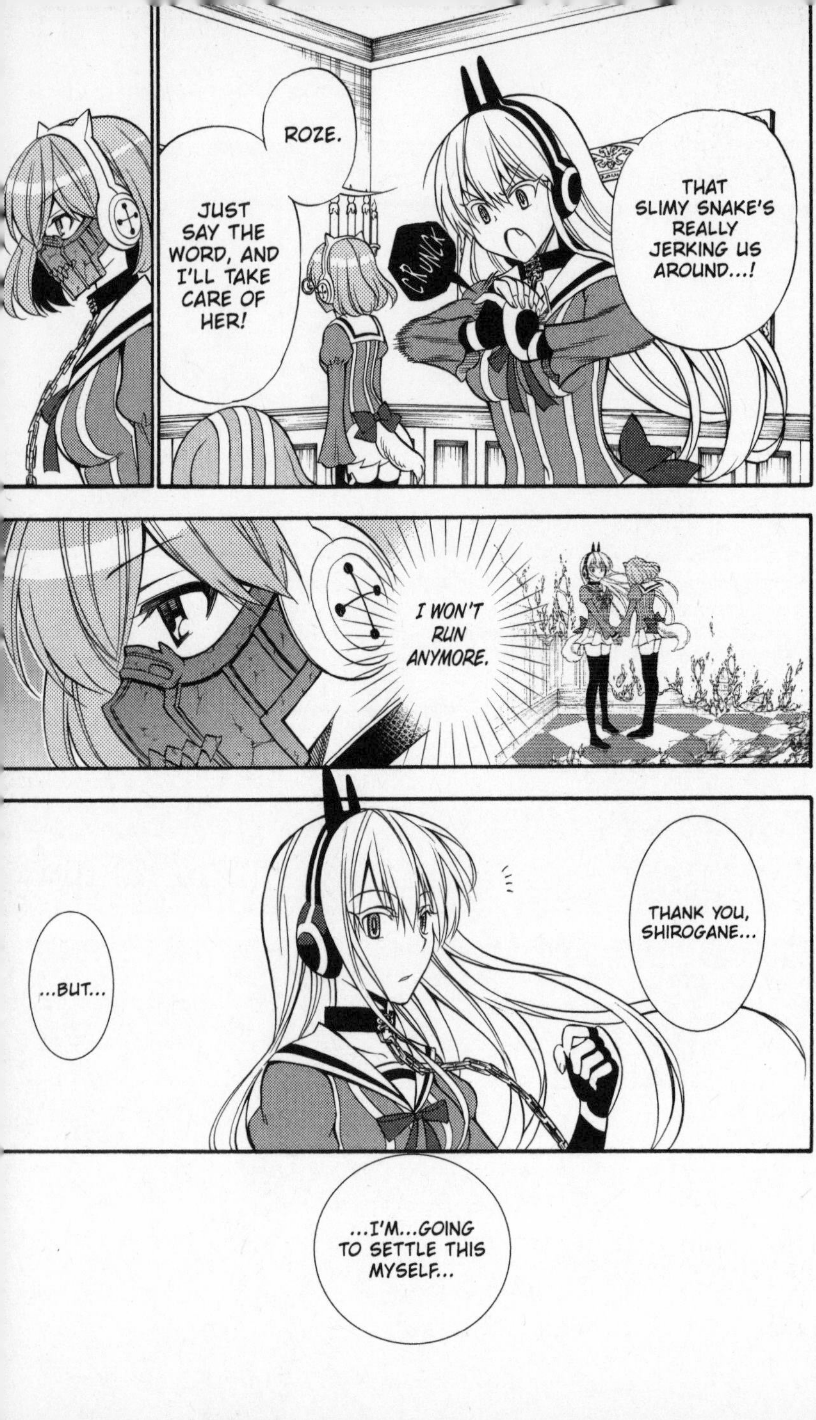
THAT SLIMY SNAKE'S REALLY JERKING US AROUND...!
ROZE.
CRUNCK
JUST SAY THE WORD, AND I'LL TAKE CARE OF HER!
I WON'T RUN ANYMORE.
THANK YOU, SHIROGANE...
...BUT...
...I'M...GOING TO SETTLE THIS MYSELF...

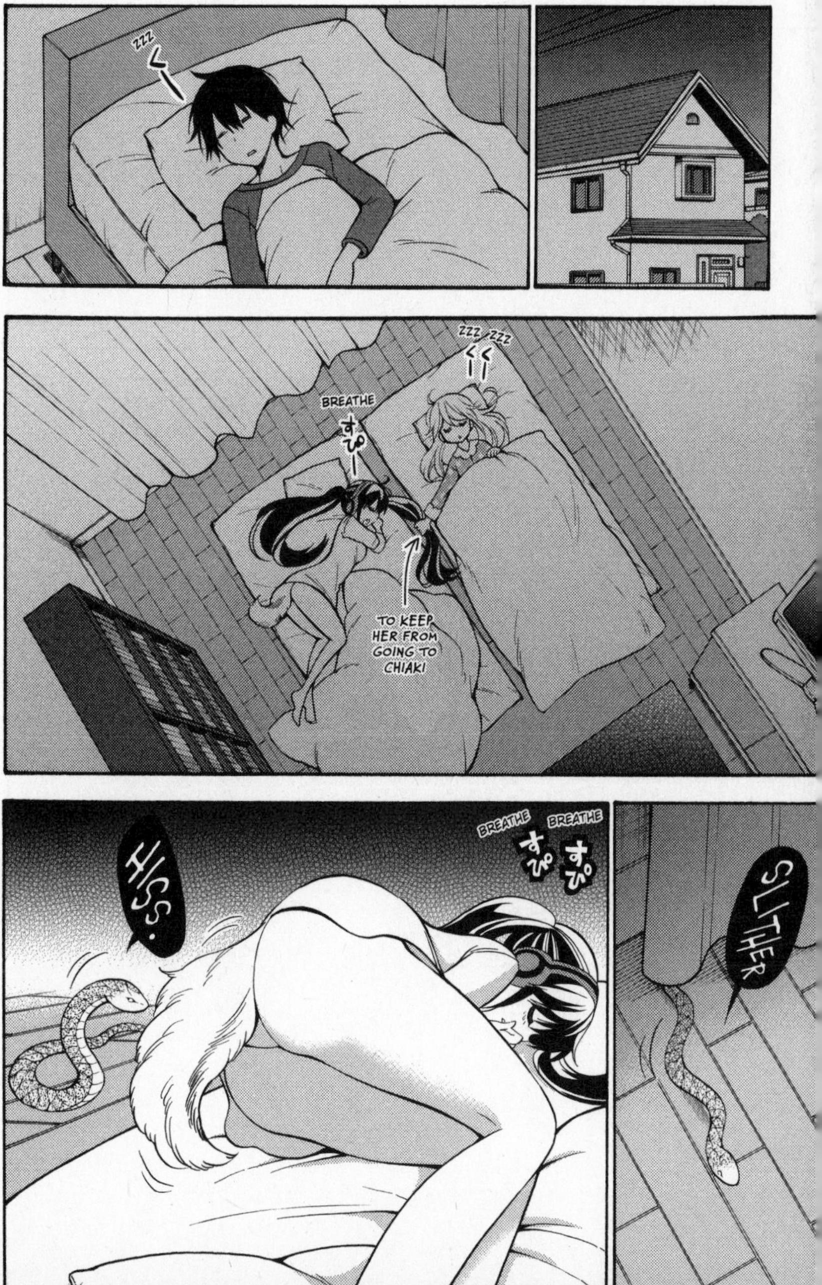
ZZZ
くー
ZZZ ZZZ
くー くー
BREATHE
すぴー
TO KEEP HER FROM GOING TO CHIAKI
SLITHER
BREATHE BREATHE
すぴ すぴ
HISS.

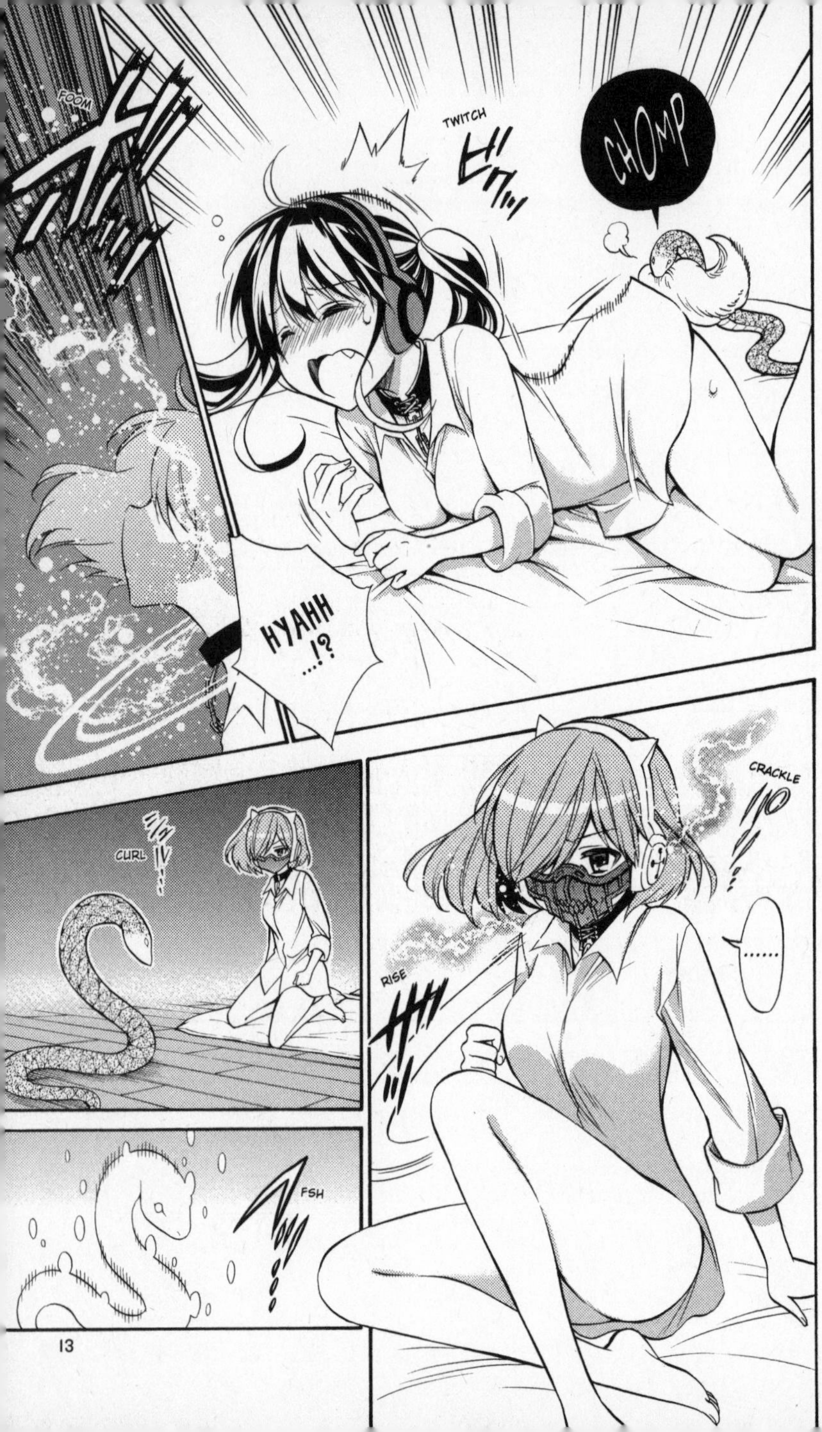
CHOMP
TWITCH
FOOM
HYAHH ...!?
CRACKLE
......
RISE
CURL
FSH

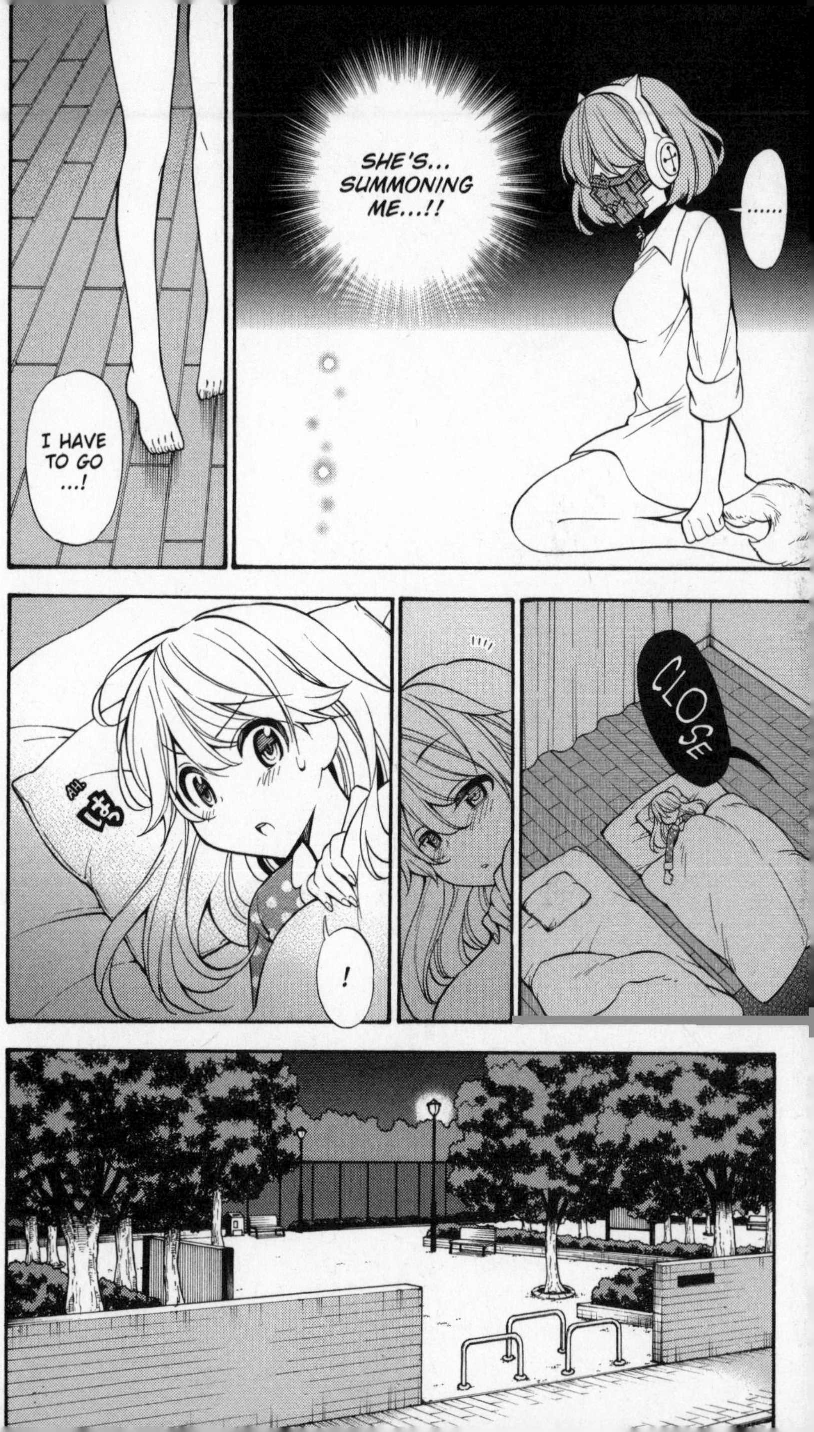
......
SHE'S... SUMMONING ME...!!
I HAVE TO GO ...!
CLOSE
!

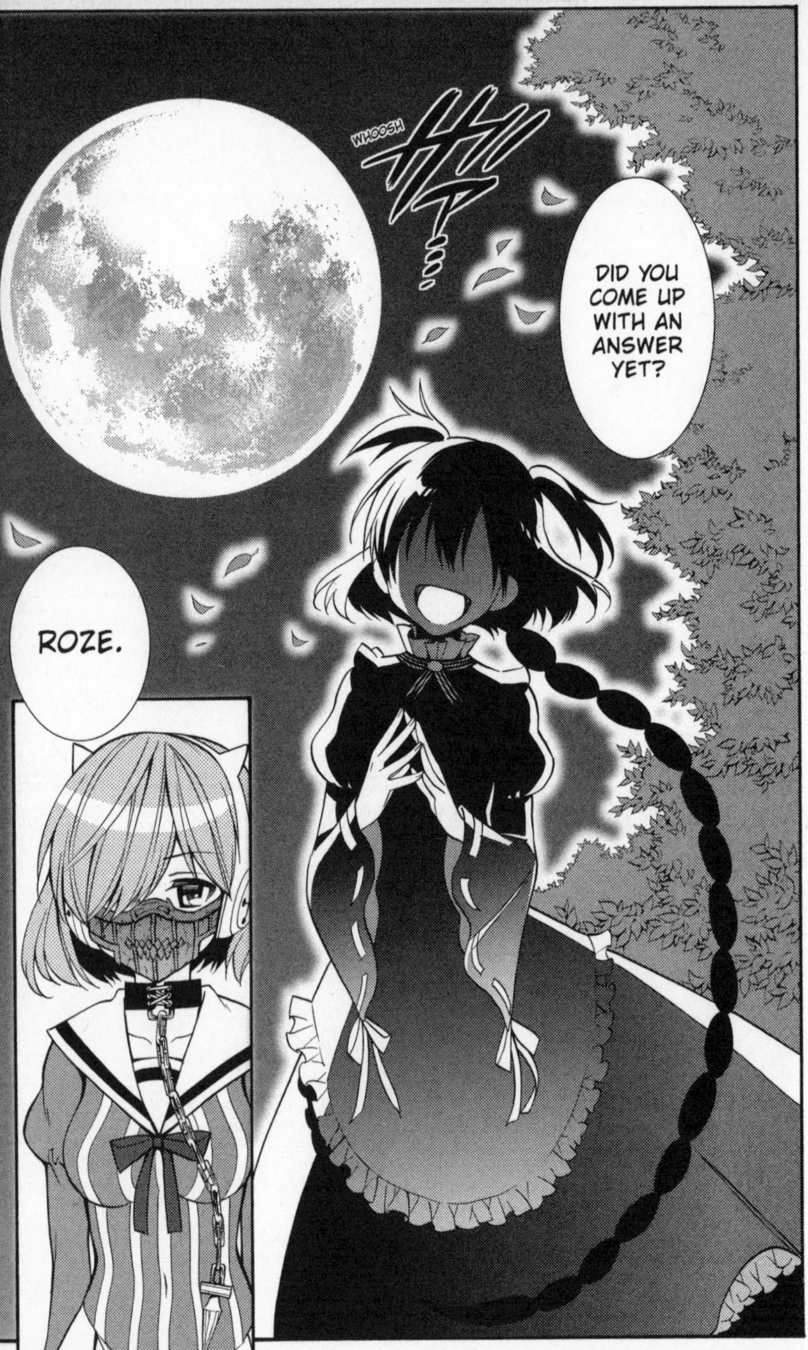
WHOOSH
DID YOU COME UP WITH AN ANSWER YET?
ROZE.

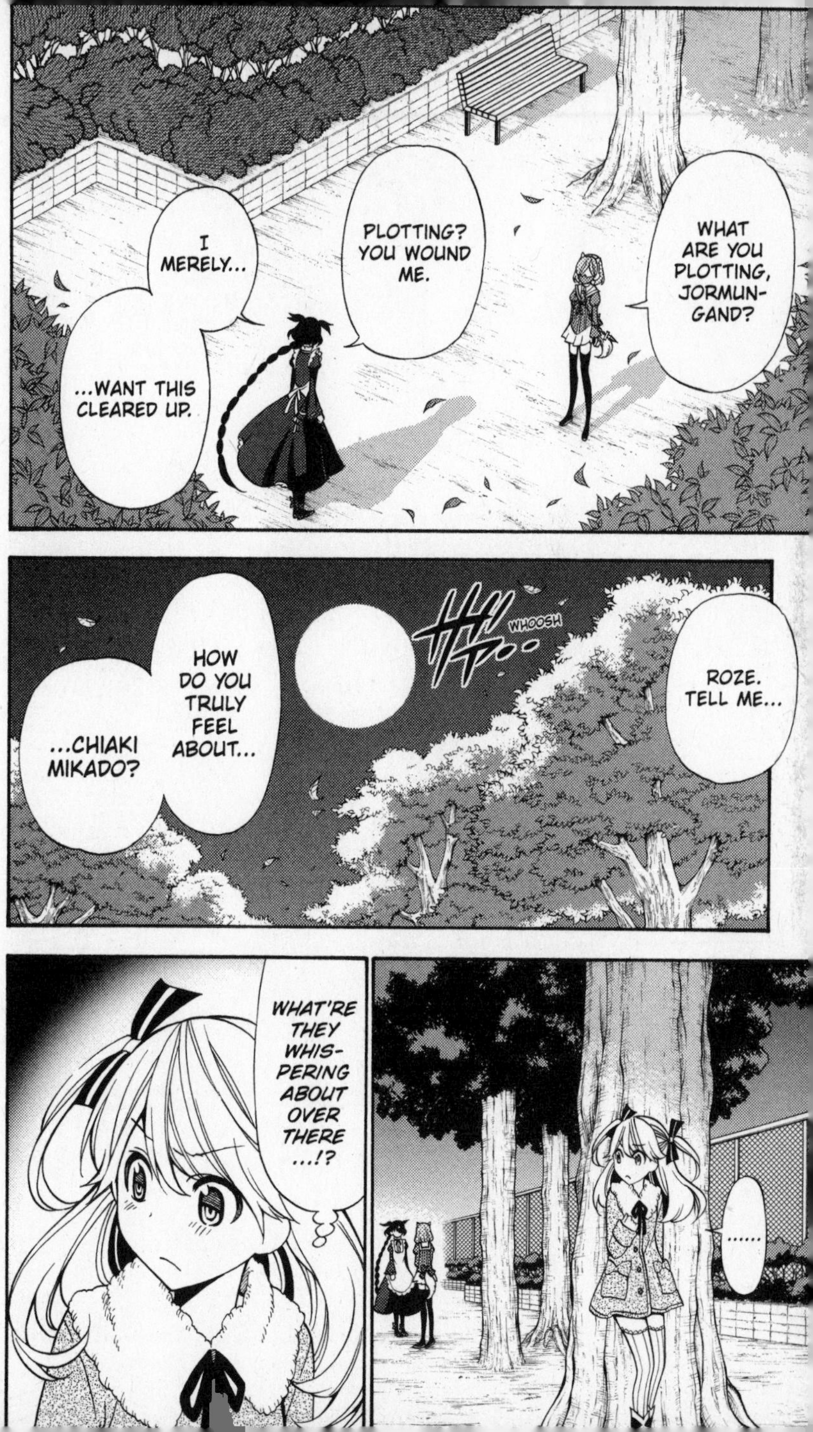
WHAT ARE YOU PLOTTING, JORMUNGAND?
PLOTTING? YOU WOUND ME.
I MERELY...
...WANT THIS CLEARED UP.
ROZE. TELL ME...
WHOOSH
HOW DO YOU TRULY FEEL ABOUT...
...CHIAKI MIKADO?
......
WHAT'RE THEY WHISPERING ABOUT OVER THERE...!?

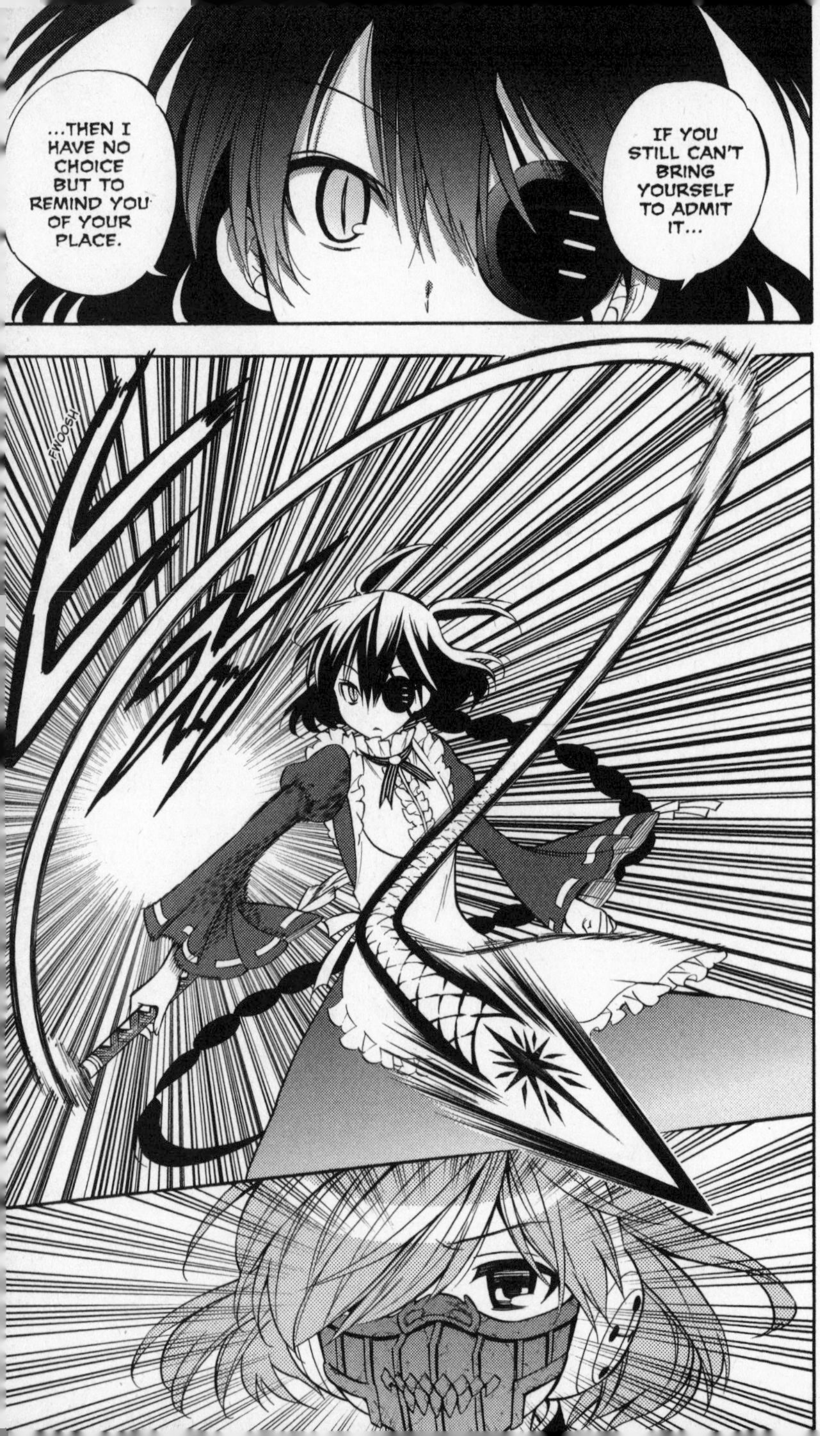
IF YOU STILL CAN'T BRING YOURSELF TO ADMIT IT...
...THEN I HAVE NO CHOICE BUT TO REMIND YOU OF YOUR PLACE.
FWOOSH

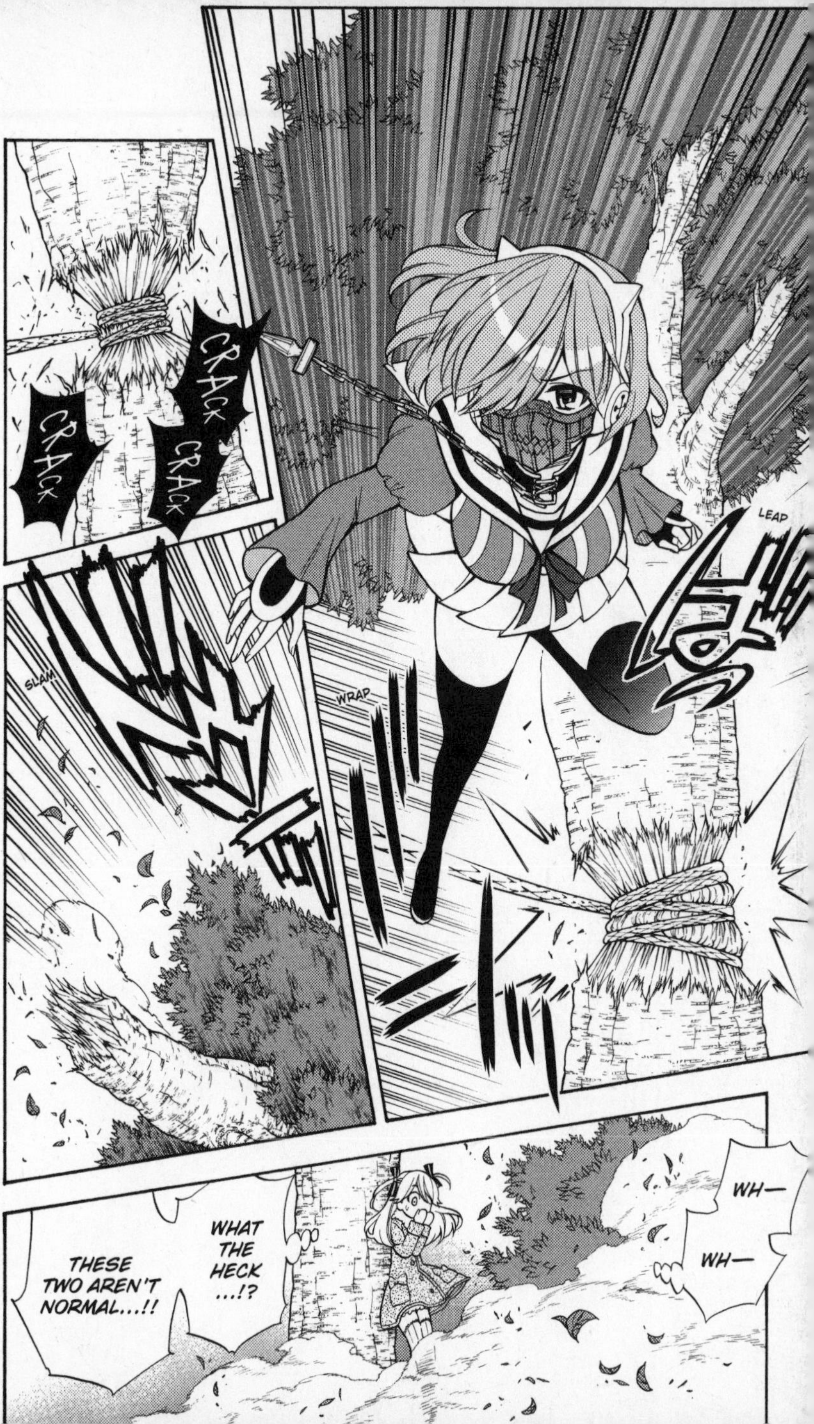
LEAP
CRACK
CRACK
CRACK
WRAP
SLAM
WH—
WH—
WHAT THE HECK ...!?
THESE TWO AREN'T NORMAL...!!

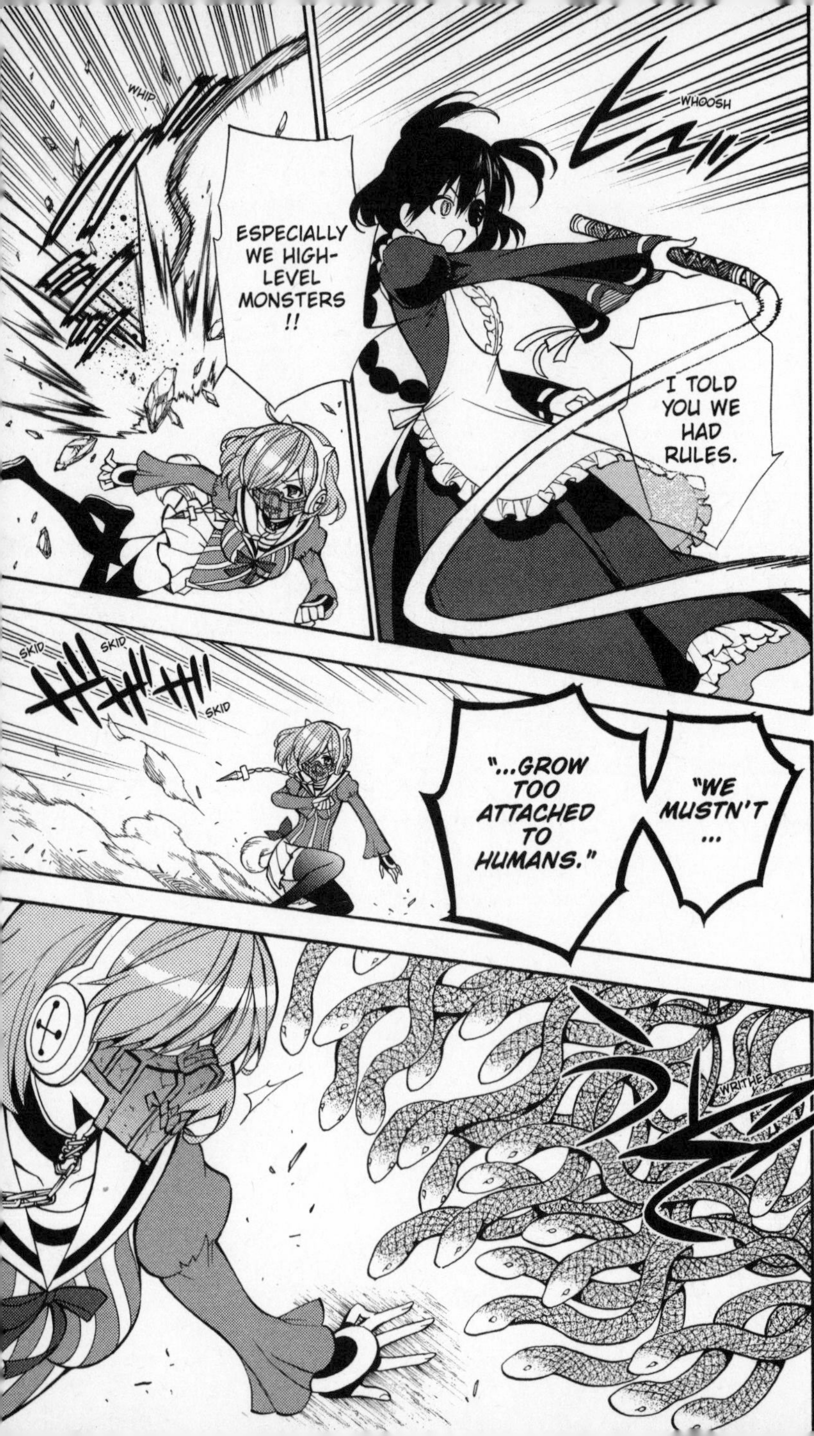
WHOOSH
I TOLD YOU WE HAD RULES.
WHIP
ESPECIALLY WE HIGH-LEVEL MONSTERS !!
"WE MUSTN'T ...
"...GROW TOO ATTACHED TO HUMANS."
SKID
SKID
SKID
WRITHE

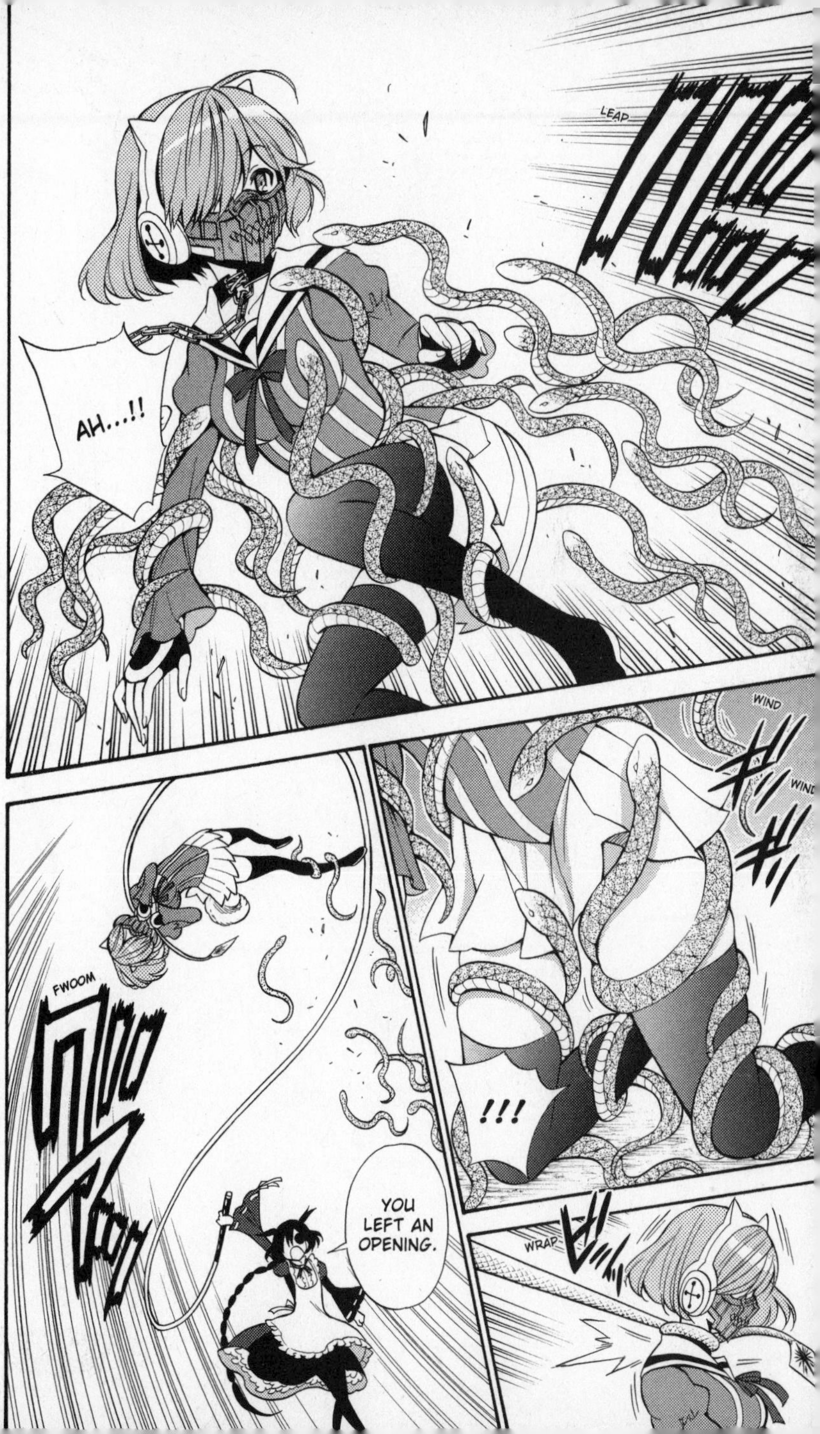
LEAP
AH...!!
WIND
WIND
!!!
WRAP
FWOOM
YOU LEFT AN OPENING.

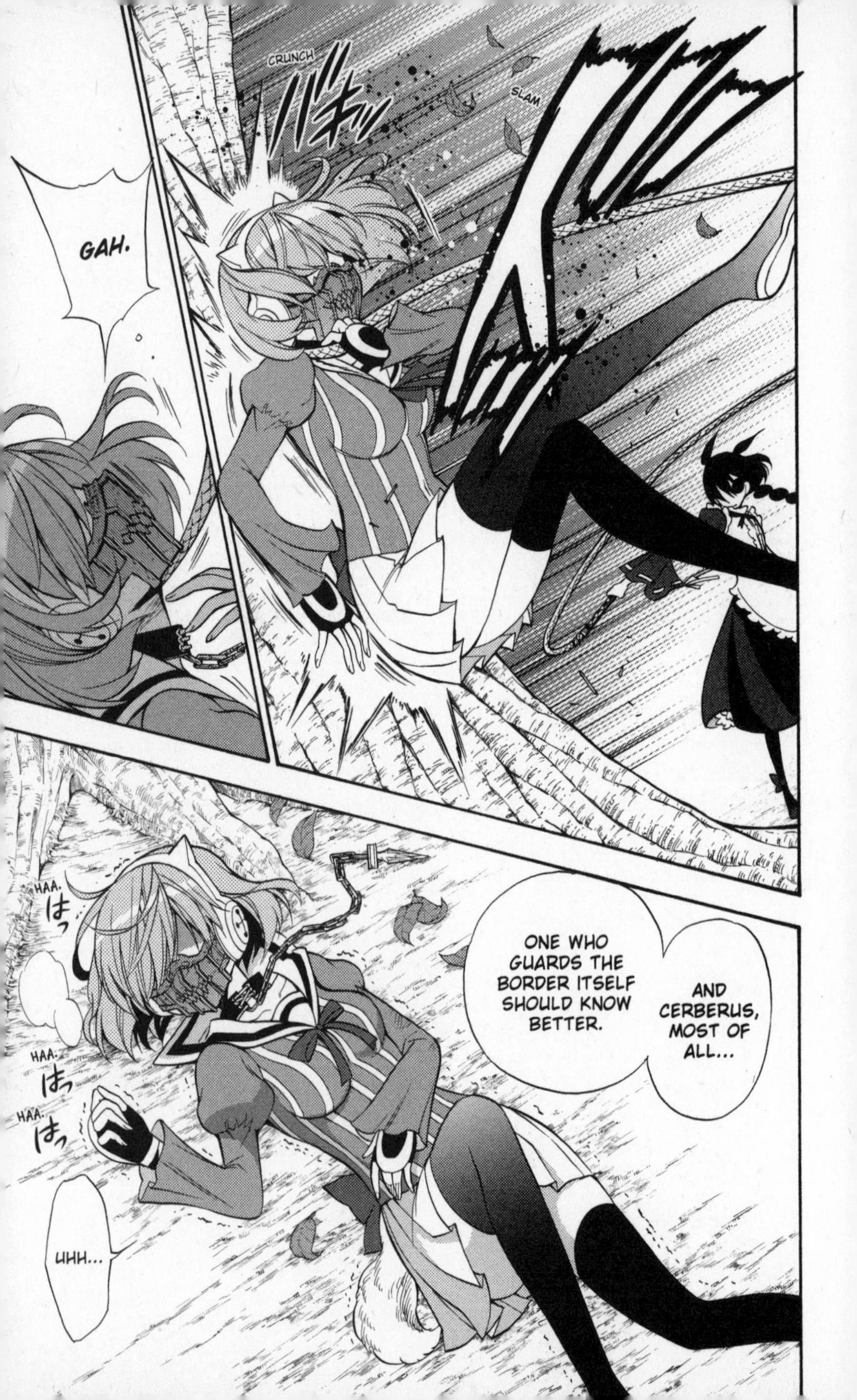
SLAM
CRUNCH
バキッ
GAH.
AND CERBERUS, MOST OF ALL...
ONE WHO GUARDS THE BORDER ITSELF SHOULD KNOW BETTER.
HAA.
はっ
HAA.
はっ
HAA.
はっ
UHH...

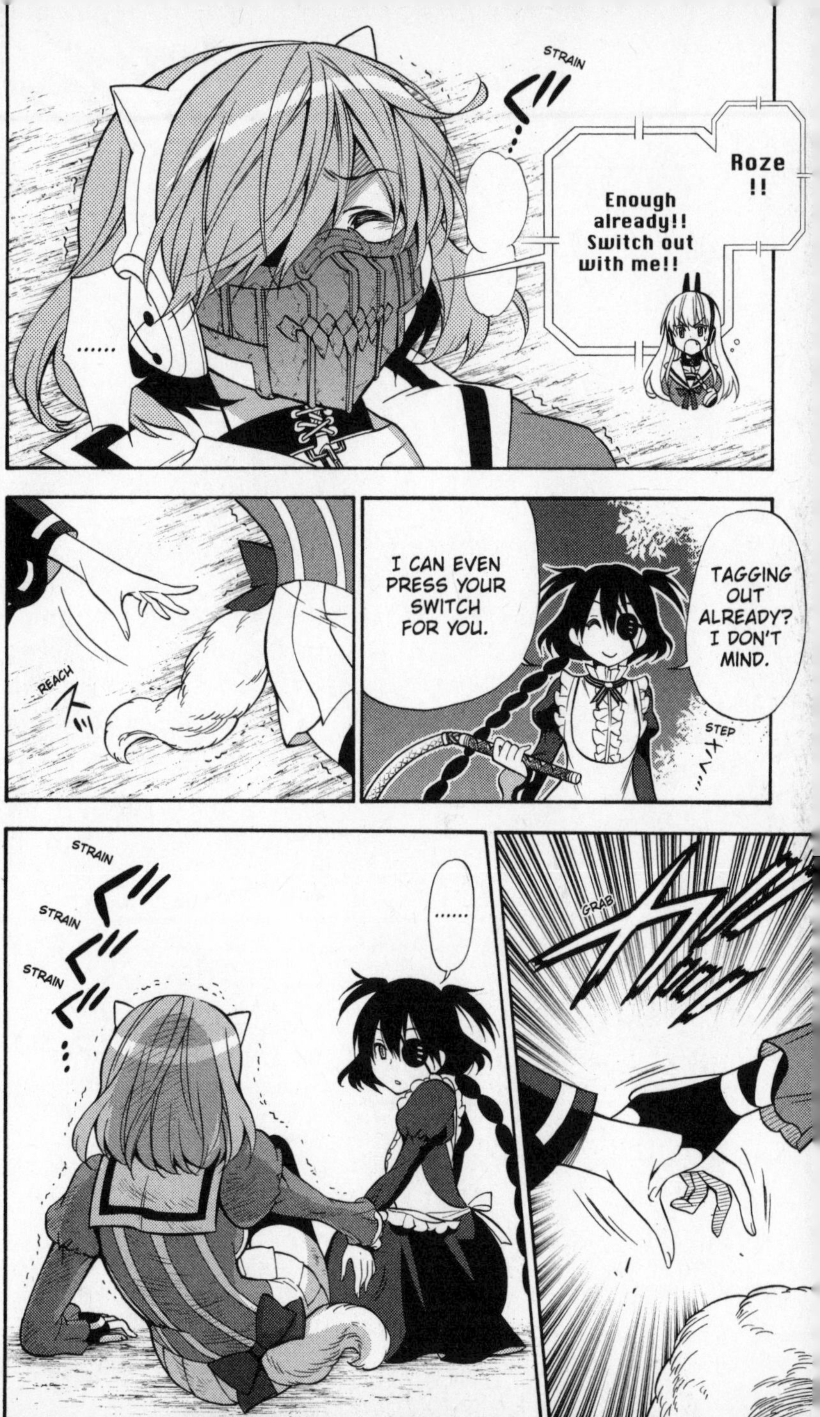

STRAIN
Roze !!
Enough already!! Switch out with me!!
......
TAGGING OUT ALREADY? I DON'T MIND.
STEP
I CAN EVEN PRESS YOUR SWITCH FOR YOU.
REACH
GRAB
......
STRAIN
STRAIN
STRAIN

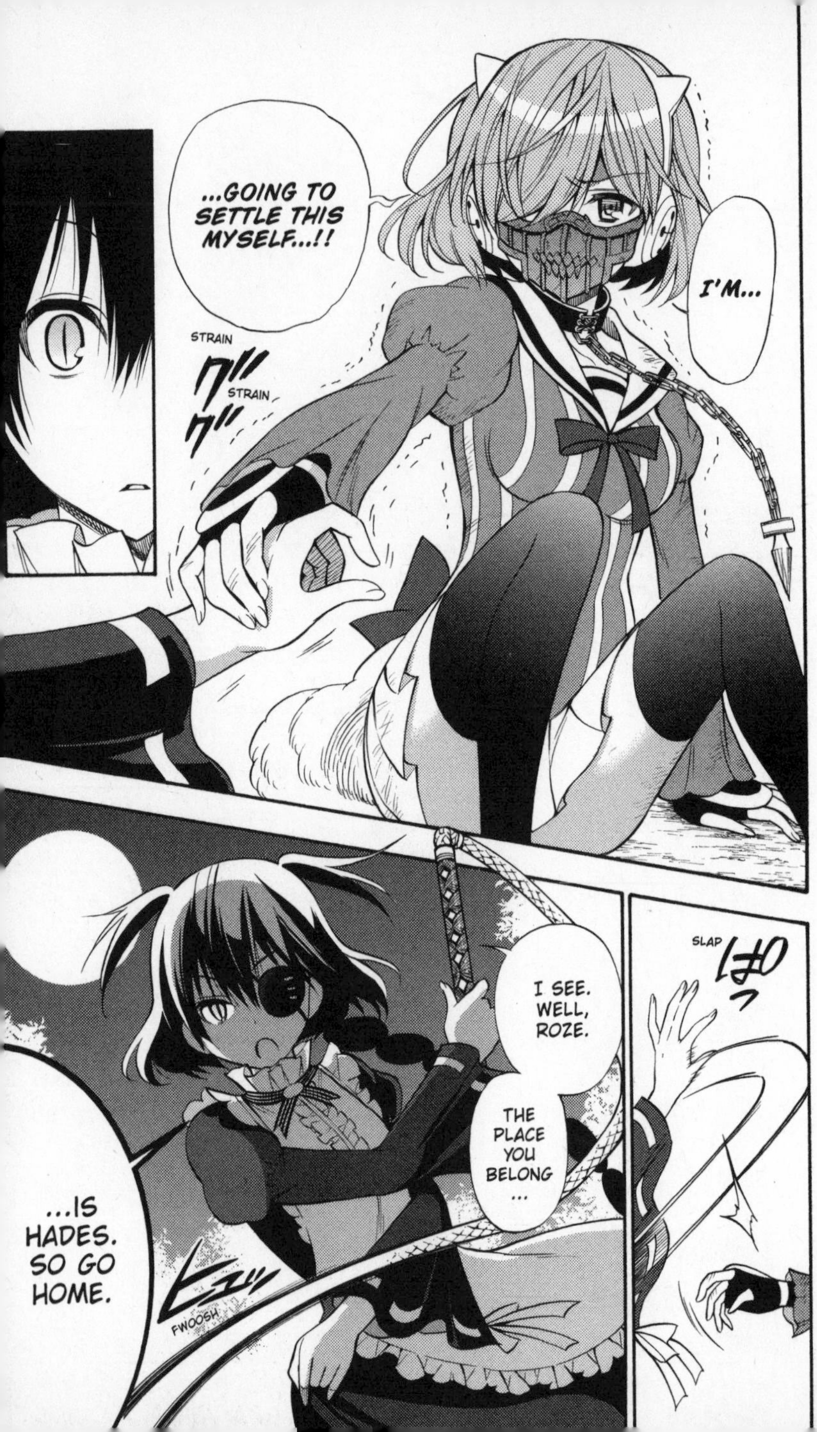
I'M...
...GOING TO SETTLE THIS MYSELF...!!
STRAIN
STRAIN
SLAP
I SEE. WELL, ROZE.
THE PLACE YOU BELONG ...
...IS HADES. SO GO HOME.
FWOOSH

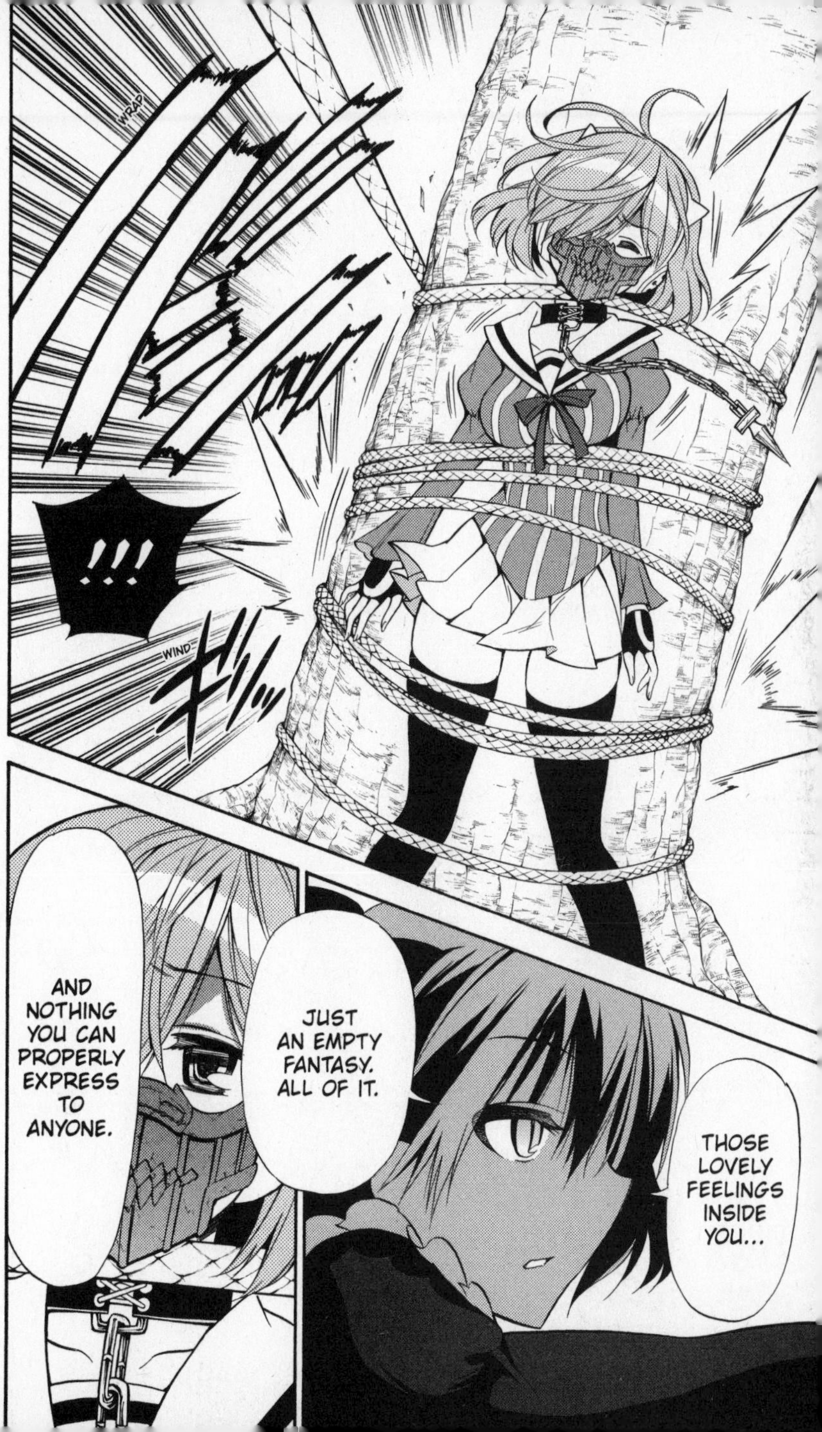
WRAP
!!!
WIND
THOSE LOVELY FEELINGS INSIDE YOU...
JUST AN EMPTY FANTASY. ALL OF IT.
AND NOTHING YOU CAN PROPERLY EXPRESS TO ANYONE.

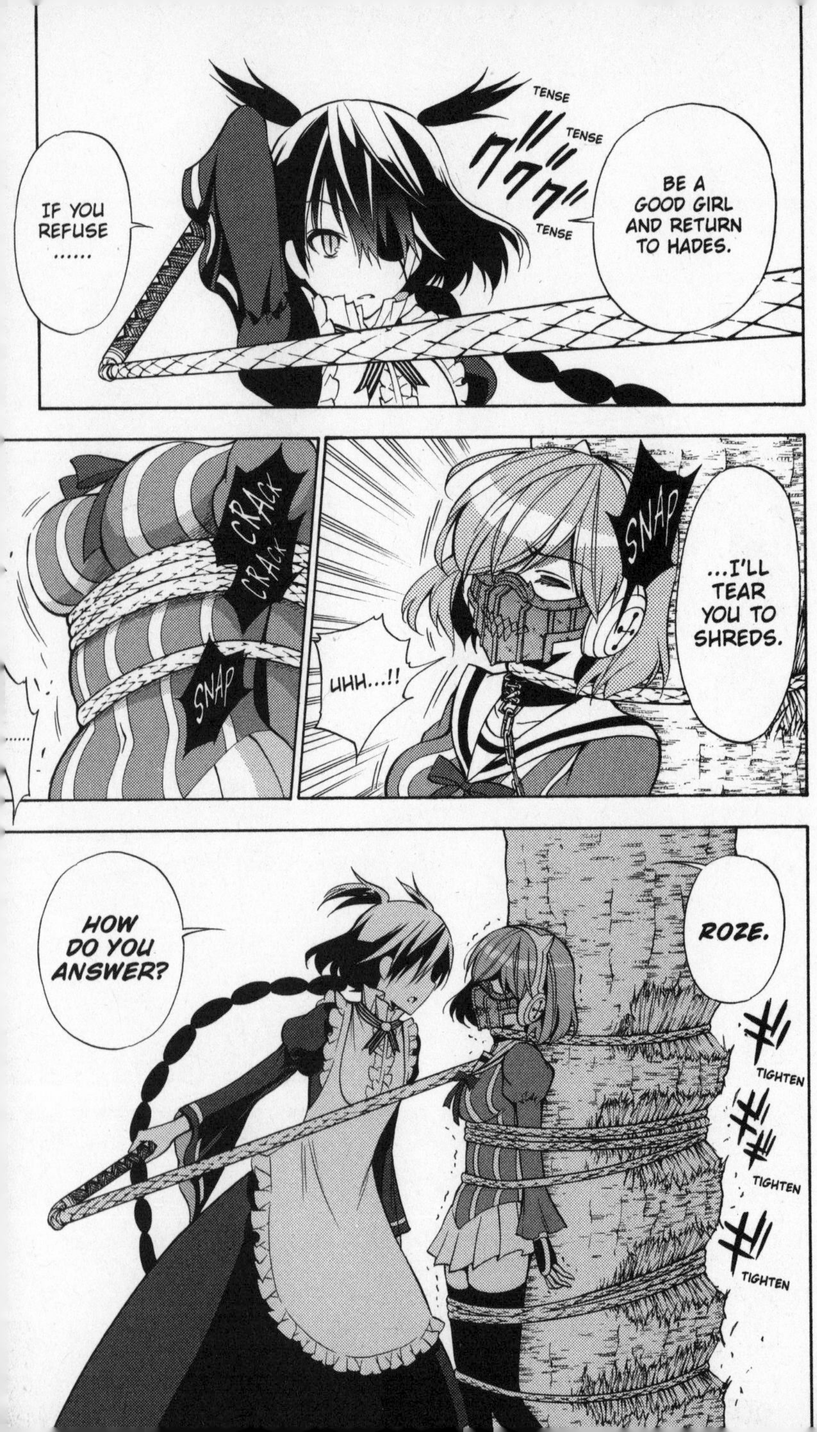
TENSE
TENSE
TENSE
BE A GOOD GIRL AND RETURN TO HADES.
IF YOU REFUSE ......
SNAP
...I'LL TEAR YOU TO SHREDS.
UHH...!!
CRACK
CRACK
SNAP
ROZE.
HOW DO YOU ANSWER?
TIGHTEN
TIGHTEN
TIGHTEN

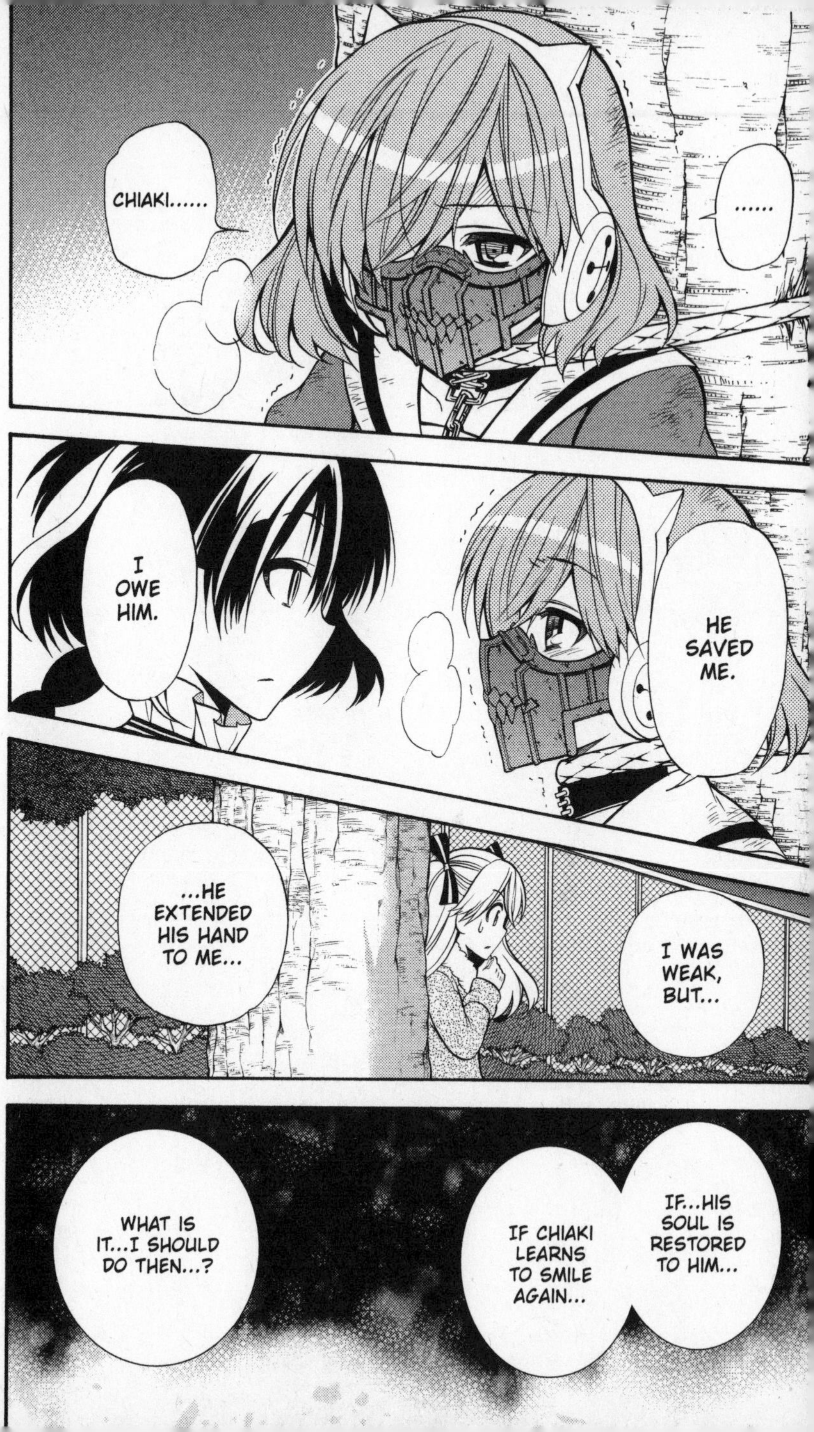
......
CHIAKI......
HE SAVED ME.
I OWE HIM.
I WAS WEAK, BUT...
...HE EXTENDED HIS HAND TO ME...
IF...HIS SOUL IS RESTORED TO HIM...
IF CHIAKI LEARNS TO SMILE AGAIN...
WHAT IS IT...I SHOULD DO THEN...?

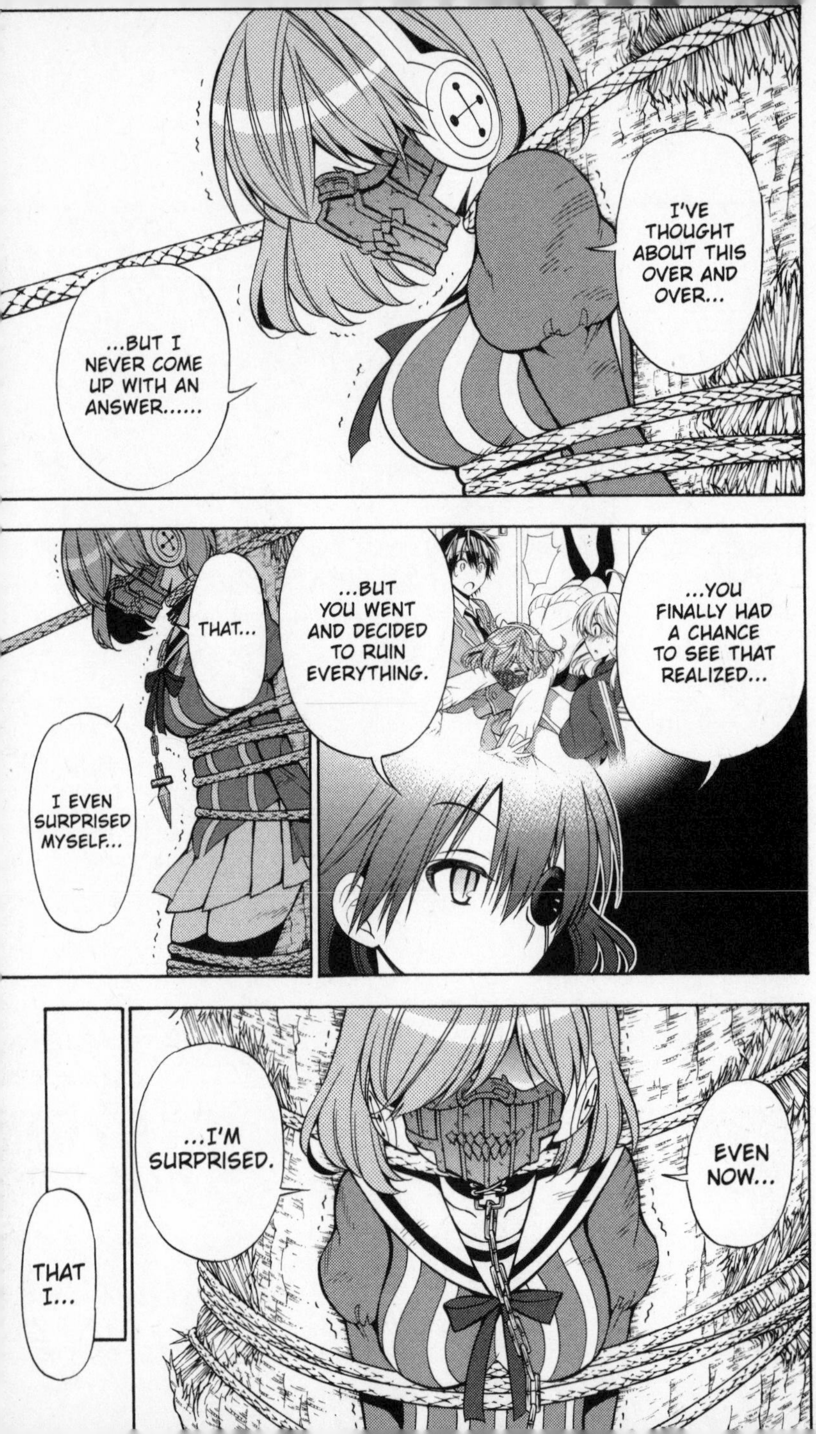
I'VE THOUGHT ABOUT THIS OVER AND OVER...
...BUT I NEVER COME UP WITH AN ANSWER......
...YOU FINALLY HAD A CHANCE TO SEE THAT REALIZED...
...BUT YOU WENT AND DECIDED TO RUIN EVERYTHING.
THAT...
I EVEN SURPRISED MYSELF...
EVEN NOW...
...I'M SURPRISED.
THAT I...

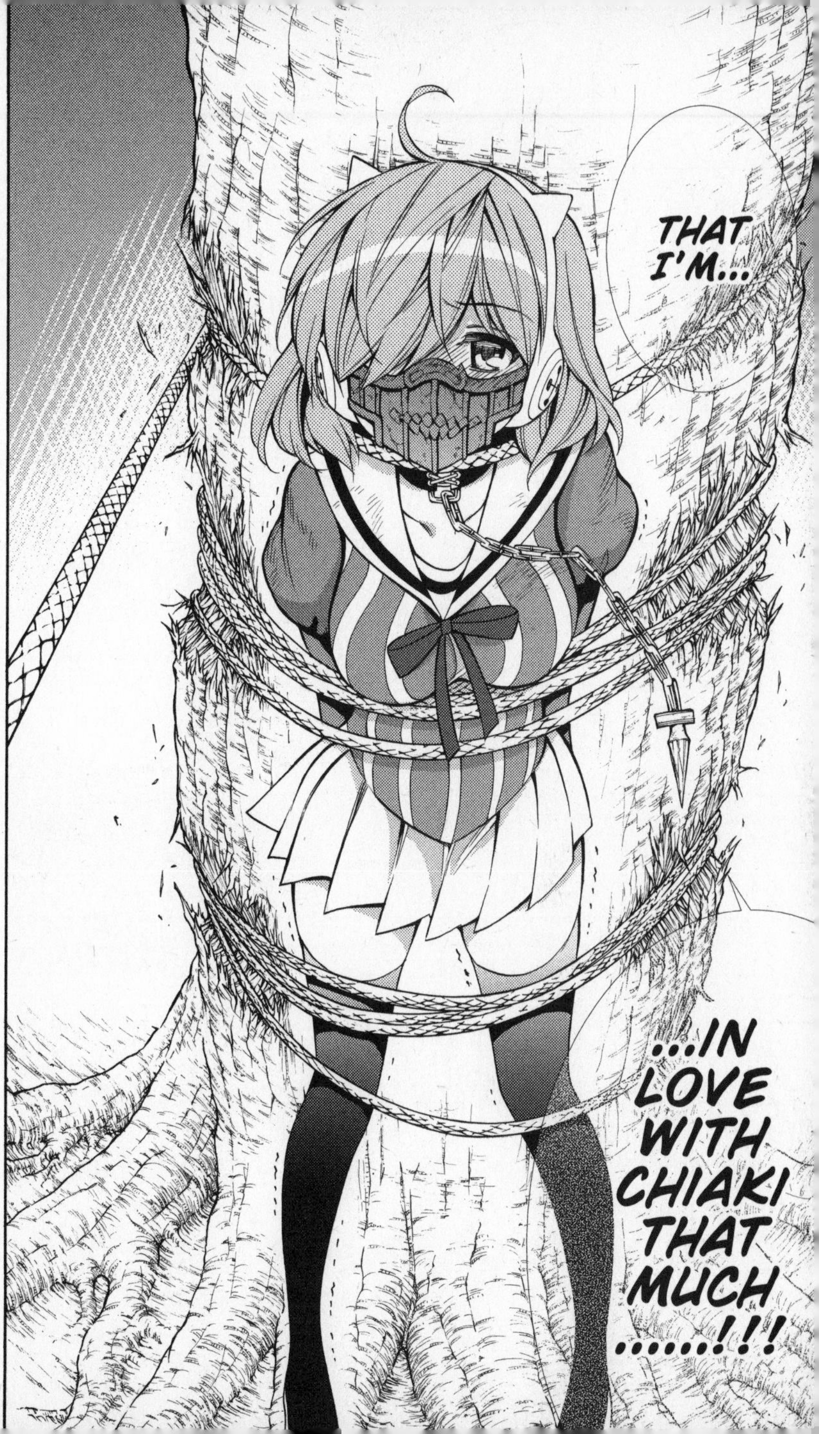
THAT I'M...
...IN LOVE WITH CHIAKI THAT MUCH......!!!

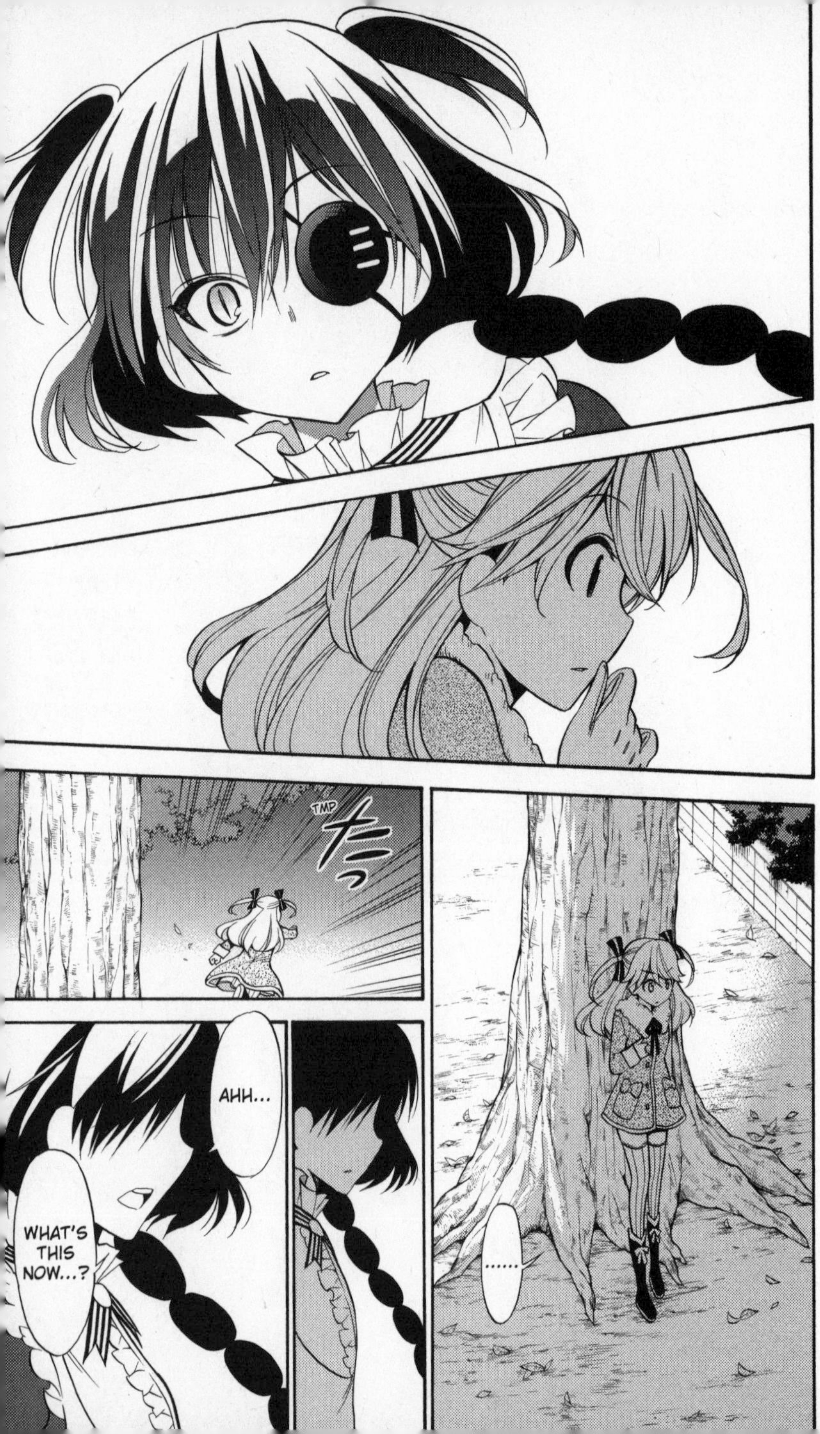
......
TMP
たっ
AHH...
WHAT'S THIS NOW...?

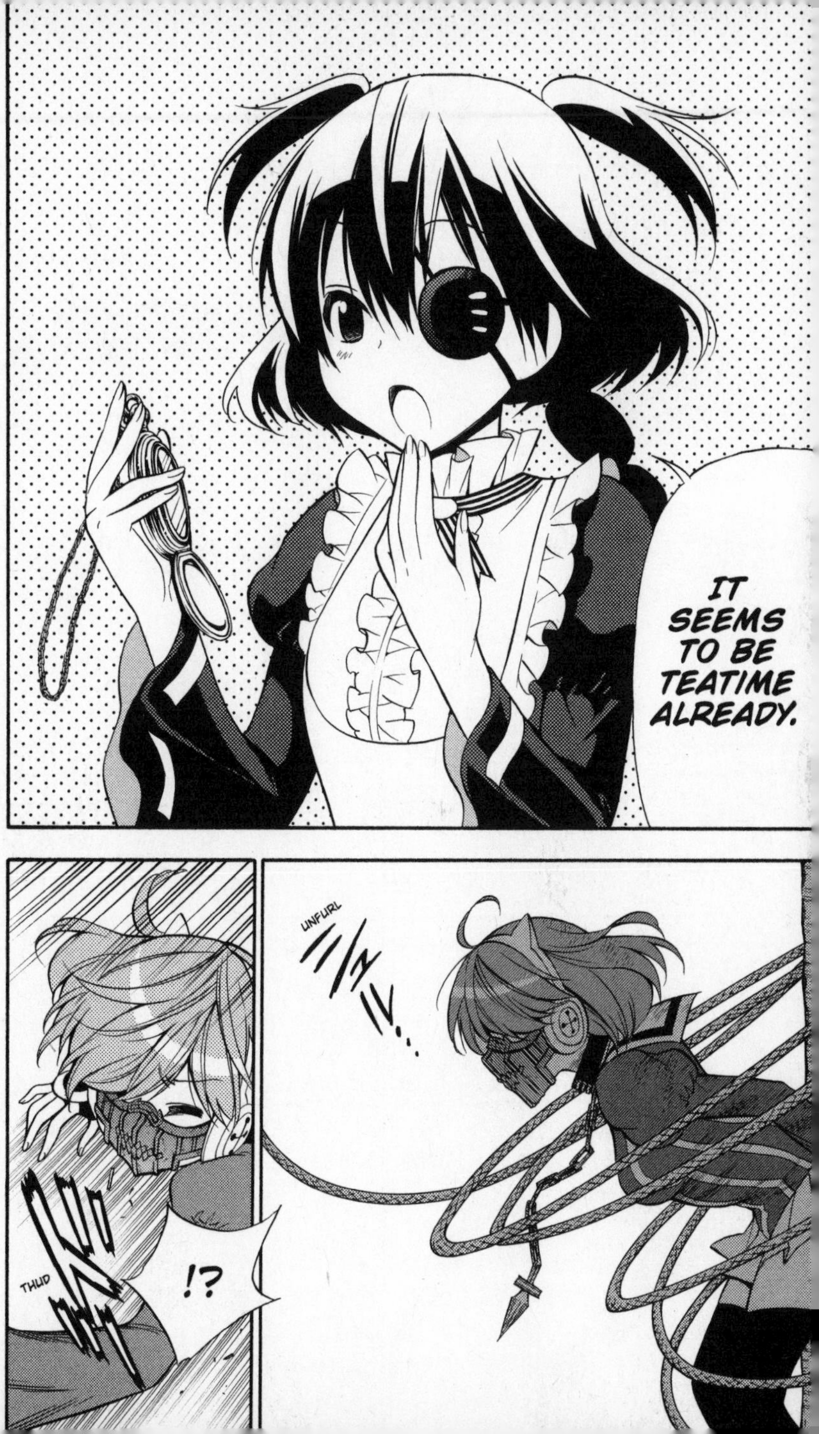
IT SEEMS TO BE TEATIME ALREADY.
UNFURL
!?
THUD

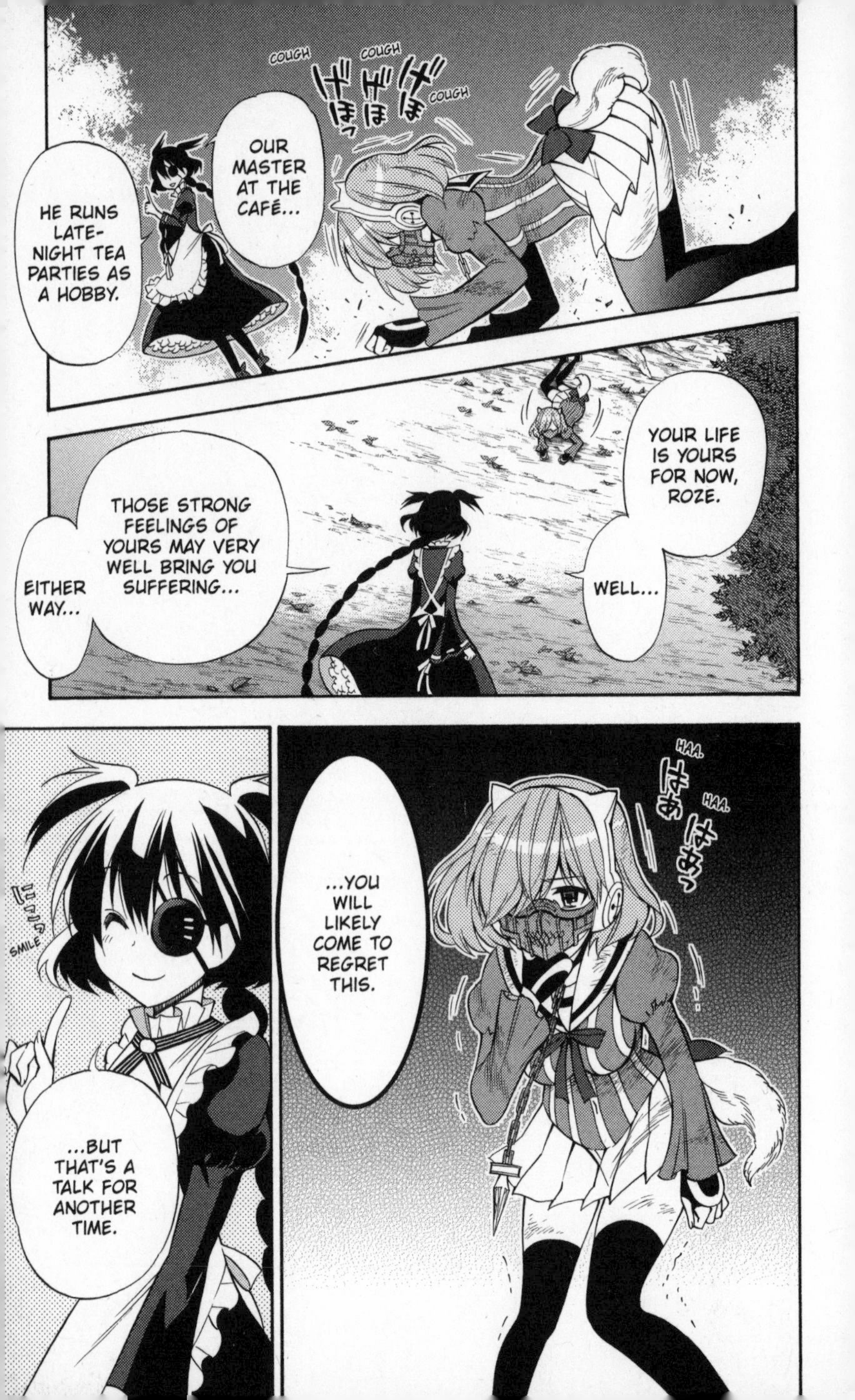
げほ げほ げほっ
COUGH COUGH COUGH
OUR MASTER AT THE CAFÉ...
HE RUNS LATE-NIGHT TEA PARTIES AS A HOBBY.
YOUR LIFE IS YOURS FOR NOW, ROZE.
WELL...
THOSE STRONG FEELINGS OF YOURS MAY VERY WELL BRING YOU SUFFERING...
EITHER WAY...
はあ はあっ
HAA. HAA.
...YOU WILL LIKELY COME TO REGRET THIS.
SMILE
...BUT THAT'S A TALK FOR ANOTHER TIME.

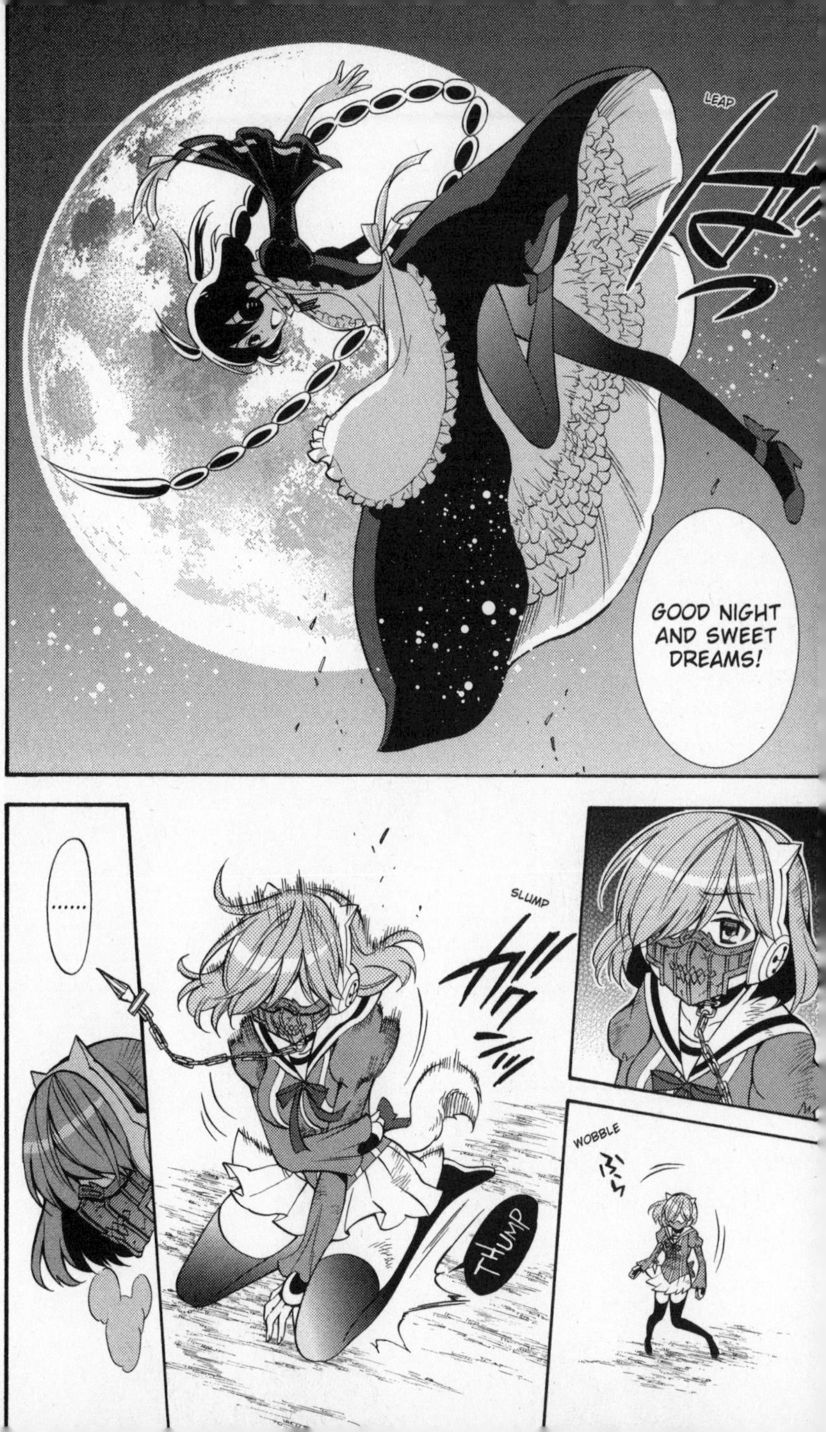
LEAP
GOOD NIGHT AND SWEET DREAMS!
WOBBLE
SLUMP
......
THUMP

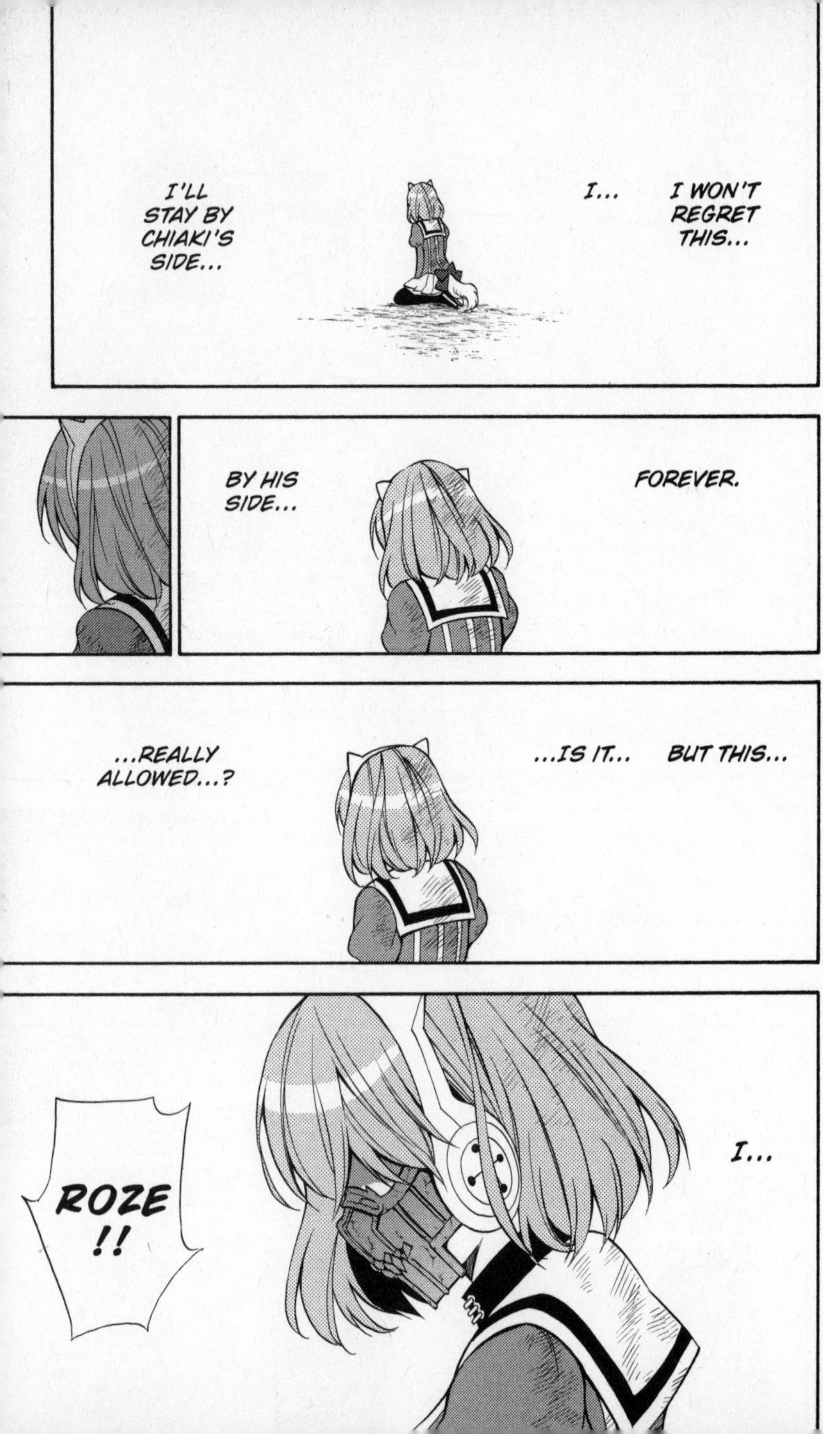
I WON'T REGRET THIS...
I...
I'LL STAY BY CHIAKI'S SIDE...
FOREVER.
BY HIS SIDE...
BUT THIS...
...IS IT...
...REALLY ALLOWED...?
I...
ROZE !!

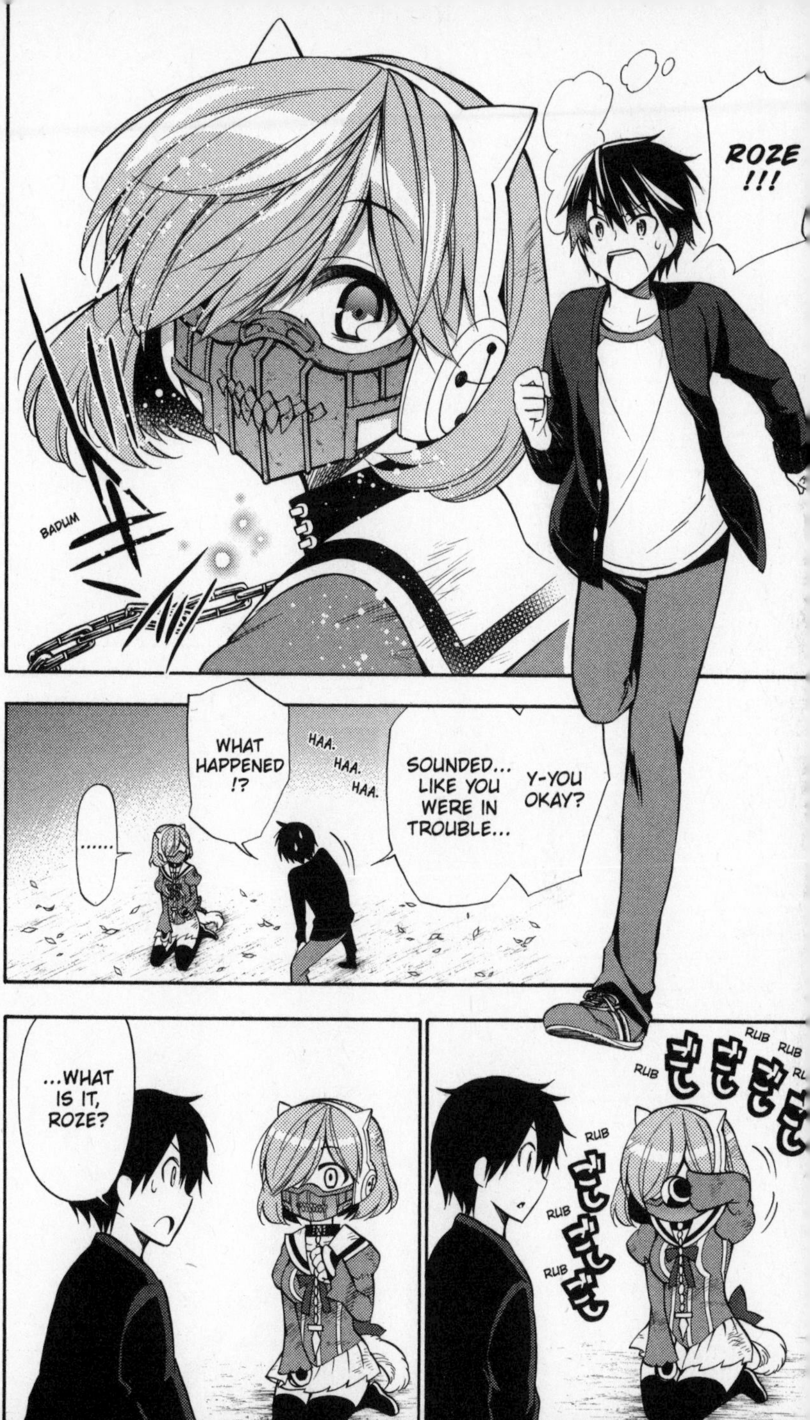
ROZE !!!
BADUM
Y-YOU OKAY?
SOUNDED... LIKE YOU WERE IN TROUBLE...
HAA. HAA. HAA.
WHAT HAPPENED !?
......
RUB RUB RUB
RUB RUB RUB
...WHAT IS IT, ROZE?

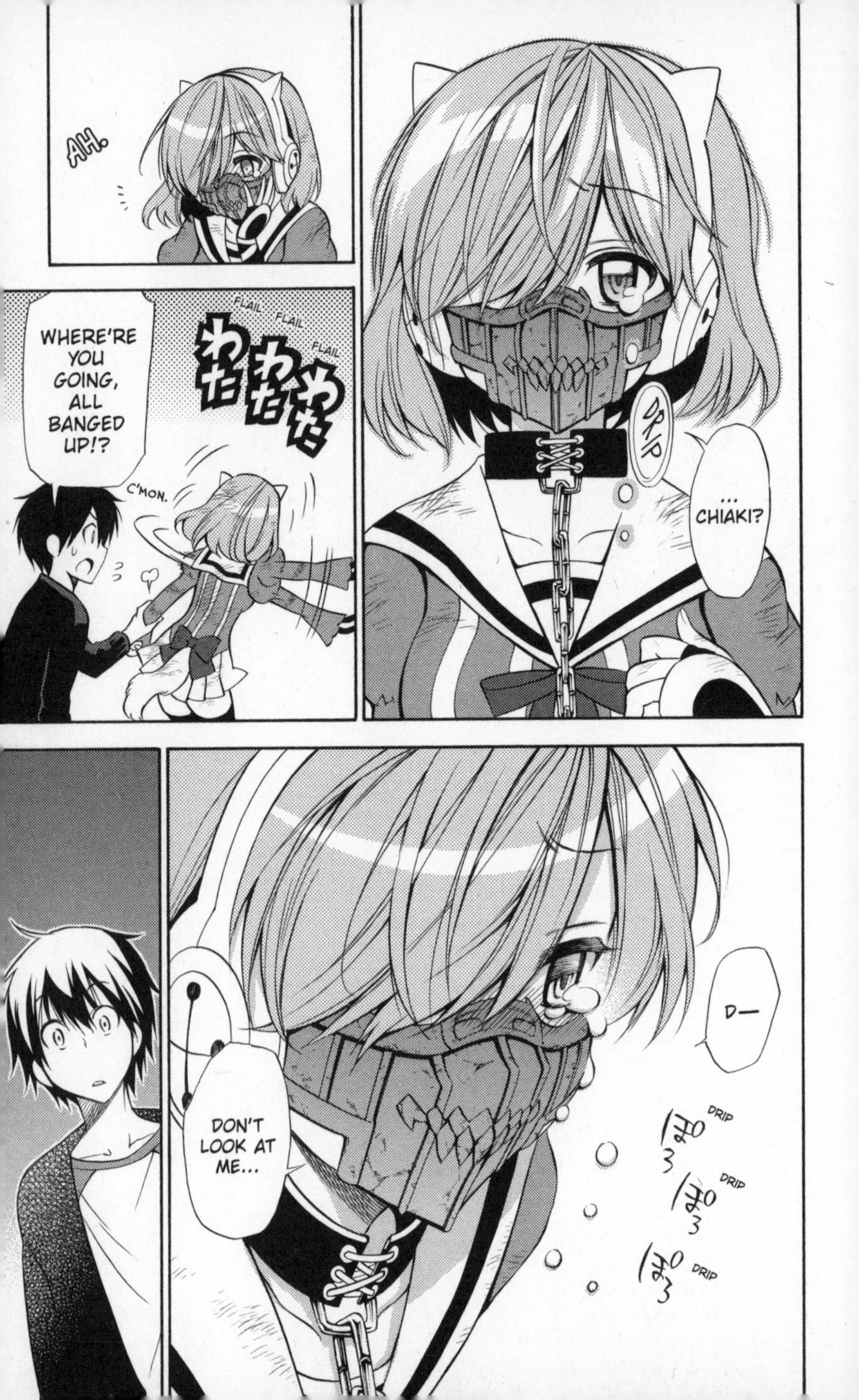
...CHIAKI?
DRIP
AH.
FLAIL
FLAIL
FLAIL
わたわたわた
WHERE'RE YOU GOING, ALL BANGED UP!?
C'MON.
D—
DRIP
ぽろ
DRIP
ぽろ
DRIP
ぽろ
DON'T LOOK AT ME...

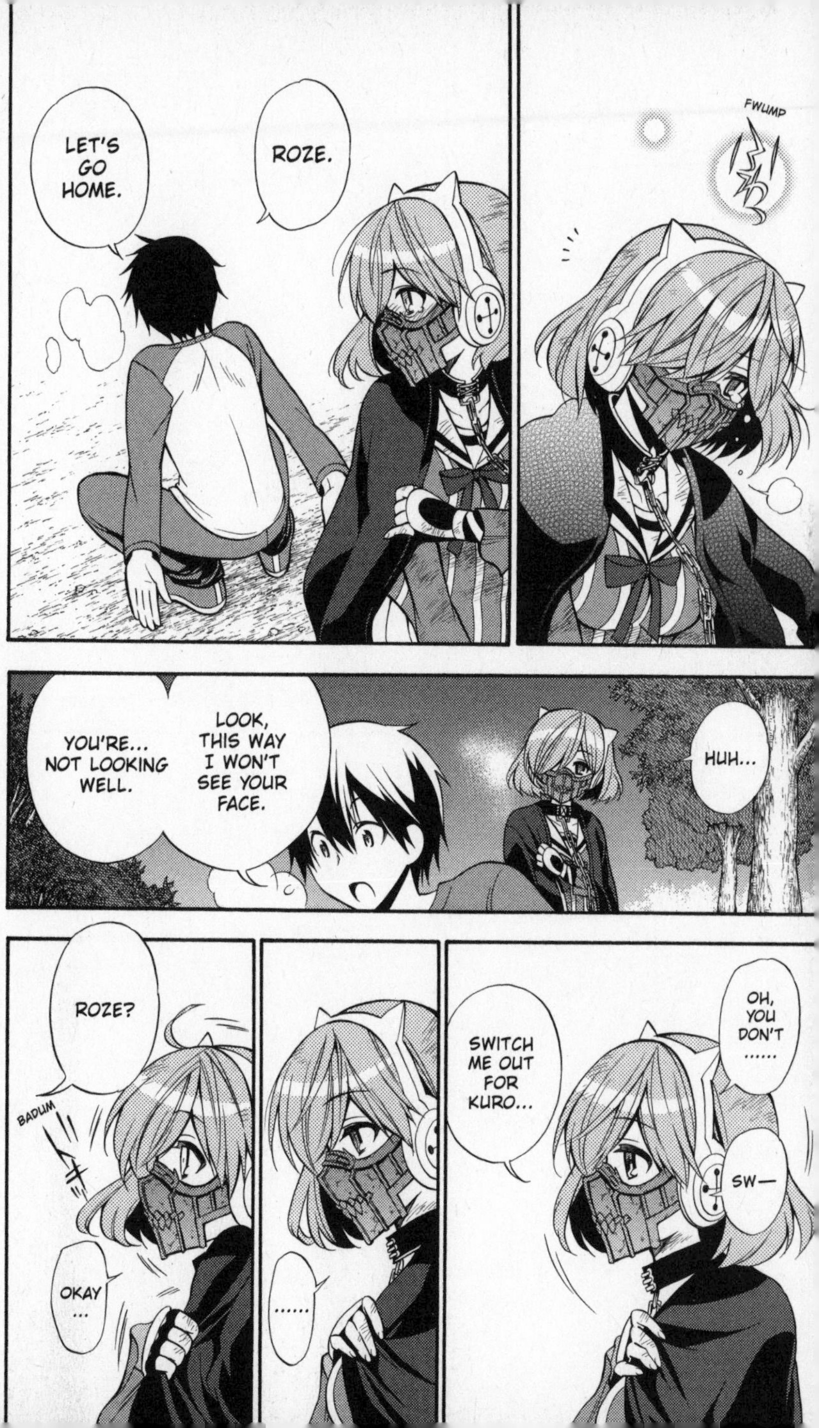
FWUMP
ROZE.
LET'S GO HOME.
HUH...
LOOK, THIS WAY I WON'T SEE YOUR FACE.
YOU'RE... NOT LOOKING WELL.
OH, YOU DON'T ......
SWITCH ME OUT FOR KURO...
SW—
......
ROZE?
BADUM
OKAY ...

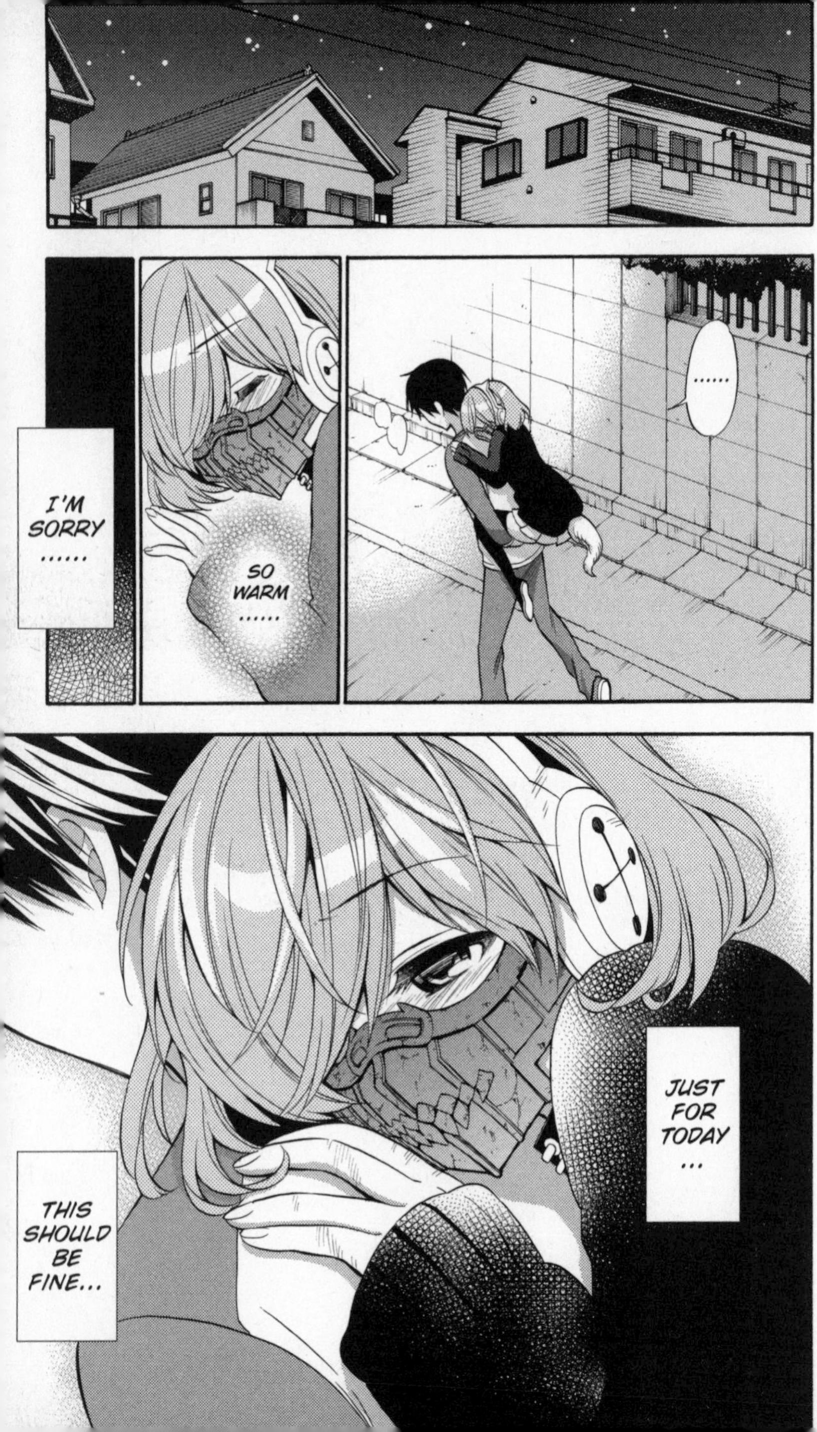
……
SO WARM ……
I'M SORRY ……
JUST FOR TODAY …
THIS SHOULD BE FINE…

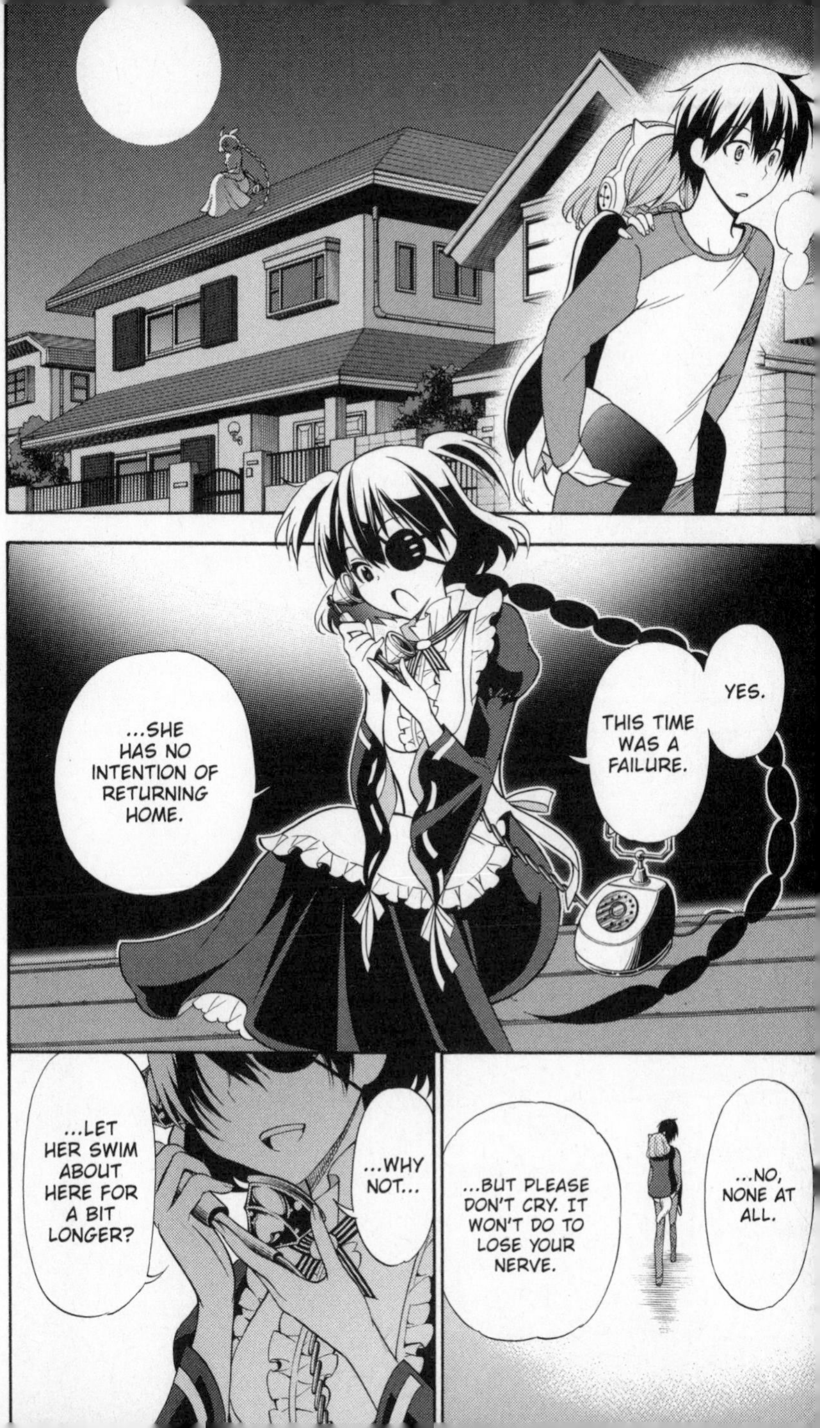
YES.
THIS TIME WAS A FAILURE.
...SHE HAS NO INTENTION OF RETURNING HOME.
...NO, NONE AT ALL.
...BUT PLEASE DON'T CRY. IT WON'T DO TO LOSE YOUR NERVE.
...WHY NOT...
...LET HER SWIM ABOUT HERE FOR A BIT LONGER?

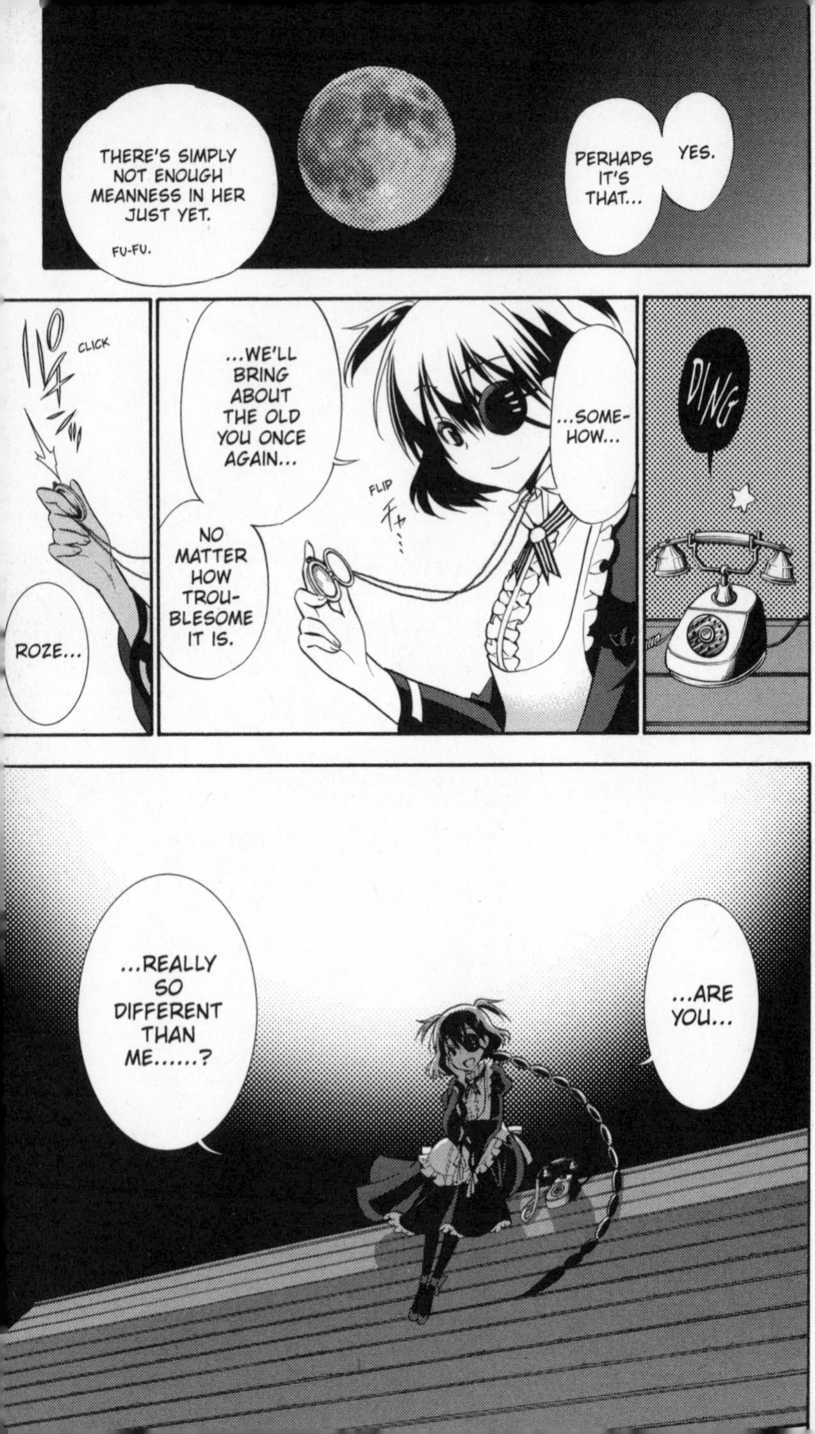
YES.
PERHAPS IT'S THAT...
THERE'S SIMPLY NOT ENOUGH MEANNESS IN HER JUST YET.
FU-FU.
DING
...SOME-HOW...
...WE'LL BRING ABOUT THE OLD YOU ONCE AGAIN...
NO MATTER HOW TROU-BLESOME IT IS.
FLIP
CLICK
ROZE...
...ARE YOU...
...REALLY SO DIFFERENT THAN ME......?

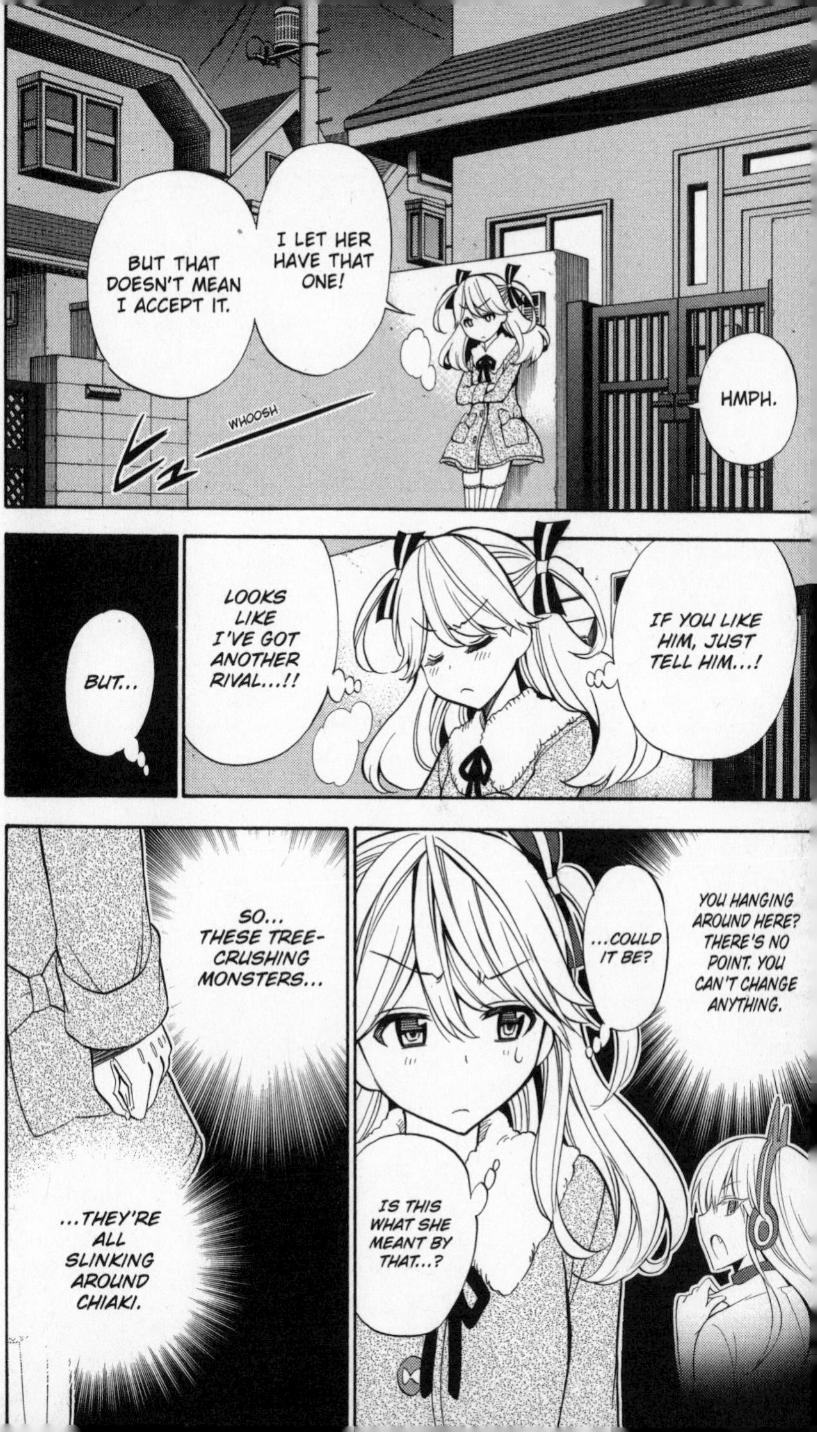
I LET HER HAVE THAT ONE!
BUT THAT DOESN'T MEAN I ACCEPT IT.
WHOOSH
HMPH.
IF YOU LIKE HIM, JUST TELL HIM...!
LOOKS LIKE I'VE GOT ANOTHER RIVAL...!!
BUT...
YOU HANGING AROUND HERE? THERE'S NO POINT. YOU CAN'T CHANGE ANYTHING.
...COULD IT BE?
IS THIS WHAT SHE MEANT BY THAT...?
SO... THESE TREE-CRUSHING MONSTERS...
...THEY'RE ALL SLINKING AROUND CHIAKI.

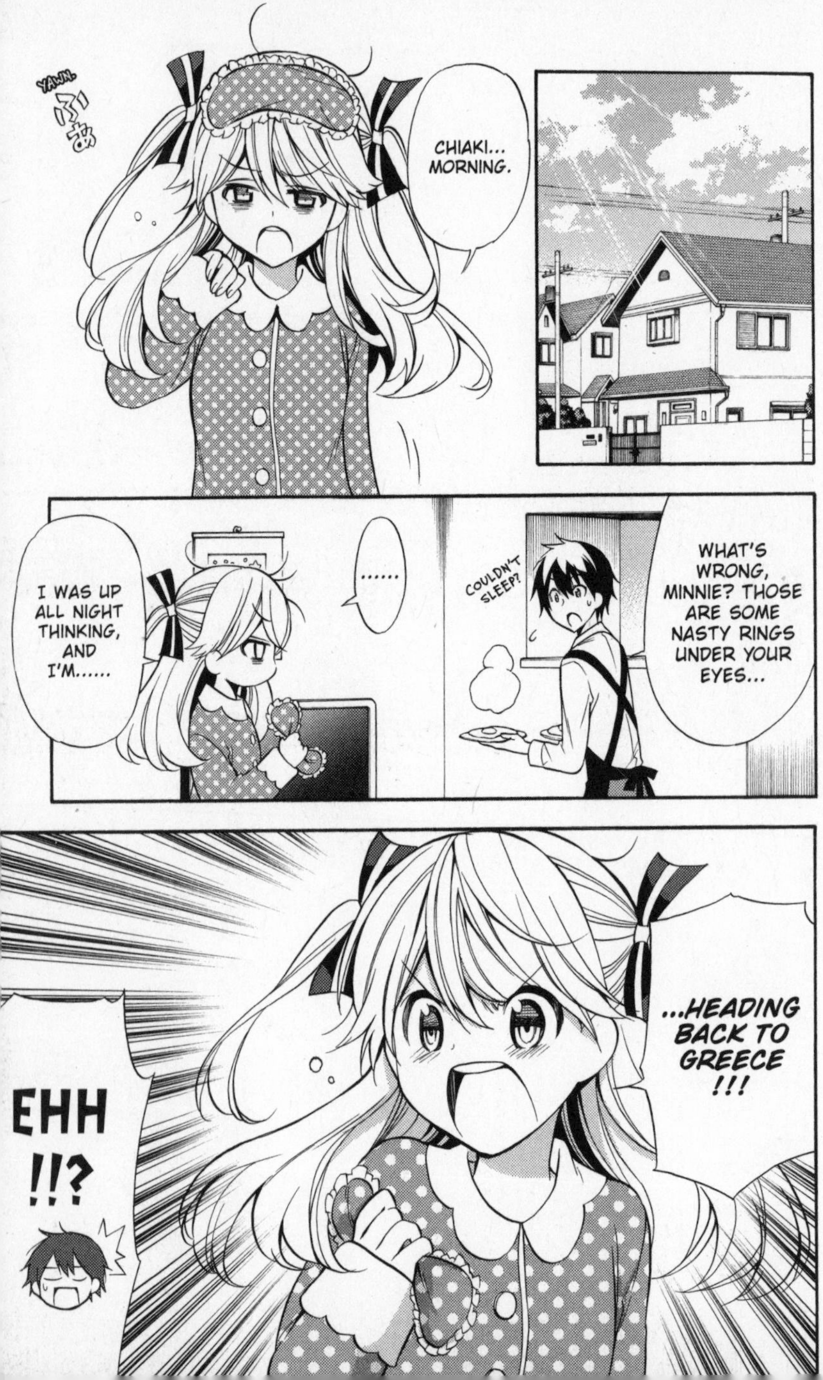
CHIAKI... MORNING.
YAWN.
ふあ
WHAT'S WRONG, MINNIE? THOSE ARE SOME NASTY RINGS UNDER YOUR EYES...
COULDN'T SLEEP?
......
I WAS UP ALL NIGHT THINKING, AND I'M......
...HEADING BACK TO GREECE!!!
EHH!!?

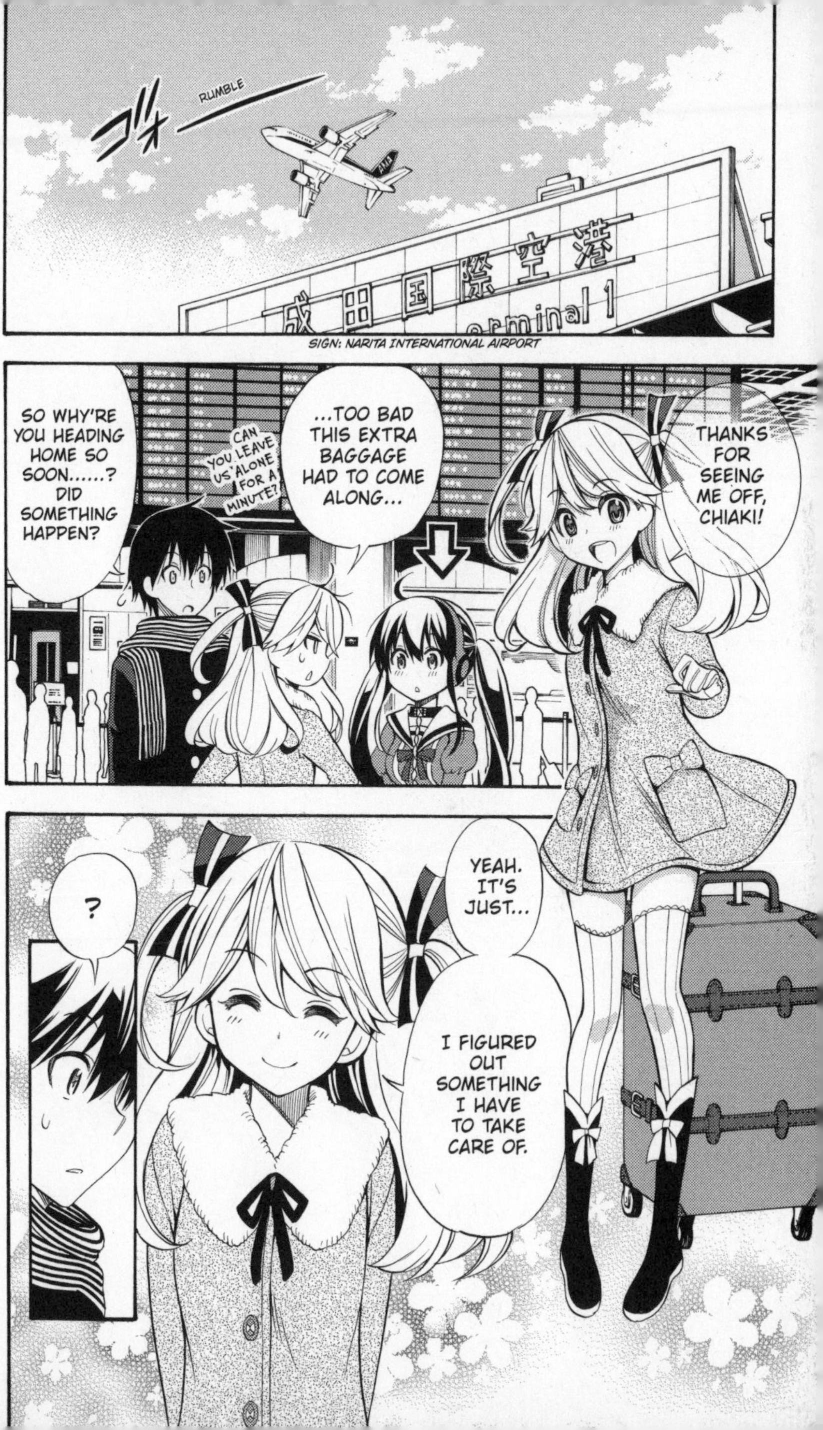

RUMBLE
成田国際空港
erminal 1
SIGN: NARITA INTERNATIONAL AIRPORT
THANKS FOR SEEING ME OFF, CHIAKI!
...TOO BAD THIS EXTRA BAGGAGE HAD TO COME ALONG...
CAN YOU LEAVE US ALONE FOR A MINUTE?
SO WHY'RE YOU HEADING HOME SO SOON......? DID SOMETHING HAPPEN?
YEAH. IT'S JUST...
I FIGURED OUT SOMETHING I HAVE TO TAKE CARE OF.
?

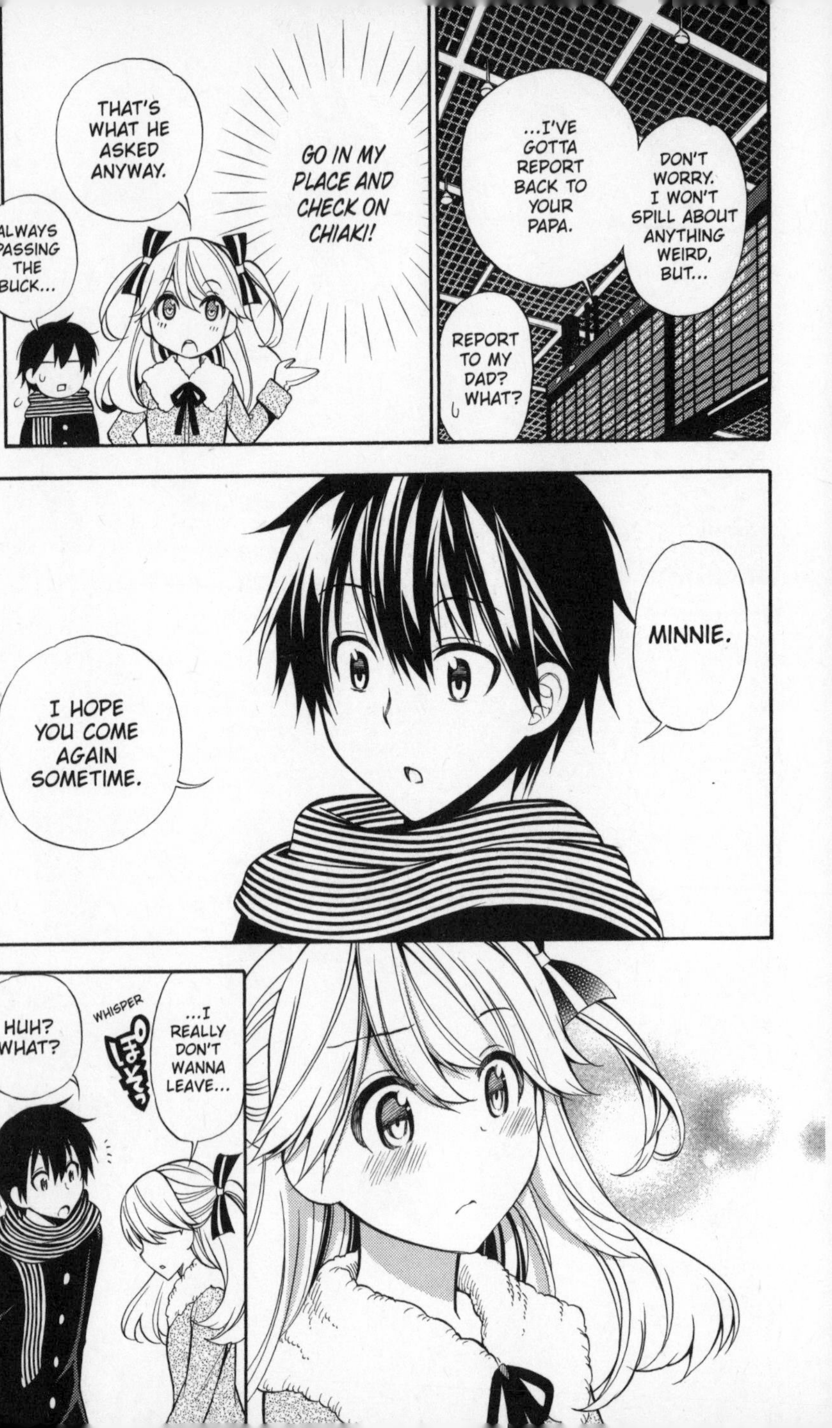
DON'T WORRY. I WON'T SPILL ABOUT ANYTHING WEIRD, BUT...
...I'VE GOTTA REPORT BACK TO YOUR PAPA.
REPORT TO MY DAD? WHAT?
GO IN MY PLACE AND CHECK ON CHIAKI!
THAT'S WHAT HE ASKED ANYWAY.
ALWAYS PASSING THE BUCK...
MINNIE.
I HOPE YOU COME AGAIN SOMETIME.
...I REALLY DON'T WANNA LEAVE...
WHISPER
HUH? WHAT?

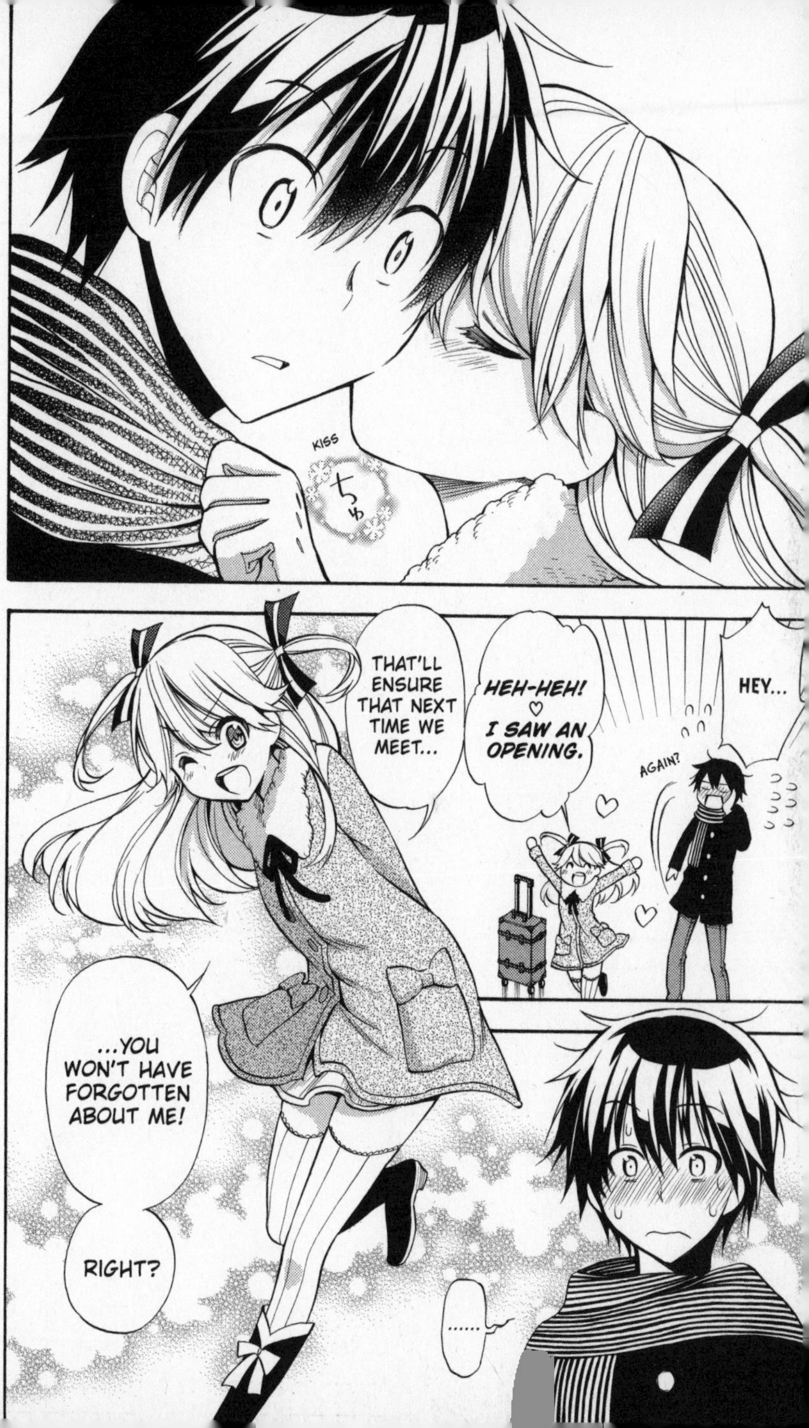
KISS
ちゅ
HEY...
AGAIN?
HEH-HEH! ♡ I SAW AN OPENING.
......
THAT'LL ENSURE THAT NEXT TIME WE MEET...
...YOU WON'T HAVE FORGOTTEN ABOUT ME!
RIGHT?

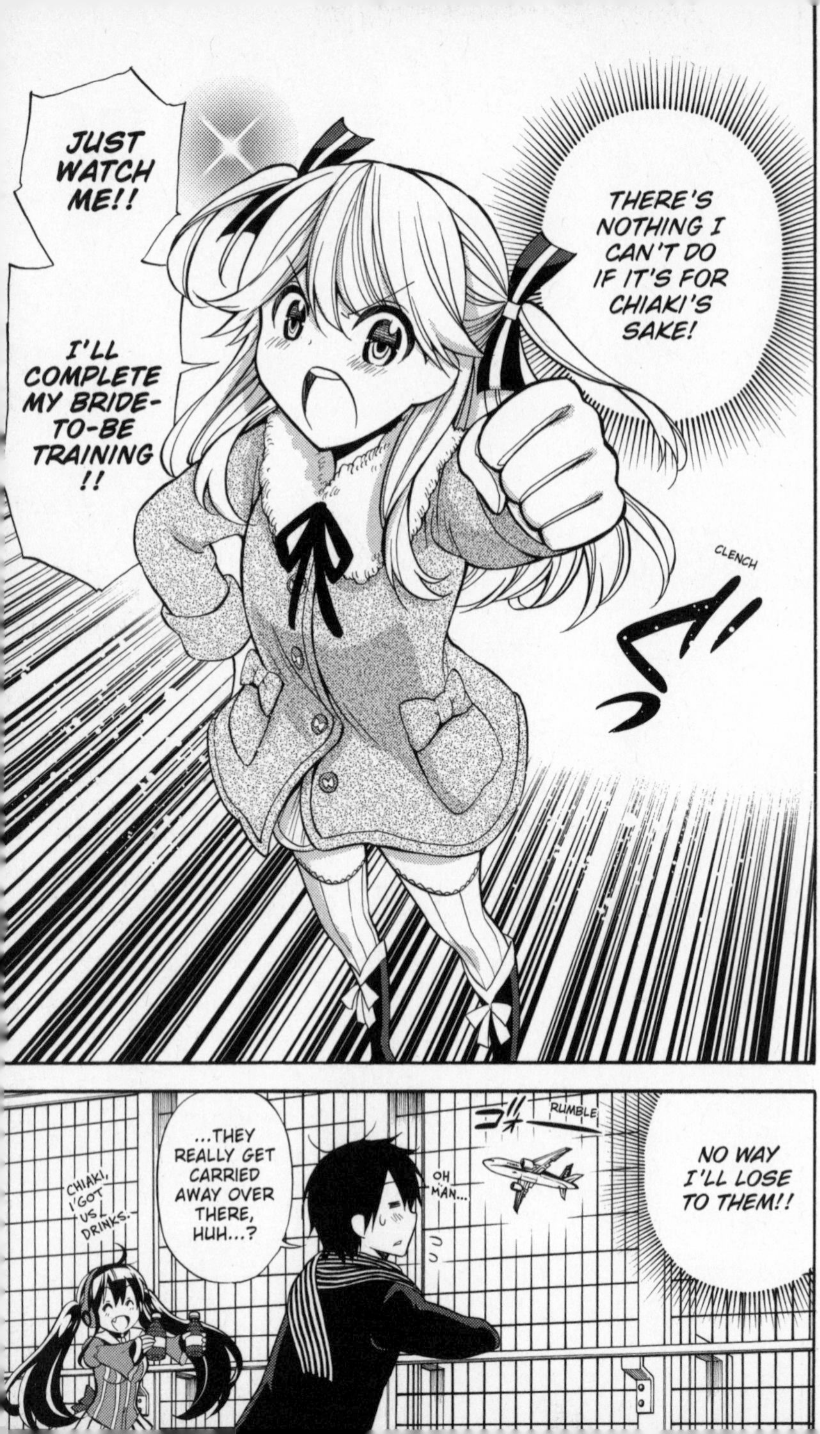
THERE'S NOTHING I CAN'T DO IF IT'S FOR CHIAKI'S SAKE!
JUST WATCH ME!!
I'LL COMPLETE MY BRIDE-TO-BE TRAINING!!
CLENCH
NO WAY I'LL LOSE TO THEM!!
RUMBLE
OH MAN...
...THEY REALLY GET CARRIED AWAY OVER THERE, HUH...?
CHIAKI, I GOT US DRINKS.

TODAY'S CERBERUS 🐾

I'M DEFINITELY GONNA BE BACK. MARK MY WORDS.

SO DON'T YOU DARE FORGET ABOUT ME.

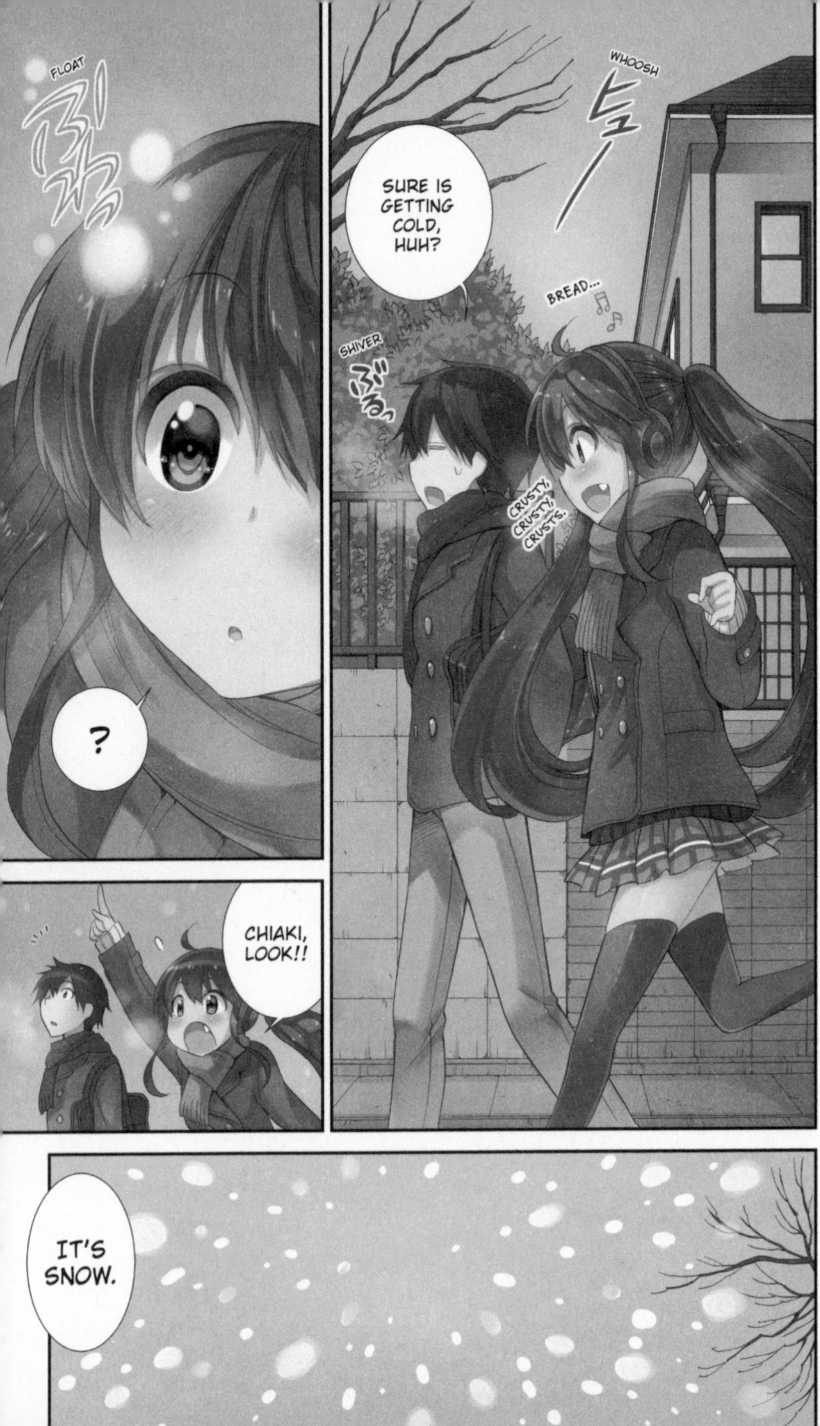
WHOOSH
SURE IS GETTING COLD, HUH?
BREAD...
SHIVER
CRUSTY, CRUSTY, CRUSTS.
FLOAT
?
CHIAKI, LOOK!!
IT'S SNOW.

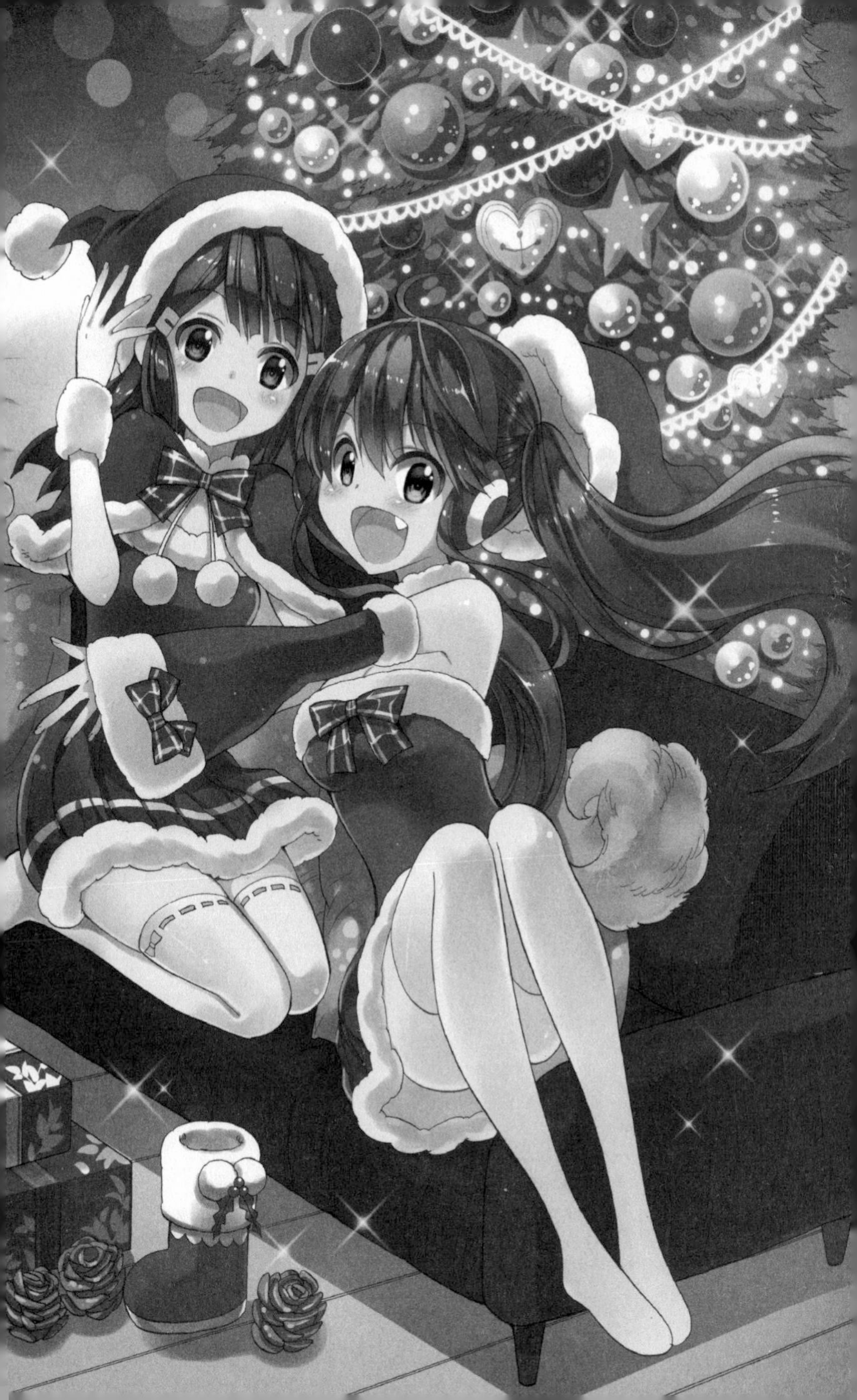

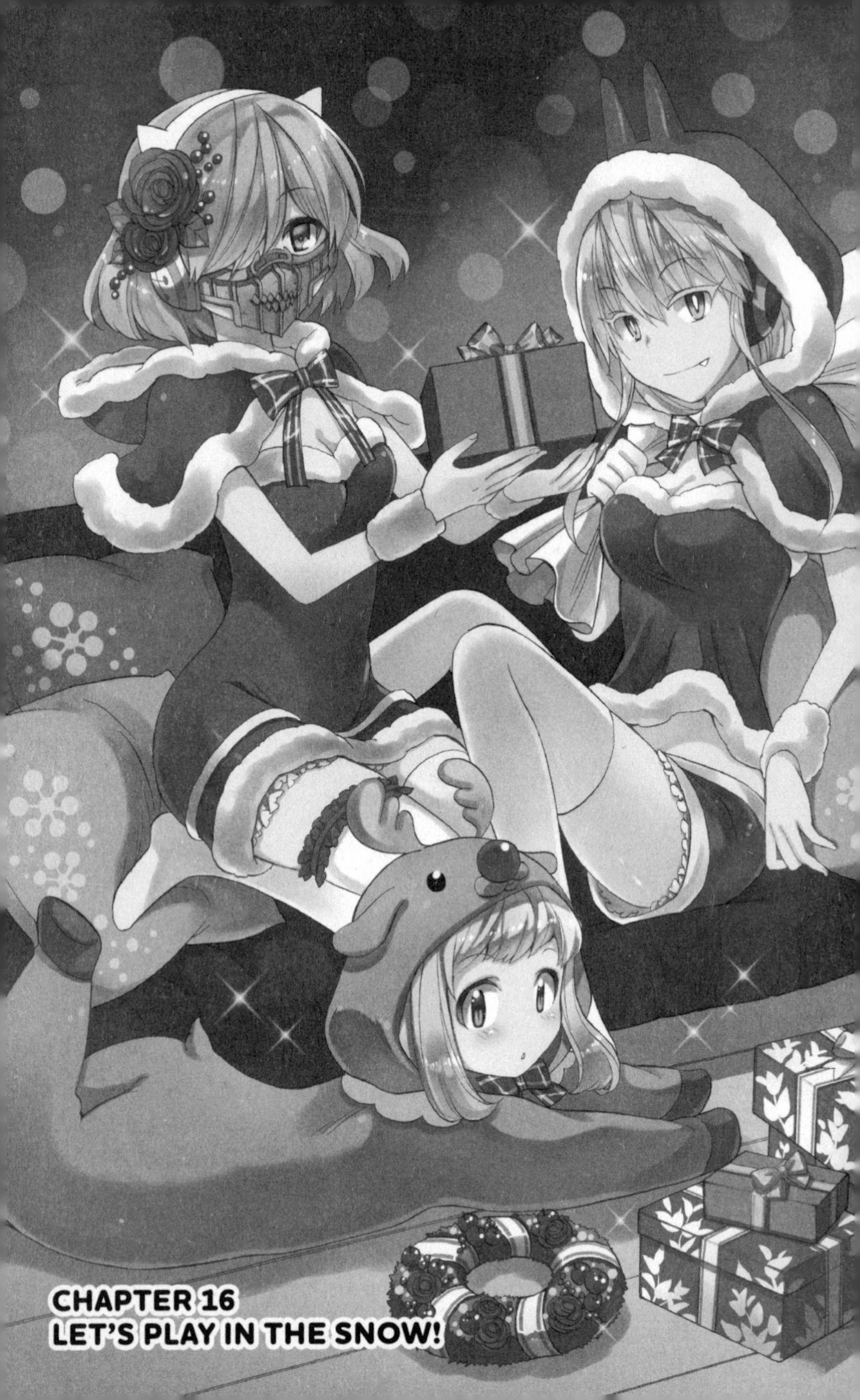

CHAPTER 16
LET'S PLAY IN THE SNOW!

TODAY'S CERBERUS 🐾

※CERBERUS'
ROOM

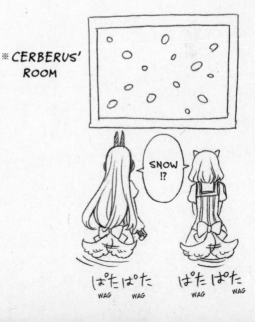

SNOW
!?

ぱたぱた
WAG   WAG

ぱたぱた
WAG   WAG

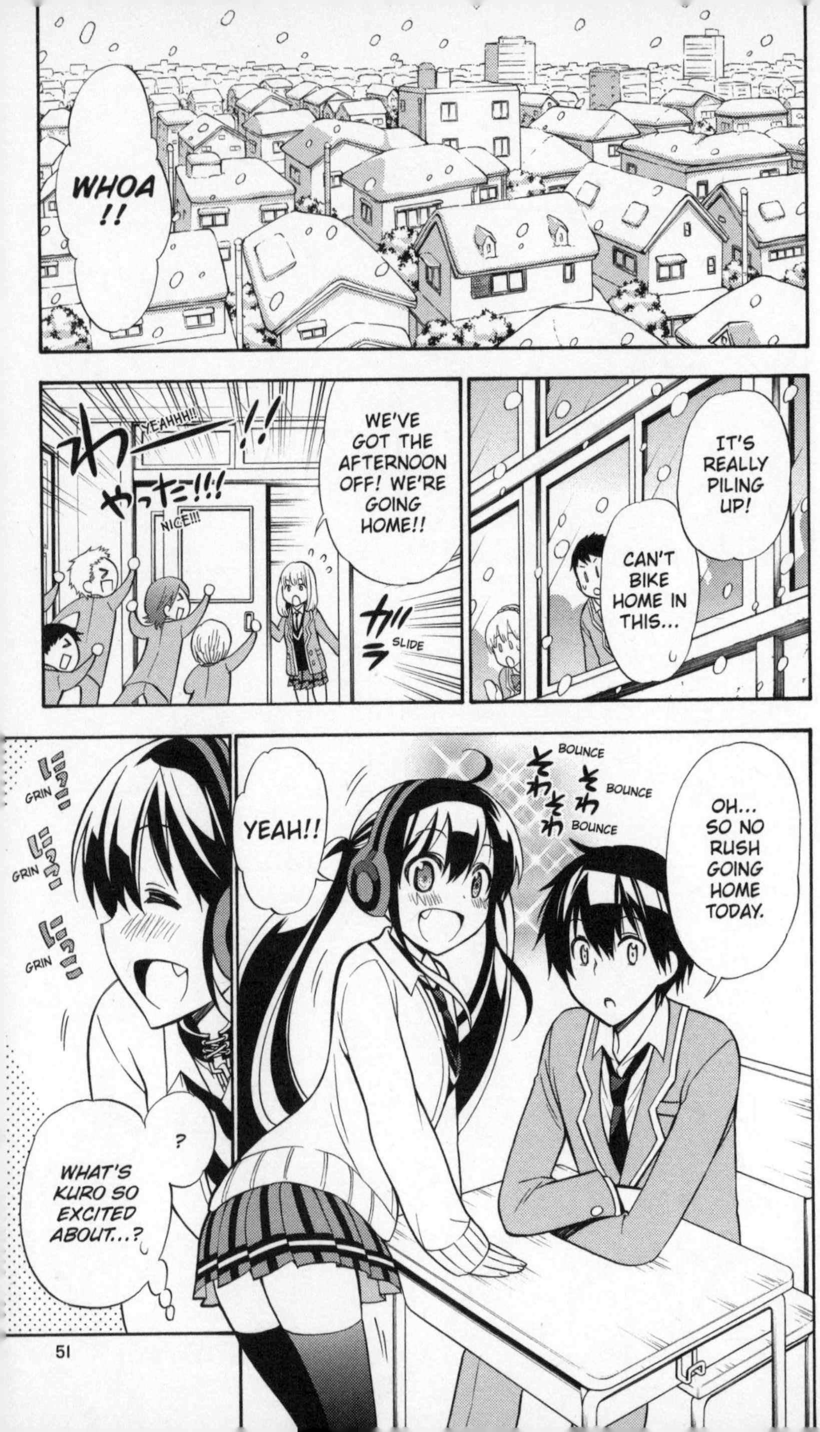
WHOA!!
IT'S REALLY PILING UP!
CAN'T BIKE HOME IN THIS...
WE'VE GOT THE AFTERNOON OFF! WE'RE GOING HOME!!
わーー!!
YEAHHH!!
やったー!!!
NICE!!!
ガラ
SLIDE
OH... SO NO RUSH GOING HOME TODAY.
そわそわそわ
BOUNCE
BOUNCE
BOUNCE
YEAH!!
にこー
GRIN
にこー
GRIN
にこー
GRIN
?
WHAT'S KURO SO EXCITED ABOUT...?

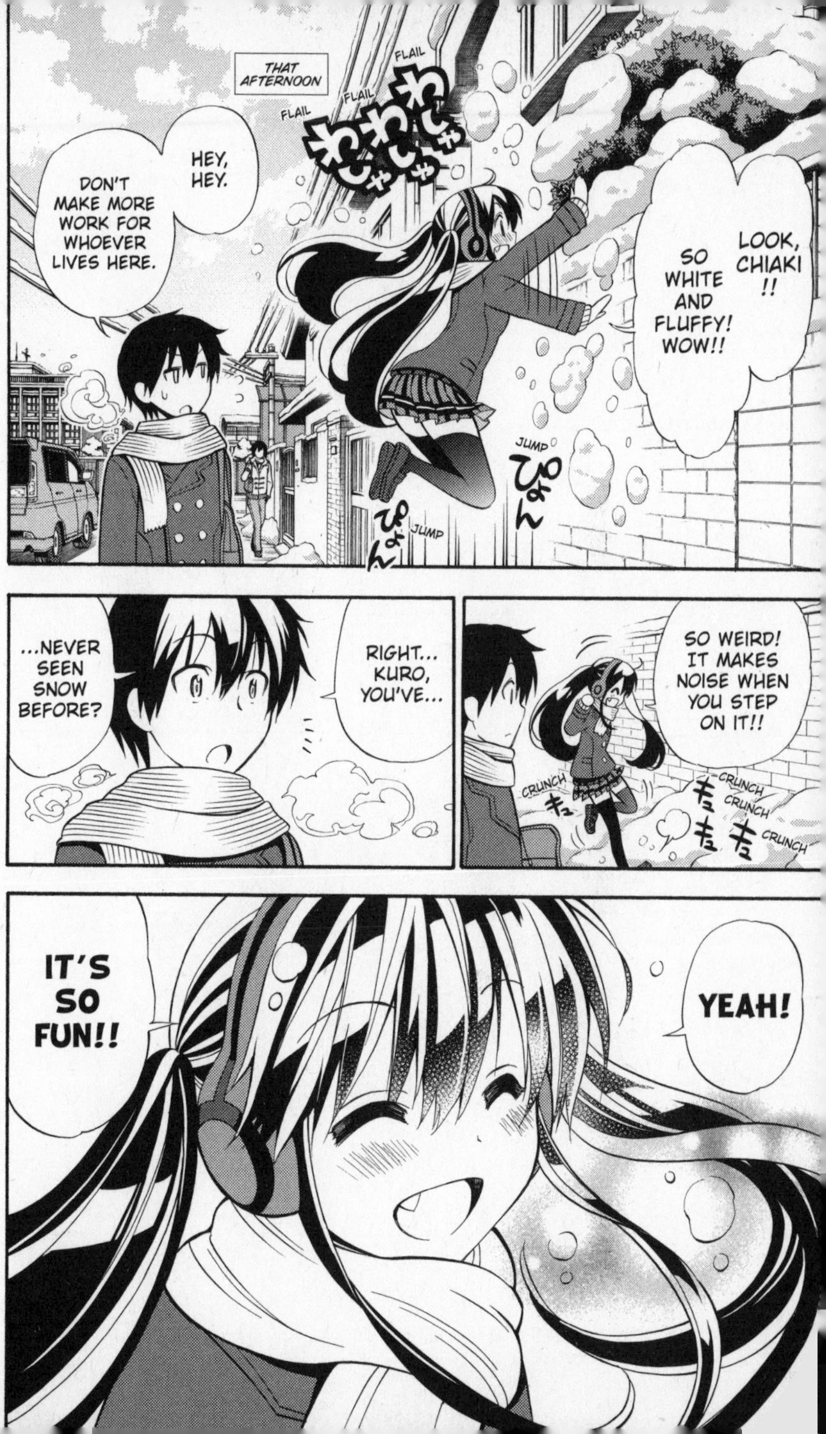
THAT AFTERNOON
LOOK, CHIAKI!!
SO WHITE AND FLUFFY! WOW!!
FLAIL
FLAIL
FLAIL
JUMP
JUMP
HEY, HEY.
DON'T MAKE MORE WORK FOR WHOEVER LIVES HERE.
SO WEIRD! IT MAKES NOISE WHEN YOU STEP ON IT!!
CRUNCH
CRUNCH
CRUNCH
CRUNCH
RIGHT... KURO, YOU'VE...
...NEVER SEEN SNOW BEFORE?
YEAH!
IT'S SO FUN!!

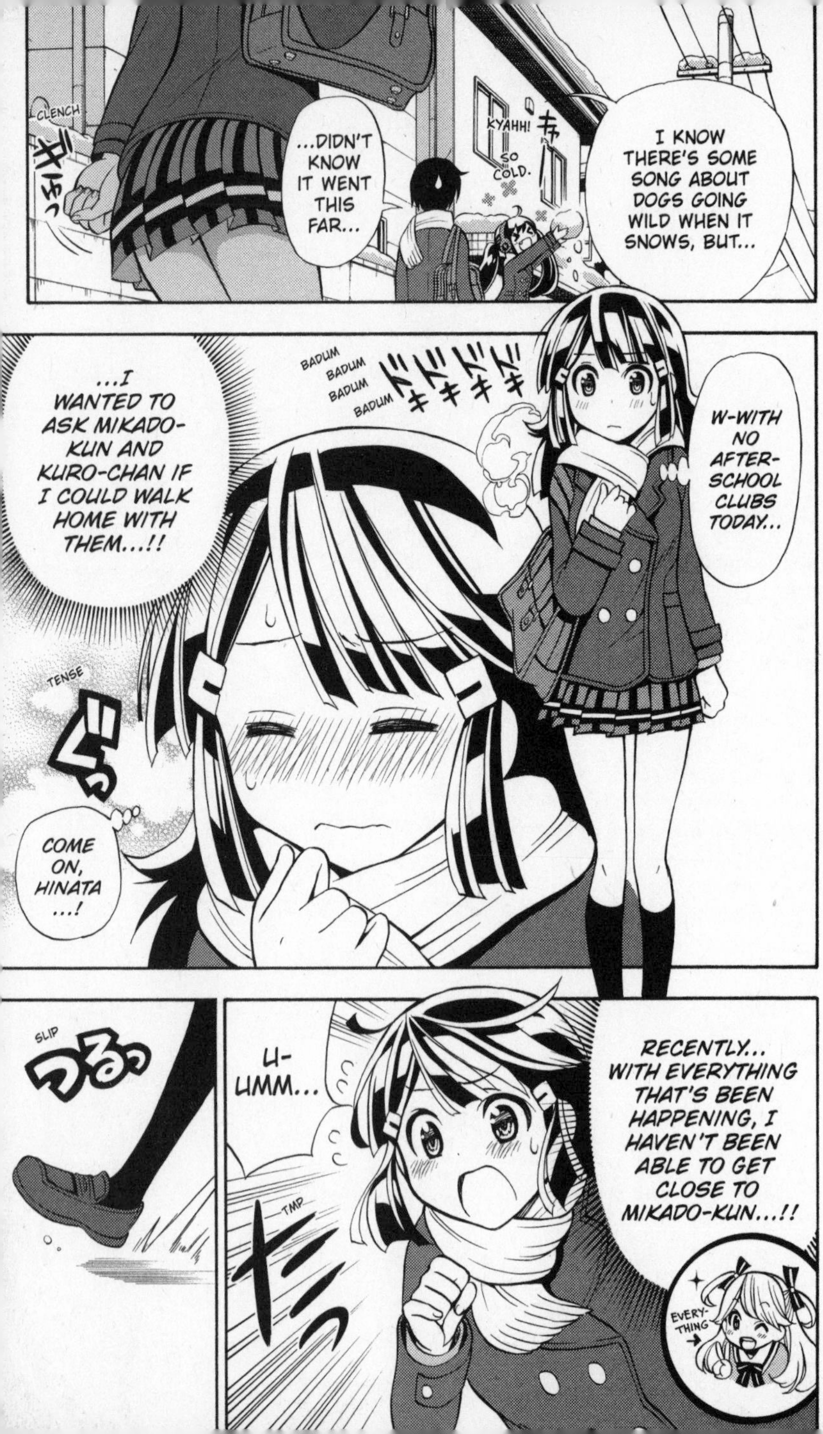
I KNOW THERE'S SOME SONG ABOUT DOGS GOING WILD WHEN IT SNOWS, BUT...
KYAHH!
SO COLD.
...DIDN'T KNOW IT WENT THIS FAR...
CLENCH
W-WITH NO AFTER-SCHOOL CLUBS TODAY...
BADUM BADUM BADUM BADUM
...I WANTED TO ASK MIKADO-KUN AND KURO-CHAN IF I COULD WALK HOME WITH THEM...!!
TENSE
COME ON, HINATA...!
RECENTLY... WITH EVERYTHING THAT'S BEEN HAPPENING, I HAVEN'T BEEN ABLE TO GET CLOSE TO MIKADO-KUN...!!
EVERY-THING
U-UMM...
TMP
SLIP

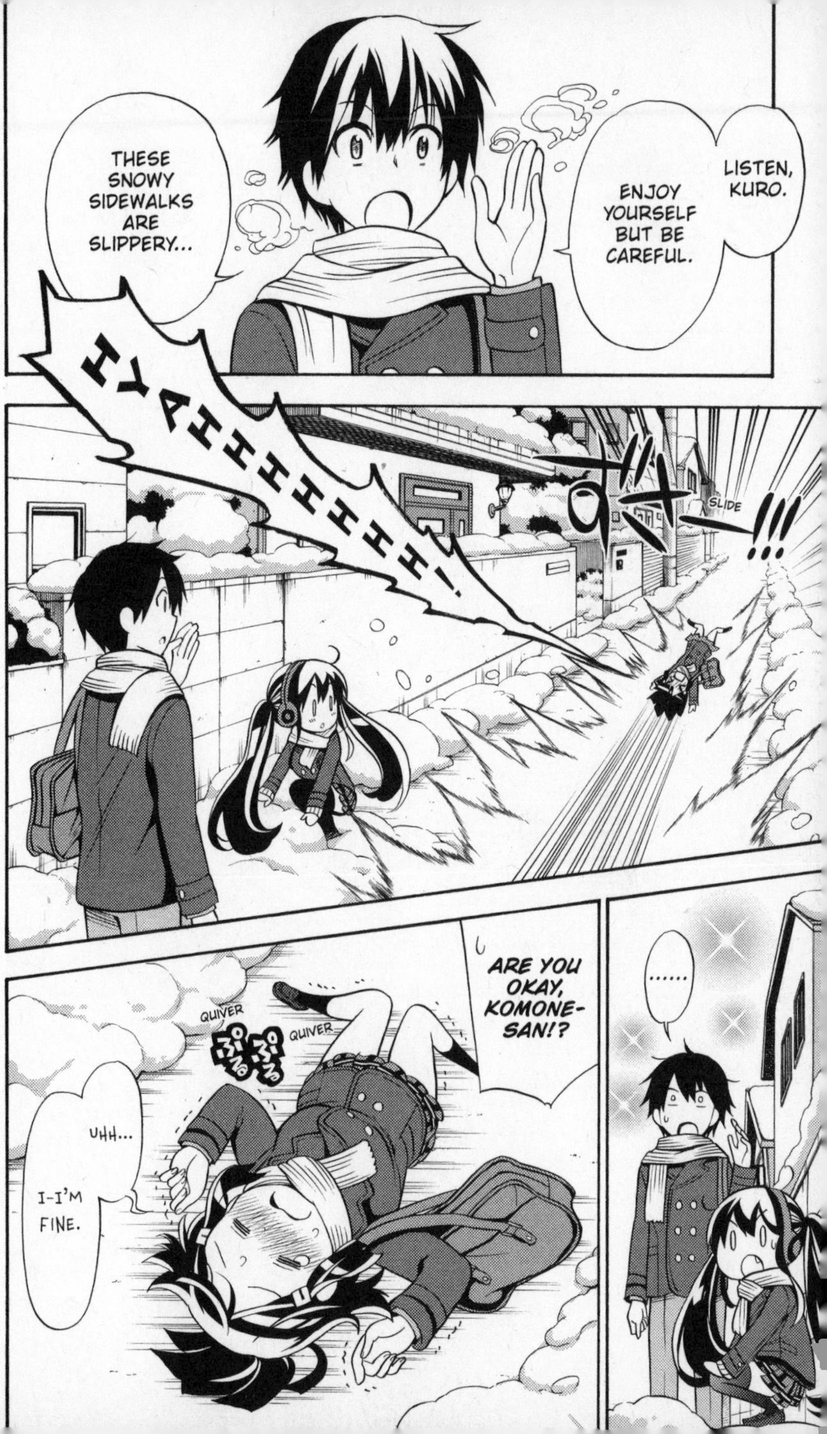

LISTEN, KURO.
ENJOY YOURSELF BUT BE CAREFUL.
THESE SNOWY SIDEWALKS ARE SLIPPERY...
HYAIIIIIIII!
SLIDE
!!!
......
ARE YOU OKAY, KOMONE-SAN!?
QUIVER
QUIVER
UHH...
I-I'M FINE.

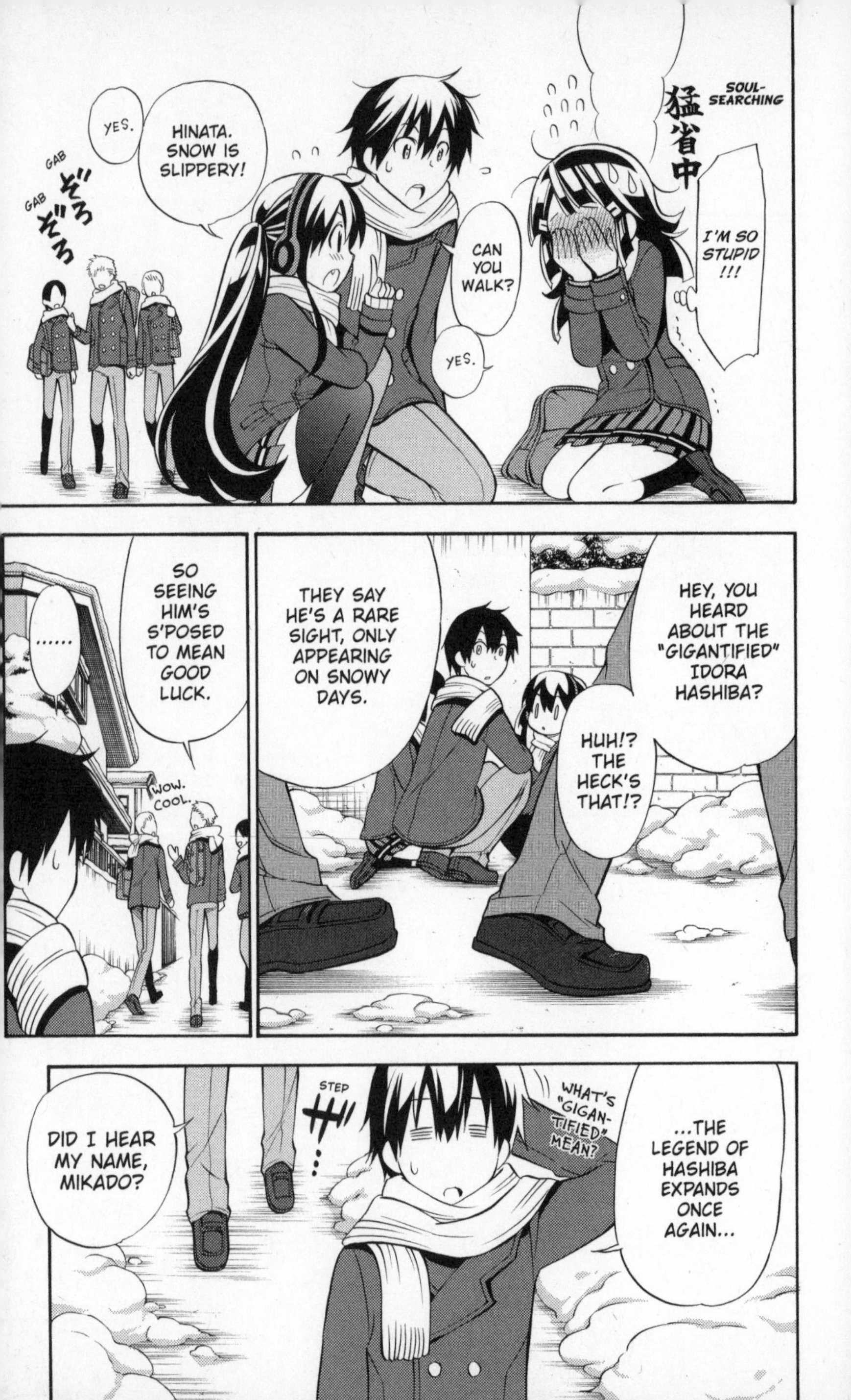
猛省中
SOUL-SEARCHING
I'M SO STUPID!!!
HINATA. SNOW IS SLIPPERY!
YES.
CAN YOU WALK?
YES.
ぞろぞろ
GAB GAB
HEY, YOU HEARD ABOUT THE "GIGANTIFIED" IDORA HASHIBA?
HUH!? THE HECK'S THAT!?
THEY SAY HE'S A RARE SIGHT, ONLY APPEARING ON SNOWY DAYS.
SO SEEING HIM'S S'POSED TO MEAN GOOD LUCK.
WOW. COOL.
......
...THE LEGEND OF HASHIBA EXPANDS ONCE AGAIN...
WHAT'S "GIGANTIFIED" MEAN?
ザッ
STEP
DID I HEAR MY NAME, MIKADO?

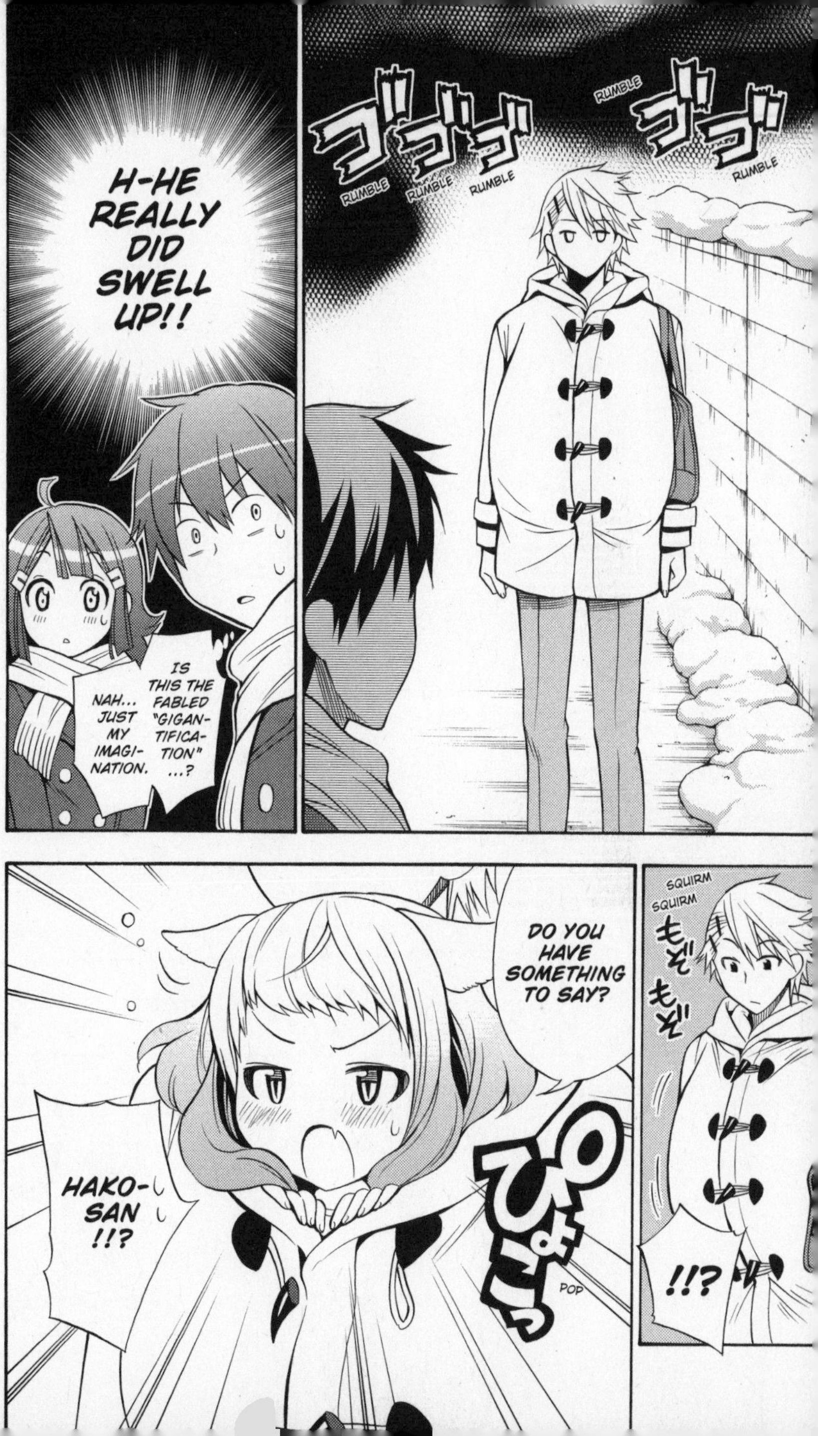

ゴゴゴ
RUMBLE RUMBLE RUMBLE
ゴゴ
RUMBLE RUMBLE
H-HE REALLY DID SWELL UP!!
IS THIS THE FABLED "GIGANTIFICATION"...?
NAH... JUST MY IMAGINATION.
もぞもぞ
SQUIRM SQUIRM
!!?
DO YOU HAVE SOMETHING TO SAY?
ぴょこっ
POP
HAKO-SAN!!?

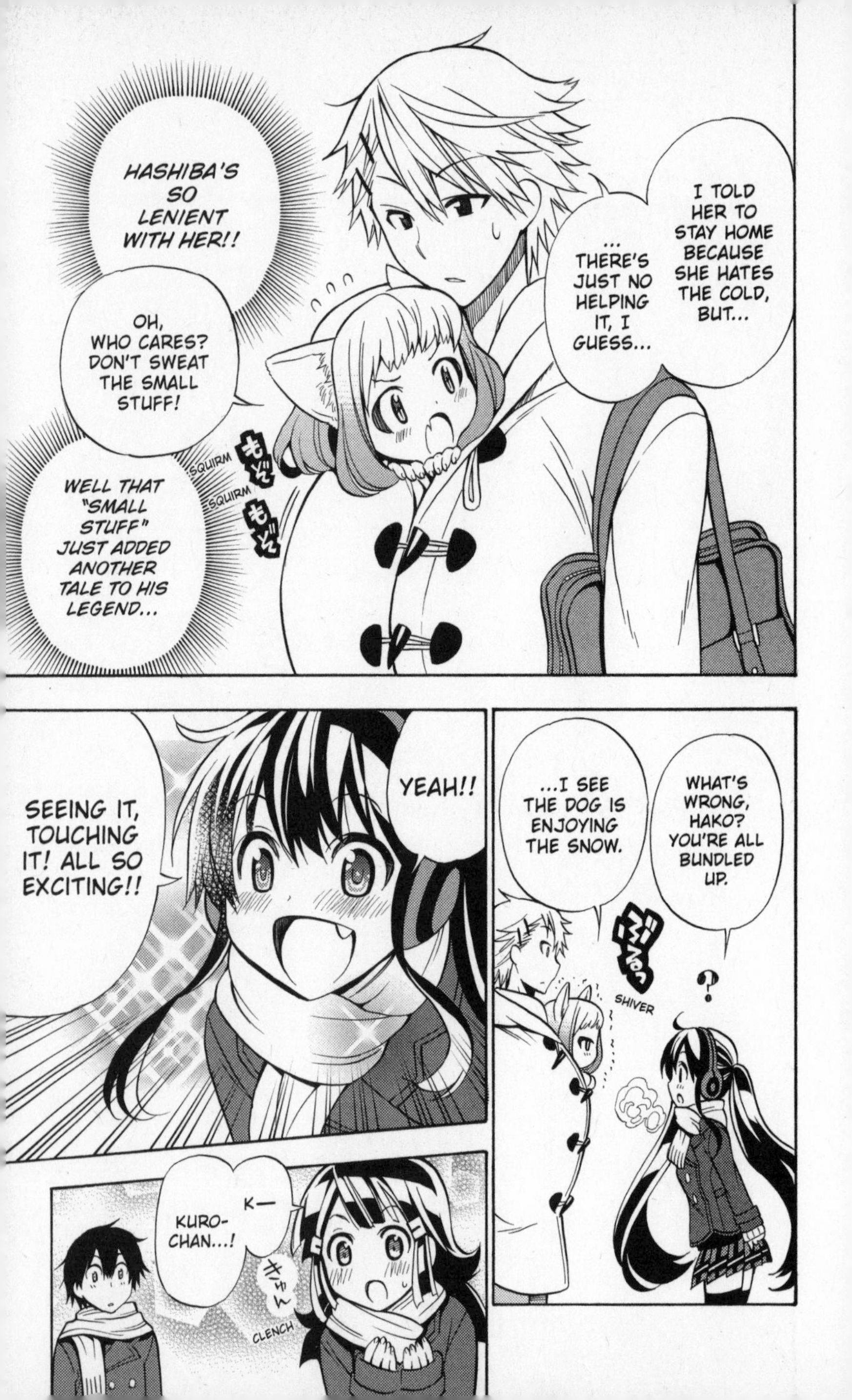
I TOLD HER TO STAY HOME BECAUSE SHE HATES THE COLD, BUT...
... THERE'S JUST NO HELPING IT, I GUESS...
HASHIBA'S SO LENIENT WITH HER!!
OH, WHO CARES? DON'T SWEAT THE SMALL STUFF!
もぞ
SQUIRM
もぞ
SQUIRM
WELL THAT "SMALL STUFF" JUST ADDED ANOTHER TALE TO HIS LEGEND...
WHAT'S WRONG, HAKO? YOU'RE ALL BUNDLED UP.
...I SEE THE DOG IS ENJOYING THE SNOW.
SHIVER
?
YEAH!!
SEEING IT, TOUCHING IT! ALL SO EXCITING!!
K— KURO-CHAN...!
きゅん
CLENCH

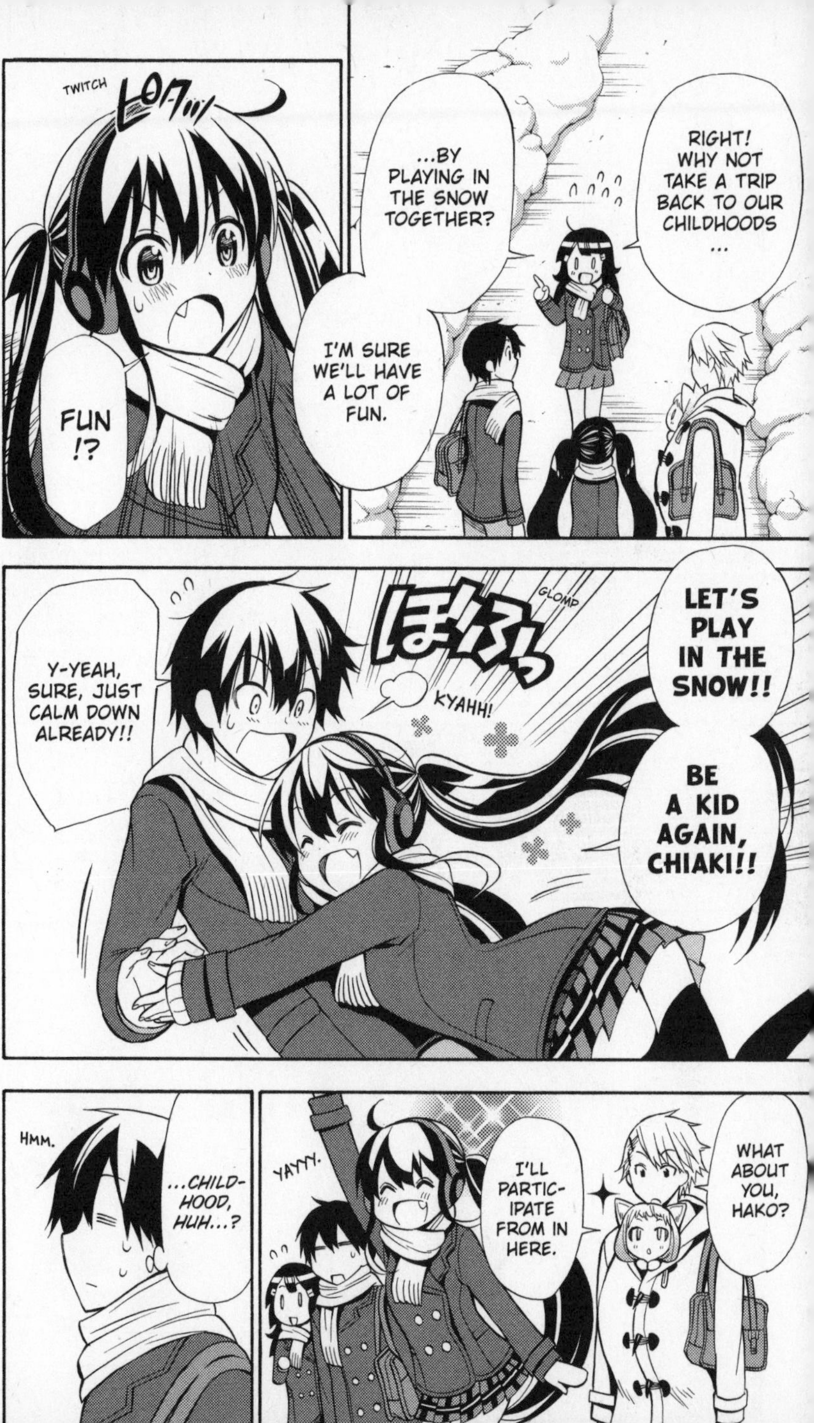
RIGHT! WHY NOT TAKE A TRIP BACK TO OUR CHILDHOODS ...
...BY PLAYING IN THE SNOW TOGETHER?
I'M SURE WE'LL HAVE A LOT OF FUN.
TWITCH
FUN !?
LET'S PLAY IN THE SNOW!!
BE A KID AGAIN, CHIAKI!!
GLOMP
KYAHH!
Y-YEAH, SURE, JUST CALM DOWN ALREADY!!
WHAT ABOUT YOU, HAKO?
I'LL PARTIC-IPATE FROM IN HERE.
YAYYY.
HMM.
...CHILD-HOOD, HUH...?

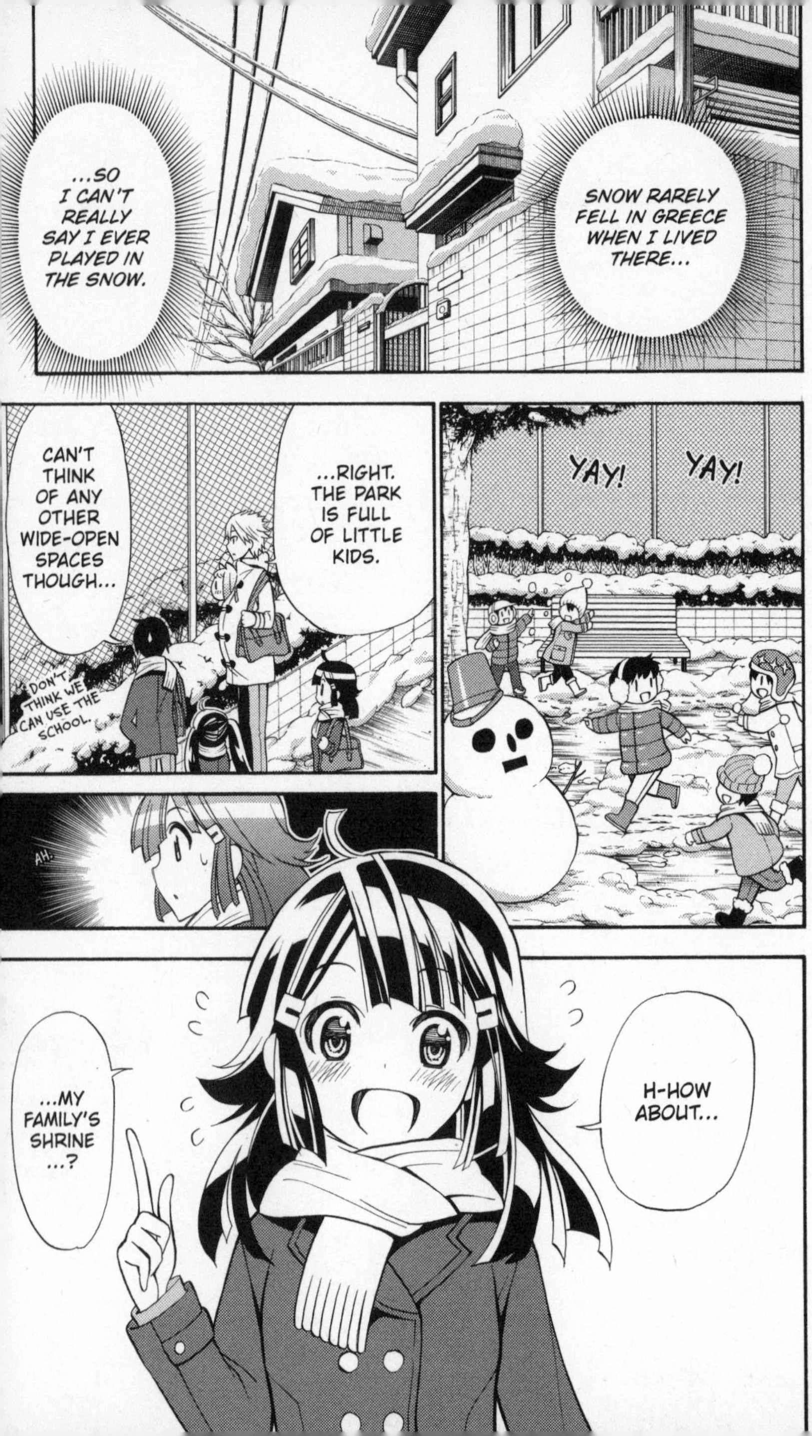
SNOW RARELY FELL IN GREECE WHEN I LIVED THERE...
...SO I CAN'T REALLY SAY I EVER PLAYED IN THE SNOW.
YAY!
YAY!
...RIGHT. THE PARK IS FULL OF LITTLE KIDS.
CAN'T THINK OF ANY OTHER WIDE-OPEN SPACES THOUGH...
DON'T THINK WE CAN USE THE SCHOOL.
AH.
H-HOW ABOUT...
...MY FAMILY'S SHRINE ...?

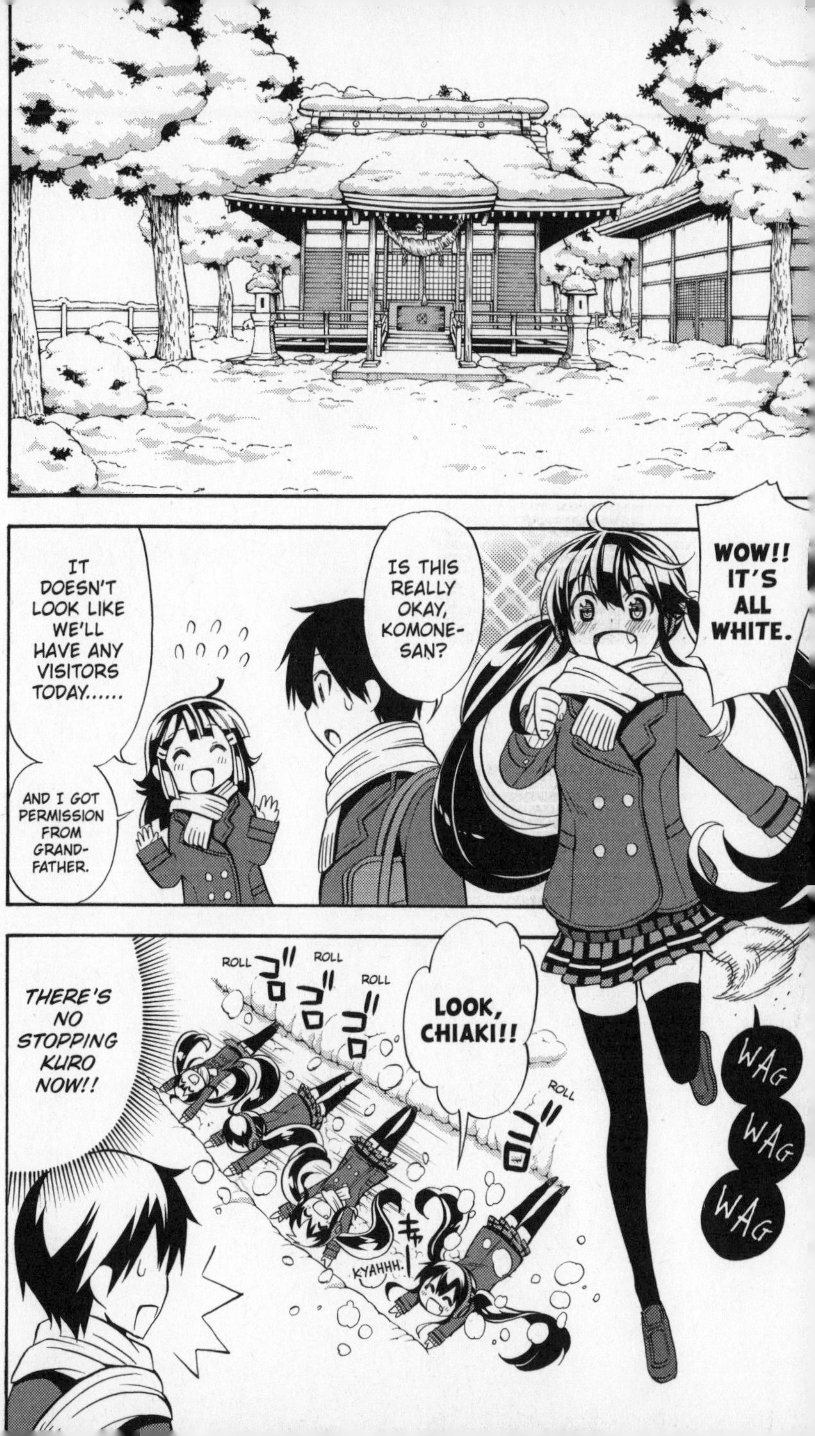
WOW!! IT'S ALL WHITE.
IS THIS REALLY OKAY, KOMONE-SAN?
IT DOESN'T LOOK LIKE WE'LL HAVE ANY VISITORS TODAY......
AND I GOT PERMISSION FROM GRAND-FATHER.
WAG WAG WAG
LOOK, CHIAKI!!
ROLL ゴロ
ROLL ゴロ
ROLL ゴロ
ROLL ゴロ
キャー KYAHHH!
THERE'S NO STOPPING KURO NOW!!

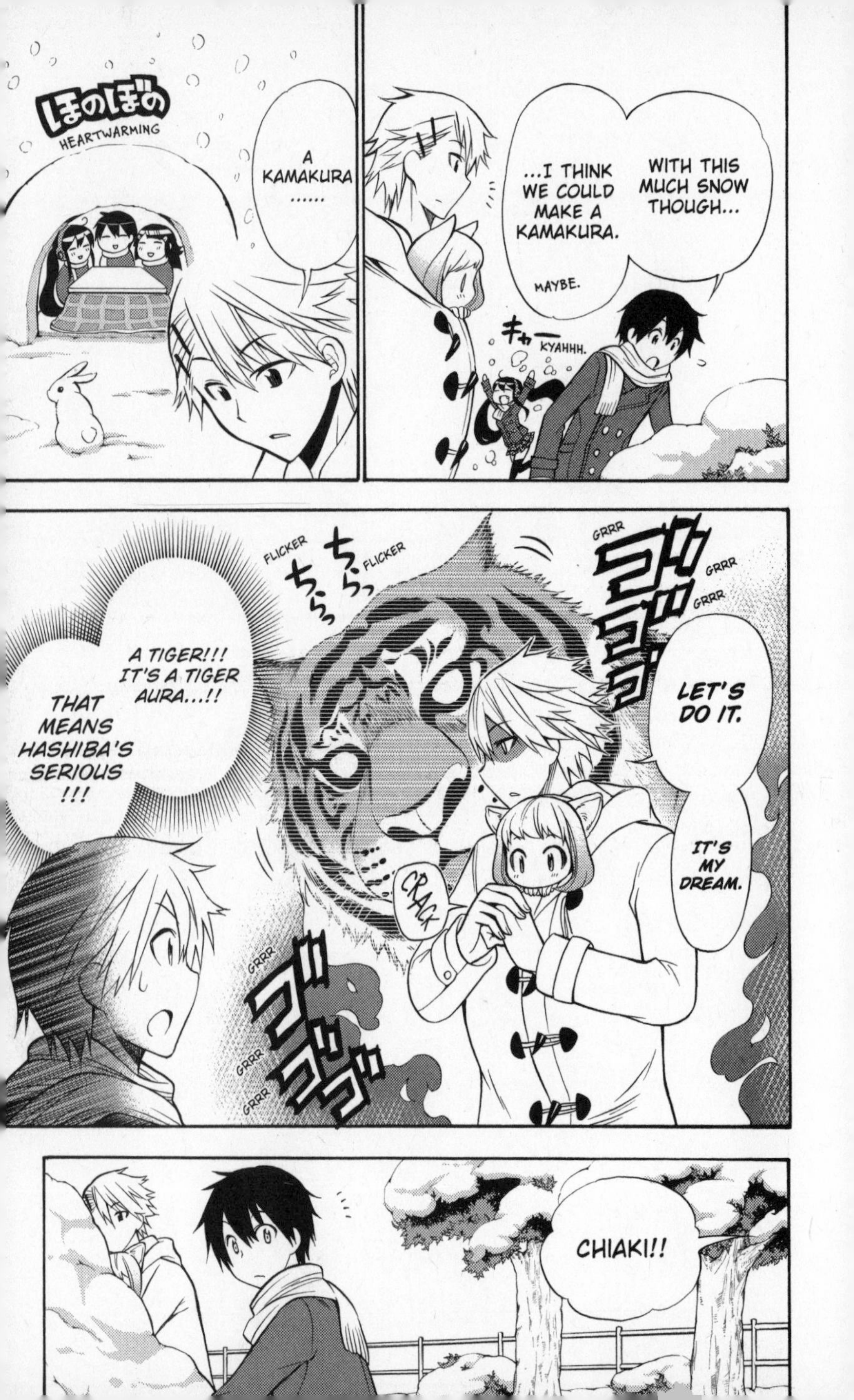
WITH THIS MUCH SNOW THOUGH...
...I THINK WE COULD MAKE A KAMAKURA.
MAYBE.
キャー KYAHHH.
ほのぼの HEARTWARMING
A KAMAKURA ......
GRRR GRRR GRRR
LET'S DO IT.
IT'S MY DREAM.
ちらっ FLICKER
ちらっ FLICKER
A TIGER!!! IT'S A TIGER AURA...!!
THAT MEANS HASHIBA'S SERIOUS!!!
CRACK
GRRR GRRR GRRR
CHIAKI!!

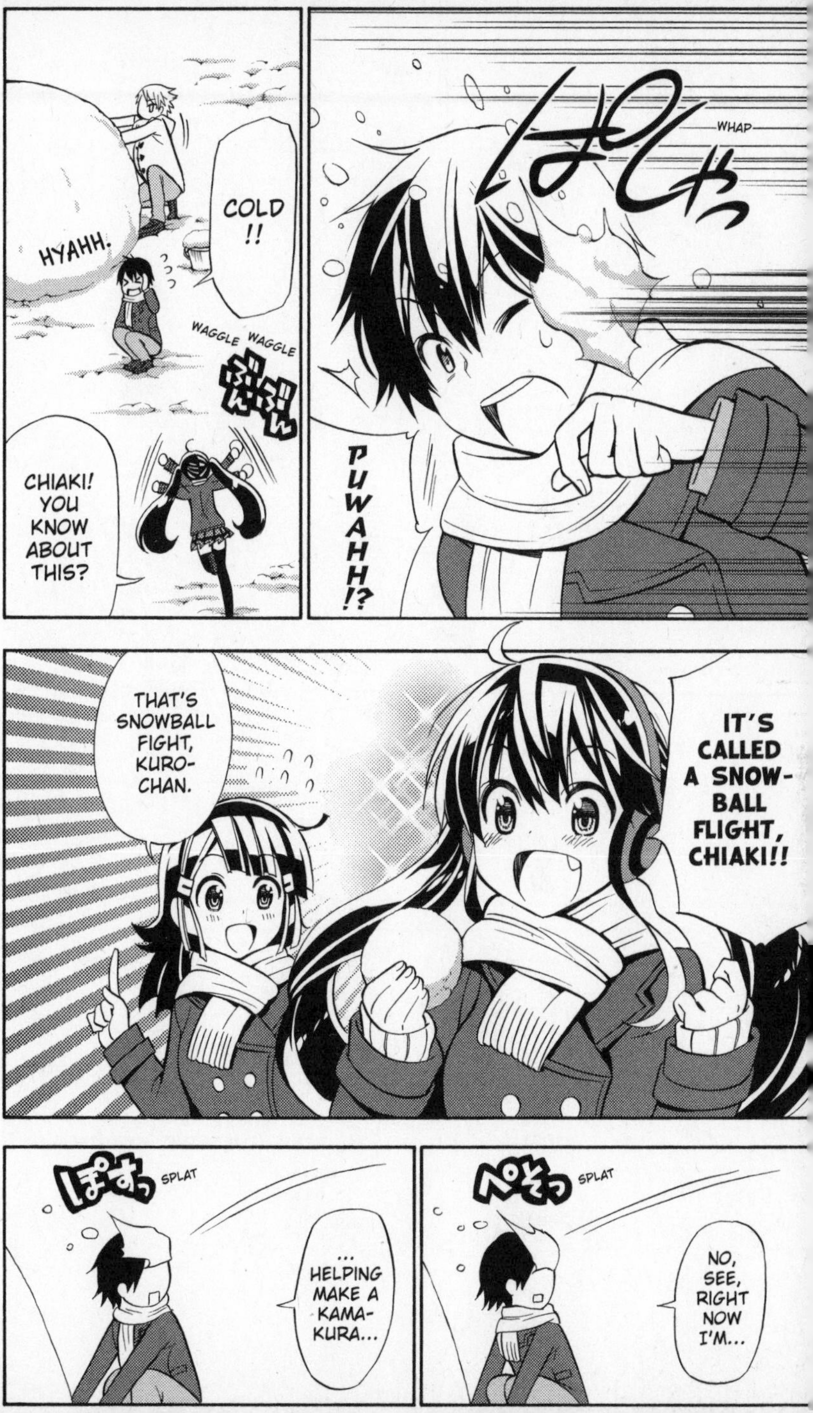
ぱしゃっ
WHAP
PUWAHH!?
COLD!!
WAGGLE WAGGLE
ぶんぶん
HYAHH.
CHIAKI! YOU KNOW ABOUT THIS?
IT'S CALLED A SNOW-BALL FLIGHT, CHIAKI!!
THAT'S SNOWBALL FIGHT, KURO-CHAN.
ぺそっ
SPLAT
NO, SEE, RIGHT NOW I'M...
ぽすっ
SPLAT
...HELPING MAKE A KAMA-KURA...

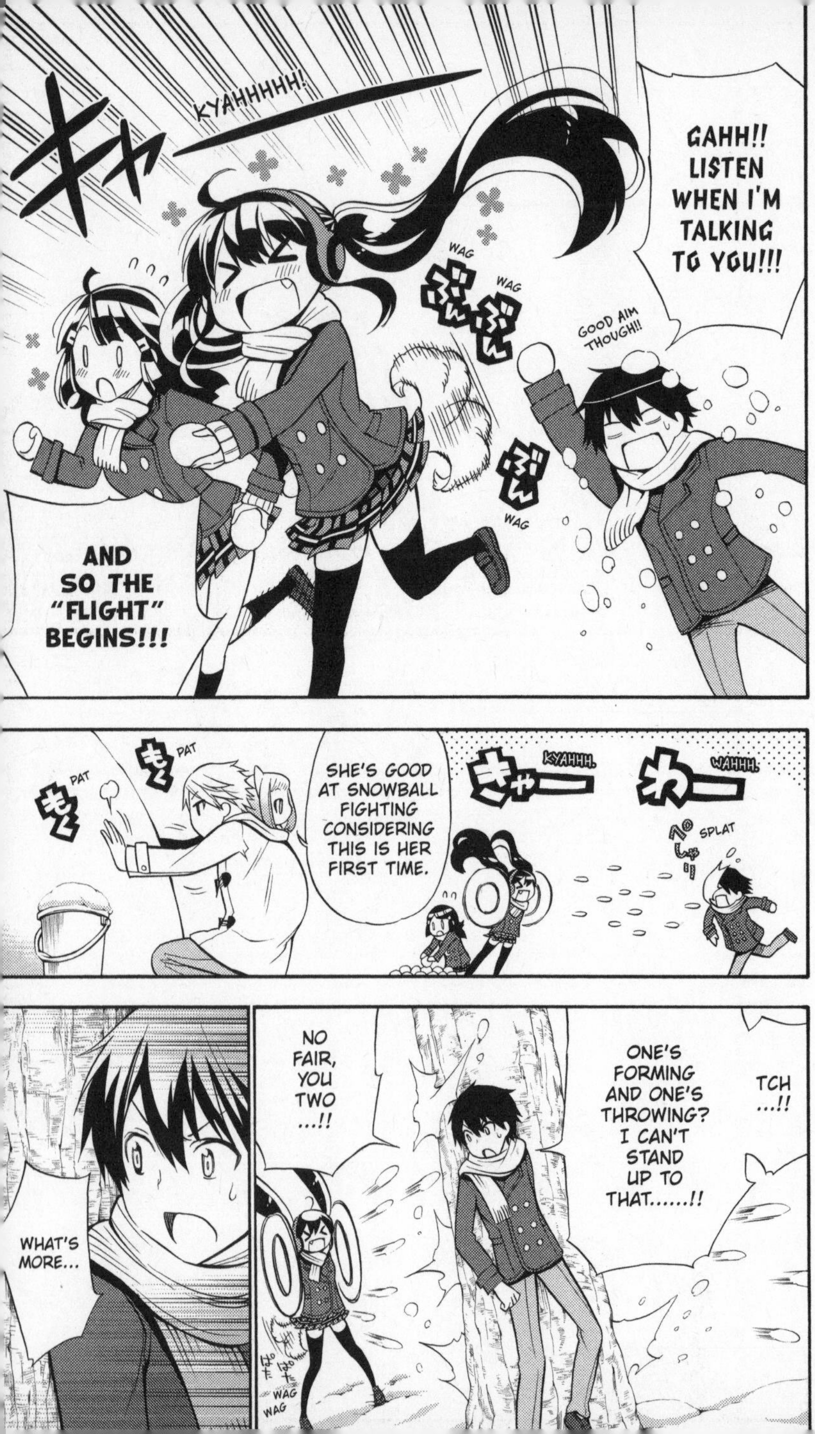
GAHH!! LISTEN WHEN I'M TALKING TO YOU!!!
GOOD AIM THOUGH!!
WAG
WAG
WAG
キャ
KYAHHHHH!
AND SO THE "FLIGHT" BEGINS!!!
わー
WAHHH.
きゃー
KYAHHH.
SPLAT
SHE'S GOOD AT SNOWBALL FIGHTING CONSIDERING THIS IS HER FIRST TIME.
PAT
PAT
TCH ...!!
ONE'S FORMING AND ONE'S THROWING? I CAN'T STAND UP TO THAT......!!
NO FAIR, YOU TWO ...!!
WAG
WAG
WHAT'S MORE...

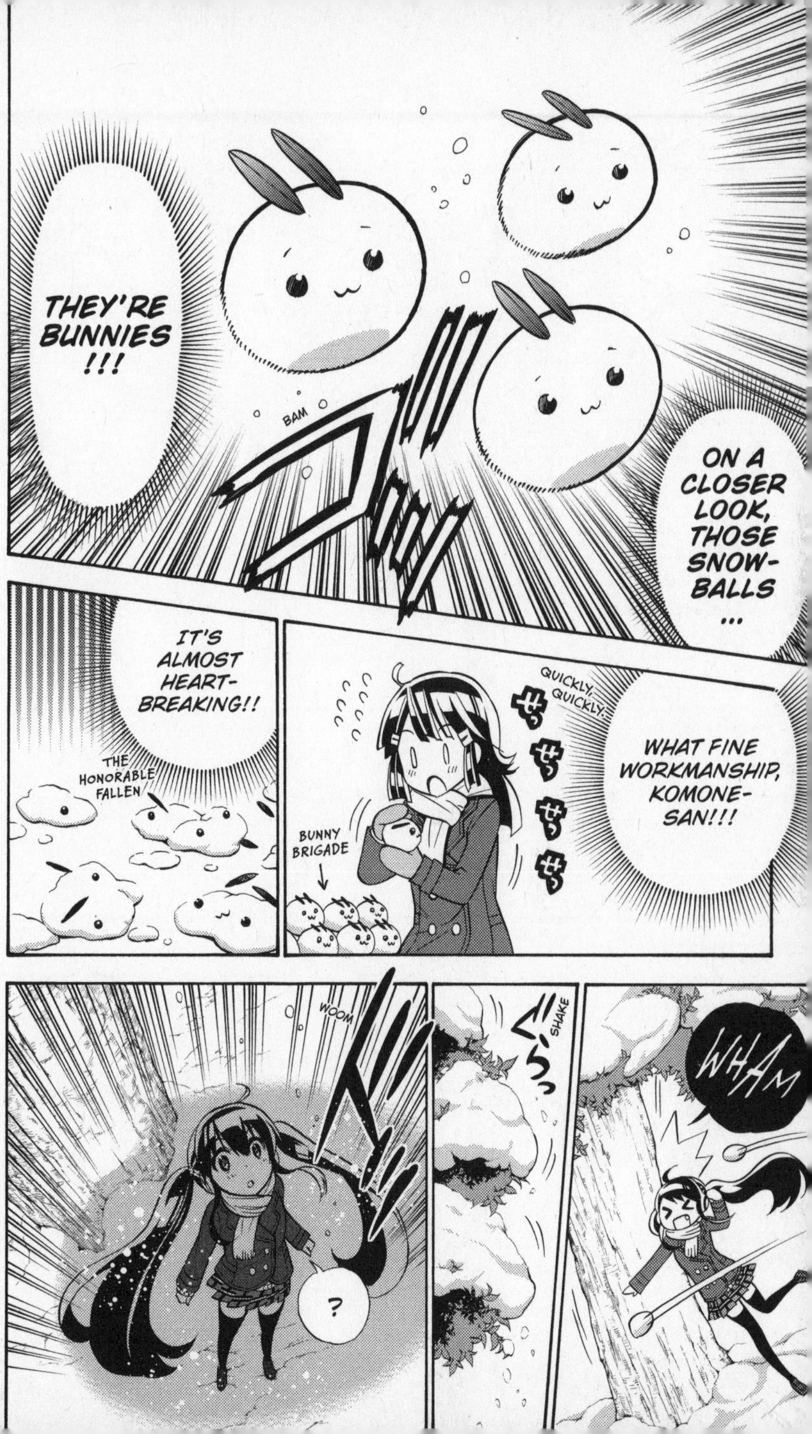
ON A CLOSER LOOK, THOSE SNOW-BALLS...
BAM
THEY'RE BUNNIES!!!
QUICKLY, QUICKLY.
WHAT FINE WORKMANSHIP, KOMONE-SAN!!!
BUNNY BRIGADE
IT'S ALMOST HEART-BREAKING!!
THE HONORABLE FALLEN
WHAM
SHAKE
WOOM
?

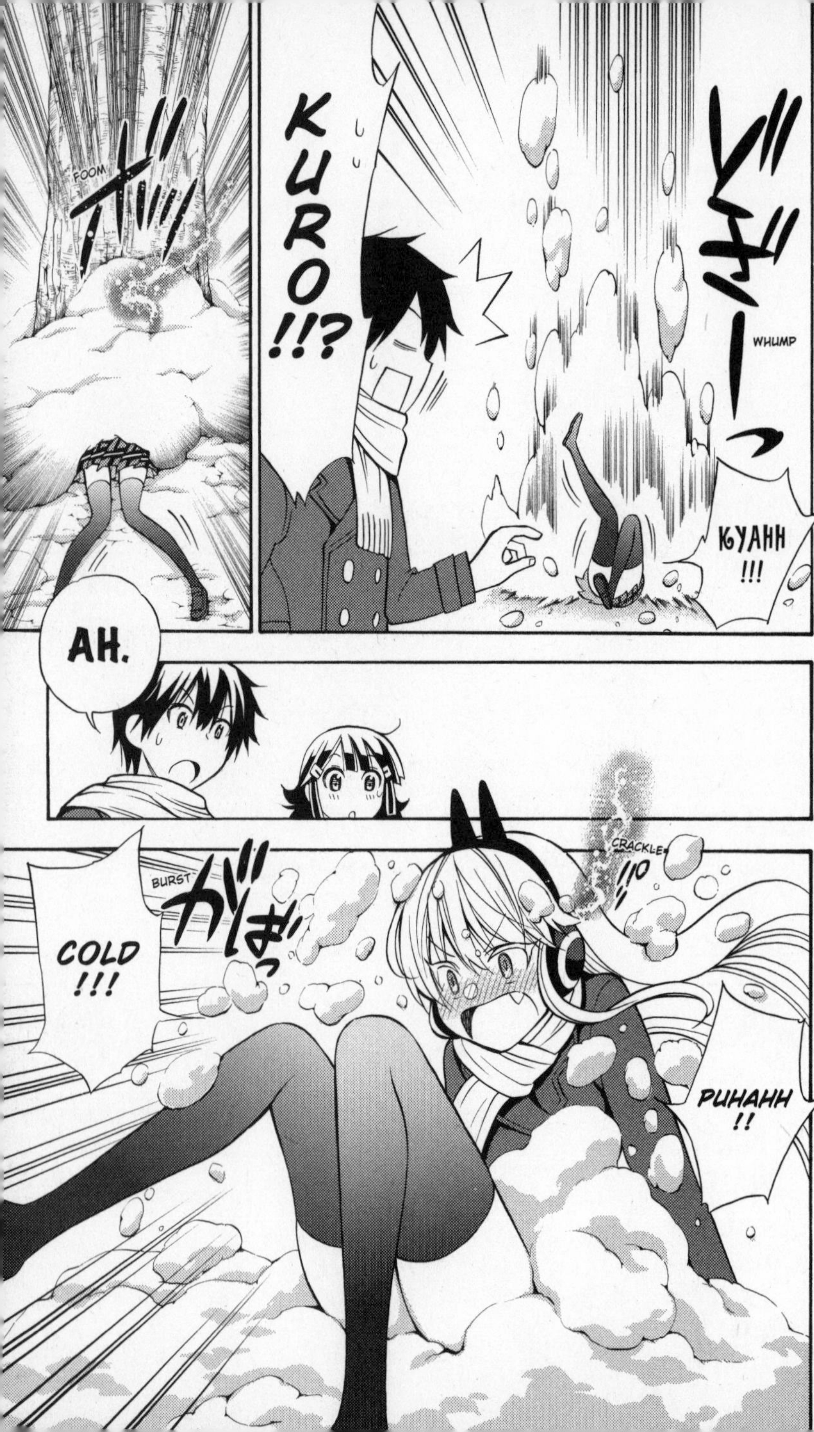

WHUMP
KURO!!?
KYAHH!!!
FOOM
AH.
CRACKLE
PUHAHH!!
BURST
COLD!!!

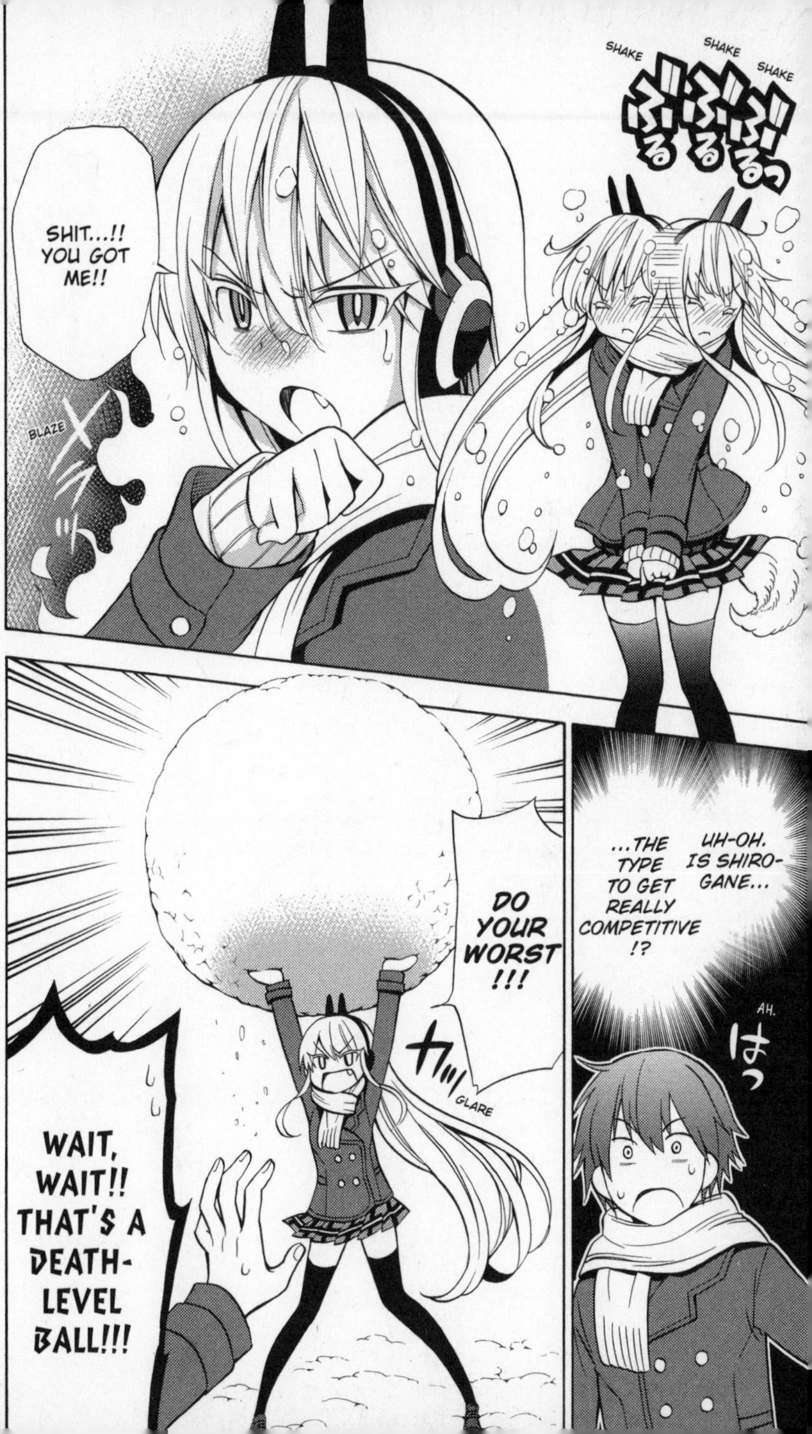
SHAKE SHAKE SHAKE
ぶるぶるぶるっ
SHIT...!! YOU GOT ME!!
BLAZE
UH-OH. IS SHIRO-GANE...
...THE TYPE TO GET REALLY COMPETITIVE !?
AH.
はっ
DO YOUR WORST !!!
GLARE
WAIT, WAIT!! THAT'S A DEATH-LEVEL BALL!!!

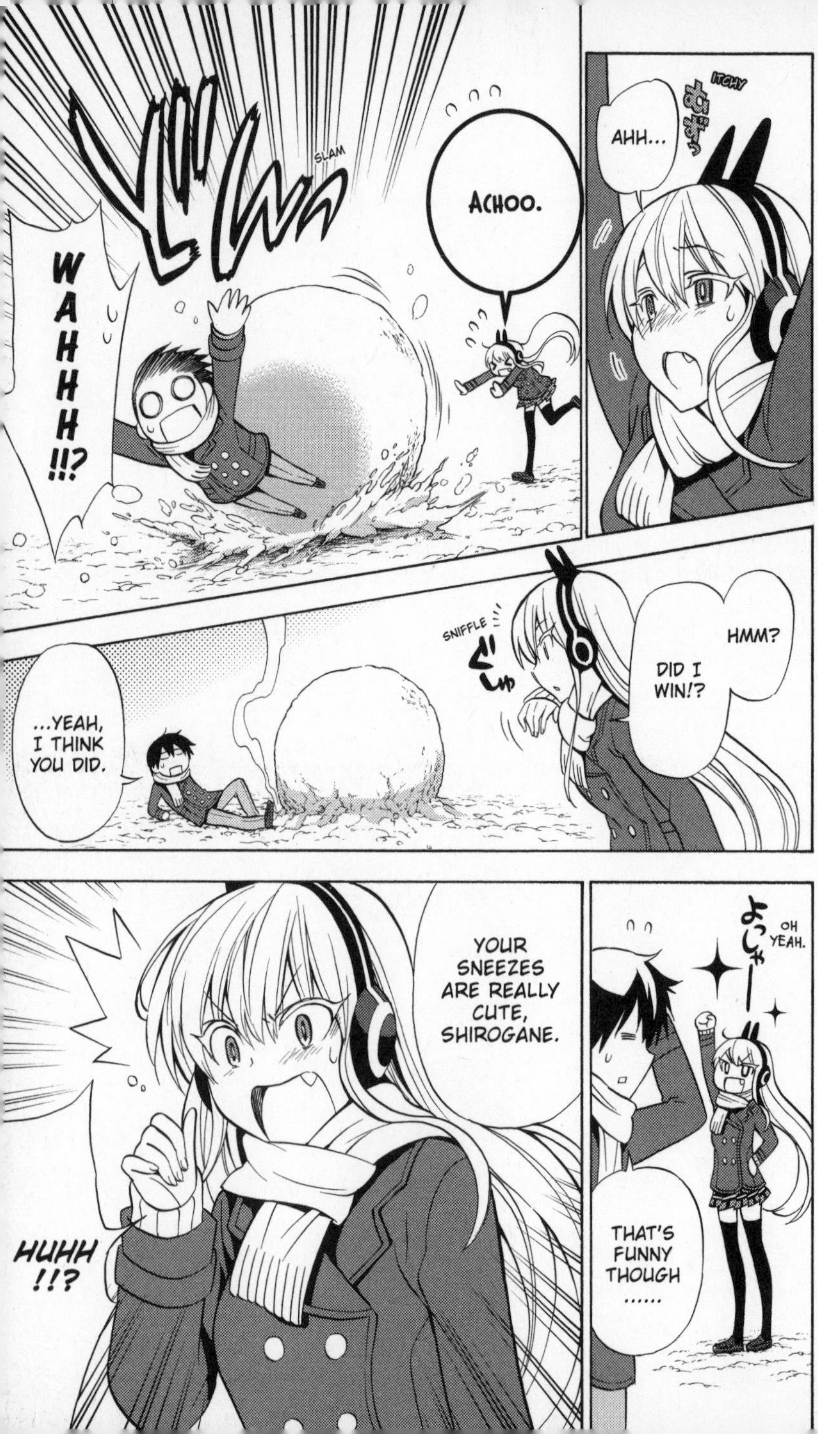
ITCHY
AHH...
ACHOO.
SLAM
WAHHHH!!?
HMM?
DID I WIN!?
SNIFFLE
ぐしゅ
...YEAH, I THINK YOU DID.
よっしゃー
OH YEAH.
THAT'S FUNNY THOUGH ......
YOUR SNEEZES ARE REALLY CUTE, SHIROGANE.
HUHH!!?

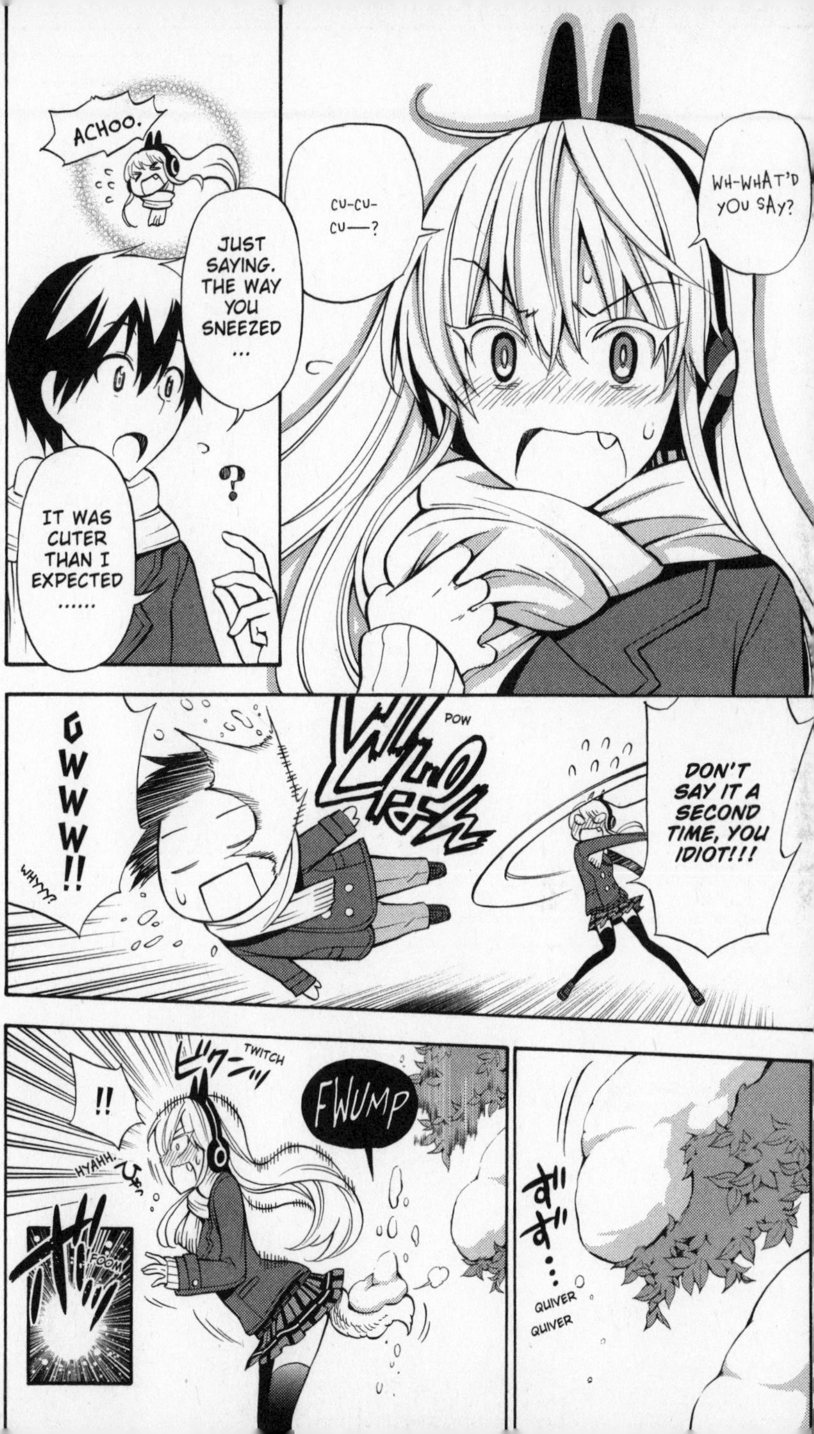
WH-WHAT'D YOU SAY?
CU-CU-CU—?
ACHOO.
JUST SAYING. THE WAY YOU SNEEZED ...
IT WAS CUTER THAN I EXPECTED ......
DON'T SAY IT A SECOND TIME, YOU IDIOT!!!
POW
GWWWW!!
WHYYY?
QUIVER QUIVER
TWITCH
FWUMP
!!
HYAHH.
FOOM

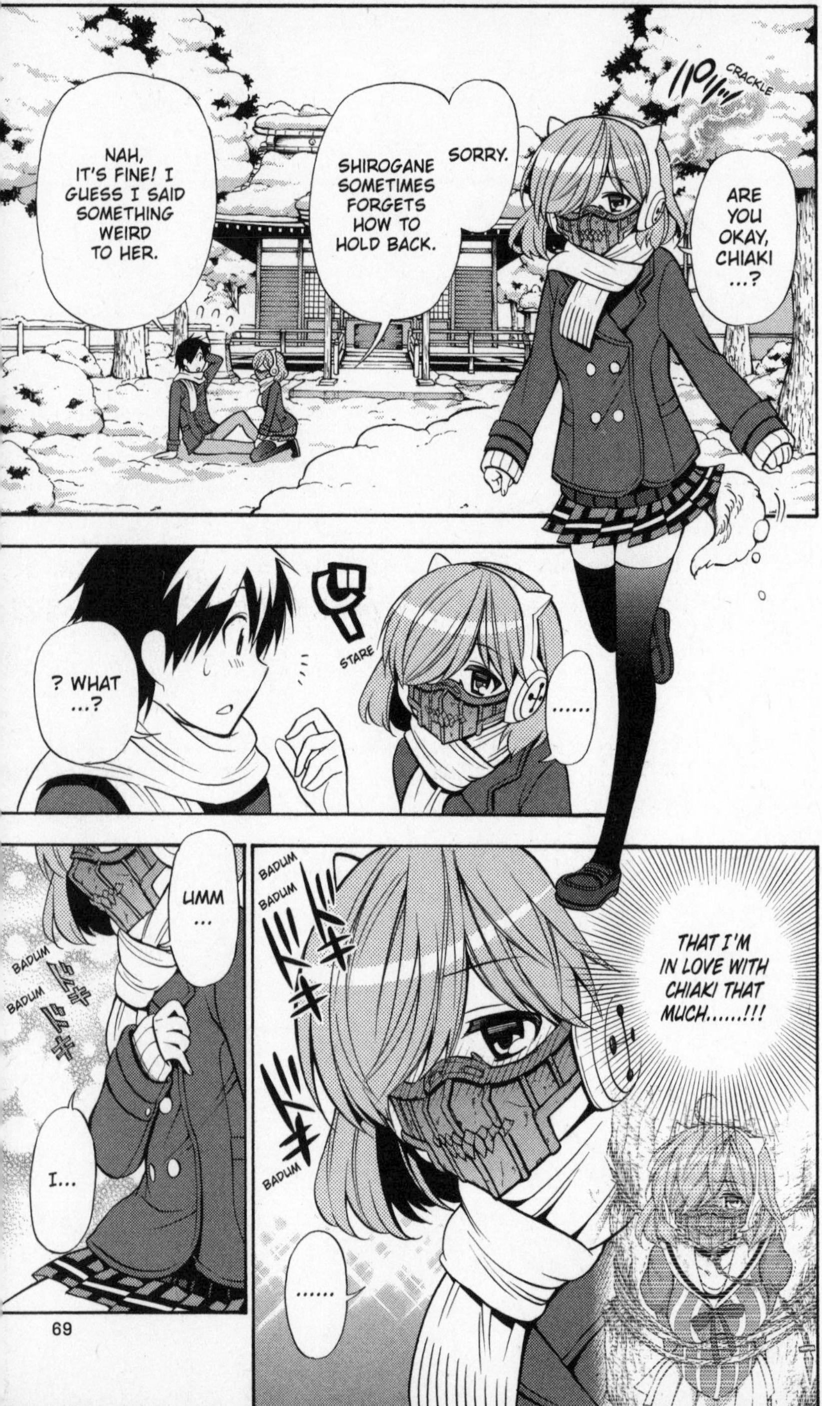
CRACKLE
ARE YOU OKAY, CHIAKI ...?
SORRY.
SHIROGANE SOMETIMES FORGETS HOW TO HOLD BACK.
NAH, IT'S FINE! I GUESS I SAID SOMETHING WEIRD TO HER.
......
STARE
? WHAT ...?
BADUM
BADUM
THAT I'M IN LOVE WITH CHIAKI THAT MUCH......!!!
BADUM
......
UMM ...
BADUM
BADUM
I...

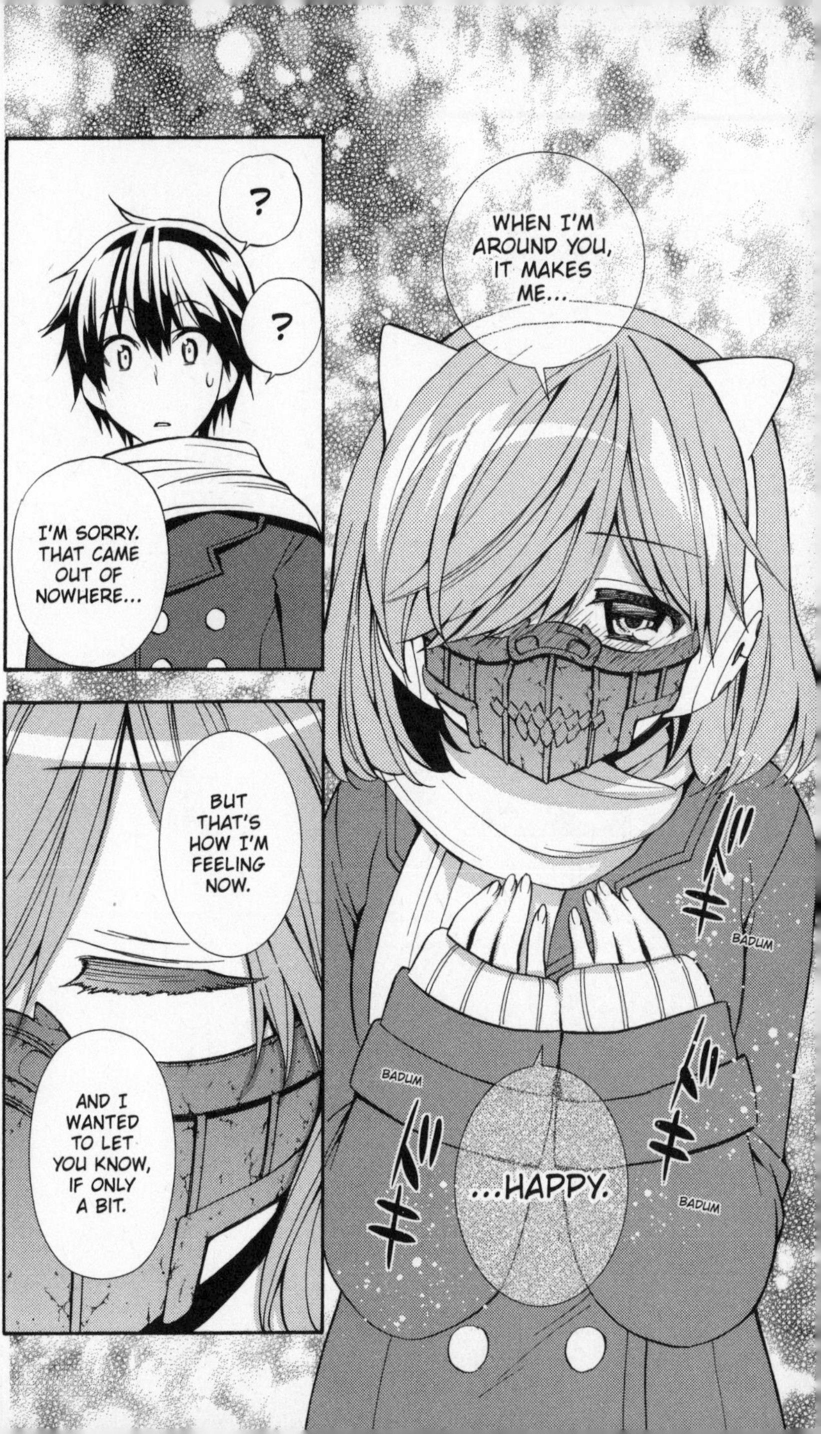
WHEN I'M AROUND YOU, IT MAKES ME...
BADUM
BADUM
BADUM
...HAPPY.
?
?
I'M SORRY. THAT CAME OUT OF NOWHERE...
BUT THAT'S HOW I'M FEELING NOW.
AND I WANTED TO LET YOU KNOW, IF ONLY A BIT.

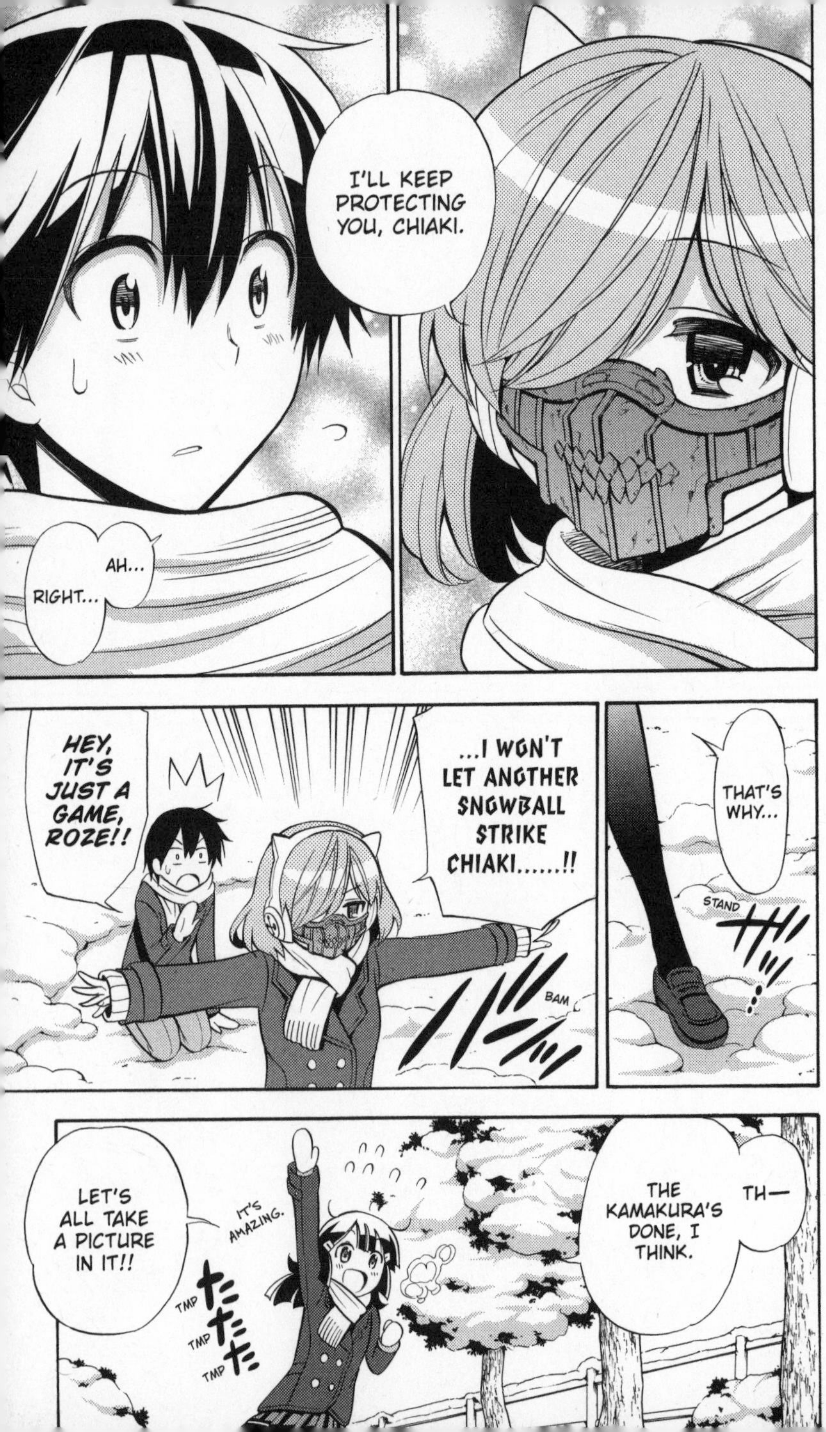
I'LL KEEP PROTECTING YOU, CHIAKI.
AH... RIGHT...
THAT'S WHY...
STAND
...I WON'T LET ANOTHER SNOWBALL STRIKE CHIAKI......!!
BAM
HEY, IT'S JUST A GAME, ROZE!!
TH—
THE KAMAKURA'S DONE, I THINK.
IT'S AMAZING.
LET'S ALL TAKE A PICTURE IN IT!!
TMP TMP TMP

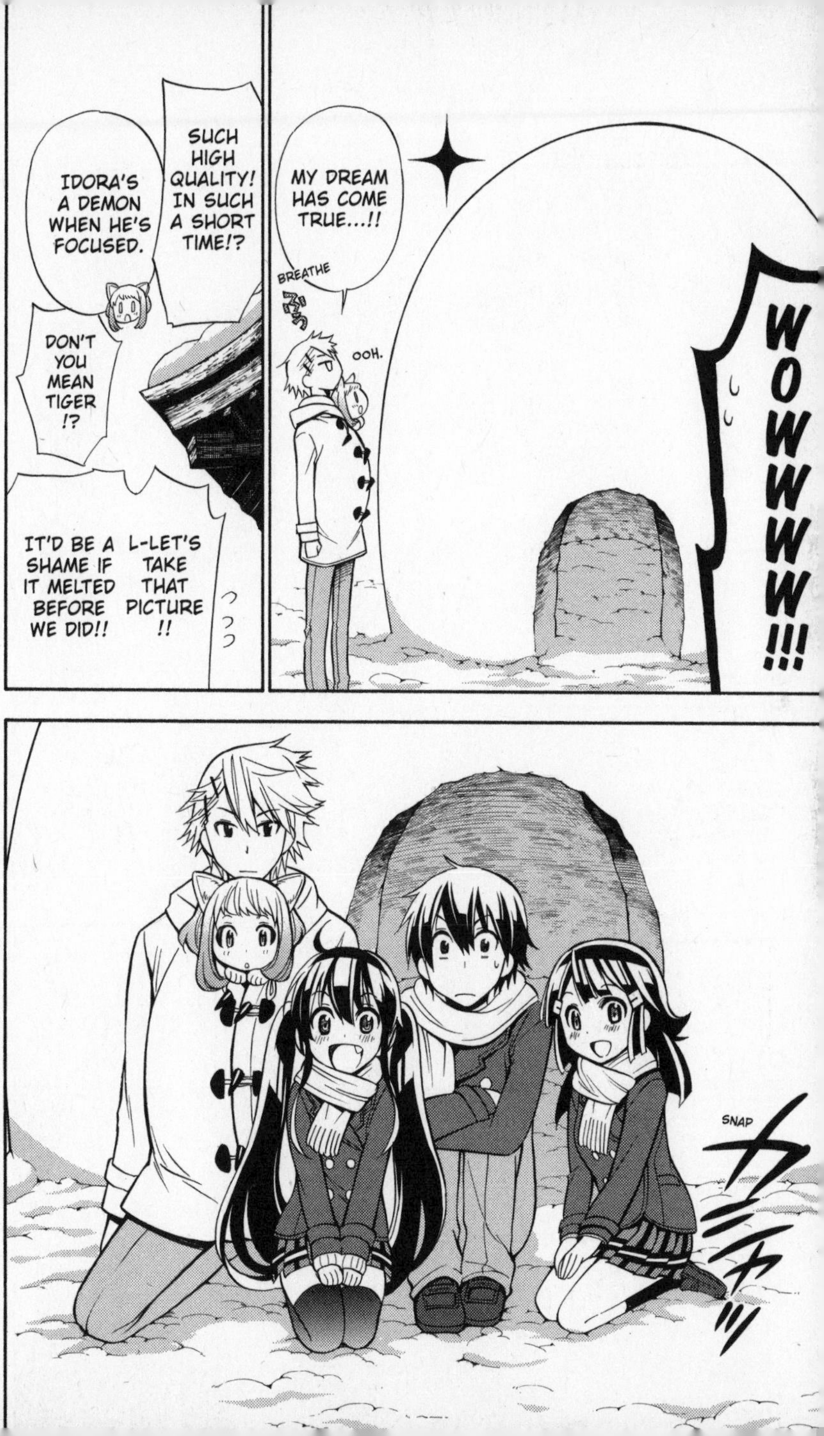
WOWWWWW!!!
MY DREAM HAS COME TRUE...!!
BREATHE
OOH.
SUCH HIGH QUALITY! IN SUCH A SHORT TIME!?
IDORA'S A DEMON WHEN HE'S FOCUSED.
DON'T YOU MEAN TIGER!?
L-LET'S TAKE THAT PICTURE!!
IT'D BE A SHAME IF IT MELTED BEFORE WE DID!!
SNAP

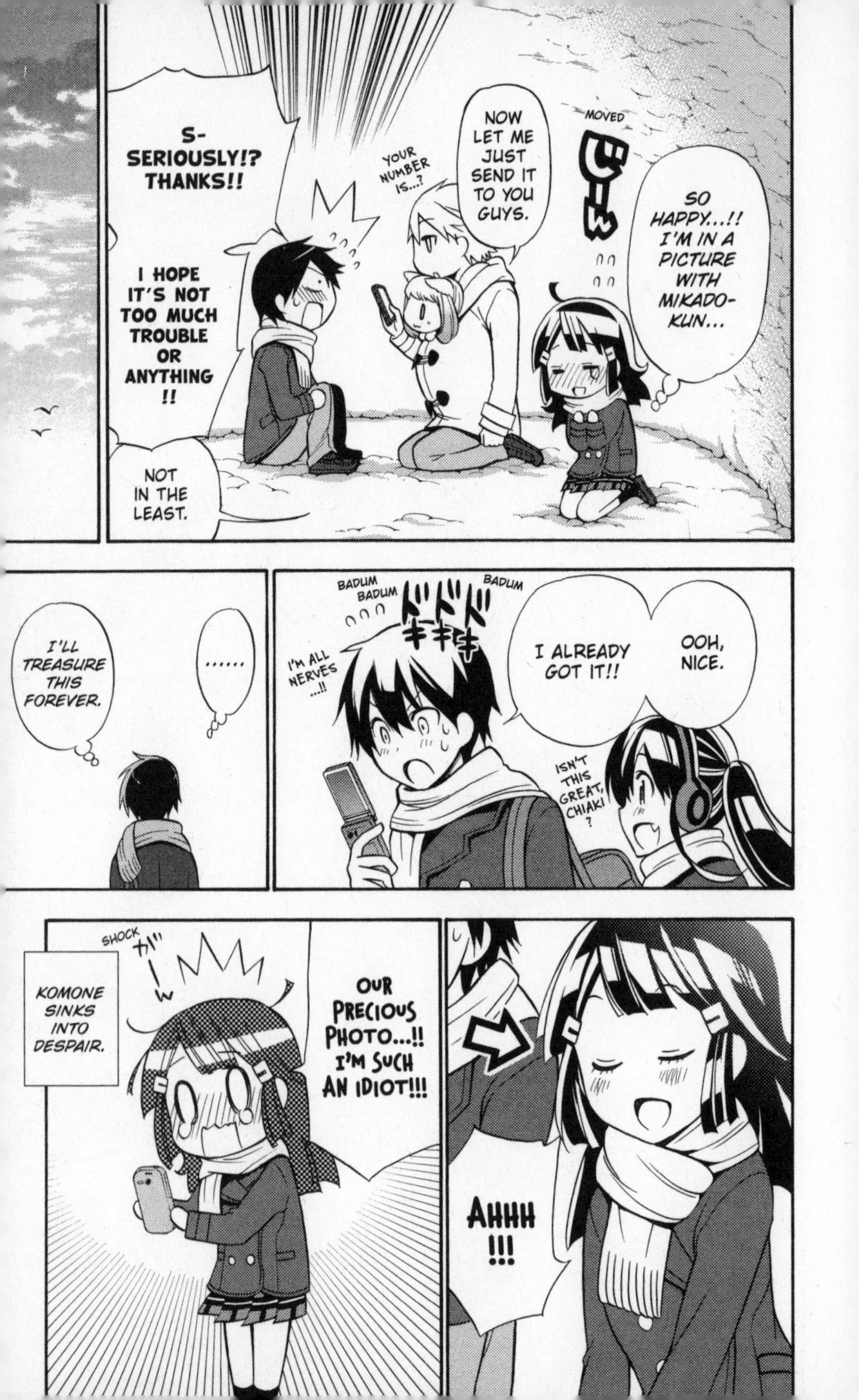
SO HAPPY...!! I'M IN A PICTURE WITH MIKADO-KUN...
MOVED
NOW LET ME JUST SEND IT TO YOU GUYS.
YOUR NUMBER IS...?
S-SERIOUSLY!? THANKS!!
I HOPE IT'S NOT TOO MUCH TROUBLE OR ANYTHING !!
NOT IN THE LEAST.
BADUM
OOH, NICE.
I ALREADY GOT IT!!
BADUM BADUM
I'M ALL NERVES ...!!
ISN'T THIS GREAT, CHIAKI ?
......
I'LL TREASURE THIS FOREVER.
AHHH !!!
OUR PRECIOUS PHOTO...!! I'M SUCH AN IDIOT!!!
SHOCK
KOMONE SINKS INTO DESPAIR.

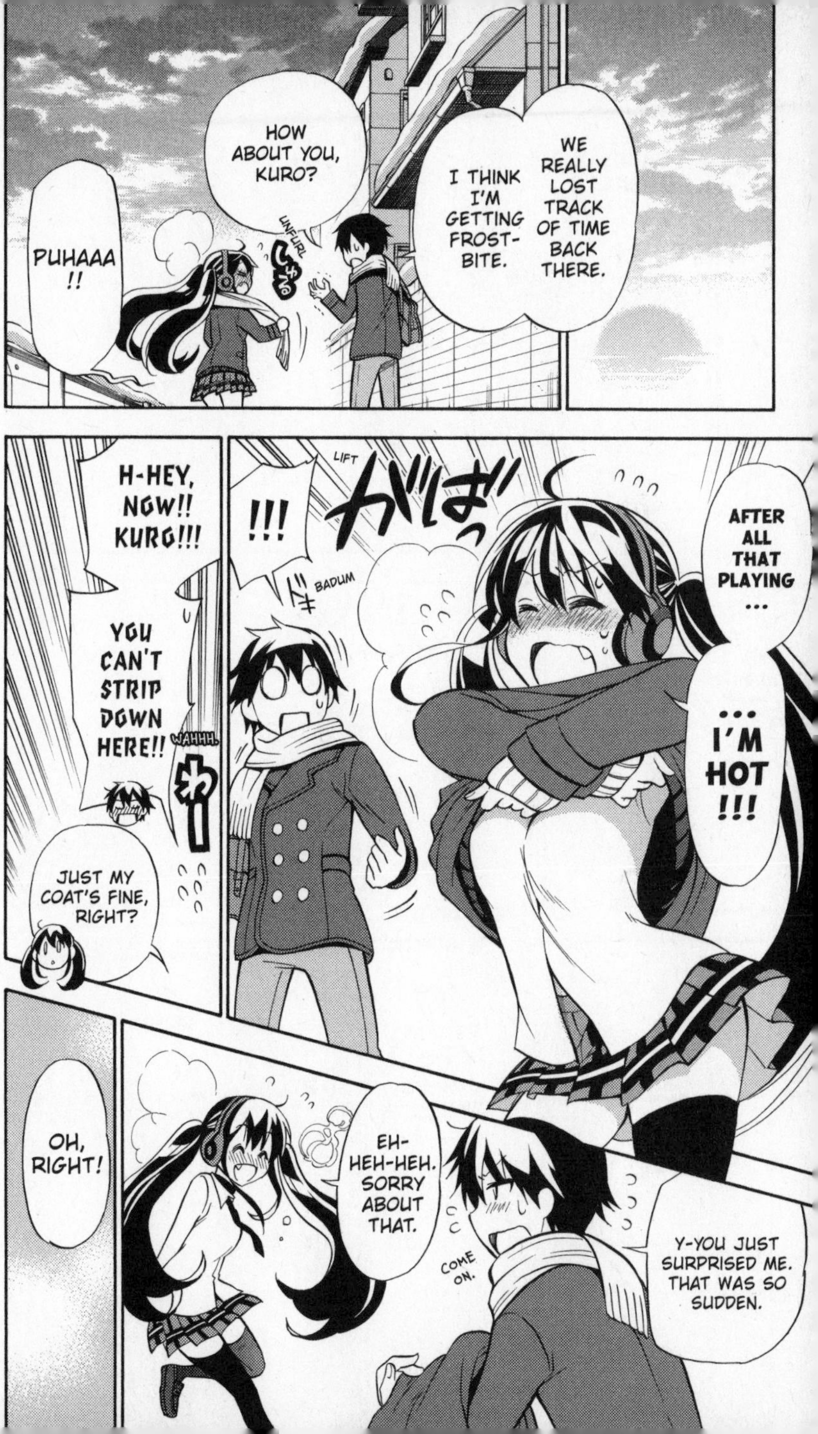
WE REALLY LOST TRACK OF TIME BACK THERE.
I THINK I'M GETTING FROST-BITE.
HOW ABOUT YOU, KURO?
UNFURL
PUHAAA!!
AFTER ALL THAT PLAYING...
...I'M HOT!!!
LIFT
!!!
BADUM
H-HEY, NOW!! KURO!!!
YOU CAN'T STRIP DOWN HERE!!
WAHHH
JUST MY COAT'S FINE, RIGHT?
Y-YOU JUST SURPRISED ME. THAT WAS SO SUDDEN.
COME ON.
EH-HEH-HEH. SORRY ABOUT THAT.
OH, RIGHT!

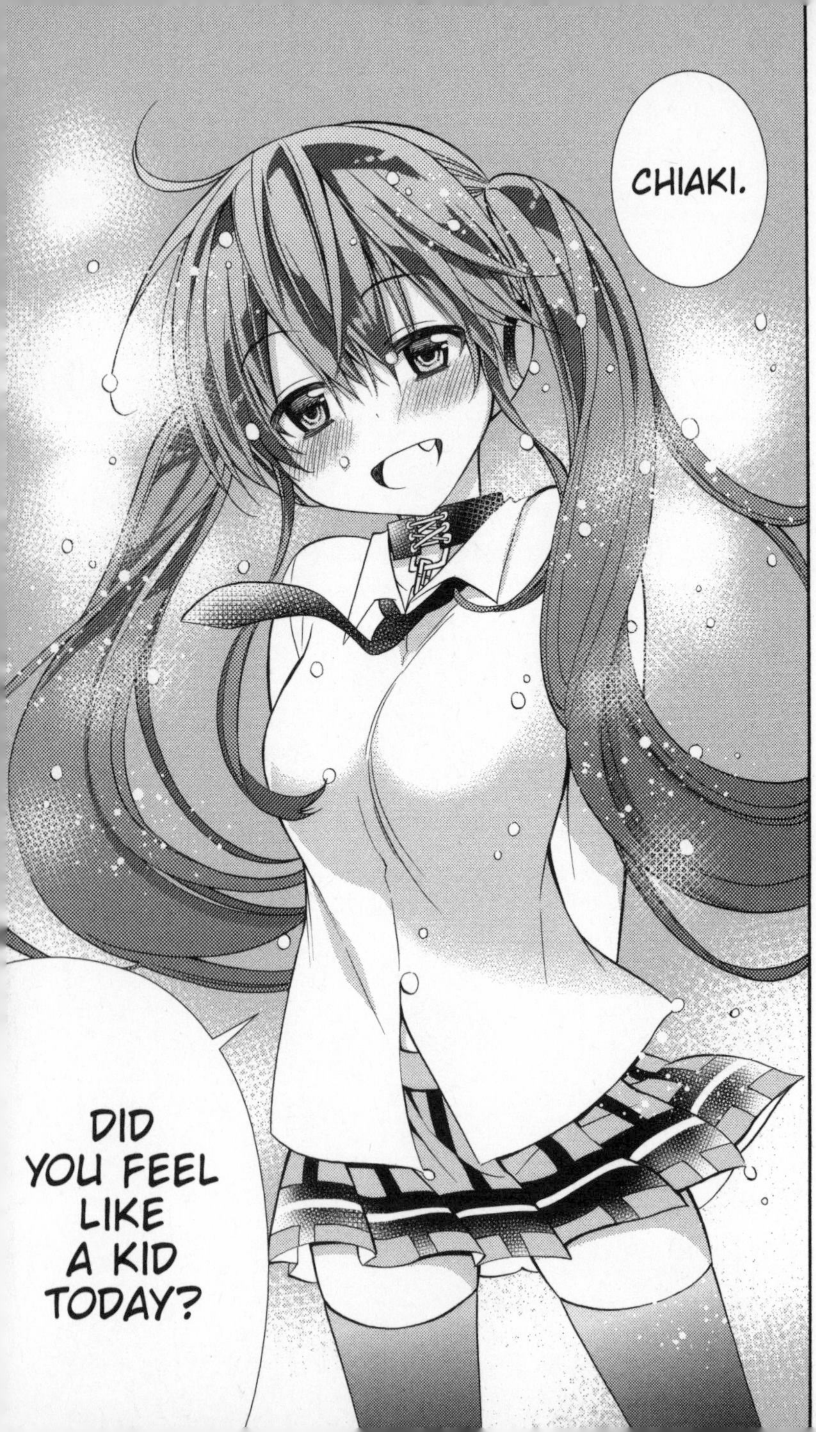
CHIAKI.
DID YOU FEEL LIKE A KID TODAY?

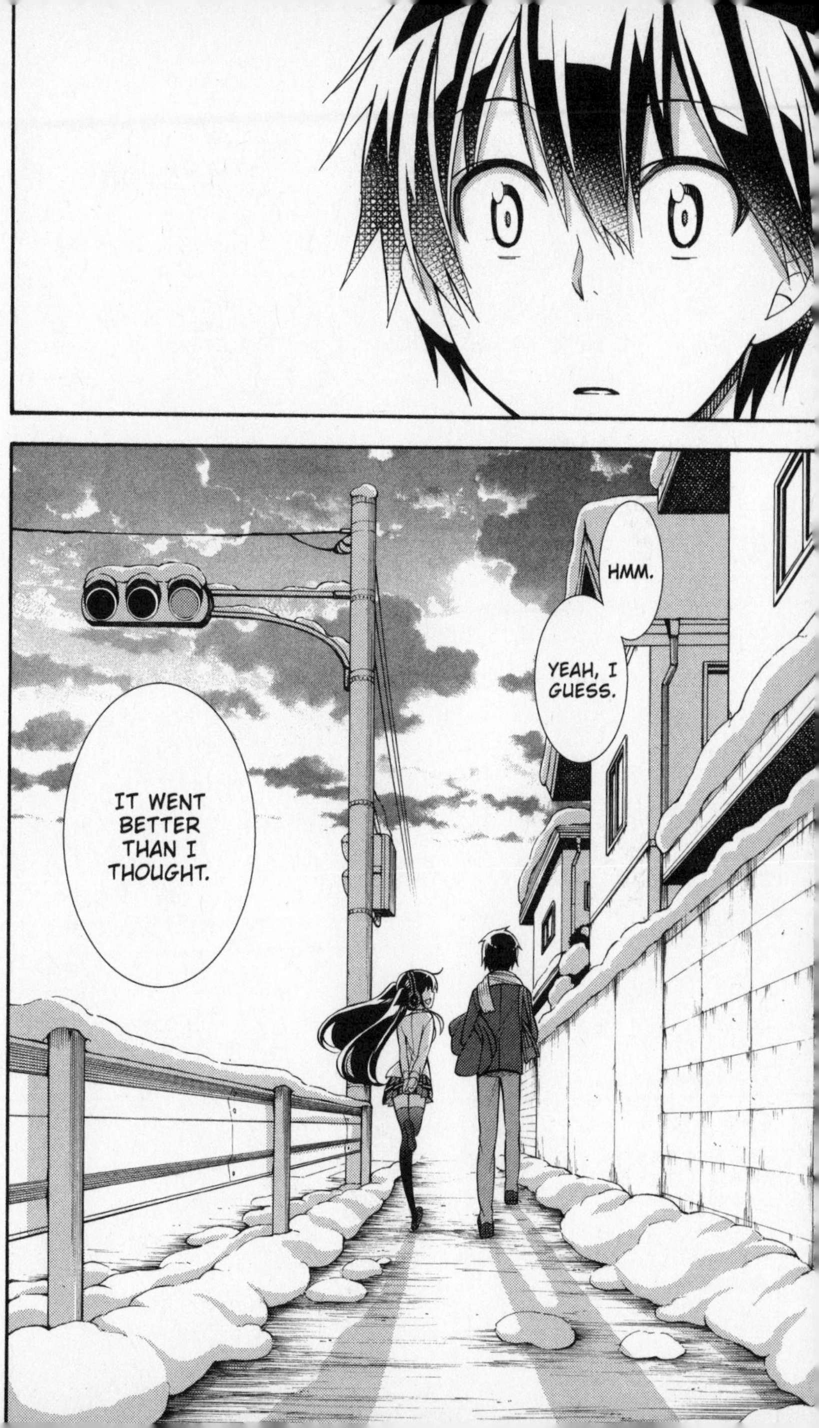
HMM.
YEAH, I GUESS.
IT WENT BETTER THAN I THOUGHT.

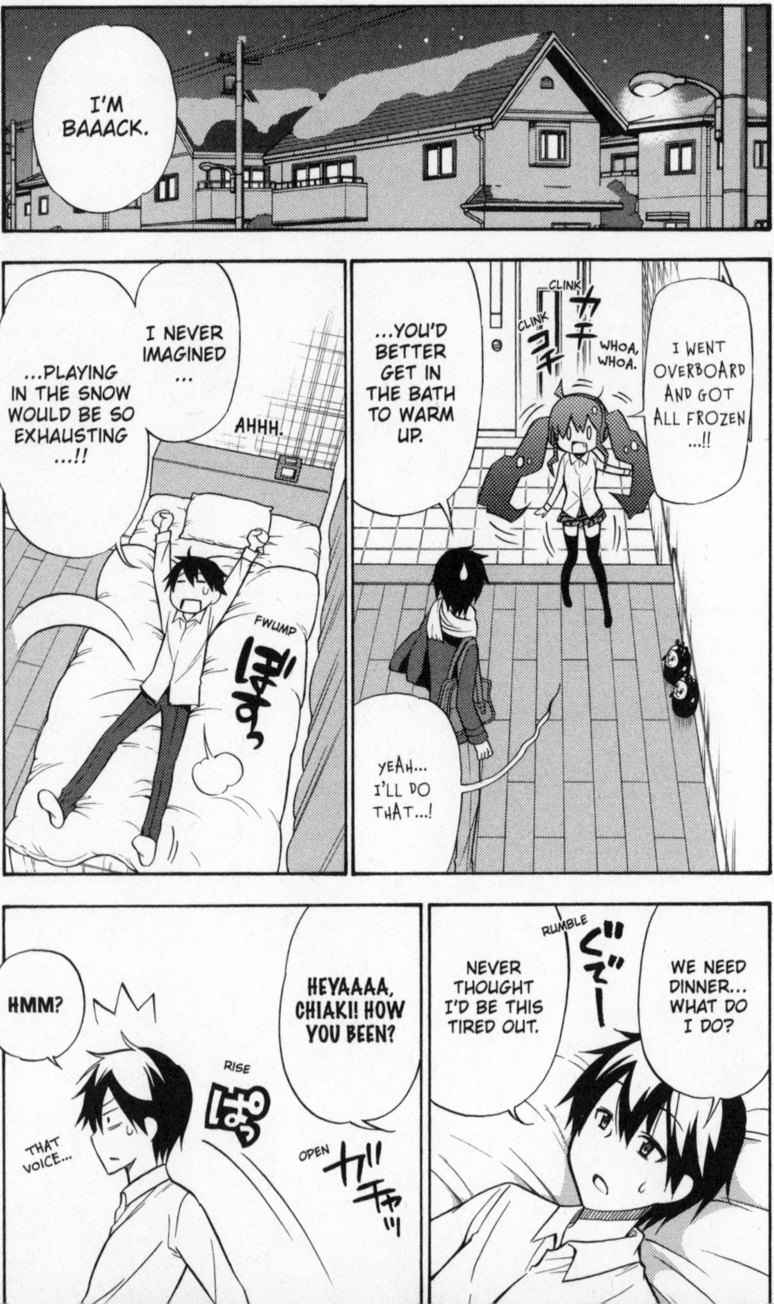

I'M BAAACK.
CLINK
カチ
CLINK
コチ
WHOA, WHOA.
I WENT OVERBOARD AND GOT ALL FROZEN ...!!
...YOU'D BETTER GET IN THE BATH TO WARM UP.
YEAH... I'LL DO THAT...!
I NEVER IMAGINED ...
...PLAYING IN THE SNOW WOULD BE SO EXHAUSTING ...!!
AHHH.
FWUMP
ぼすっ
WE NEED DINNER... WHAT DO I DO?
RUMBLE
NEVER THOUGHT I'D BE THIS TIRED OUT.
HEYAAAA, CHIAKI!! HOW YOU BEEN?
OPEN
ガチャッ
RISE
ぱっ
HMM?
THAT VOICE...

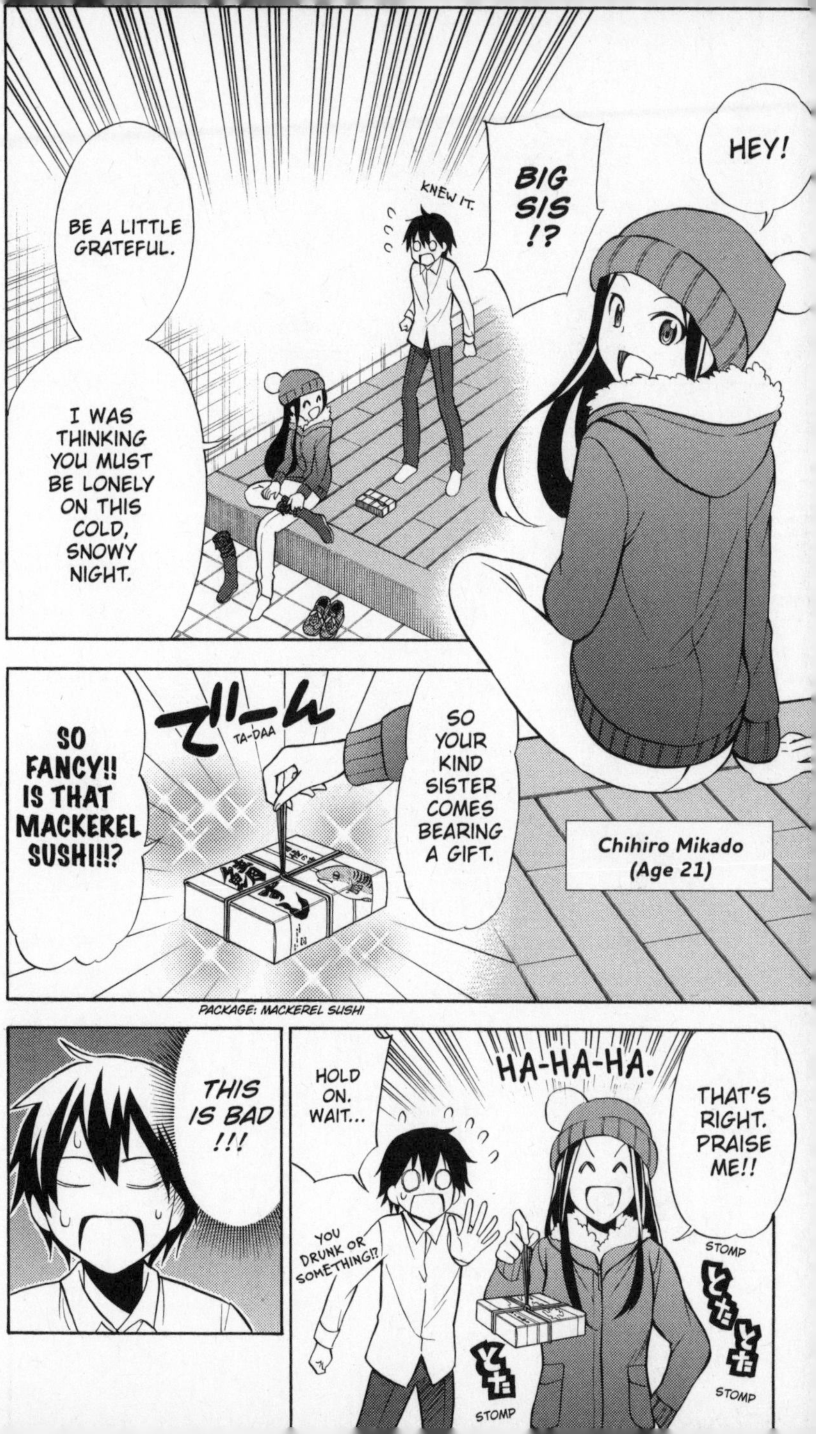
HEY!
BIG SIS !?
KNEW IT.
BE A LITTLE GRATEFUL.
I WAS THINKING YOU MUST BE LONELY ON THIS COLD, SNOWY NIGHT.
Chihiro Mikado (Age 21)
SO YOUR KIND SISTER COMES BEARING A GIFT.
でーん
TA-DAA
SO FANCY!! IS THAT MACKEREL SUSHI!!!?
PACKAGE: MACKEREL SUSHI
THAT'S RIGHT. PRAISE ME!!
HA-HA-HA.
HOLD ON. WAIT...
YOU DRUNK OR SOMETHING!?
とた
STOMP
とた
STOMP
とた
STOMP
THIS IS BAD !!!

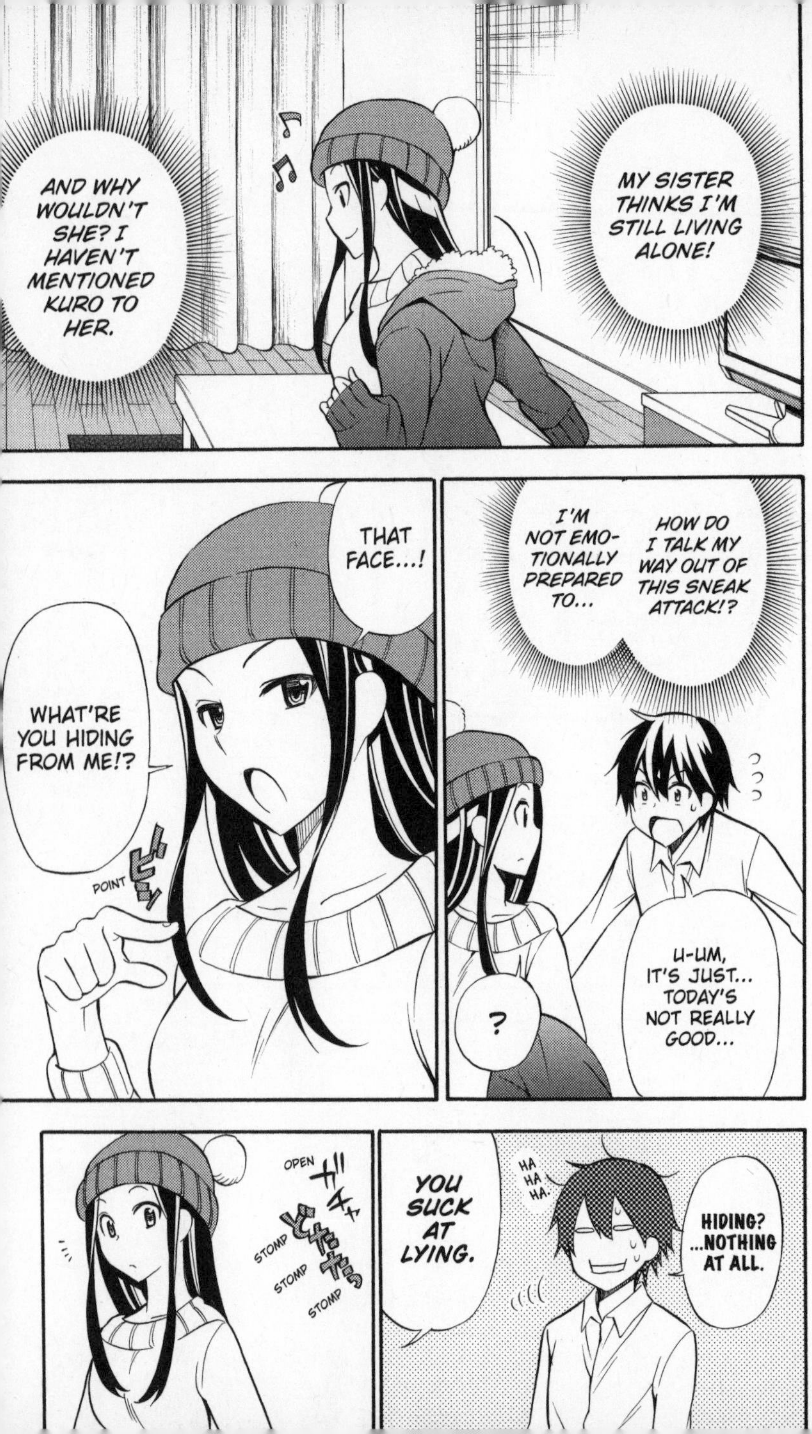
MY SISTER THINKS I'M STILL LIVING ALONE!
AND WHY WOULDN'T SHE? I HAVEN'T MENTIONED KURO TO HER.
HOW DO I TALK MY WAY OUT OF THIS SNEAK ATTACK!?
I'M NOT EMO-TIONALLY PREPARED TO...
U-UM, IT'S JUST... TODAY'S NOT REALLY GOOD...
?
THAT FACE...!
WHAT'RE YOU HIDING FROM ME!?
POINT
HA HA HA.
HIDING? ...NOTHING AT ALL.
YOU SUCK AT LYING.
OPEN
STOMP
STOMP
STOMP

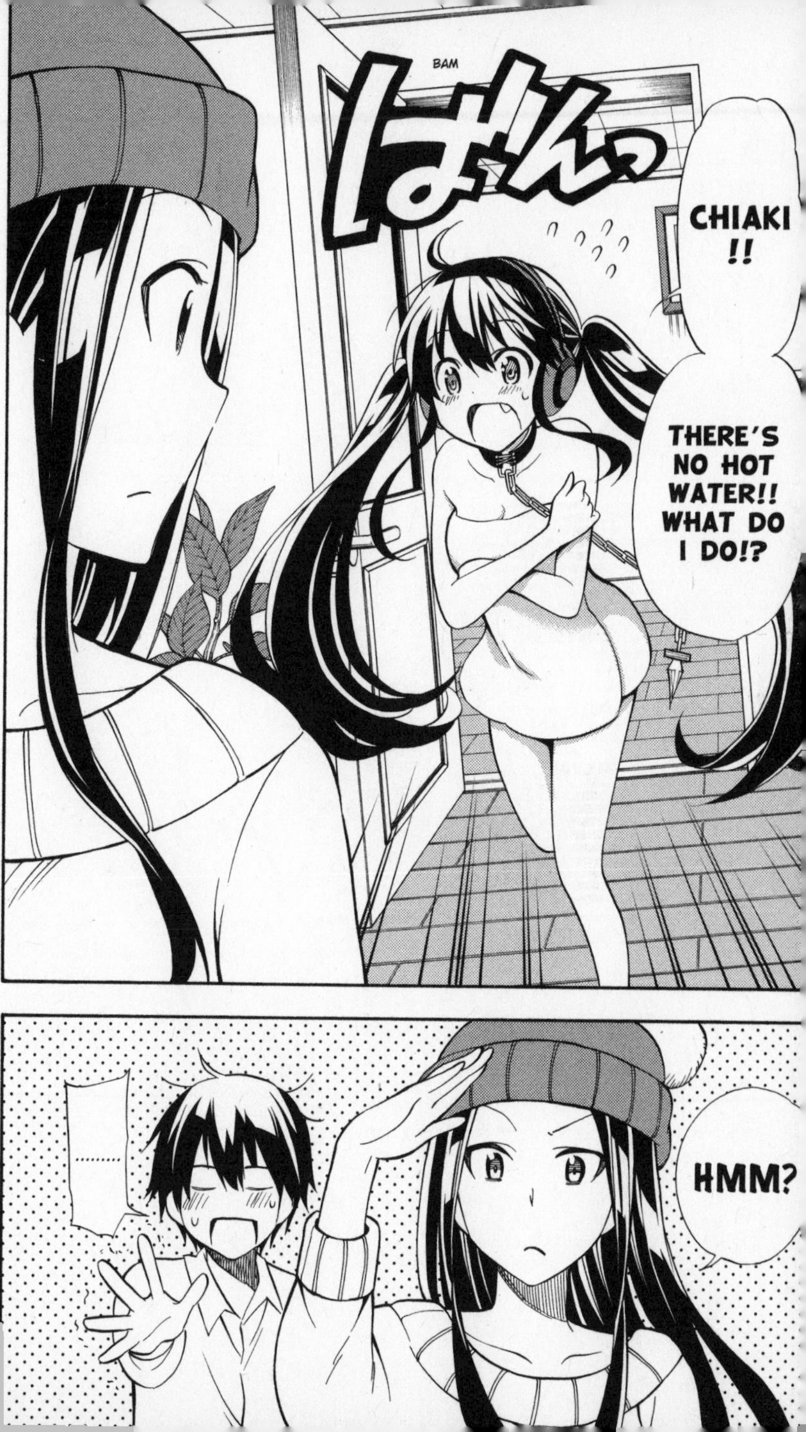
ばんっ
BAM
CHIAKI!!
THERE'S NO HOT WATER!! WHAT DO I DO!?
HMM?
……

TODAY'S CERBERUS

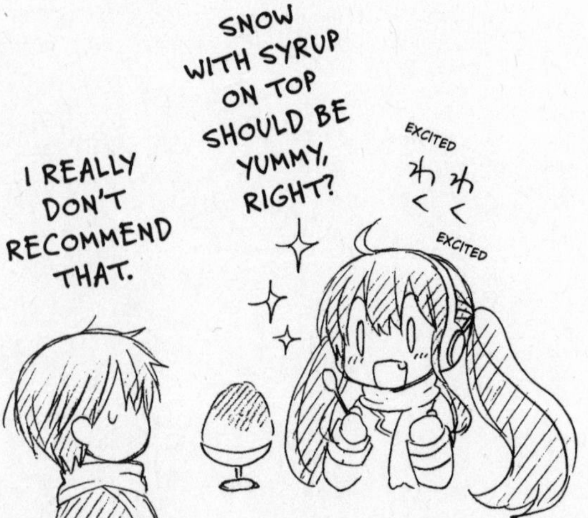
EXCITED
わくわく
EXCITED
SNOW WITH SYRUP ON TOP SHOULD BE YUMMY, RIGHT?
I REALLY DON'T RECOMMEND THAT.

TODAY'S CERBERUS

REALLY WISH MY KAMAKURA HAD A KOTATSU.
A KOTATSU... THAT WOULD BE LOVELY. LET'S DO IT.

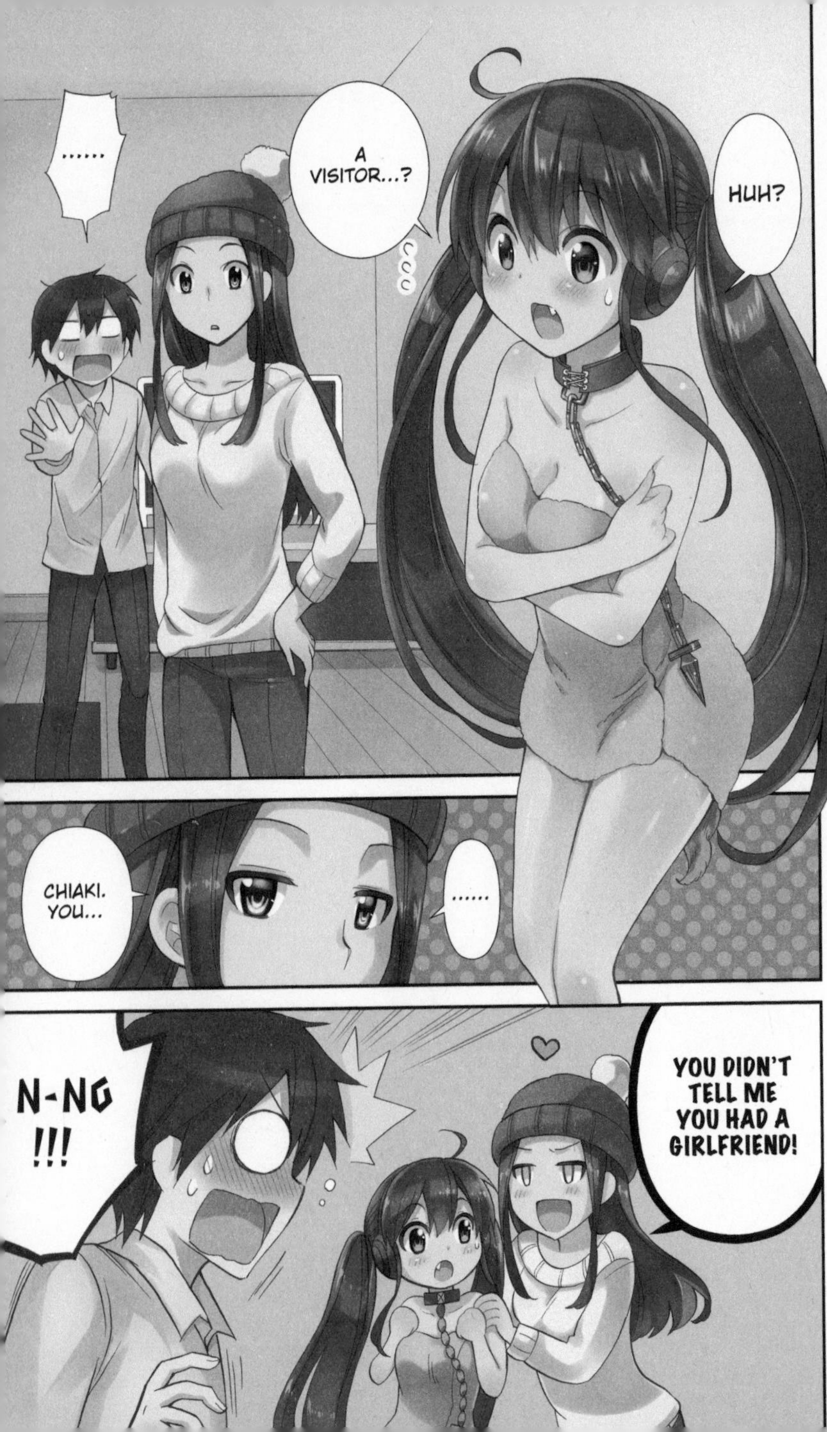
HUH?
A VISITOR...?
......
......
CHIAKI. YOU...
YOU DIDN'T TELL ME YOU HAD A GIRLFRIEND!
N-NG !!!

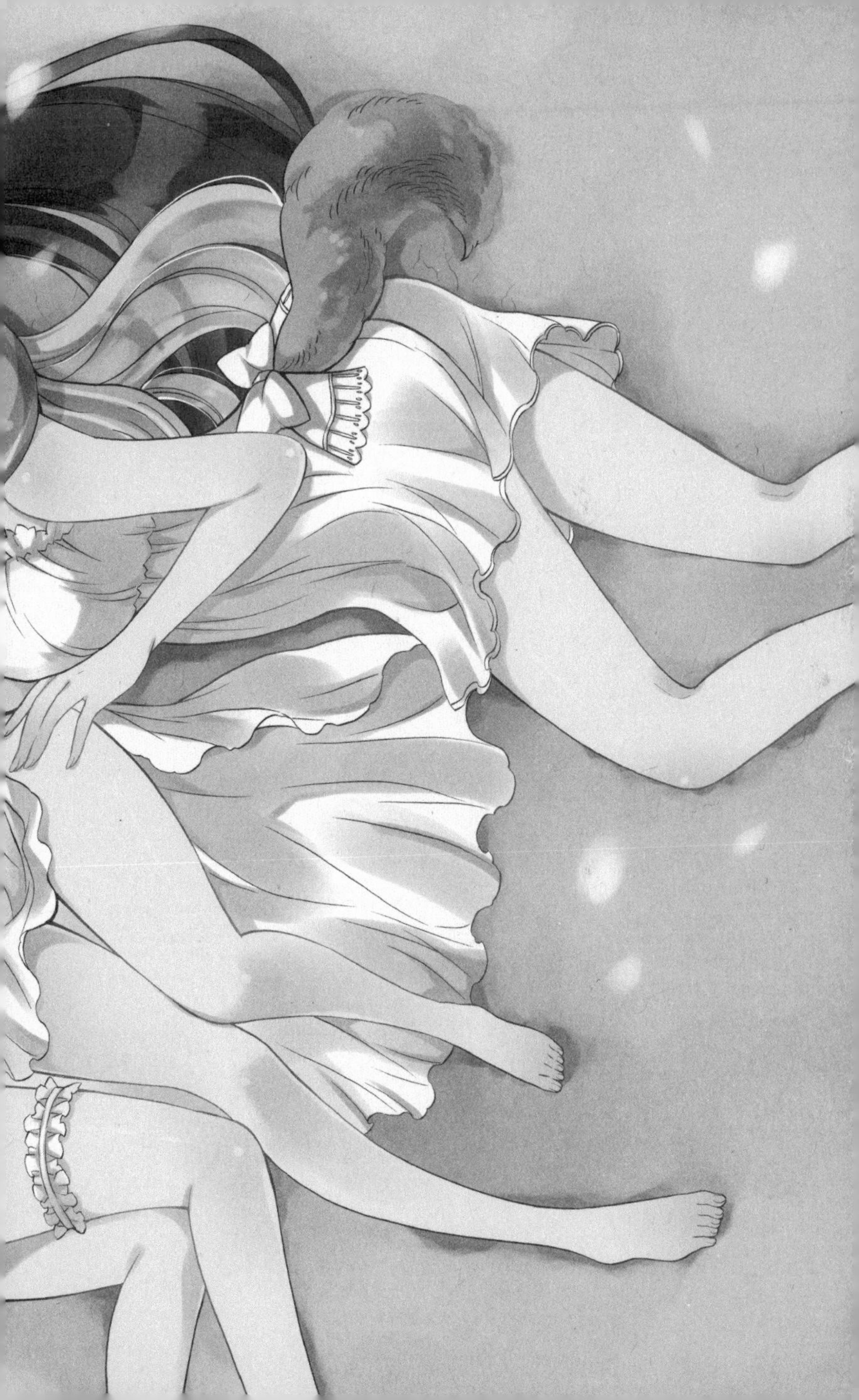

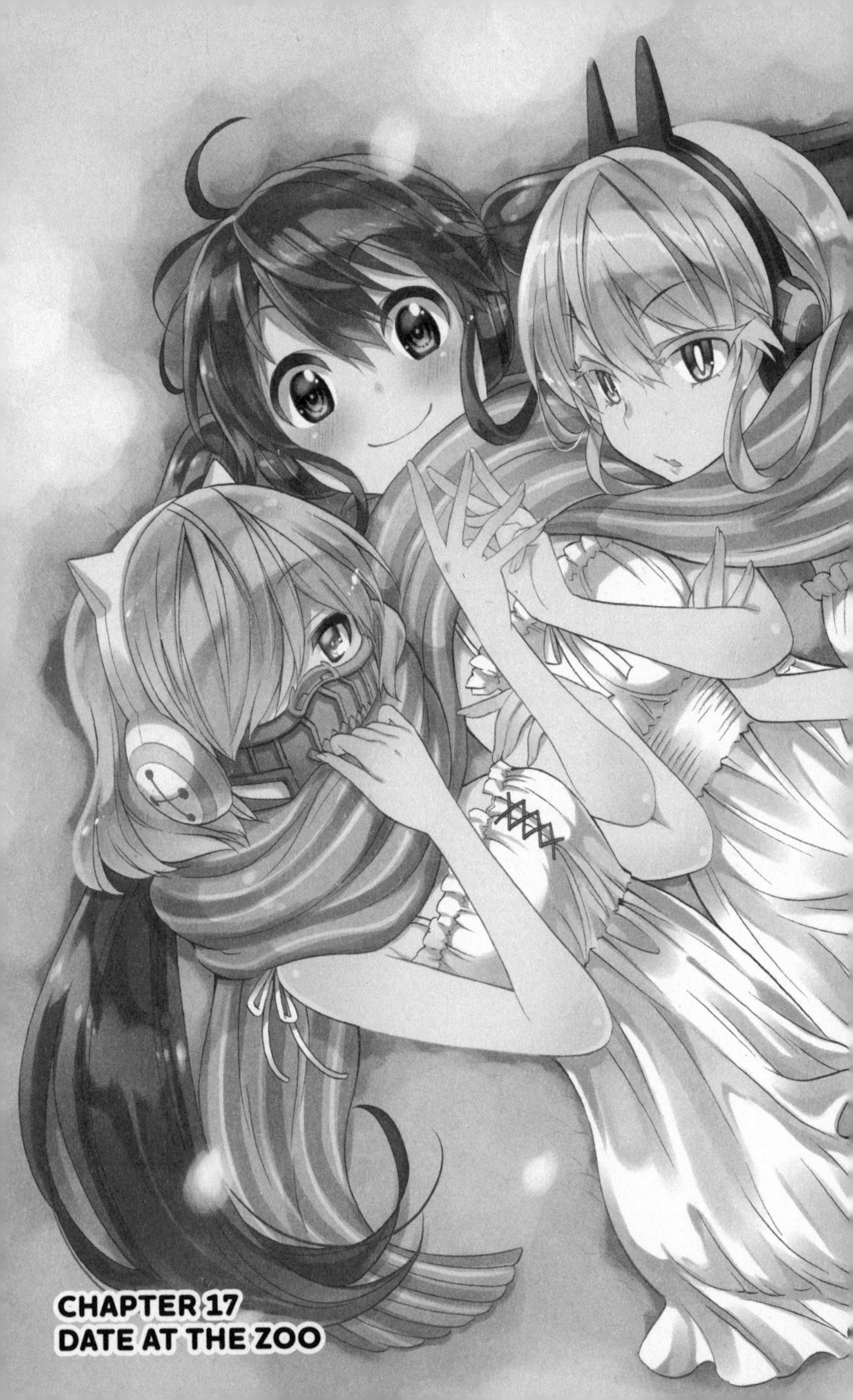

CHAPTER 17
DATE AT THE ZOO

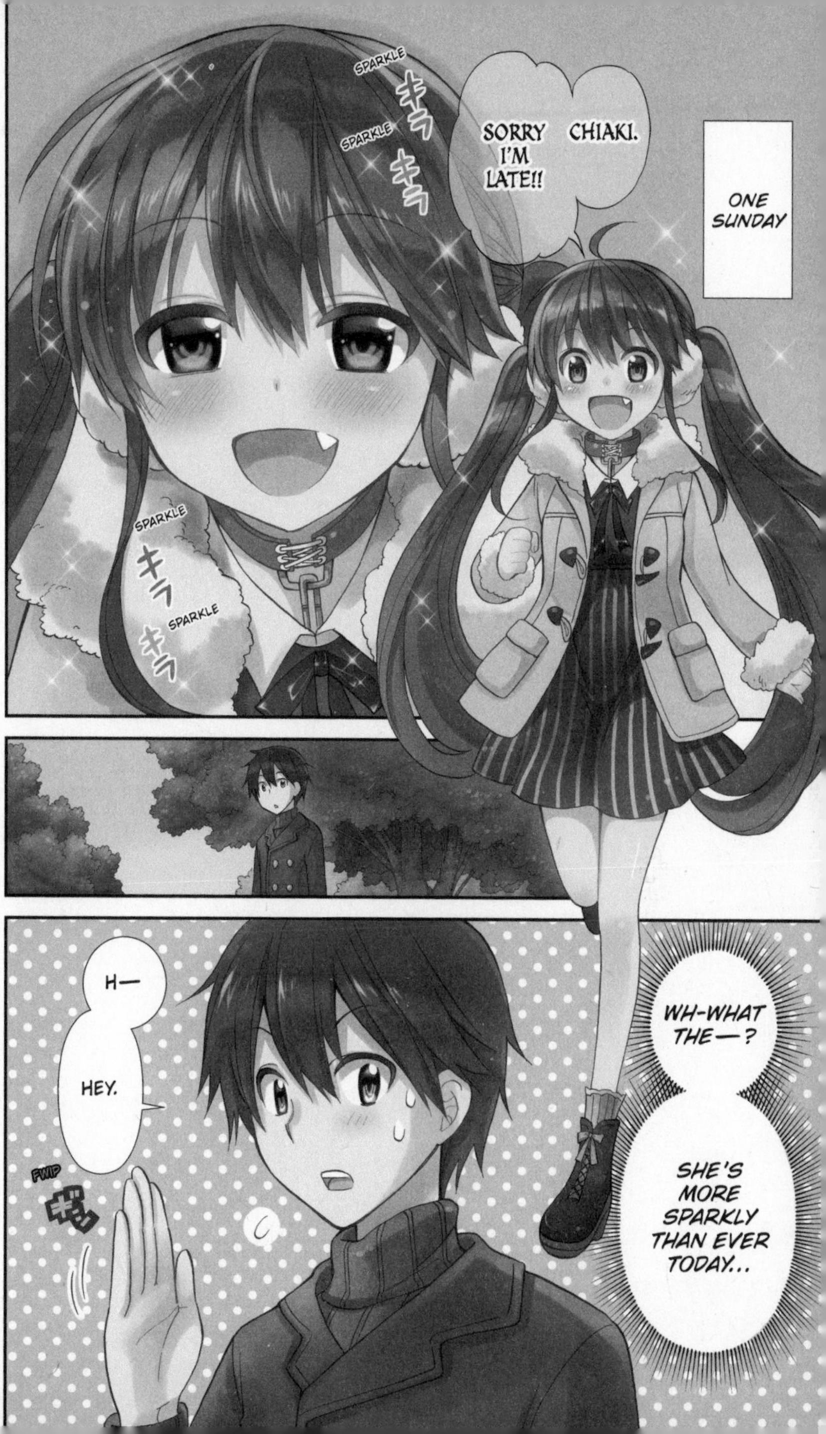

ONE SUNDAY
SORRY I'M LATE!! CHIAKI.
SPARKLE
SPARKLE
SPARKLE
SPARKLE
WH-WHAT THE—?
SHE'S MORE SPARKLY THAN EVER TODAY...
H—
HEY.
FWIP

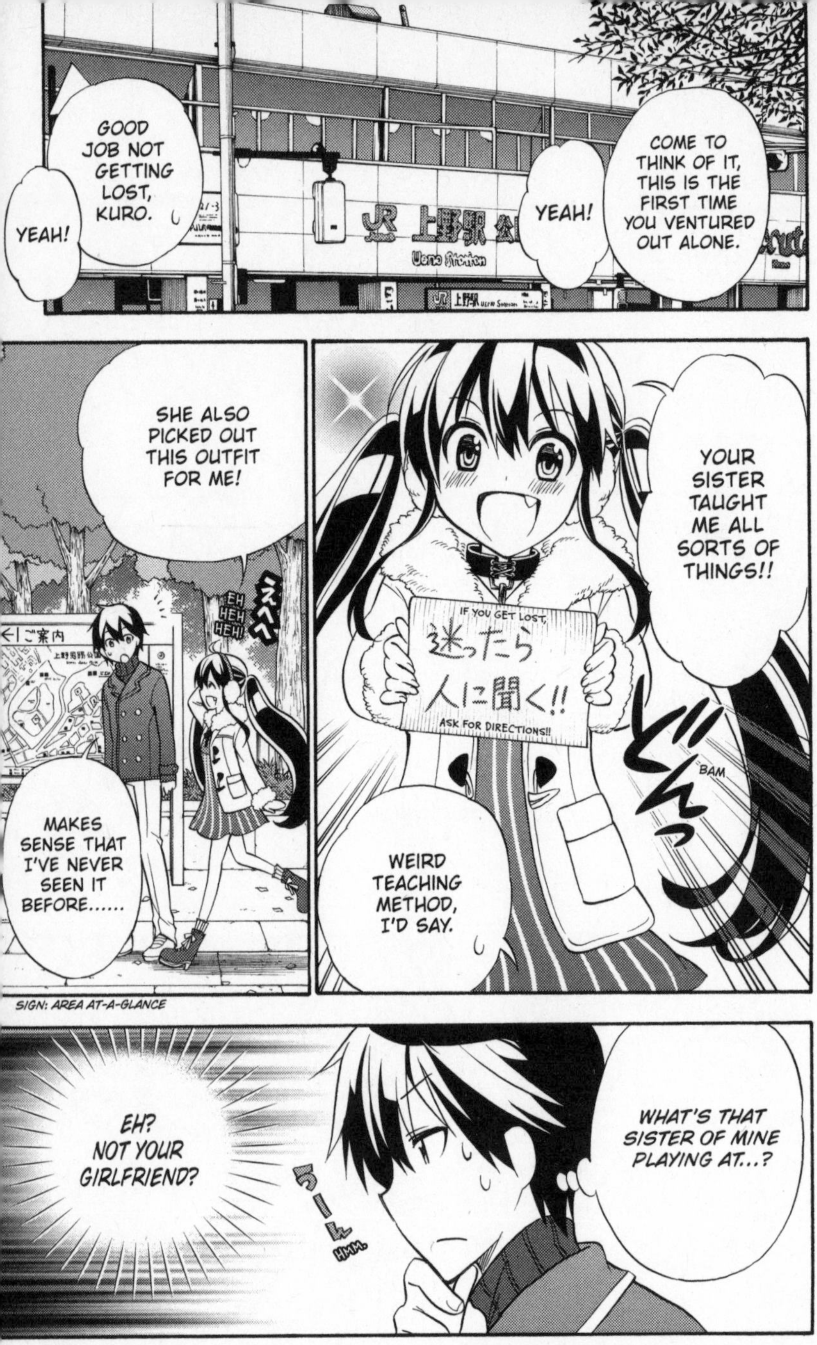
COME TO THINK OF IT, THIS IS THE FIRST TIME YOU VENTURED OUT ALONE.
YEAH!
GOOD JOB NOT GETTING LOST, KURO.
YEAH!
YOUR SISTER TAUGHT ME ALL SORTS OF THINGS!!
IF YOU GET LOST,
迷ったら
人に聞く!!
ASK FOR DIRECTIONS!!
BAM
WEIRD TEACHING METHOD, I'D SAY.
SHE ALSO PICKED OUT THIS OUTFIT FOR ME!
えへへ
EH HEH HEH!
ご案内
MAKES SENSE THAT I'VE NEVER SEEN IT BEFORE......
SIGN: AREA AT-A-GLANCE
WHAT'S THAT SISTER OF MINE PLAYING AT...?
HMM.
EH? NOT YOUR GIRLFRIEND?

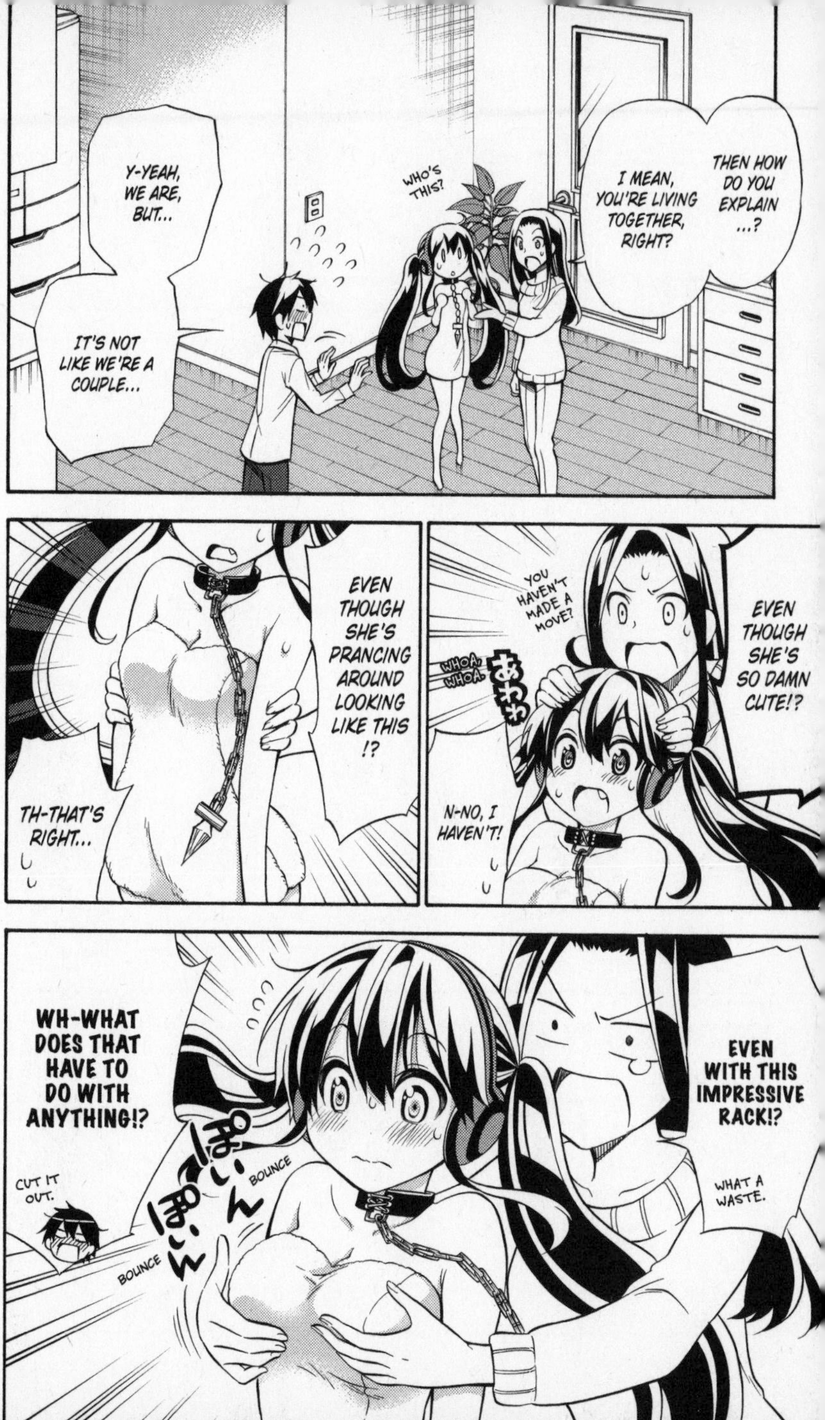
THEN HOW DO YOU EXPLAIN ...?
I MEAN, YOU'RE LIVING TOGETHER, RIGHT?
WHO'S THIS?
Y-YEAH, WE ARE, BUT...
IT'S NOT LIKE WE'RE A COUPLE...
EVEN THOUGH SHE'S SO DAMN CUTE!?
YOU HAVEN'T MADE A MOVE?
あわわ
WHOA, WHOA.
N-NO, I HAVEN'T!
EVEN THOUGH SHE'S PRANCING AROUND LOOKING LIKE THIS !?
TH-THAT'S RIGHT...
EVEN WITH THIS IMPRESSIVE RACK!?
WHAT A WASTE.
WH-WHAT DOES THAT HAVE TO DO WITH ANYTHING!?
ぽいん
BOUNCE
ぽいん
BOUNCE
CUT IT OUT.

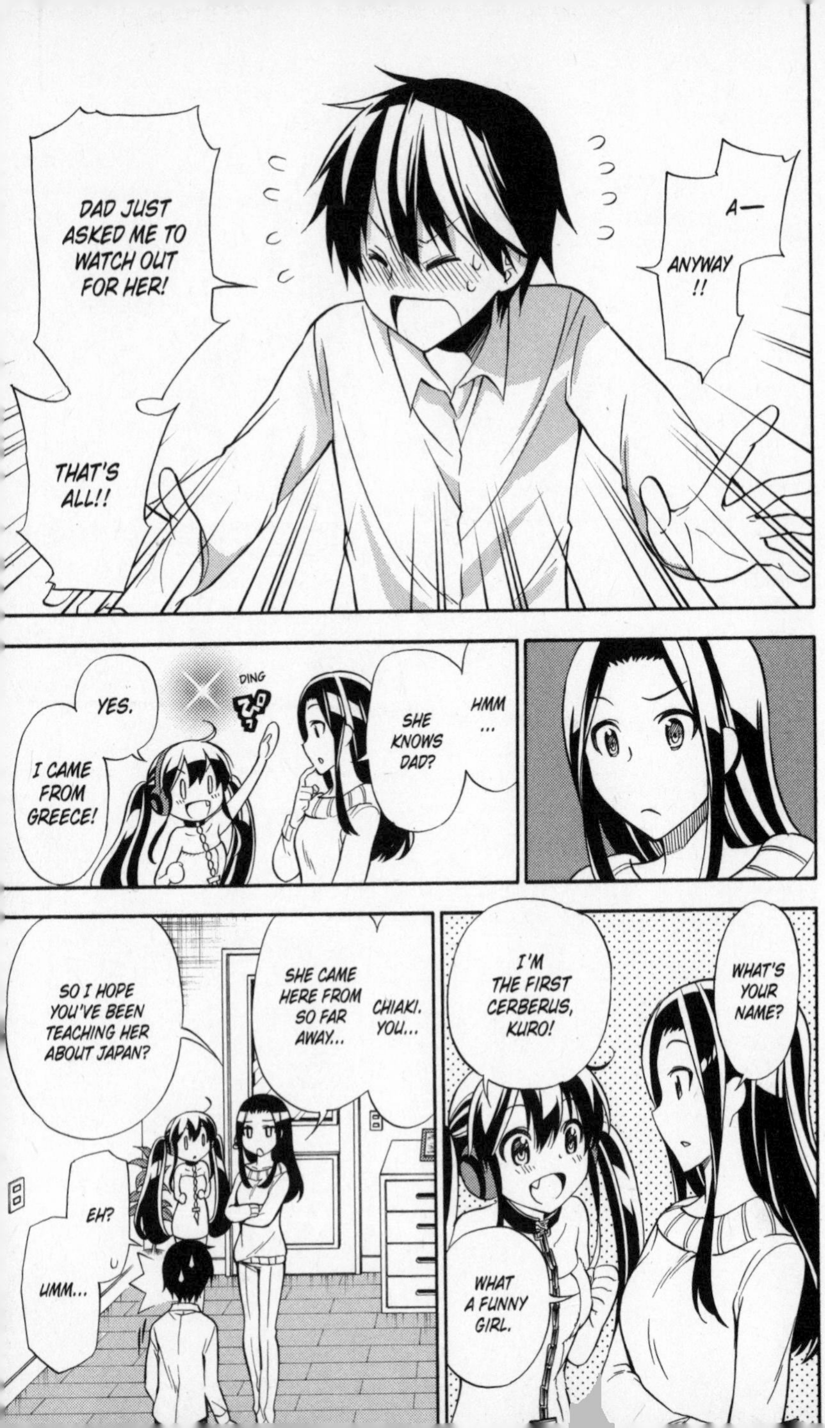
A— ANYWAY!!
DAD JUST ASKED ME TO WATCH OUT FOR HER!
THAT'S ALL!!
HMM...
SHE KNOWS DAD?
DING
YES.
I CAME FROM GREECE!
WHAT'S YOUR NAME?
I'M THE FIRST CERBERUS, KURO!
WHAT A FUNNY GIRL.
CHIAKI. YOU...
SHE CAME HERE FROM SO FAR AWAY...
SO I HOPE YOU'VE BEEN TEACHING HER ABOUT JAPAN?
EH?
UMM...

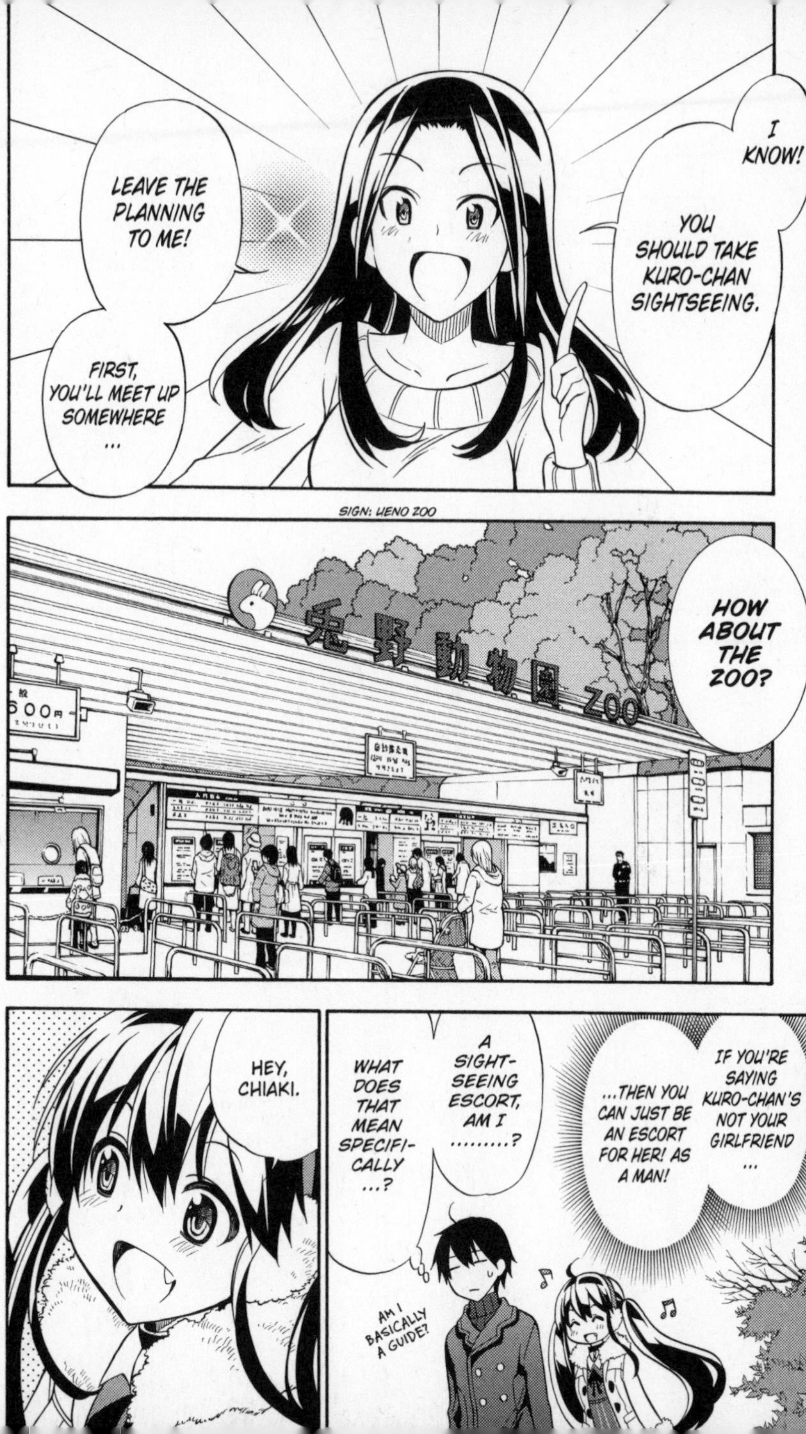
I KNOW!
YOU SHOULD TAKE KURO-CHAN SIGHTSEEING.
LEAVE THE PLANNING TO ME!
FIRST, YOU'LL MEET UP SOMEWHERE ...
SIGN: UENO ZOO
HOW ABOUT THE ZOO?
ZOO
IF YOU'RE SAYING KURO-CHAN'S NOT YOUR GIRLFRIEND ...
...THEN YOU CAN JUST BE AN ESCORT FOR HER! AS A MAN!
A SIGHT-SEEING ESCORT, AM I ....?
WHAT DOES THAT MEAN SPECIFI-CALLY ...?
AM I BASICALLY A GUIDE?
HEY, CHIAKI.

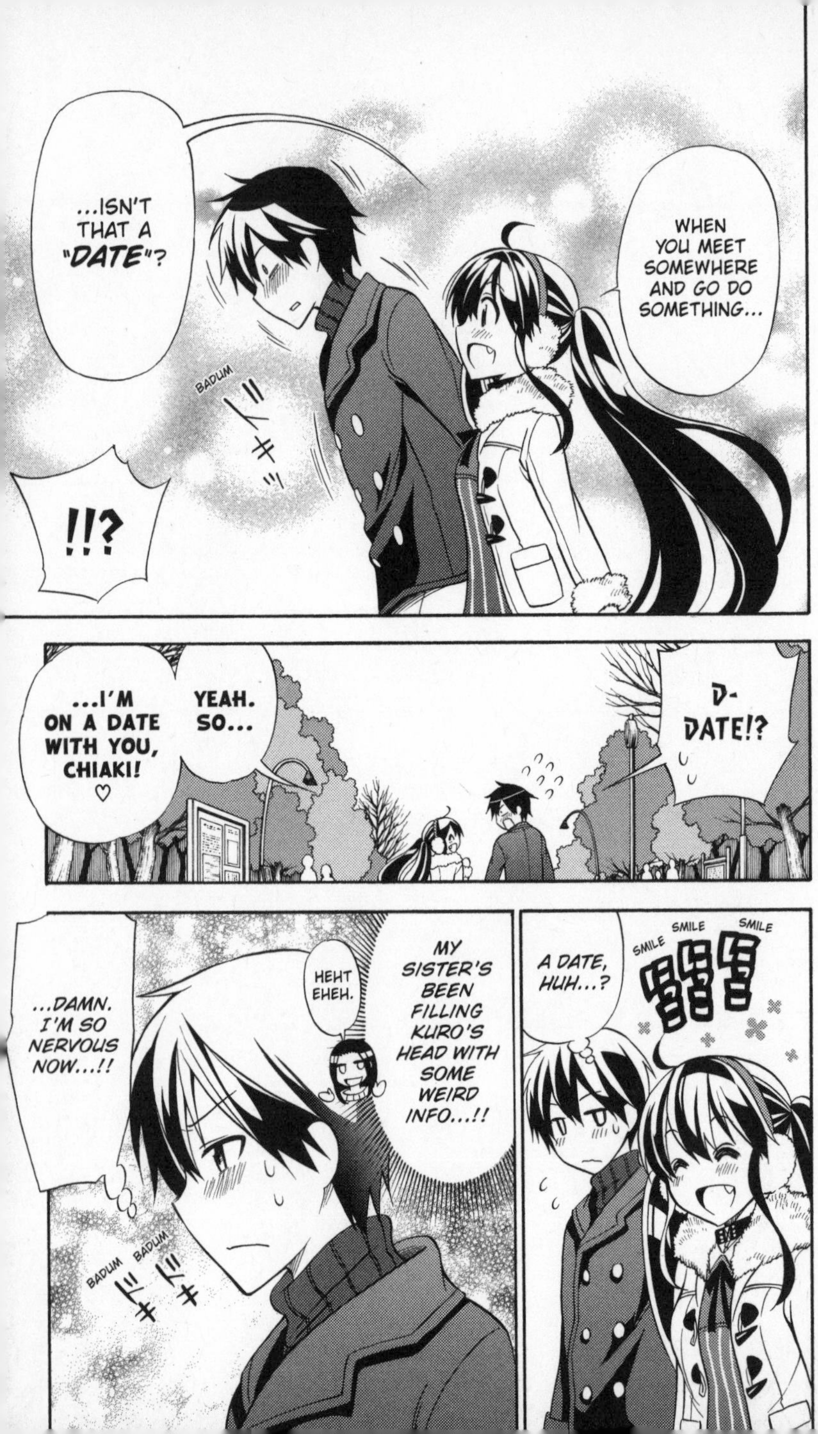
WHEN YOU MEET SOMEWHERE AND GO DO SOMETHING...
...ISN'T THAT A "DATE"?
BADUM
!!?
D-DATE!?
YEAH. SO...
...I'M ON A DATE WITH YOU, CHIAKI! ♡
SMILE SMILE SMILE
A DATE, HUH...?
MY SISTER'S BEEN FILLING KURO'S HEAD WITH SOME WEIRD INFO...!!
HEHT EHEH.
...DAMN. I'M SO NERVOUS NOW...!!
BADUM BADUM

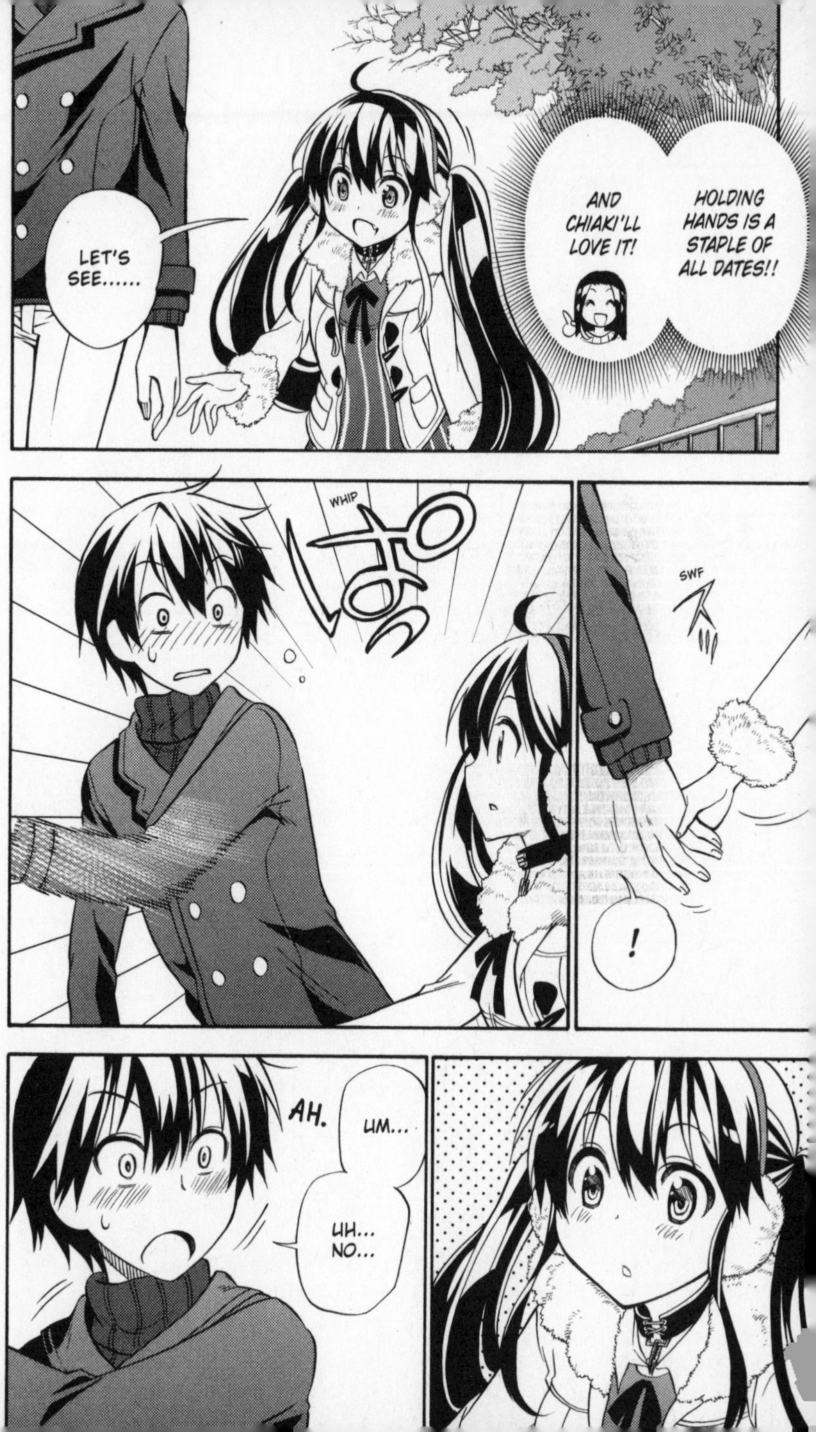
HOLDING HANDS IS A STAPLE OF ALL DATES!!
AND CHIAKI'LL LOVE IT!
LET'S SEE......
SWF
!
WHIP
AH.
UM...
UH... NO...

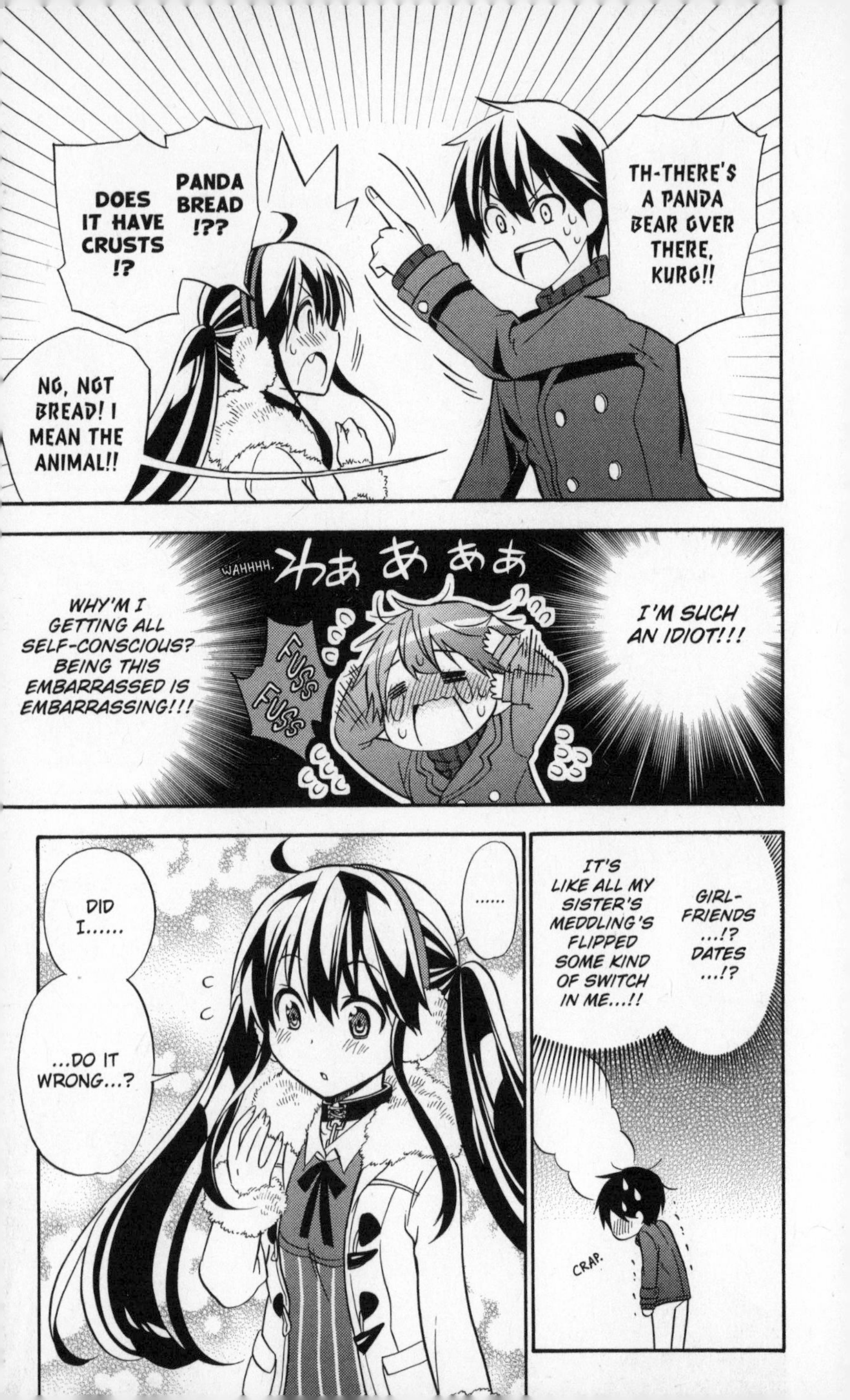
TH-THERE'S A PANDA BEAR OVER THERE, KURO!!
PANDA BREAD !??
DOES IT HAVE CRUSTS !?
NO, NOT BREAD! I MEAN THE ANIMAL!!
I'M SUCH AN IDIOT!!!
WAHHHH.
わあああ
FUSS FUSS
WHY'M I GETTING ALL SELF-CONSCIOUS? BEING THIS EMBARRASSED IS EMBARRASSING!!!
GIRL-FRIENDS ...!? DATES ...!?
IT'S LIKE ALL MY SISTER'S MEDDLING'S FLIPPED SOME KIND OF SWITCH IN ME...!!
CRAP.
......
DID I......
...DO IT WRONG...?

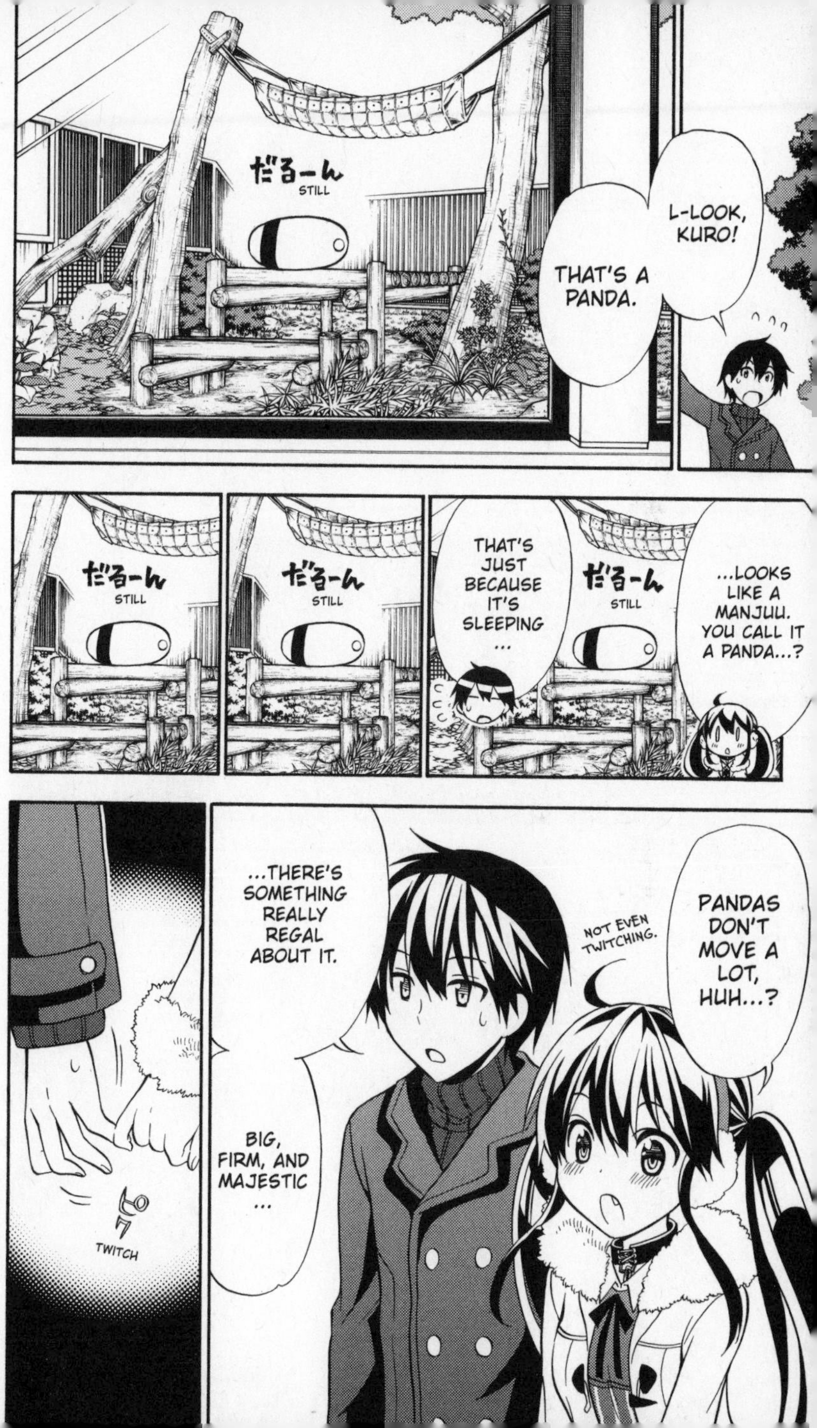
L-LOOK, KURO!
THAT'S A PANDA.
だるーん
STILL
...LOOKS LIKE A MANJUU. YOU CALL IT A PANDA...?
だるーん
STILL
THAT'S JUST BECAUSE IT'S SLEEPING...
だるーん
STILL
だるーん
STILL
PANDAS DON'T MOVE A LOT, HUH...?
NOT EVEN TWITCHING.
...THERE'S SOMETHING REALLY REGAL ABOUT IT.
BIG, FIRM, AND MAJESTIC...
ピク
TWITCH

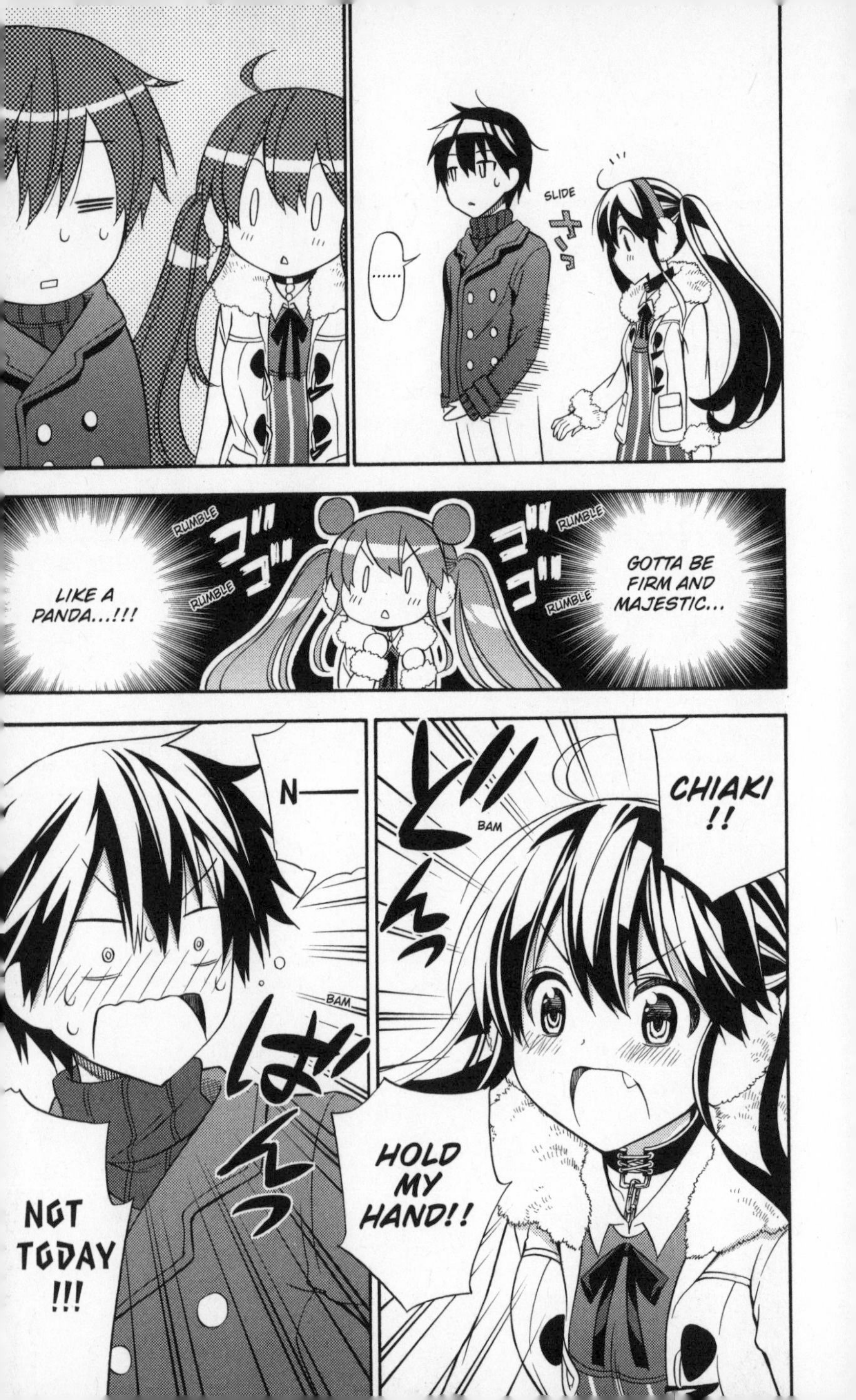
SLIDE
......
GOTTA BE FIRM AND MAJESTIC...
RUMBLE
RUMBLE
LIKE A PANDA...!!!
RUMBLE
RUMBLE
CHIAKI!!
BAM
HOLD MY HAND!!
BAM
N——
NOT TODAY!!!

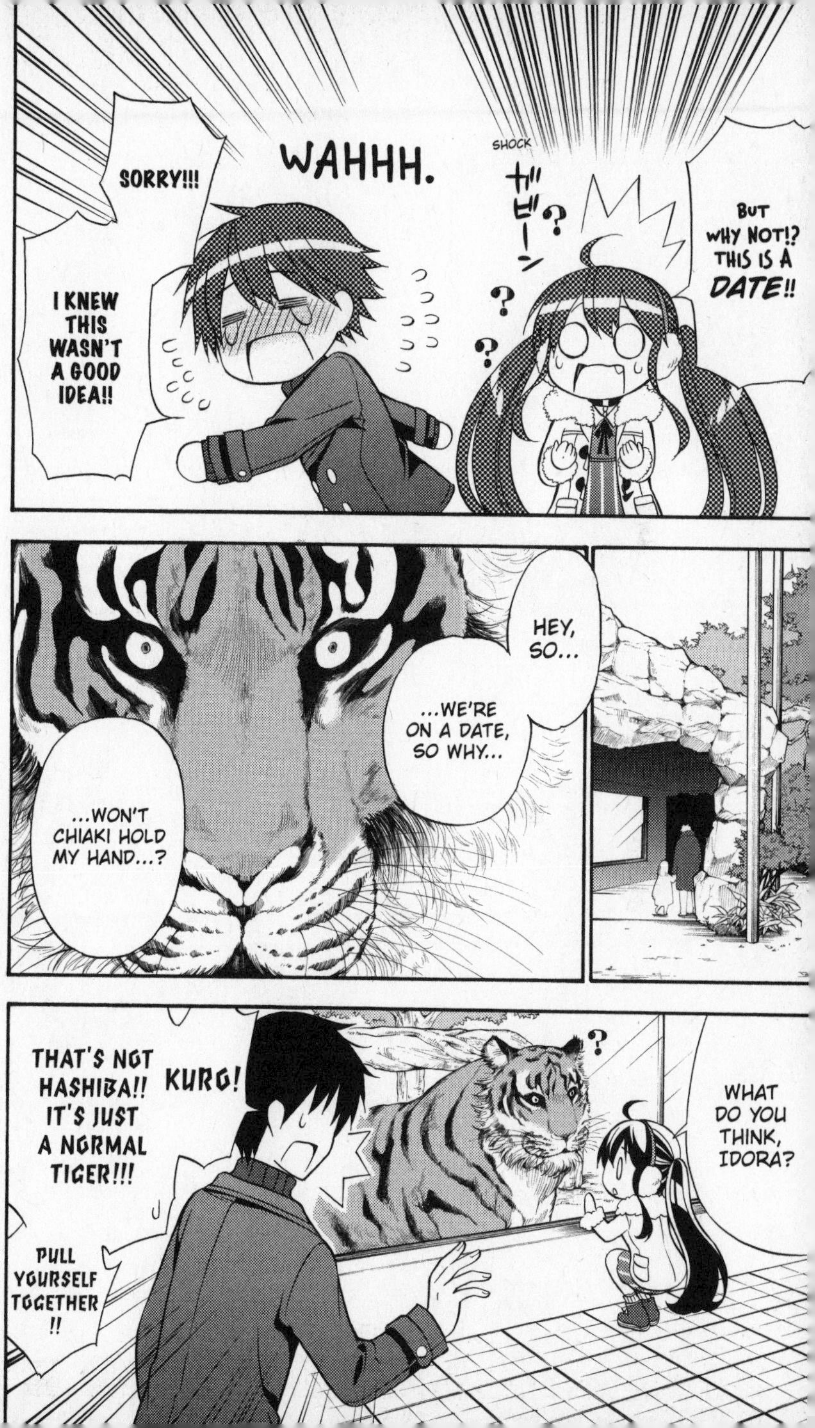
BUT WHY NOT!? THIS IS A DATE!!
SHOCK
ガビーン
WAHHH.
SORRY!!!
I KNEW THIS WASN'T A GOOD IDEA!!
HEY, SO...
...WE'RE ON A DATE, SO WHY...
...WON'T CHIAKI HOLD MY HAND...?
WHAT DO YOU THINK, IDORA?
KURG!
THAT'S NOT HASHIBA!! IT'S JUST A NORMAL TIGER!!!
PULL YOURSELF TOGETHER!!

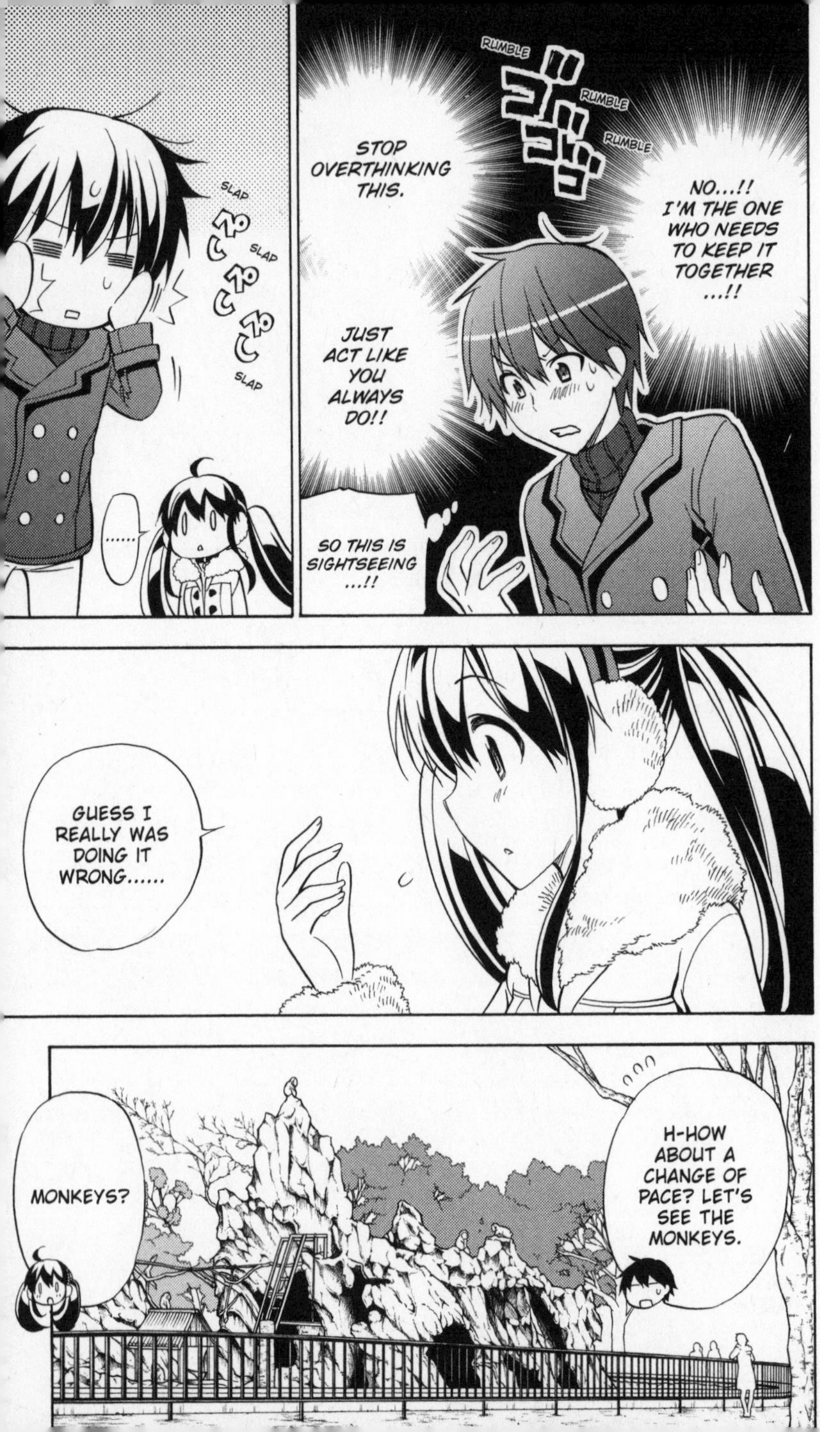
RUMBLE
RUMBLE
RUMBLE
NO...!! I'M THE ONE WHO NEEDS TO KEEP IT TOGETHER...!!
STOP OVERTHINKING THIS.
JUST ACT LIKE YOU ALWAYS DO!!
SO THIS IS SIGHTSEEING...!!
SLAP
SLAP
SLAP
......
GUESS I REALLY WAS DOING IT WRONG......
H-HOW ABOUT A CHANGE OF PACE? LET'S SEE THE MONKEYS.
MONKEYS?

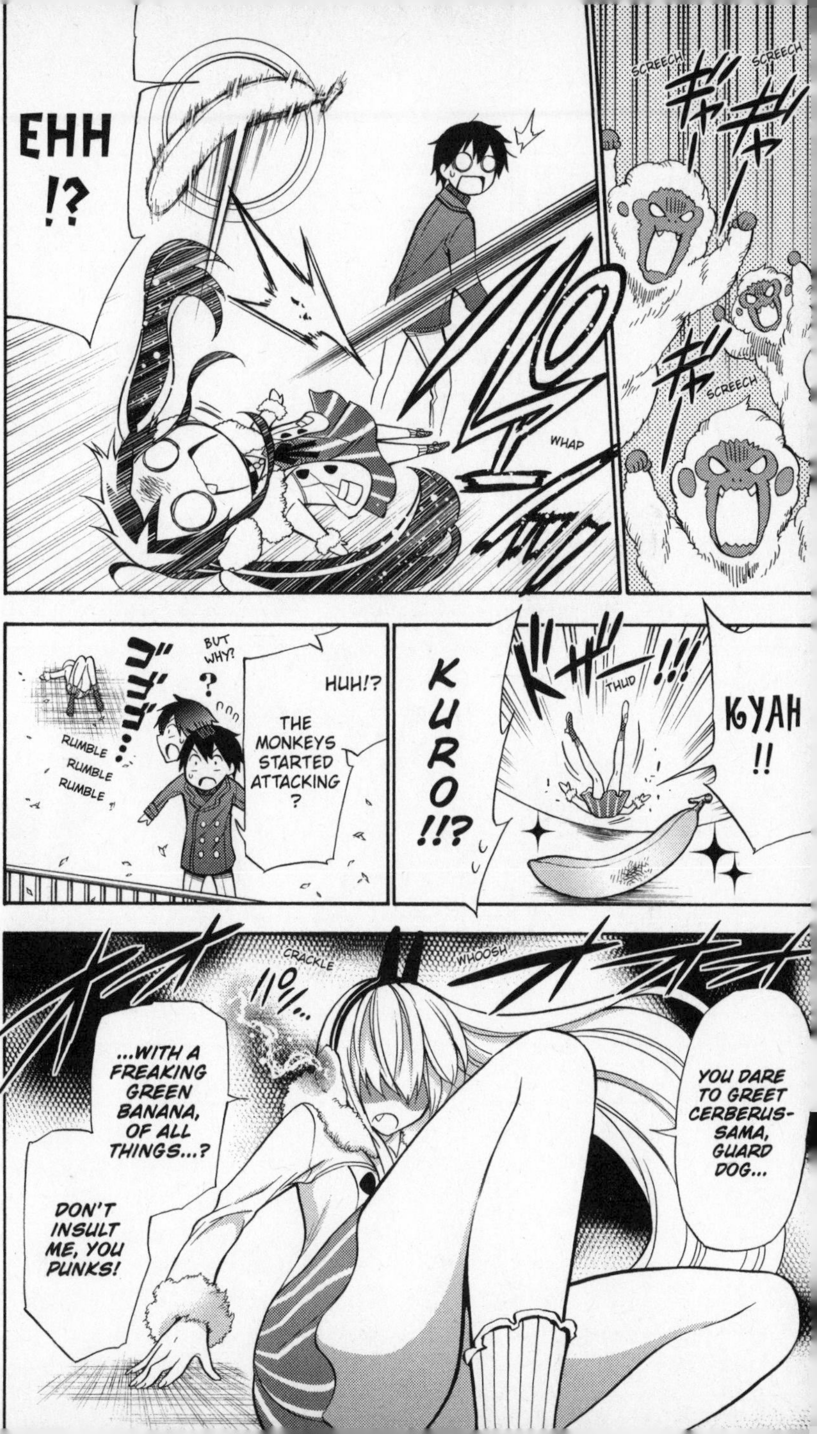
SCREECH
SCREECH
SCREECH
WHAP
EHH!?
KYAH!!
THUD
KURO!!?
HUH!?
THE MONKEYS STARTED ATTACKING?
BUT WHY?
RUMBLE RUMBLE RUMBLE
WHOOSH
CRACKLE
YOU DARE TO GREET CERBERUS-SAMA, GUARD DOG...
...WITH A FREAKING GREEN BANANA, OF ALL THINGS...?
DON'T INSULT ME, YOU PUNKS!

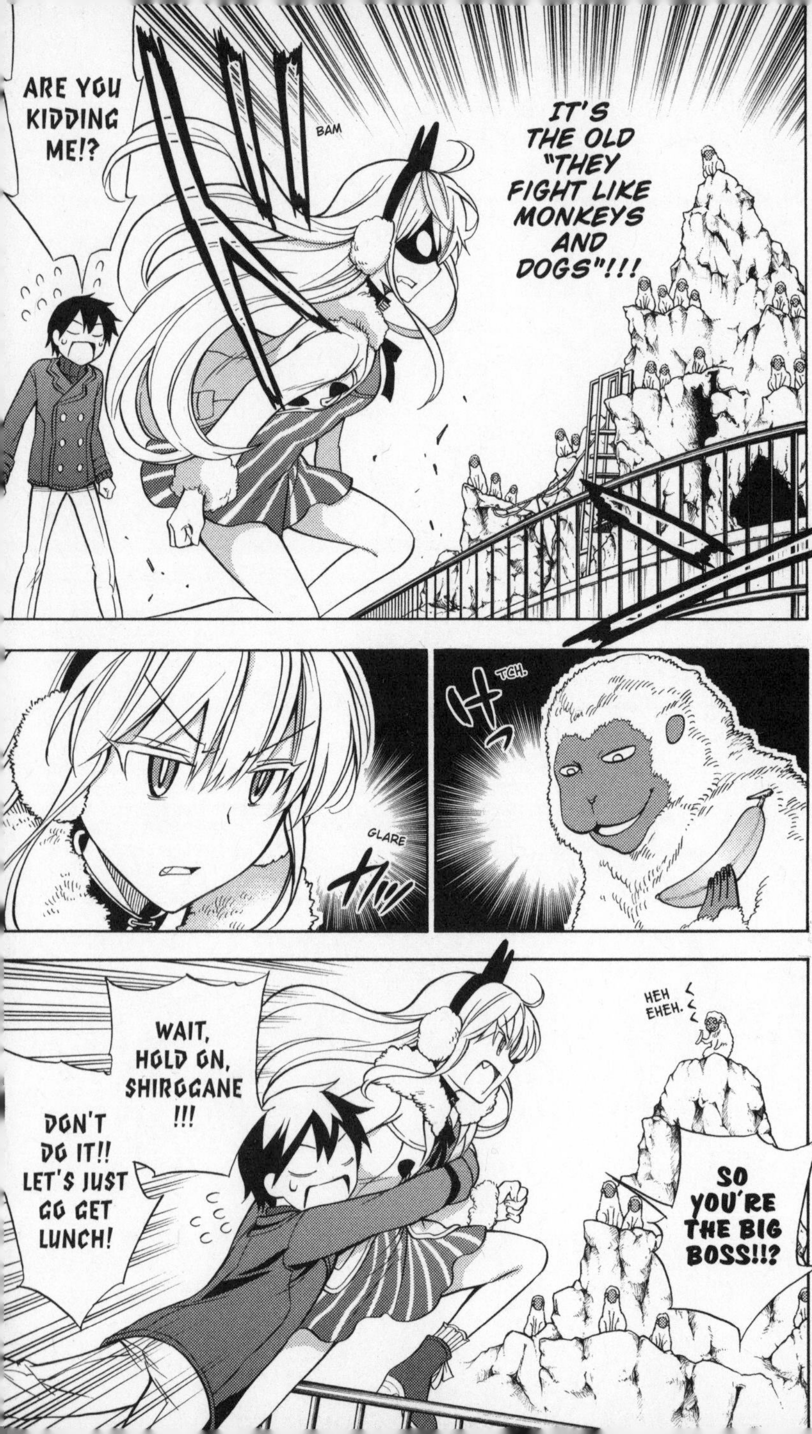
IT'S THE OLD "THEY FIGHT LIKE MONKEYS AND DOGS"!!!
BAM
ARE YOU KIDDING ME!?
TCH.
GLARE
SO YOU'RE THE BIG BOSS!!?
HEH EHEH.
WAIT, HOLD ON, SHIROGANE!!!
DON'T DO IT!! LET'S JUST GO GET LUNCH!

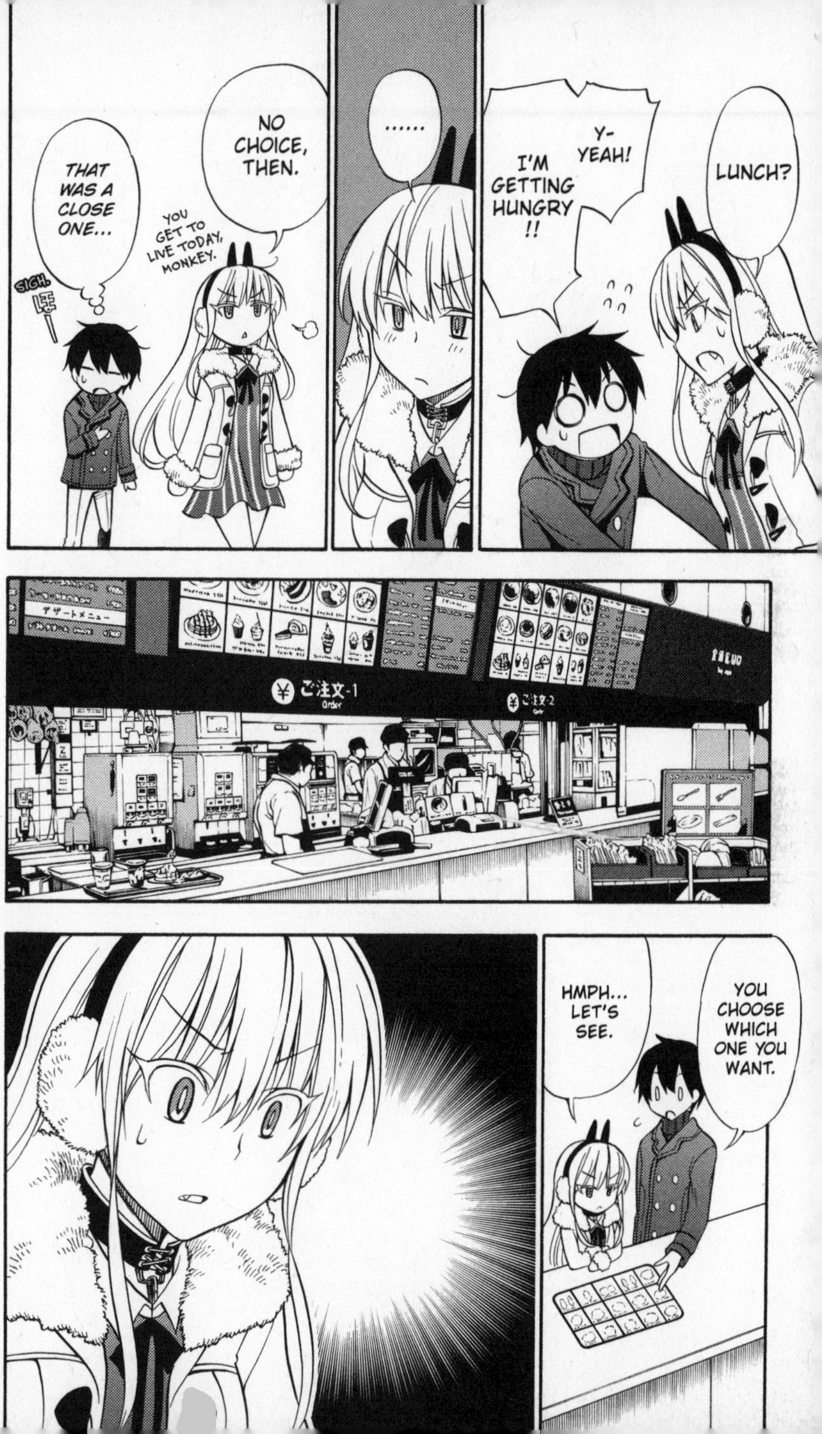
LUNCH?
Y- YEAH!
I'M GETTING HUNGRY!!
......
NO CHOICE, THEN.
YOU GET TO LIVE TODAY, MONKEY.
THAT WAS A CLOSE ONE...
SIGH.
ご注文-1
Order
YOU CHOOSE WHICH ONE YOU WANT.
HMPH... LET'S SEE.

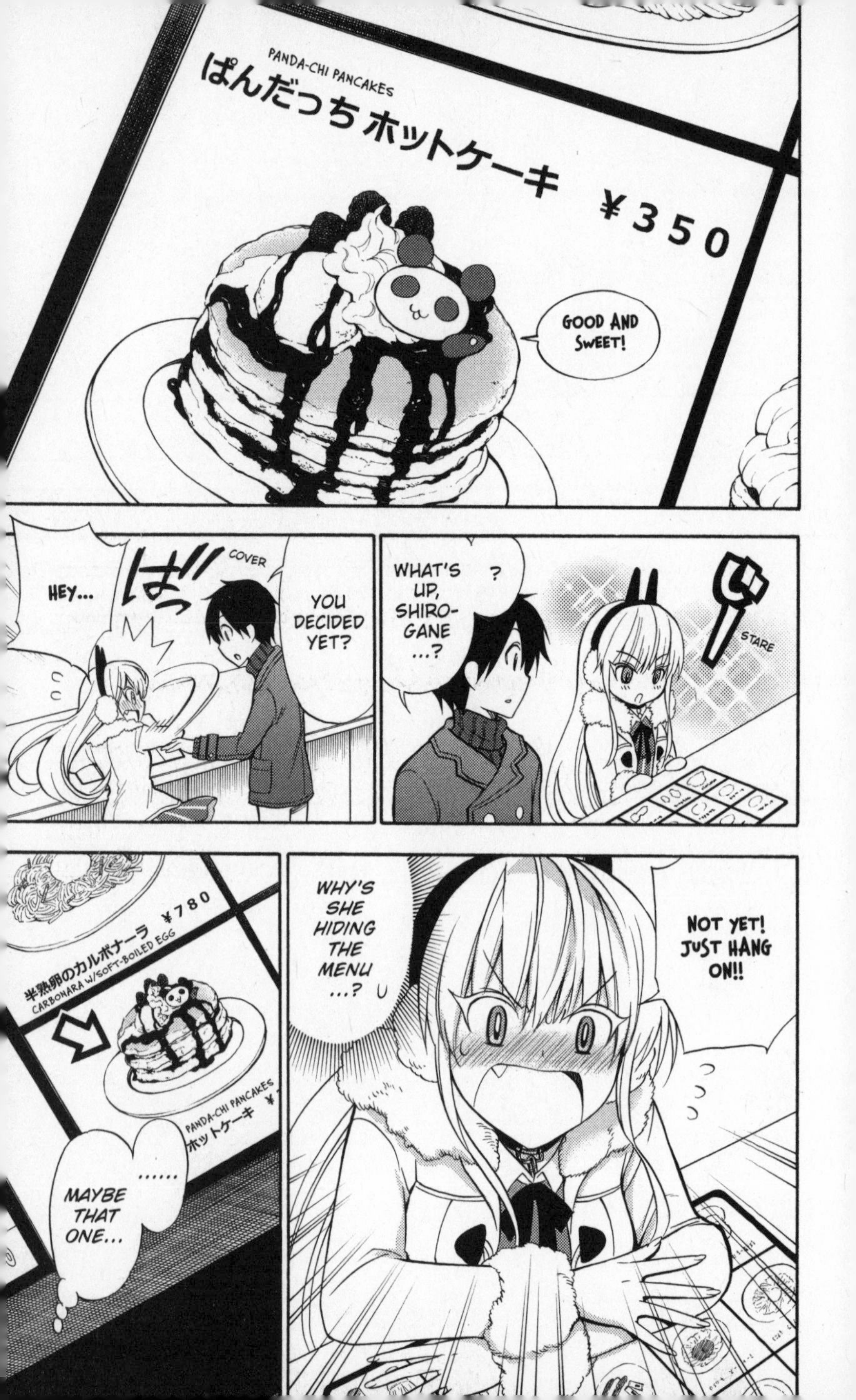
PANDA-CHI PANCAKES
ぱんだっち ホットケーキ
¥350
GOOD AND SWEET!
STARE
?
WHAT'S UP, SHIRO-GANE ...?
YOU DECIDED YET?
COVER
ばっ
HEY...
NOT YET! JUST HANG ON!!
WHY'S SHE HIDING THE MENU ...?
¥780
半熟卵のカルボナーラ
CARBONARA W/SOFT-BOILED EGG
PANDA-CHI PANCAKES
ホットケーキ
......
MAYBE THAT ONE...

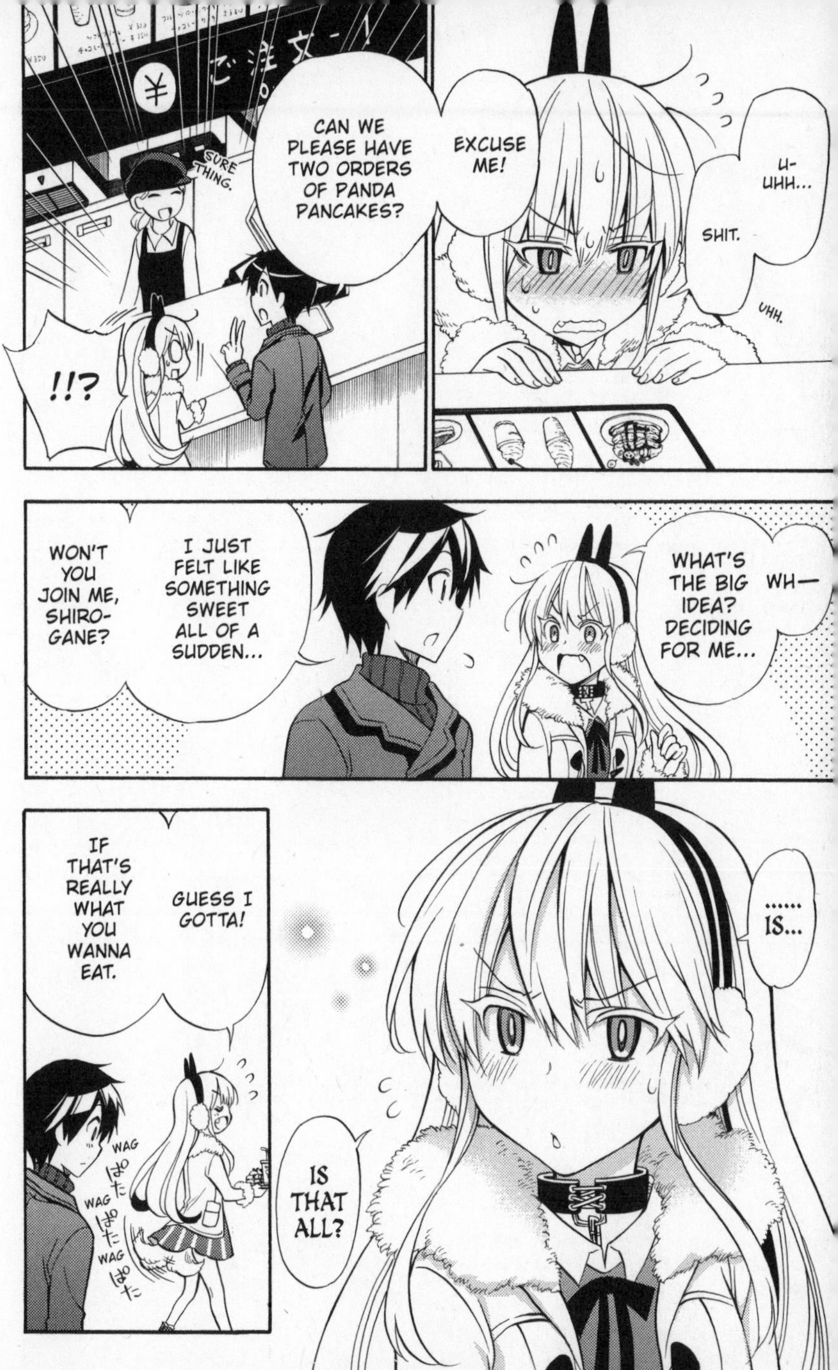
U-UHH...
SHIT.
UHH.
EXCUSE ME!
CAN WE PLEASE HAVE TWO ORDERS OF PANDA PANCAKES?
SURE THING.
!!?
WH—
WHAT'S THE BIG IDEA? DECIDING FOR ME...
I JUST FELT LIKE SOMETHING SWEET ALL OF A SUDDEN...
WON'T YOU JOIN ME, SHIRO-GANE?
......
IS...
IS THAT ALL?
GUESS I GOTTA!
IF THAT'S REALLY WHAT YOU WANNA EAT.
WAG ぱた
WAG ぱた
WAG ぱた

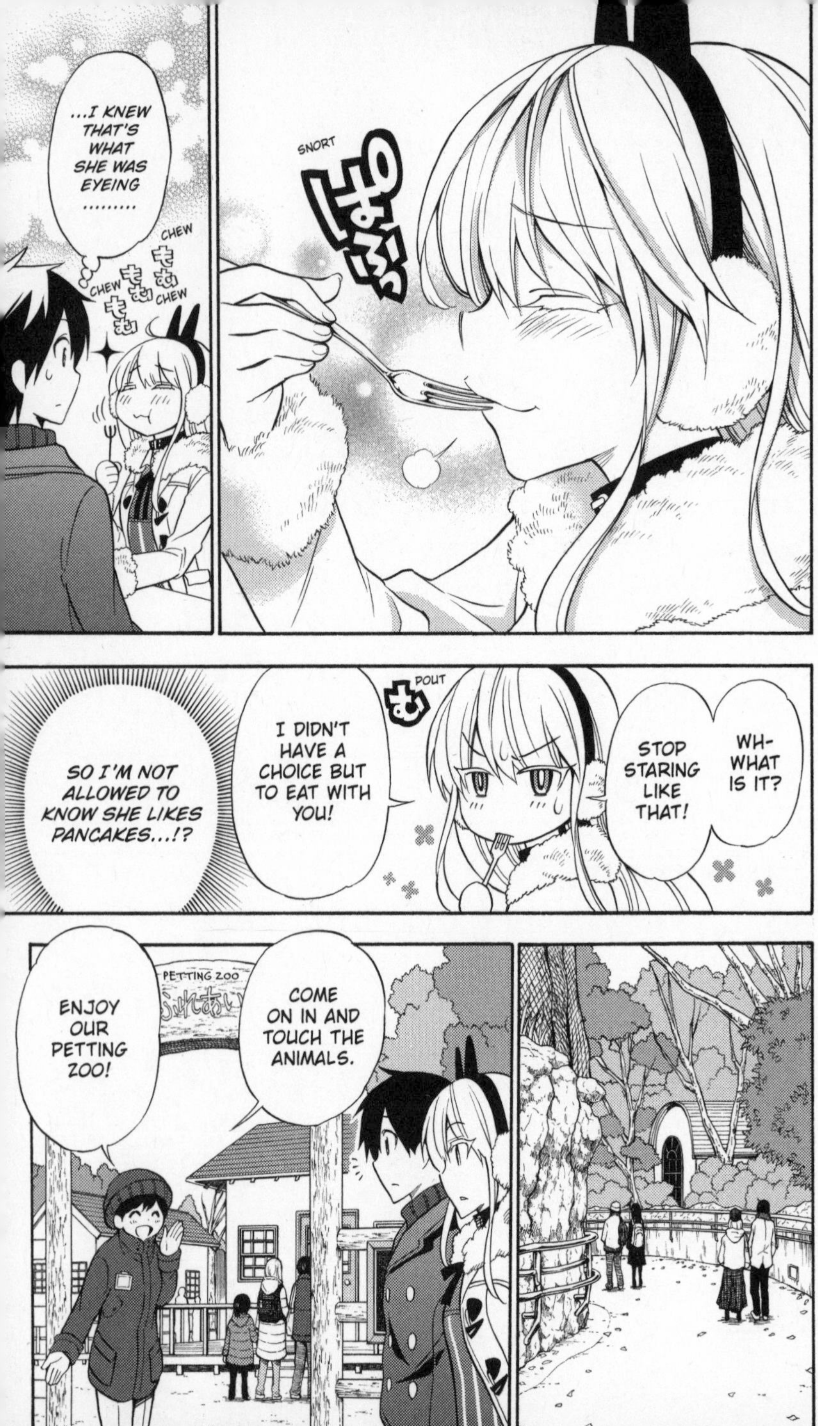
SNORT
...I KNEW THAT'S WHAT SHE WAS EYEING ....
CHEW
CHEW
CHEW
WH- WHAT IS IT?
STOP STARING LIKE THAT!
POUT
I DIDN'T HAVE A CHOICE BUT TO EAT WITH YOU!
SO I'M NOT ALLOWED TO KNOW SHE LIKES PANCAKES...!?
PETTING ZOO
COME ON IN AND TOUCH THE ANIMALS.
ENJOY OUR PETTING ZOO!

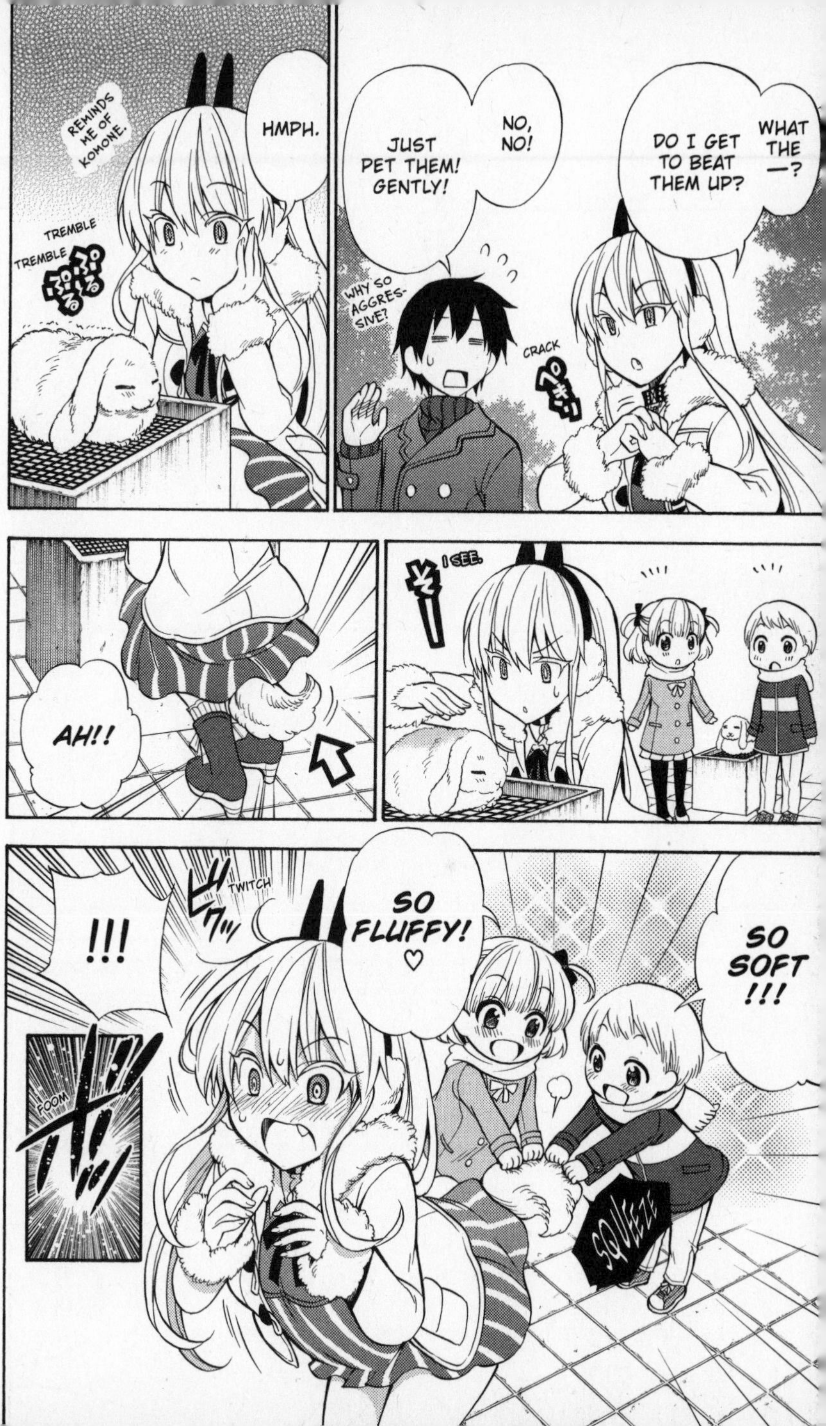
WHAT THE—?
DO I GET TO BEAT THEM UP?
NO, NO!
JUST PET THEM! GENTLY!
WHY SO AGGRES-SIVE?
CRACK
HMPH.
REMINDS ME OF KOMONE.
TREMBLE TREMBLE
I SEE.
AH!!
SO SOFT!!!
SO FLUFFY! ♡
TWITCH
SQUEEZE
!!!
FOOM

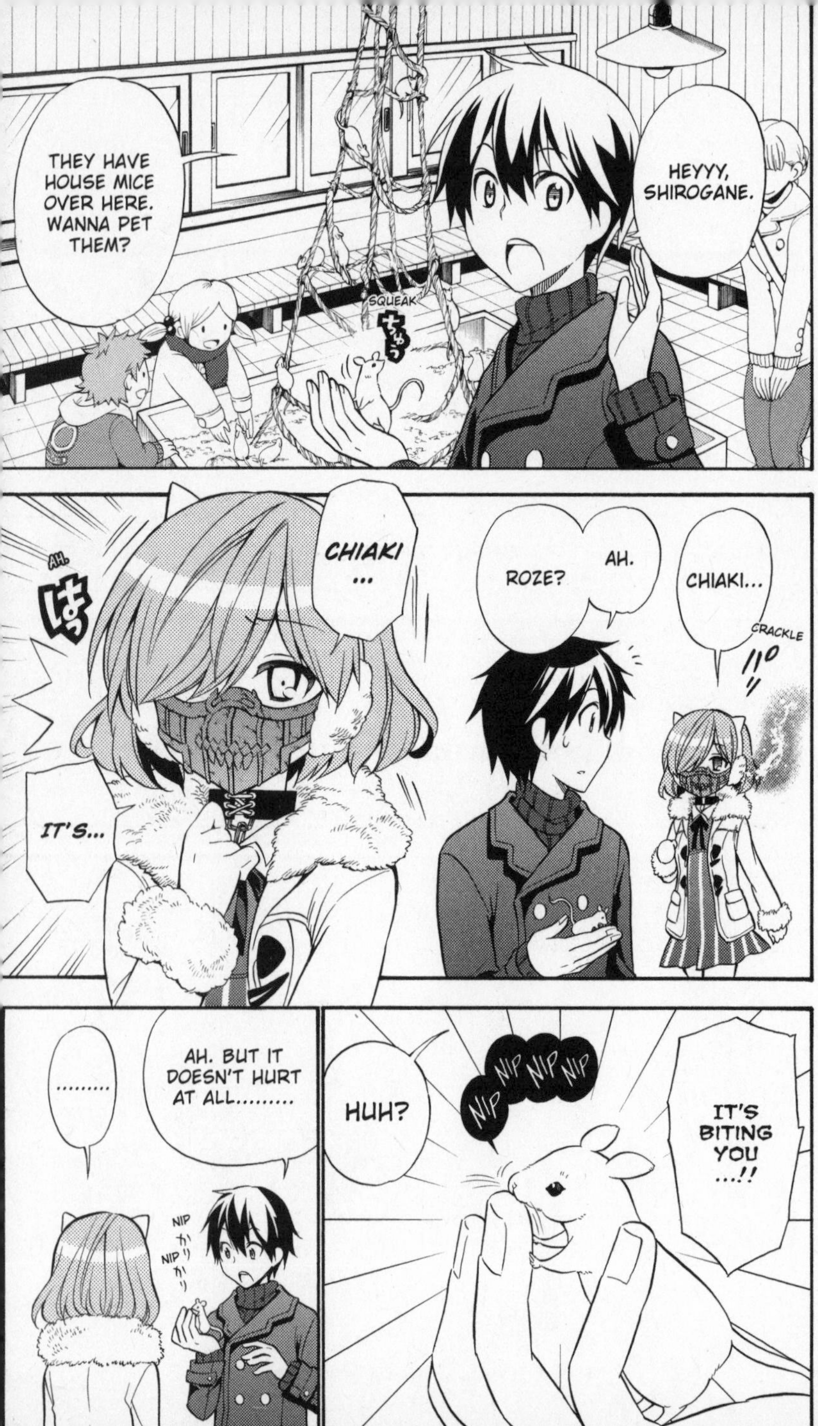
HEYYY, SHIROGANE.
THEY HAVE HOUSE MICE OVER HERE. WANNA PET THEM?
SQUEAK
CHIAKI...
CRACKLE
AH.
ROZE?
CHIAKI ...
AH.
IT'S...
IT'S BITING YOU ...!!
NIP NIP NIP NIP
HUH?
AH. BUT IT DOESN'T HURT AT ALL.........
....
NIP NIP

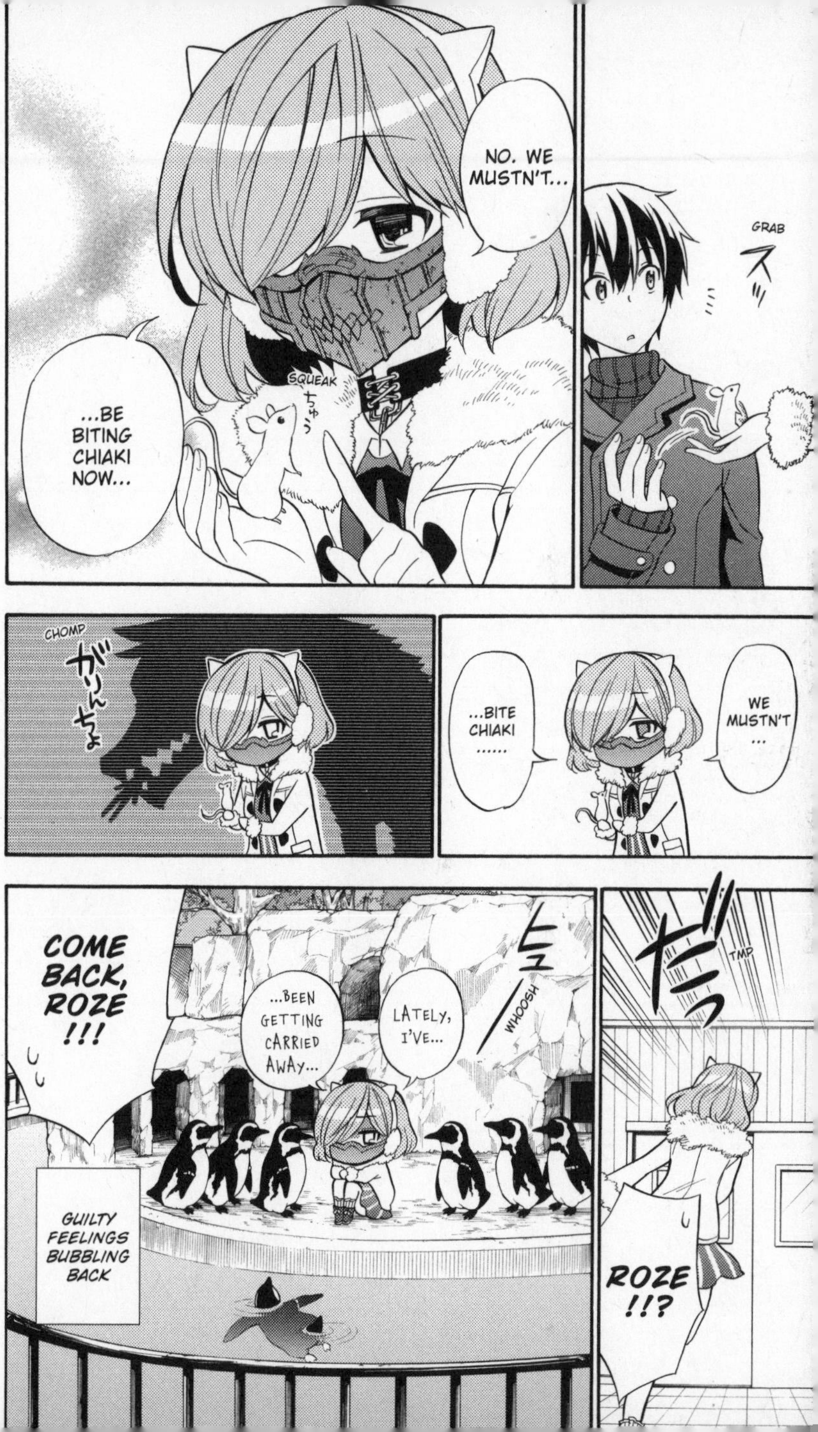
GRAB
NO. WE MUSTN'T...
SQUEAK
ちゅう
...BE BITING CHIAKI NOW...
WE MUSTN'T ...
...BITE CHIAKI ......
CHOMP
がりんちょ
TMP
ROZE !!?
WHOOSH
LATELY, I'VE...
...BEEN GETTING CARRIED AWAY...
COME BACK, ROZE !!!
GUILTY FEELINGS BUBBLING BACK

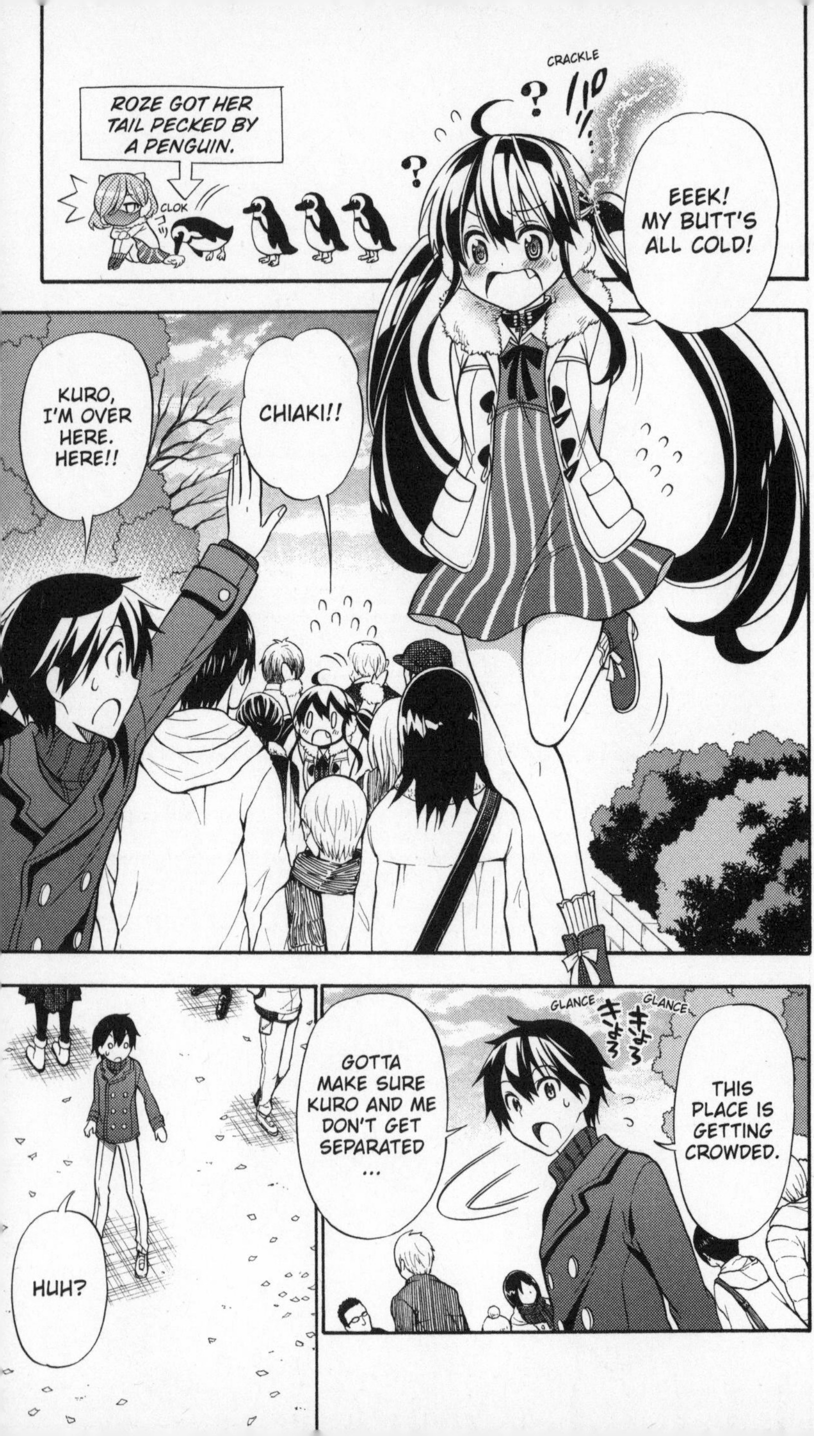
CRACKLE
EEEK! MY BUTT'S ALL COLD!
ROZE GOT HER TAIL PECKED BY A PENGUIN.
CLOK
CHIAKI!!
KURO, I'M OVER HERE. HERE!!
GLANCE GLANCE
きょろきょろ
THIS PLACE IS GETTING CROWDED.
GOTTA MAKE SURE KURO AND ME DON'T GET SEPARATED ...
HUH?

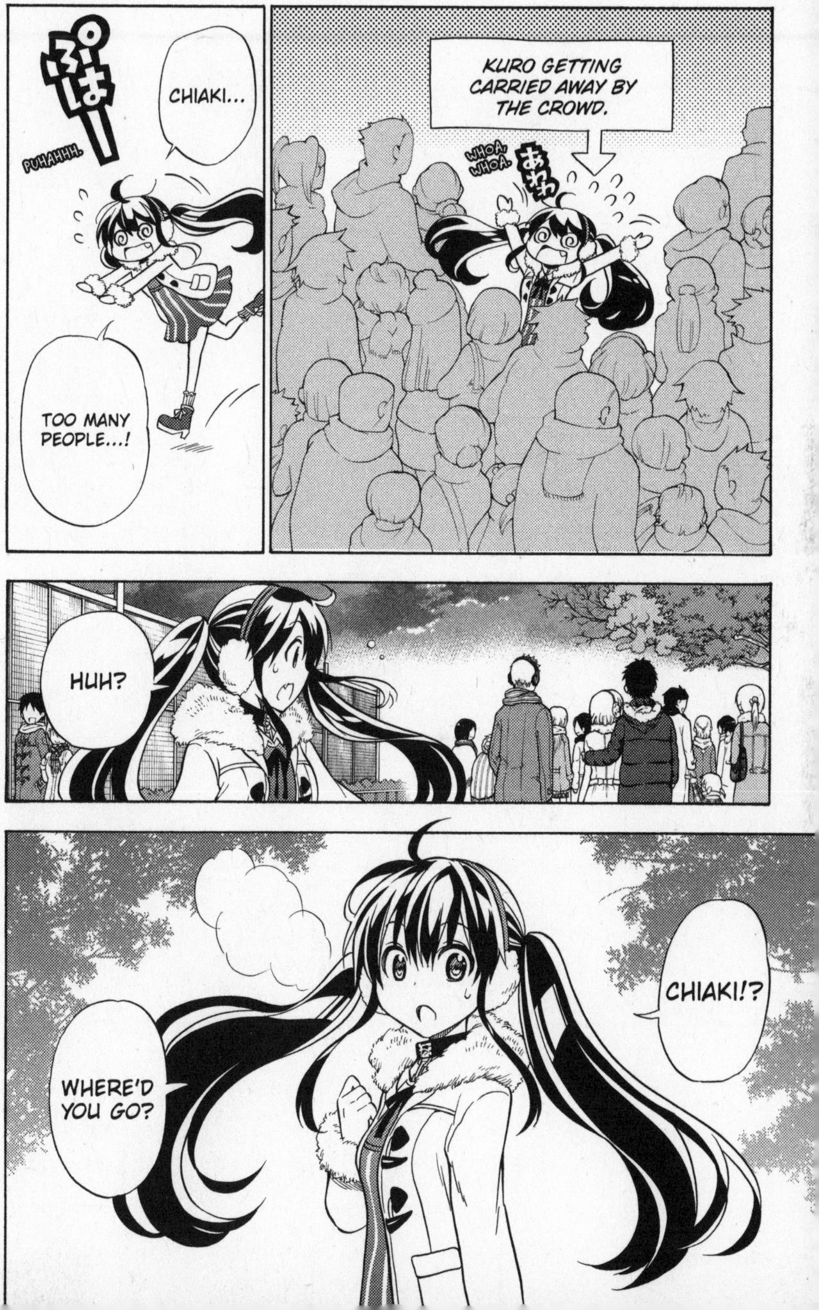
KURO GETTING CARRIED AWAY BY THE CROWD.
WHOA WHOA.
あわわ
ぷはー
PUHAHHH.
CHIAKI...
TOO MANY PEOPLE...!
HUH?
CHIAKI!?
WHERE'D YOU GO?

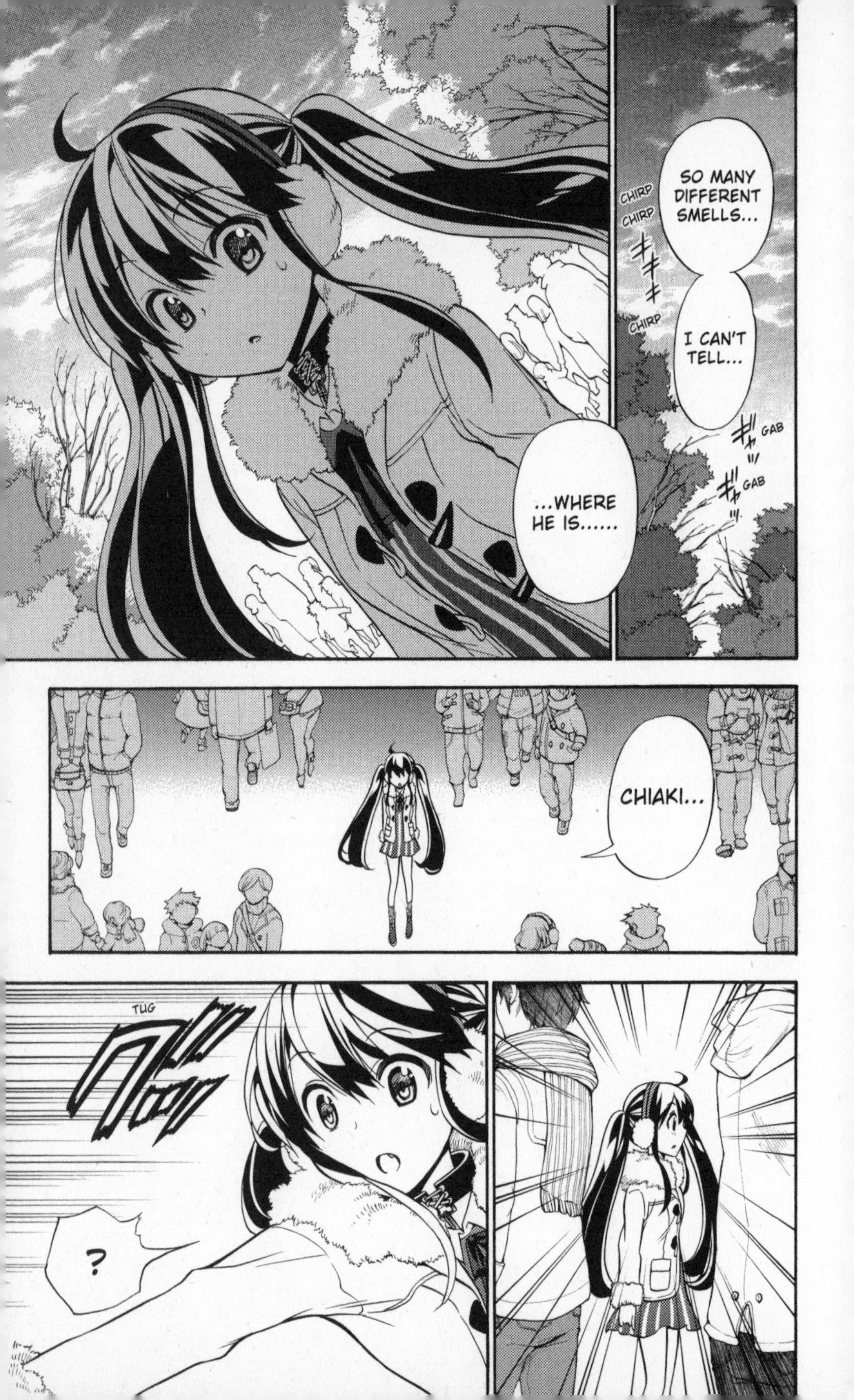
CHIRP
CHIRP
SO MANY DIFFERENT SMELLS...
CHIRP
I CAN'T TELL...
GAB
GAB
...WHERE HE IS......
CHIAKI...
TUG
?

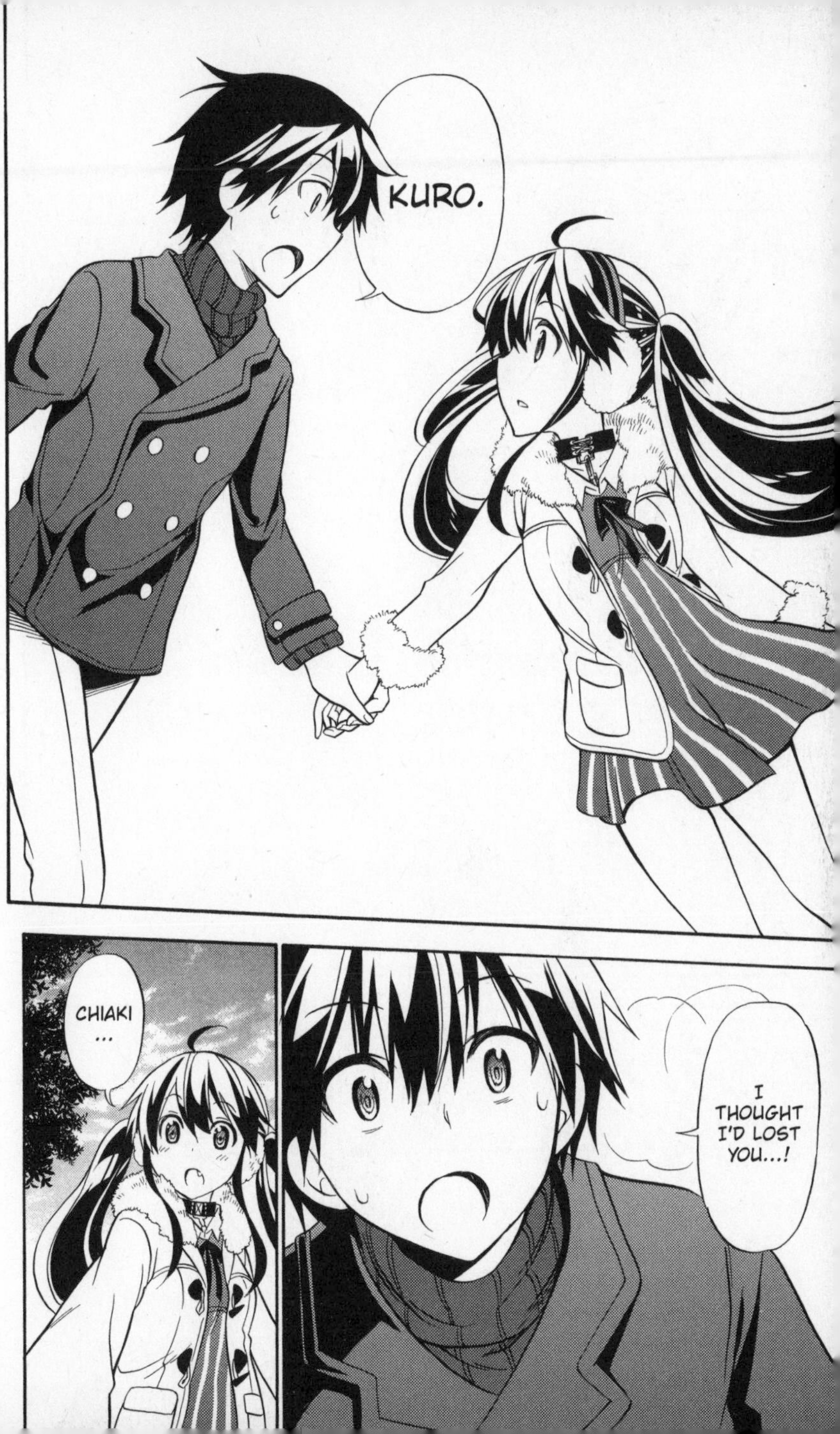
KURO.
I THOUGHT I'D LOST YOU...!
CHIAKI ...

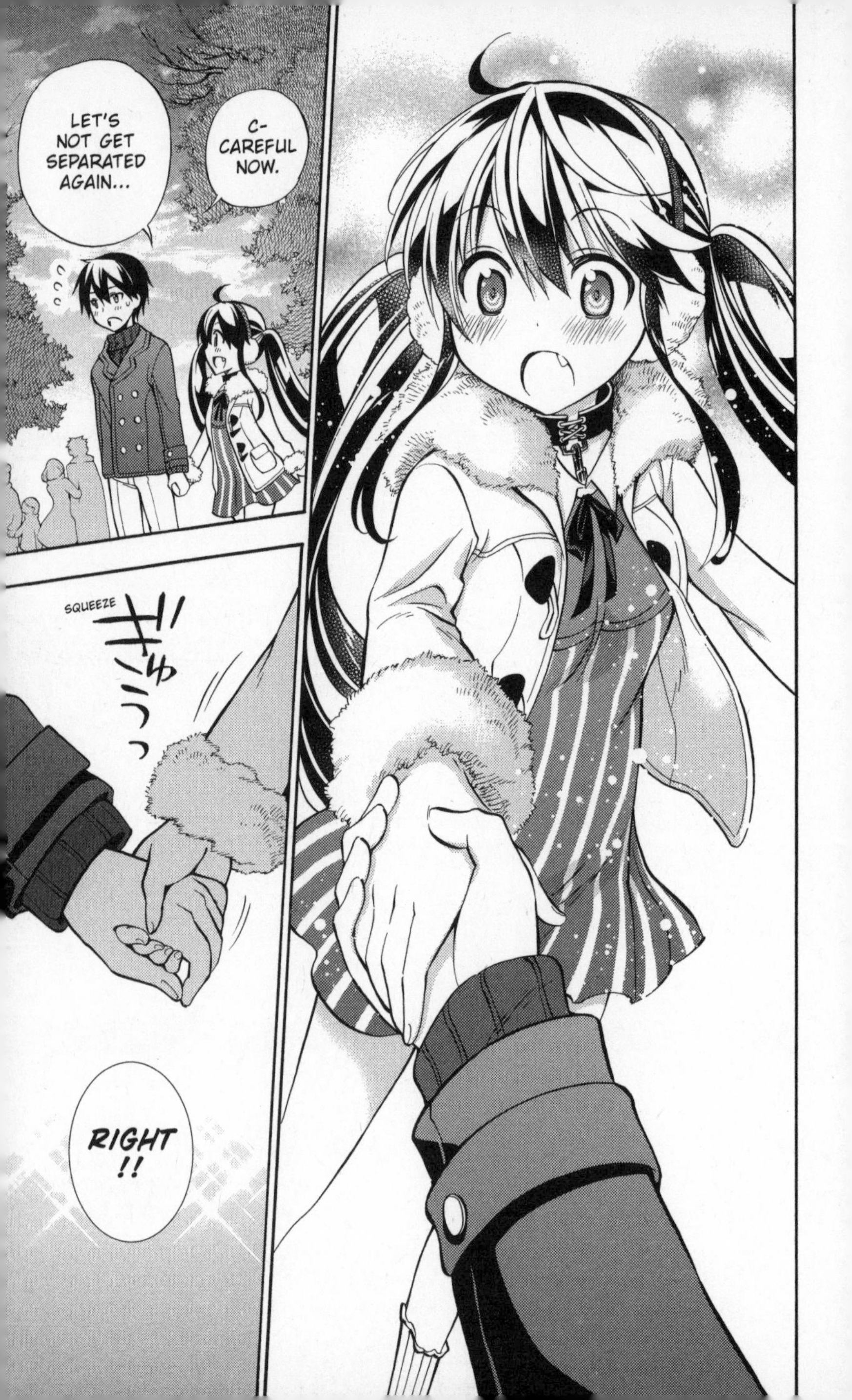
C-CAREFUL NOW.
LET'S NOT GET SEPARATED AGAIN...
SQUEEZE
ぎゅうっ
RIGHT!!

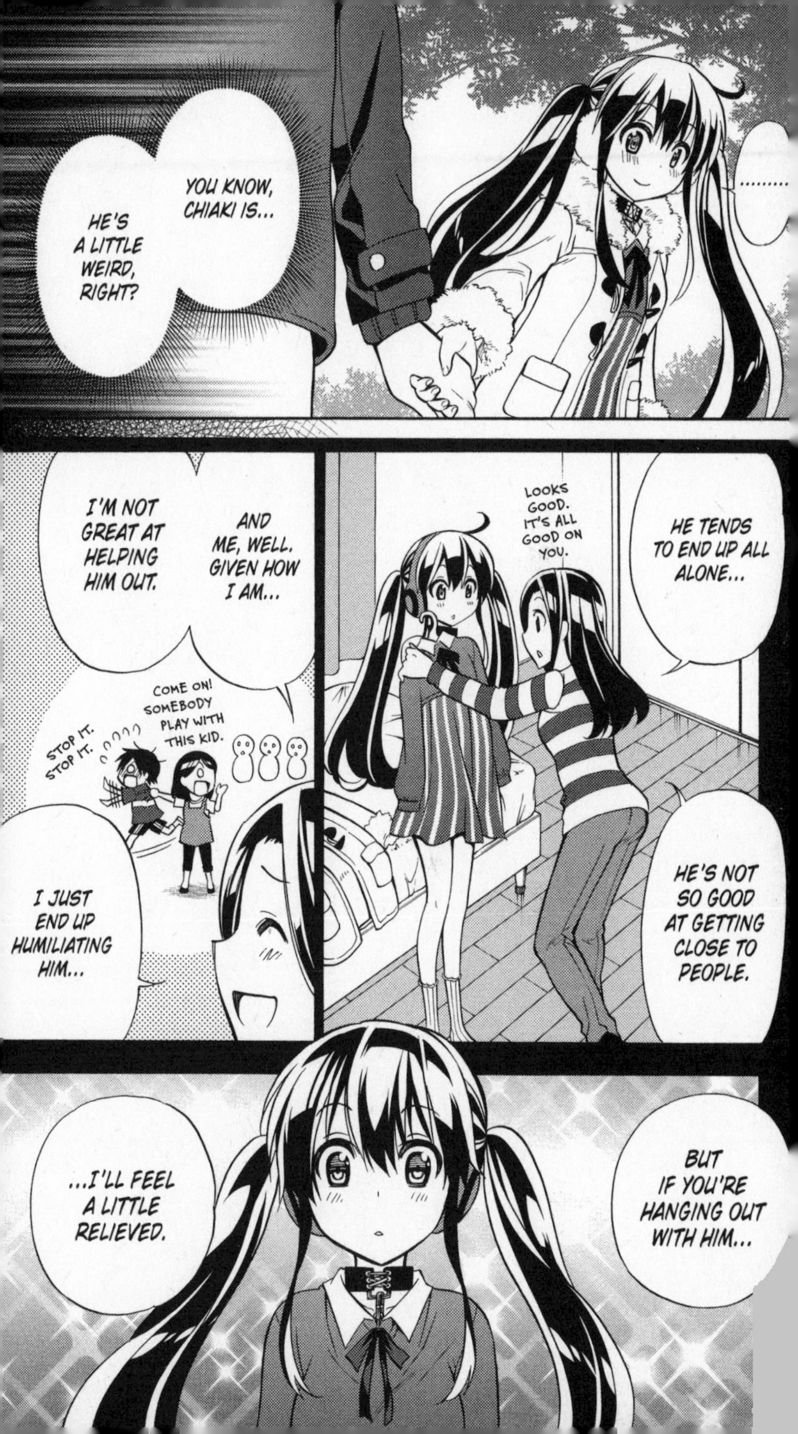
....
YOU KNOW, CHIAKI IS...
HE'S A LITTLE WEIRD, RIGHT?
HE TENDS TO END UP ALL ALONE...
LOOKS GOOD. IT'S ALL GOOD ON YOU.
HE'S NOT SO GOOD AT GETTING CLOSE TO PEOPLE.
AND ME, WELL. GIVEN HOW I AM...
I'M NOT GREAT AT HELPING HIM OUT.
COME ON! SOMEBODY PLAY WITH THIS KID.
STOP IT. STOP IT.
I JUST END UP HUMILIATING HIM...
BUT IF YOU'RE HANGING OUT WITH HIM...
...I'LL FEEL A LITTLE RELIEVED.

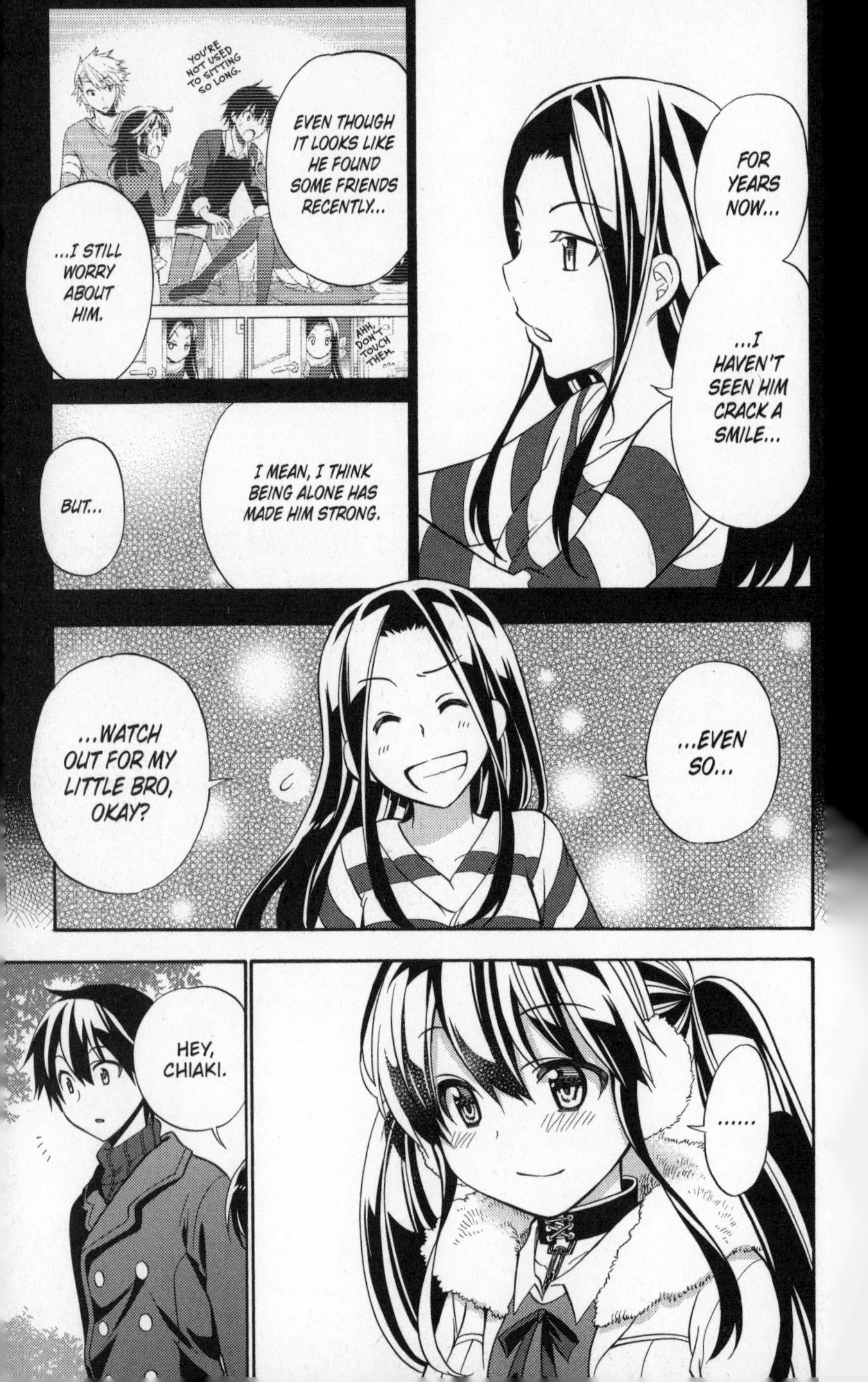
FOR YEARS NOW...
...I HAVEN'T SEEN HIM CRACK A SMILE...
EVEN THOUGH IT LOOKS LIKE HE FOUND SOME FRIENDS RECENTLY...
YOU'RE NOT USED TO SITTING SO LONG.
...I STILL WORRY ABOUT HIM.
AHH, DON'T TOUCH THEM.
I MEAN, I THINK BEING ALONE HAS MADE HIM STRONG.
BUT...
...EVEN SO...
...WATCH OUT FOR MY LITTLE BRO, OKAY?
......
HEY, CHIAKI.

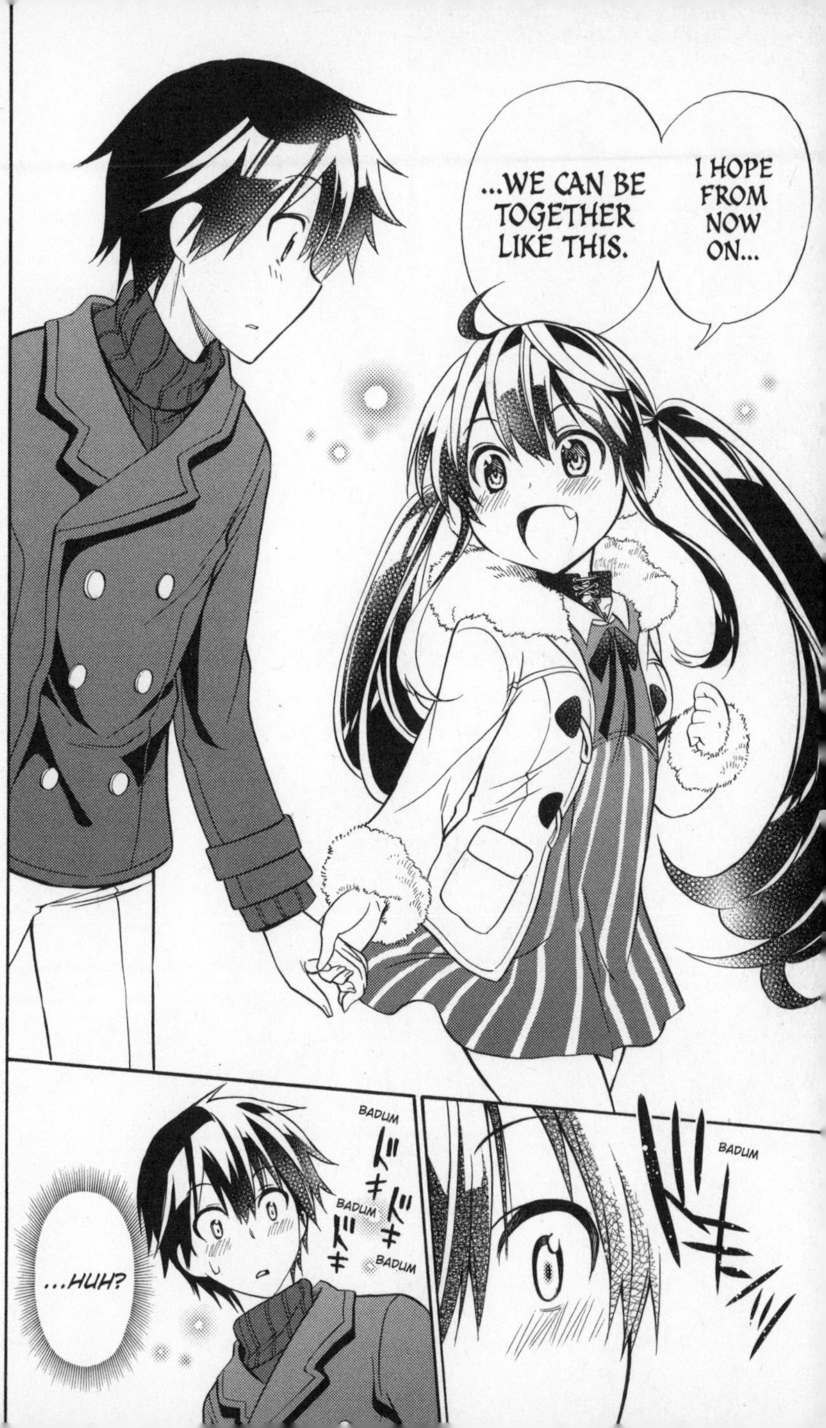
I HOPE FROM NOW ON...
...WE CAN BE TOGETHER LIKE THIS.
BADUM
ドキッ!!
BADUM
ドキ
BADUM
ドキ
BADUM
ドキ
...HUH?

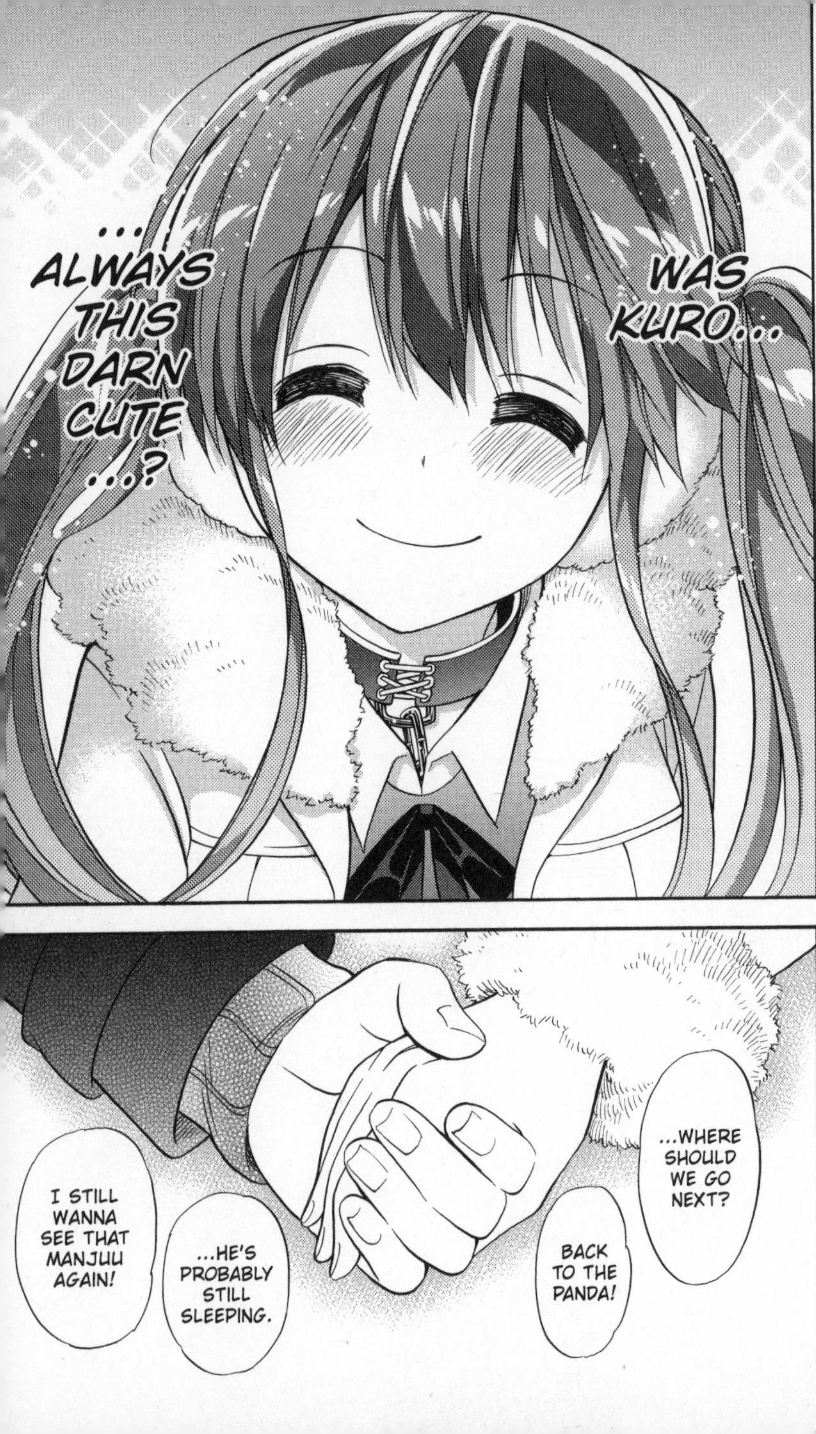
WAS KURO...
...ALWAYS THIS DARN CUTE...?
...WHERE SHOULD WE GO NEXT?
BACK TO THE PANDA!
...HE'S PROBABLY STILL SLEEPING.
I STILL WANNA SEE THAT MANJUU AGAIN!

TODAY'S CERBERUS

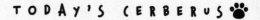

BEING A YEKNOM IS HARD. ESPECIALLY WHEN YOU'RE THE SSOB.
SOMETHING OF A NIHILIST.

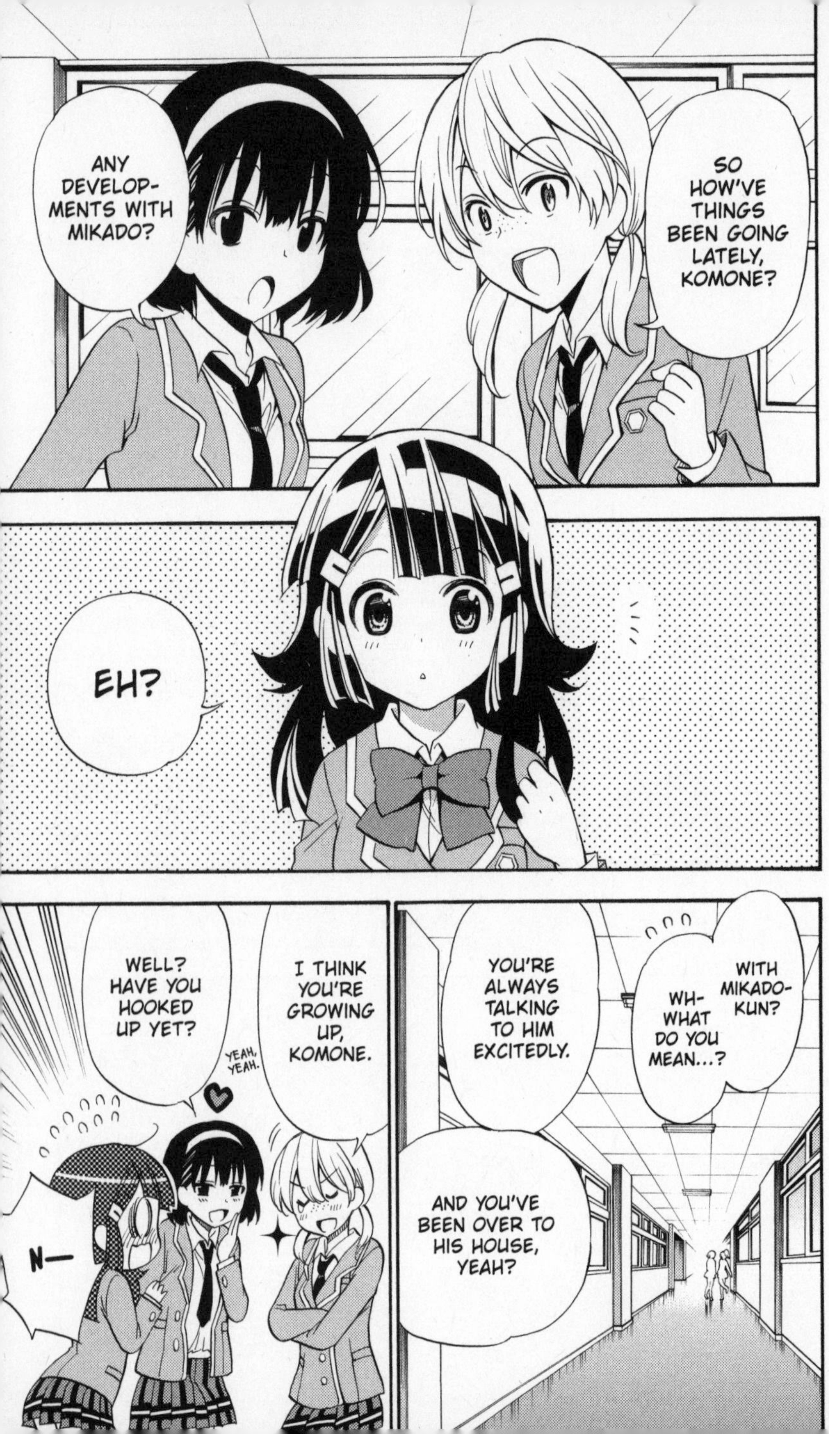
SO HOW'VE THINGS BEEN GOING LATELY, KOMONE?
ANY DEVELOP-MENTS WITH MIKADO?
EH?
WITH MIKADO-KUN?
WH-WHAT DO YOU MEAN...?
YOU'RE ALWAYS TALKING TO HIM EXCITEDLY.
AND YOU'VE BEEN OVER TO HIS HOUSE, YEAH?
I THINK YOU'RE GROWING UP, KOMONE.
YEAH, YEAH.
WELL? HAVE YOU HOOKED UP YET?
N—

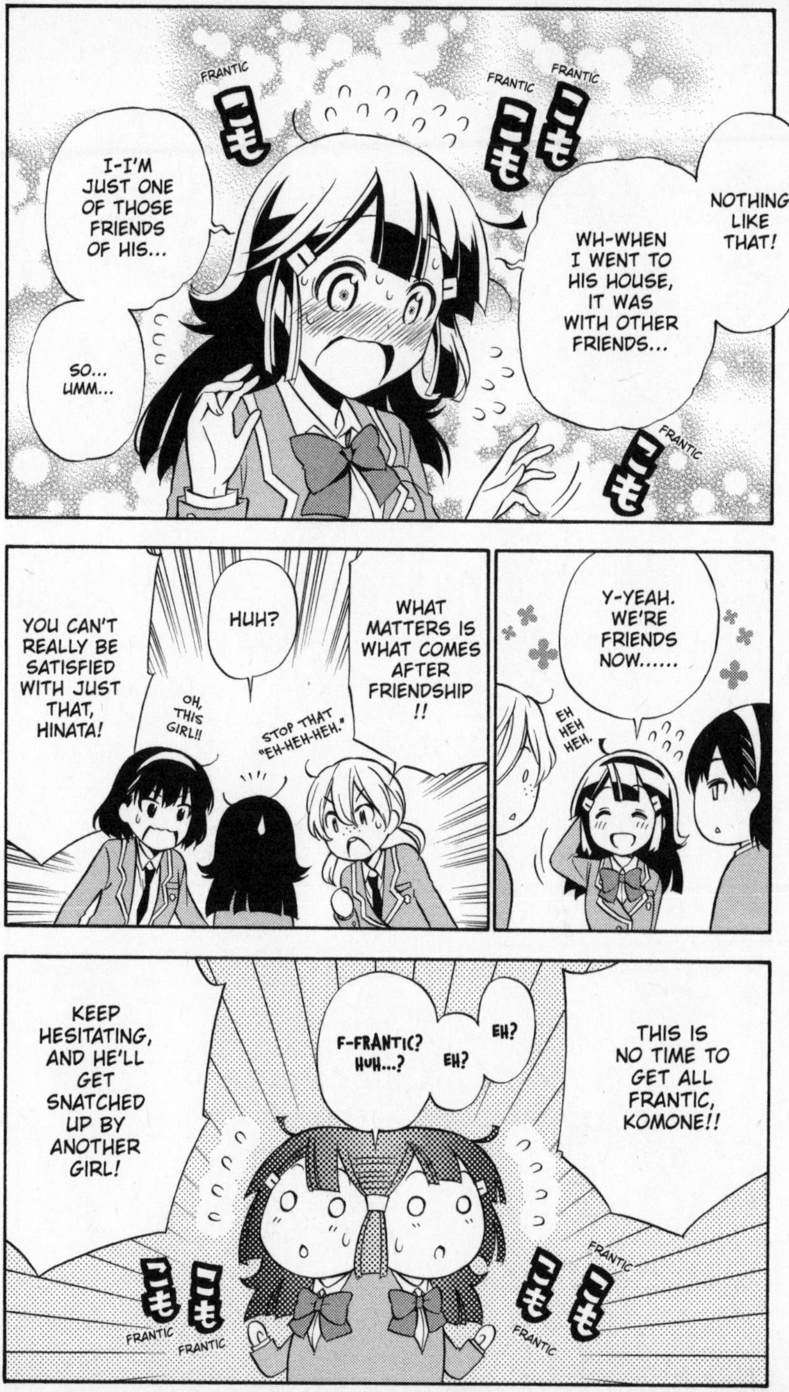
FRANTIC
こもこも
FRANTIC
NOTHING LIKE THAT!
WH-WHEN I WENT TO HIS HOUSE, IT WAS WITH OTHER FRIENDS...
FRANTIC
こも
I-I'M JUST ONE OF THOSE FRIENDS OF HIS...
SO... UMM...
FRANTIC
こも
Y-YEAH. WE'RE FRIENDS NOW......
EH HEH HEH.
WHAT MATTERS IS WHAT COMES AFTER FRIENDSHIP!!
HUH?
STOP THAT "EH-HEH-HEH."
OH, THIS GIRL!!
YOU CAN'T REALLY BE SATISFIED WITH JUST THAT, HINATA!
THIS IS NO TIME TO GET ALL FRANTIC, KOMONE!!
EH?
F-FRANTIC? HUH...?
EH?
KEEP HESITATING, AND HE'LL GET SNATCHED UP BY ANOTHER GIRL!
FRANTIC
こも
FRANTIC
こも
FRANTIC
こも
FRANTIC
こも

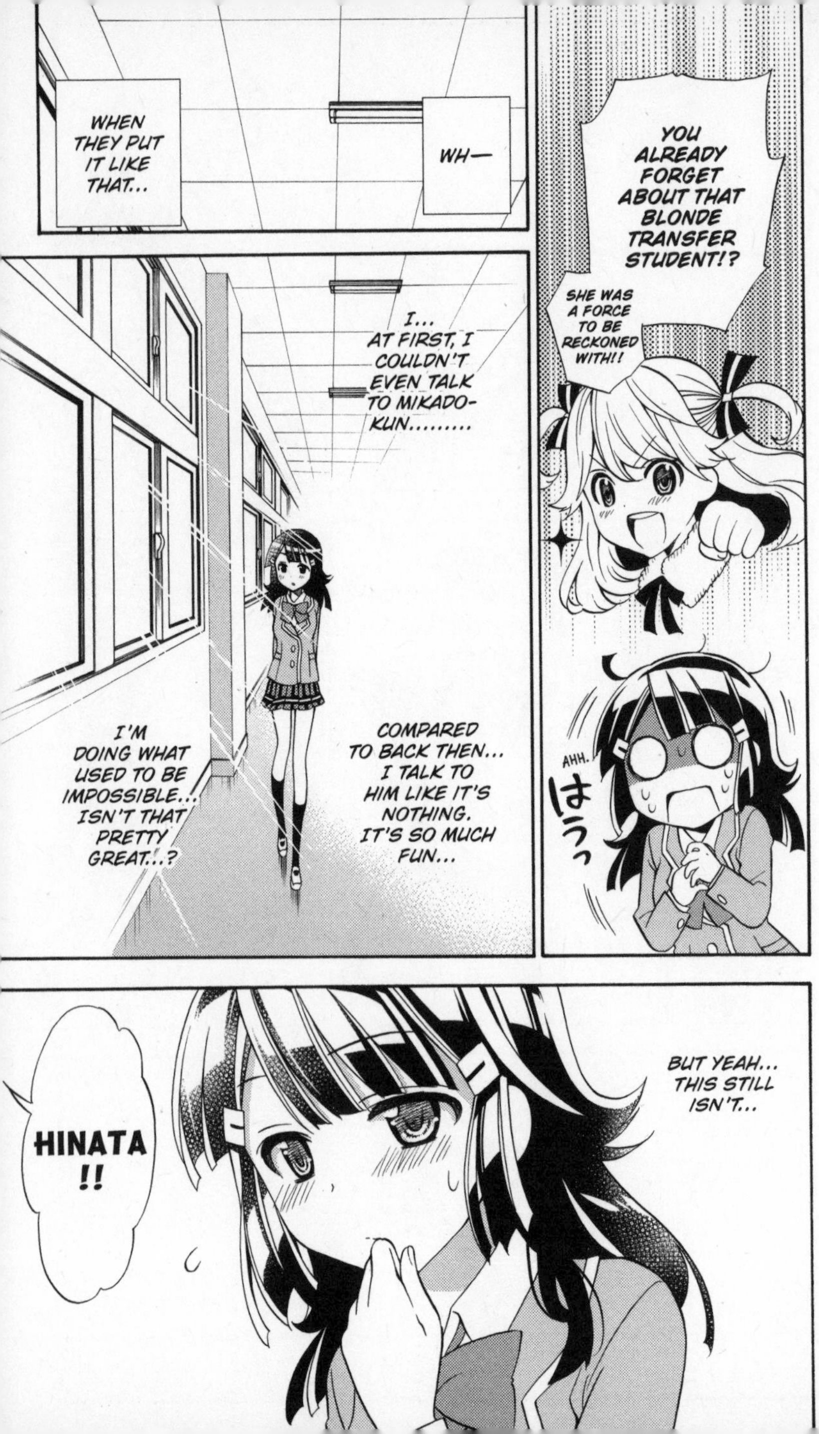

YOU ALREADY FORGET ABOUT THAT BLONDE TRANSFER STUDENT!?
SHE WAS A FORCE TO BE RECKONED WITH!!
AHH.
はうっ
WH—
WHEN THEY PUT IT LIKE THAT...
I... AT FIRST, I COULDN'T EVEN TALK TO MIKADO-KUN.........
COMPARED TO BACK THEN... I TALK TO HIM LIKE IT'S NOTHING. IT'S SO MUCH FUN...
I'M DOING WHAT USED TO BE IMPOSSIBLE... ISN'T THAT PRETTY GREAT...?
BUT YEAH... THIS STILL ISN'T...
HINATA!!

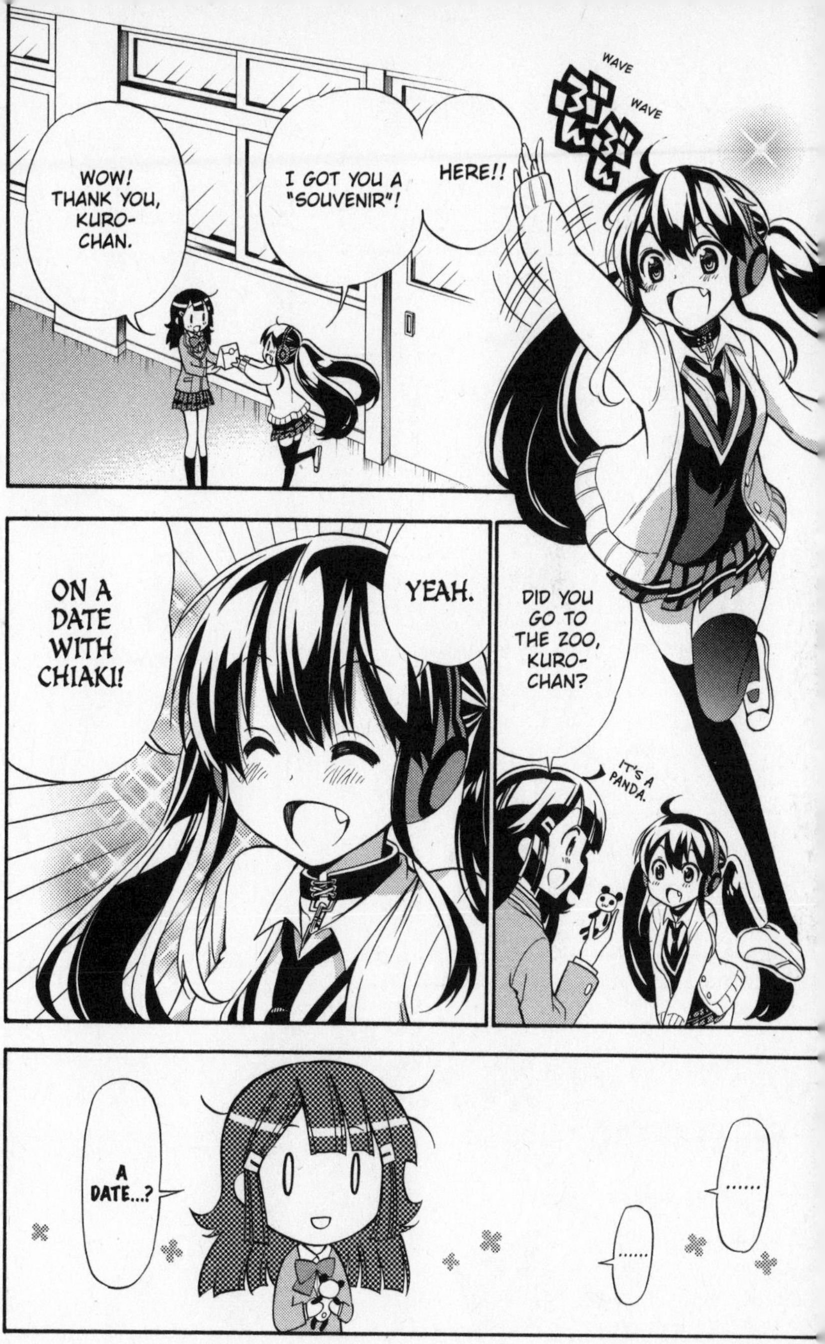
WAVE
WAVE
HERE!!
I GOT YOU A "SOUVENIR"!
WOW! THANK YOU, KURO-CHAN.
IT'S A PANDA.
DID YOU GO TO THE ZOO, KURO-CHAN?
YEAH.
ON A DATE WITH CHIAKI!
......
......
A DATE...?

CHAPTER 18
TODAY'S HINATA KOMONE

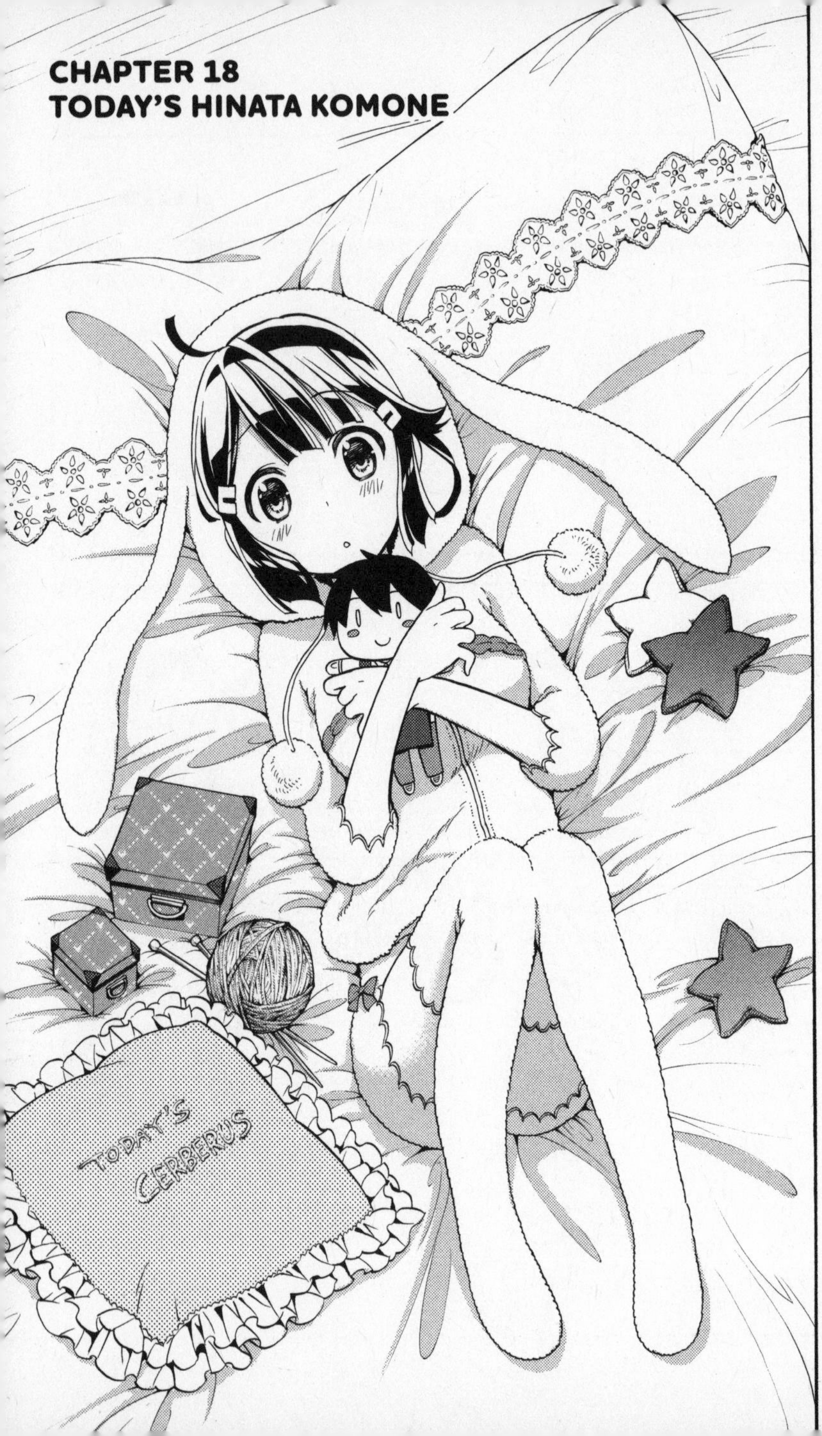
TODAY'S CERBERUS

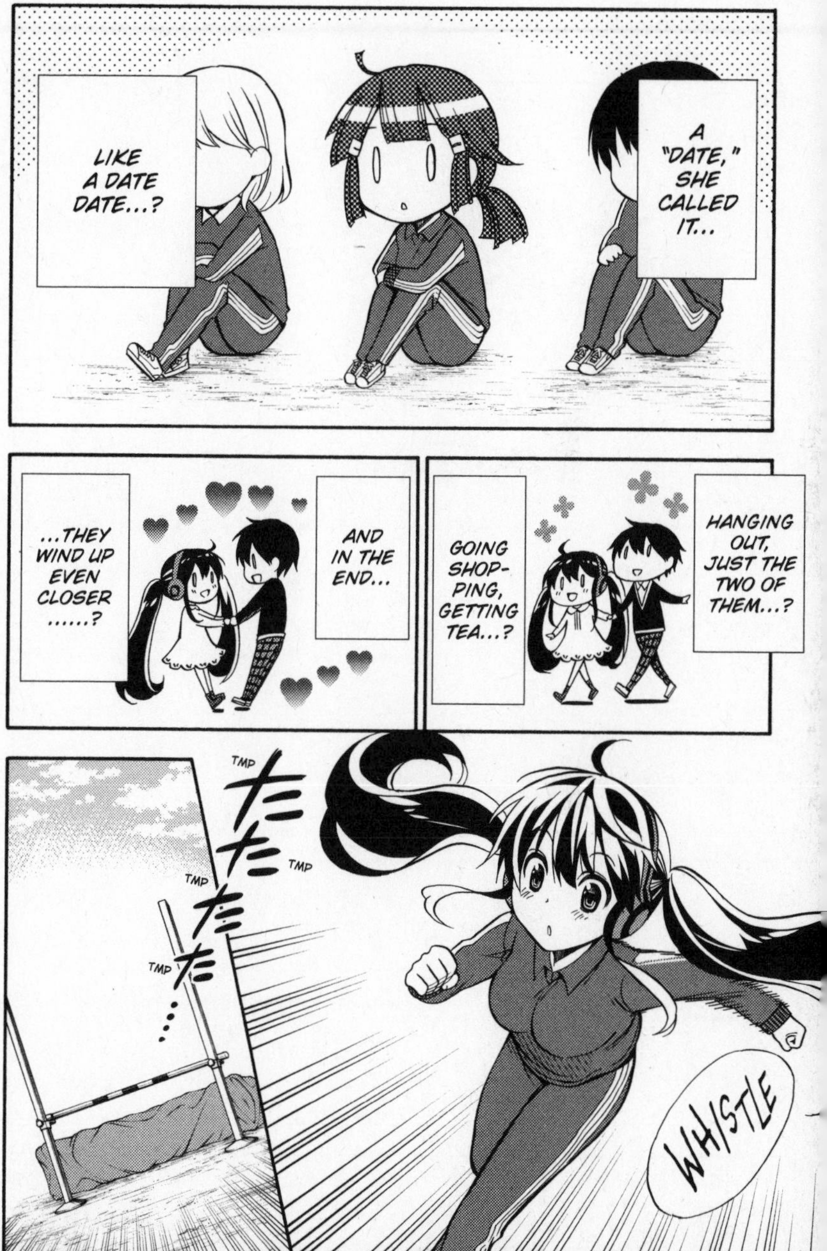
A "DATE," SHE CALLED IT...
LIKE A DATE DATE...?
HANGING OUT, JUST THE TWO OF THEM...?
GOING SHOP-PING, GETTING TEA...?
AND IN THE END...
...THEY WIND UP EVEN CLOSER ......?
TMP
TMP
TMP
TMP
WHISTLE

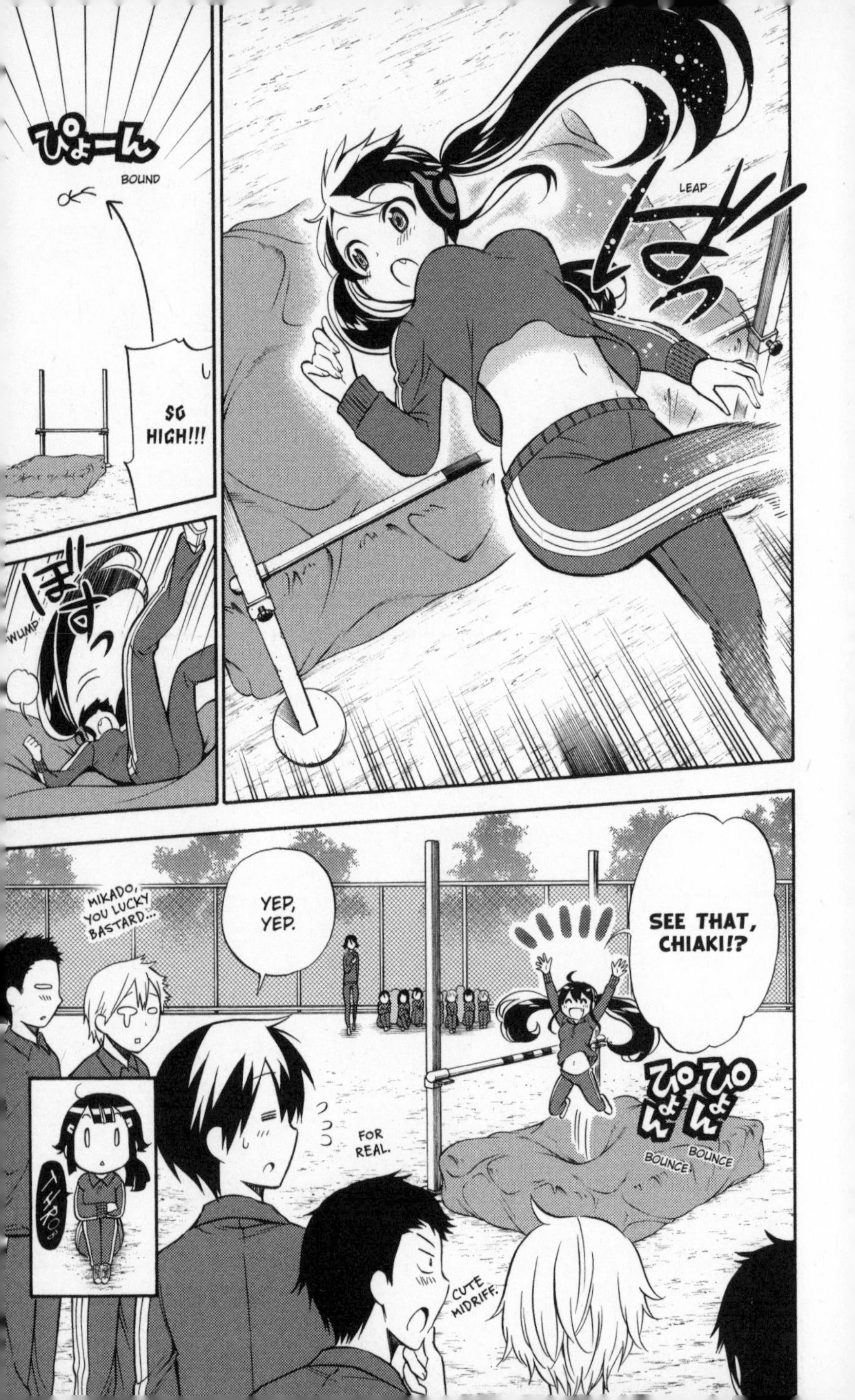
ぱっ
LEAP
ぴょーん
BOUND
SO HIGH!!!
ぼすっ
WUMP
SEE THAT, CHIAKI!?
ぴょんぴょん
BOUNCE
BOUNCE
YEP, YEP.
MIKADO, YOU LUCKY BASTARD...
FOR REAL.
CUTE MIDRIFF.

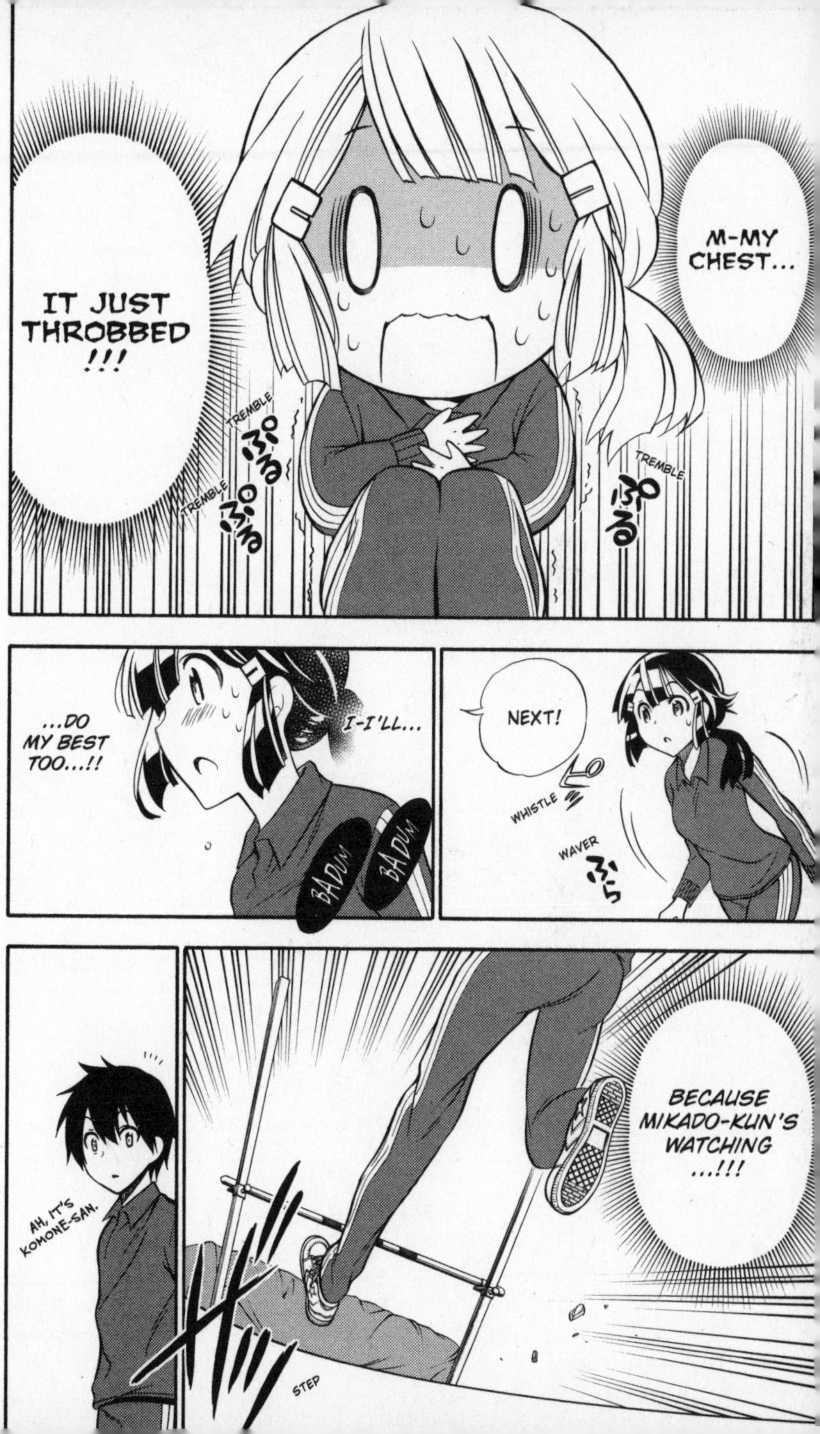
M-MY CHEST...
TREMBLE
ぷる
IT JUST THROBBED!!!
TREMBLE
ぷる
TREMBLE
ぷる
NEXT!
WHISTLE
ピッ
WAVER
ふら
I-I'LL...
...DO MY BEST TOO...!!
BADUM
BADUM
BECAUSE MIKADO-KUN'S WATCHING...!!!
STEP
AH, IT'S KOMONE-SAN.

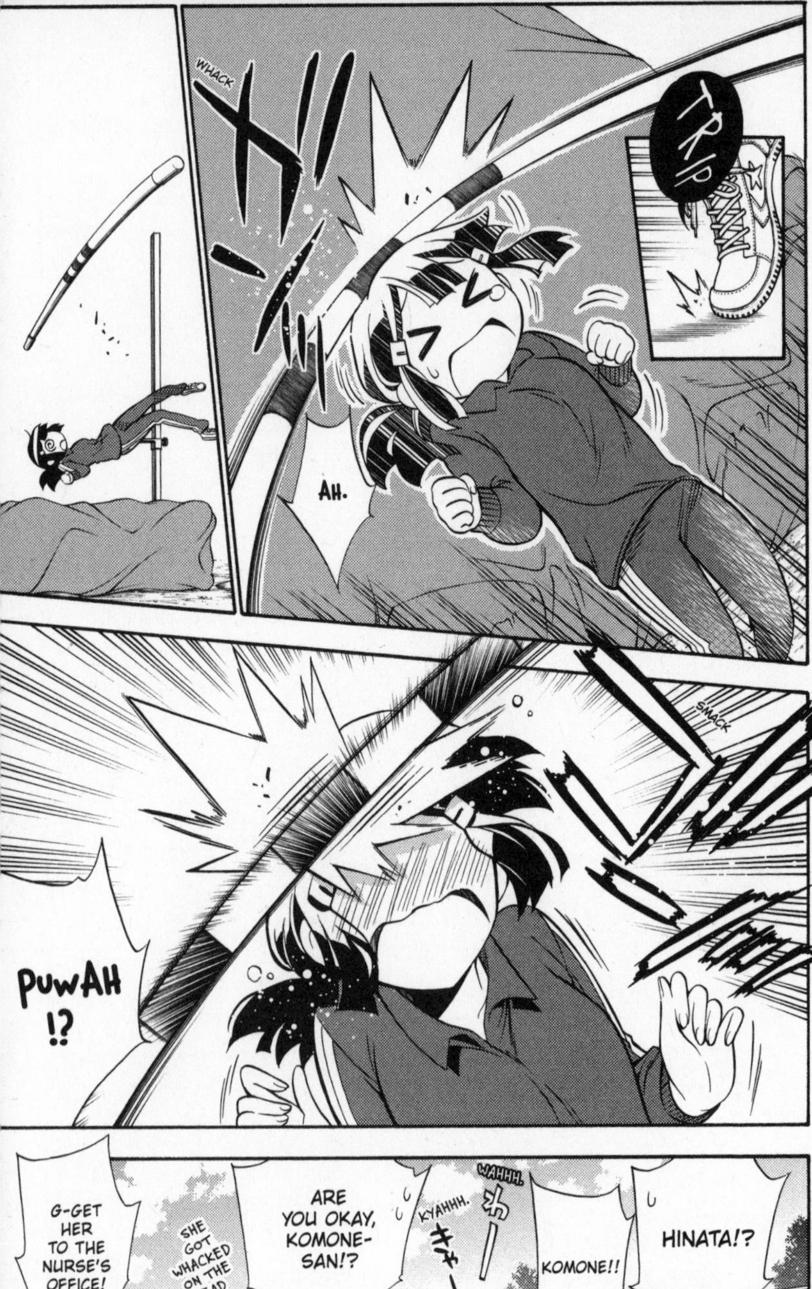

TRIP
WHACK
AH.
SMACK
PUWAH !?
HINATA!?
KOMONE!!
WAHHH.
KYAHHH.
ARE YOU OKAY, KOMONE-SAN!?
SHE GOT WHACKED ON THE HEAD TWICE.
G-GET HER TO THE NURSE'S OFFICE!

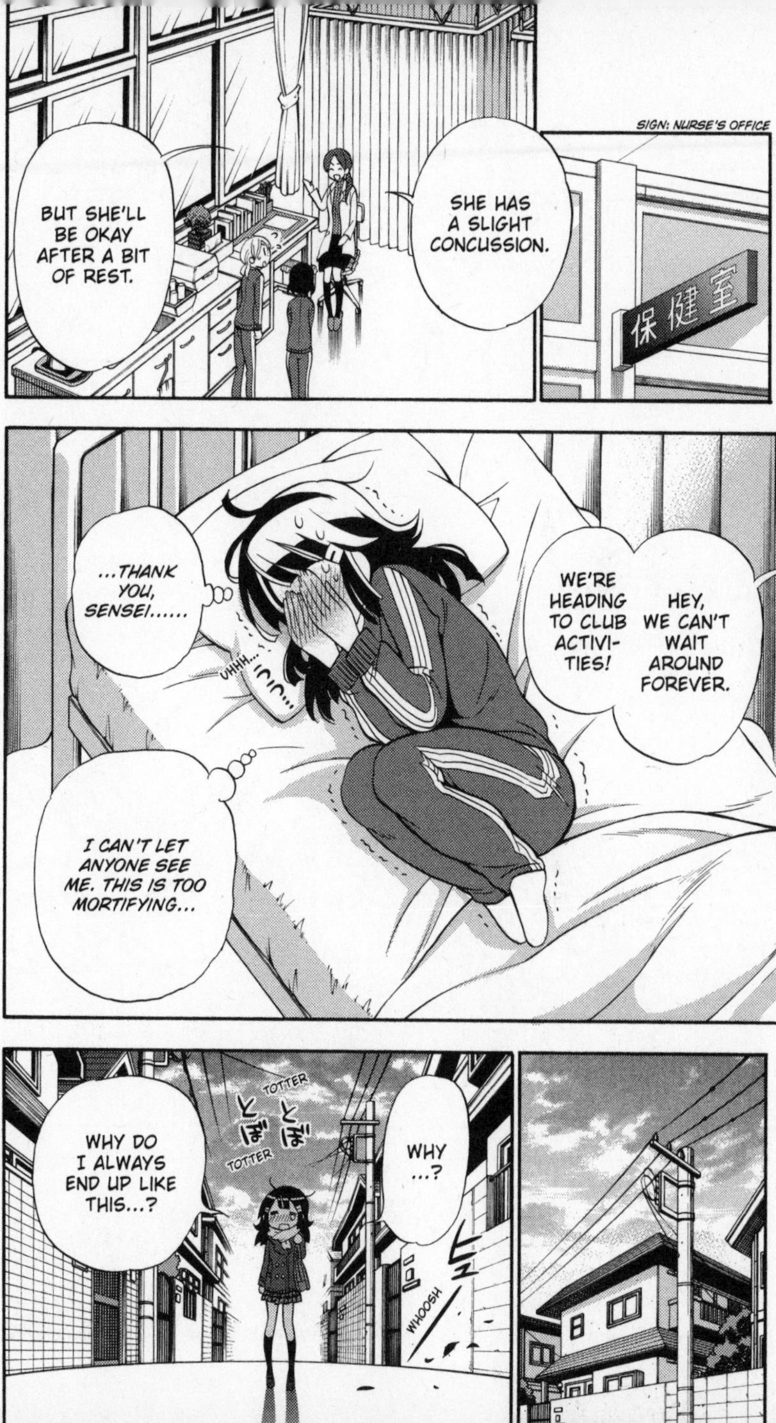
SIGN: NURSE'S OFFICE
保健室
SHE HAS A SLIGHT CONCUSSION.
BUT SHE'LL BE OKAY AFTER A BIT OF REST.
HEY, WE CAN'T WAIT AROUND FOREVER.
WE'RE HEADING TO CLUB ACTIVITIES!
...THANK YOU, SENSEI......
UHHH...
I CAN'T LET ANYONE SEE ME. THIS IS TOO MORTIFYING...
WHOOSH
WHY ...?
TOTTER
とぼとぼ
TOTTER
WHY DO I ALWAYS END UP LIKE THIS...?

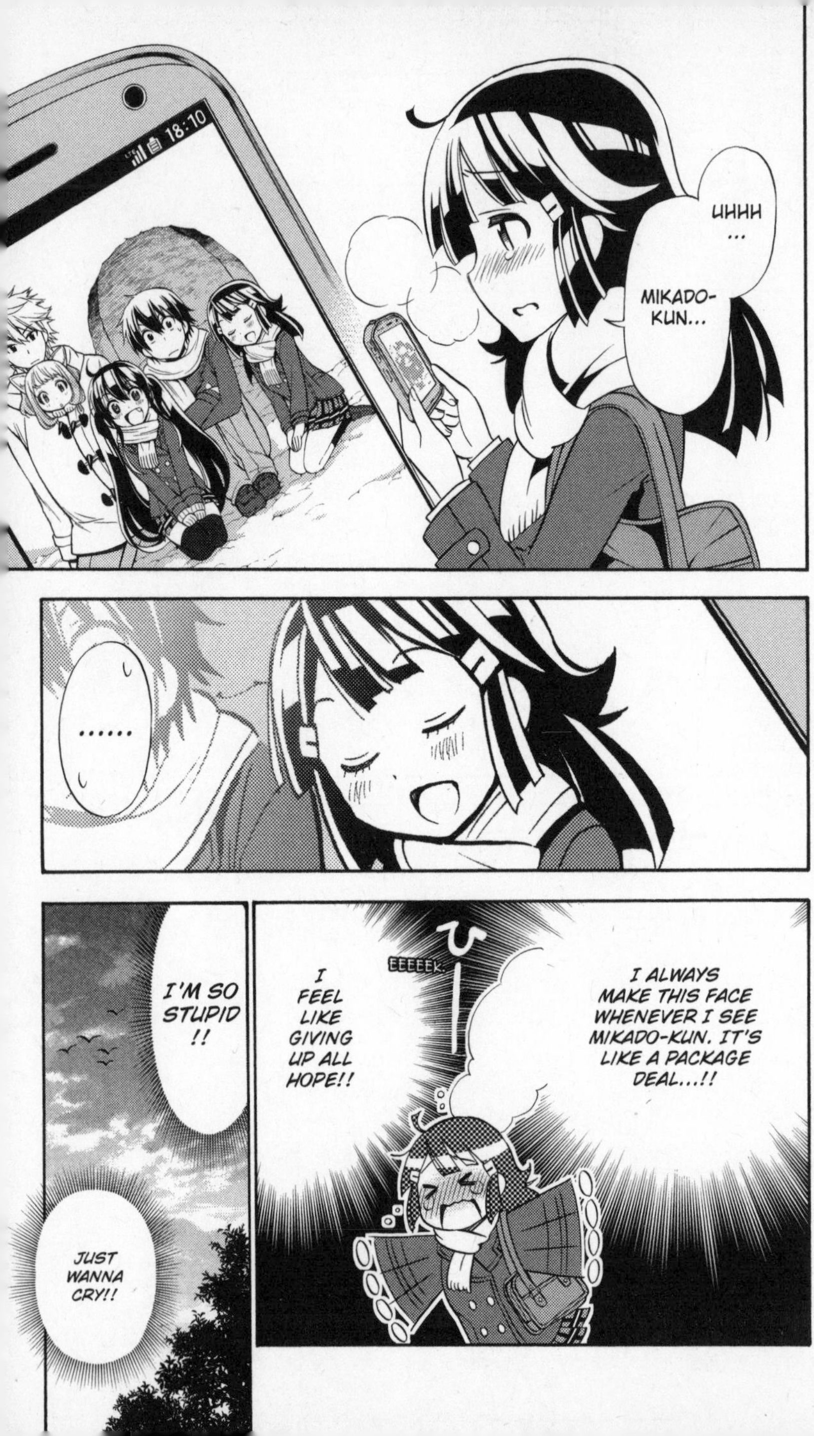
18:10
UHHH ...
MIKADO-KUN...
......
I ALWAYS MAKE THIS FACE WHENEVER I SEE MIKADO-KUN. IT'S LIKE A PACKAGE DEAL...!!
EEEEEK.
I FEEL LIKE GIVING UP ALL HOPE!!
I'M SO STUPID !!
JUST WANNA CRY!!

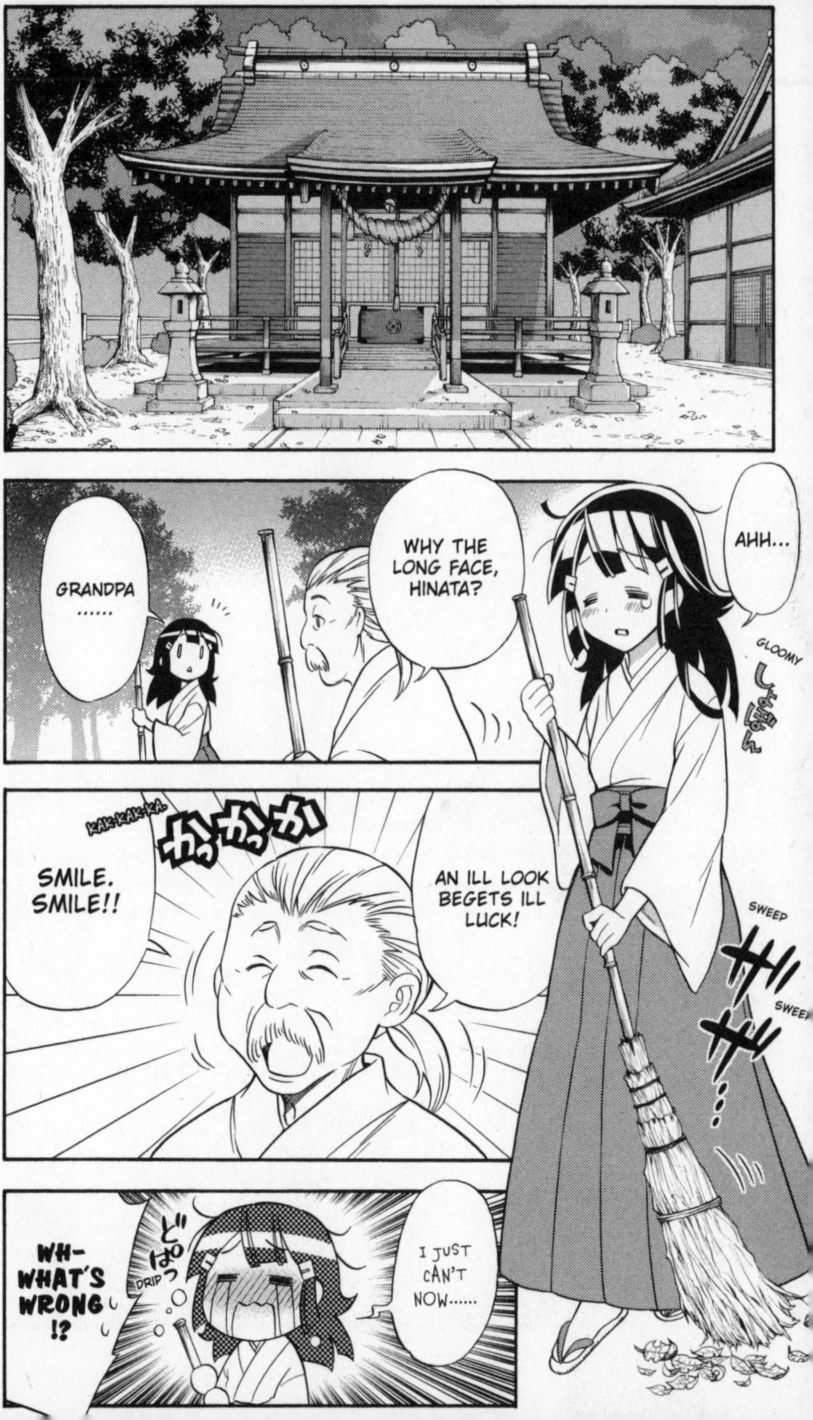
AHH...
GLOOMY
WHY THE LONG FACE, HINATA?
GRANDPA ......
SWEEP
SWEEP
KAK-KAK-KA
AN ILL LOOK BEGETS ILL LUCK!
SMILE. SMILE!!
I JUST CAN'T NOW......
DRIP
WH-WHAT'S WRONG!?

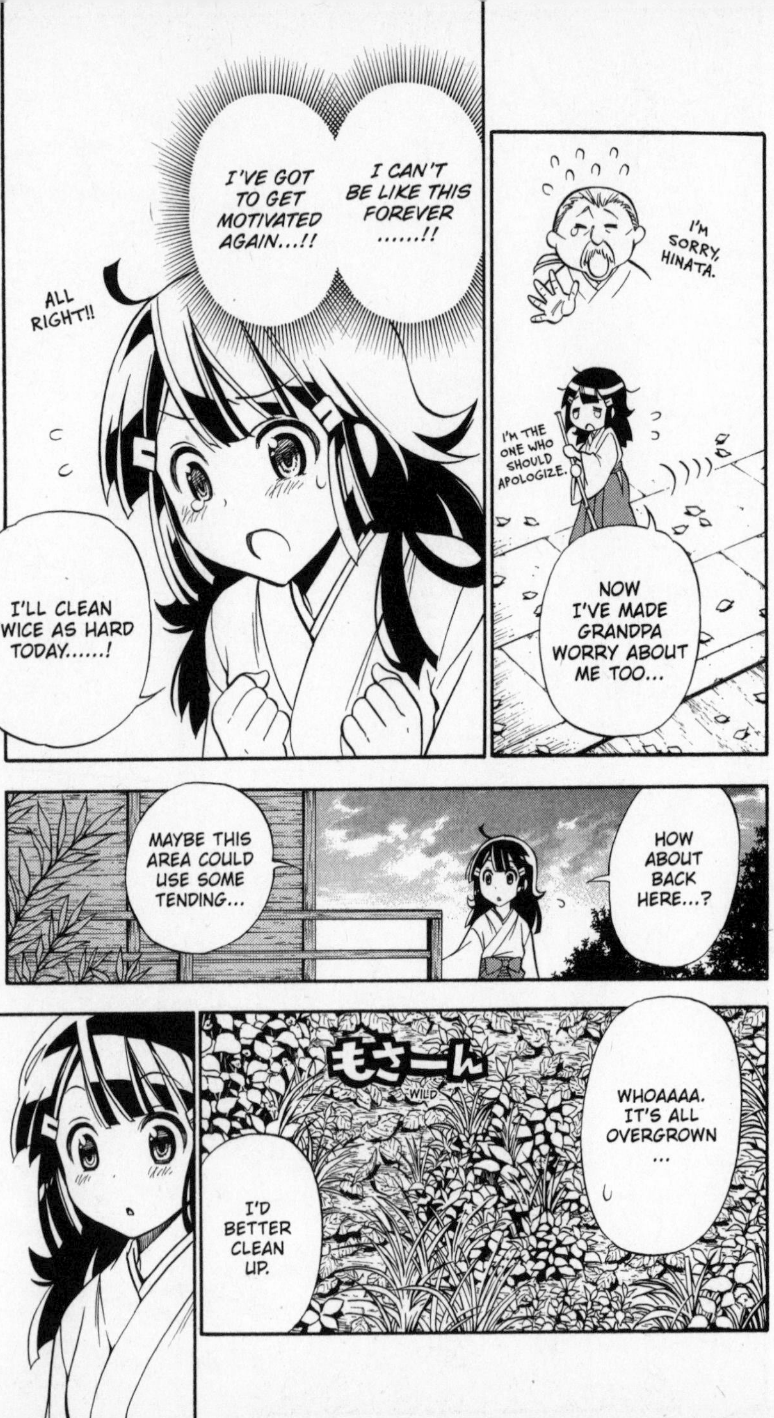
I'M SORRY, HINATA.
I'M THE ONE WHO SHOULD APOLOGIZE.
NOW I'VE MADE GRANDPA WORRY ABOUT ME TOO...
I CAN'T BE LIKE THIS FOREVER ......!!
I'VE GOT TO GET MOTIVATED AGAIN...!!
ALL RIGHT!!
I'LL CLEAN TWICE AS HARD TODAY......!
HOW ABOUT BACK HERE...?
MAYBE THIS AREA COULD USE SOME TENDING...
WHOAAAA. IT'S ALL OVERGROWN ...
もさーん
WILD
I'D BETTER CLEAN UP.

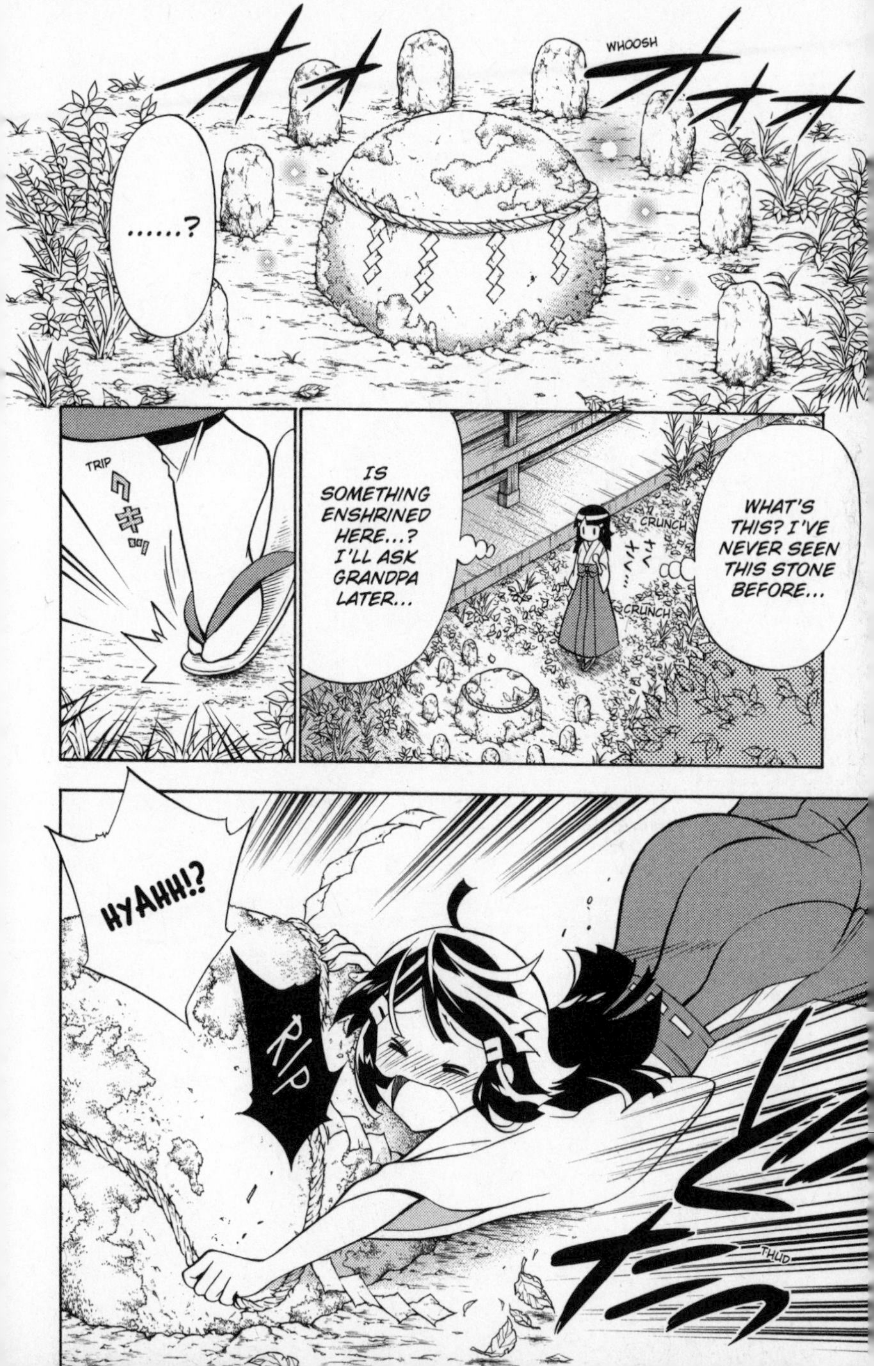

WHOOSH
......?
WHAT'S THIS? I'VE NEVER SEEN THIS STONE BEFORE...
CRUNCH
CRUNCH
IS SOMETHING ENSHRINED HERE...? I'LL ASK GRANDPA LATER...
TRIP
HYAHH!?
RIP
THUD

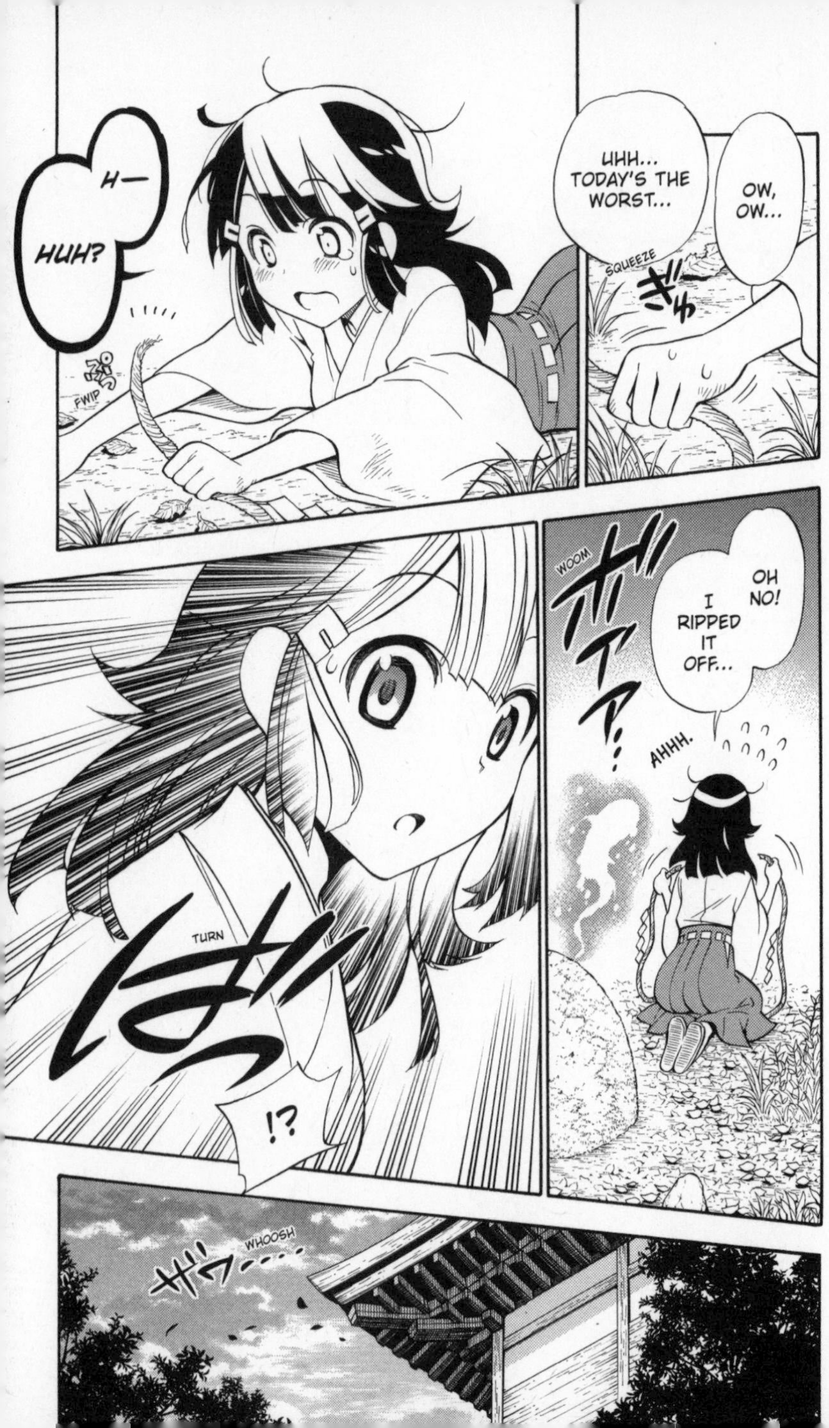
OW, OW...
UHH... TODAY'S THE WORST...
SQUEEZE
H— HUH?
FWIP
OH NO! I RIPPED IT OFF...
WOOM
AHHH.
TURN
!?
WHOOSH

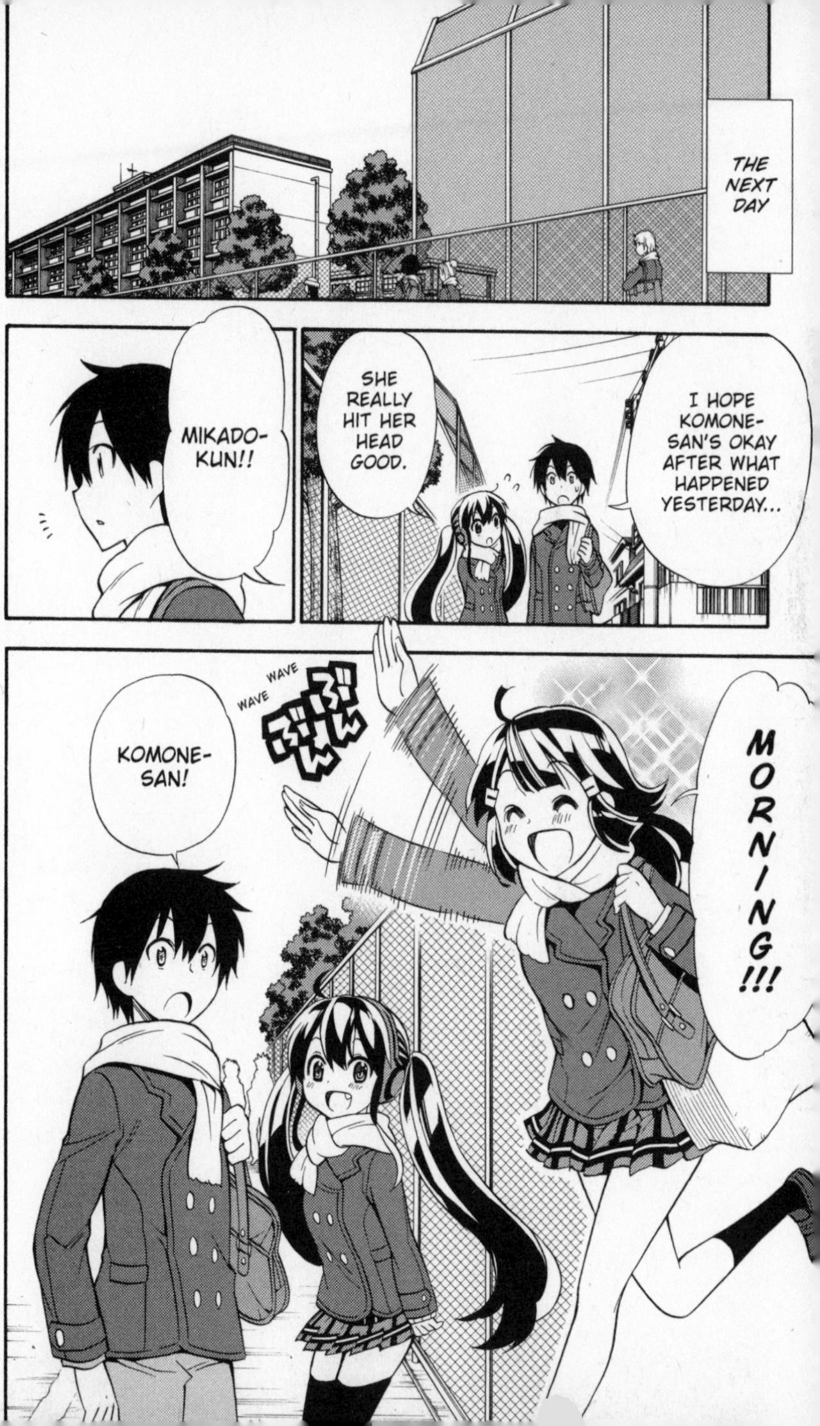
THE NEXT DAY
I HOPE KOMONE-SAN'S OKAY AFTER WHAT HAPPENED YESTERDAY...
SHE REALLY HIT HER HEAD GOOD.
MIKADO-KUN!!
MORNING!!!
ぶんぶん
WAVE WAVE
KOMONE-SAN!

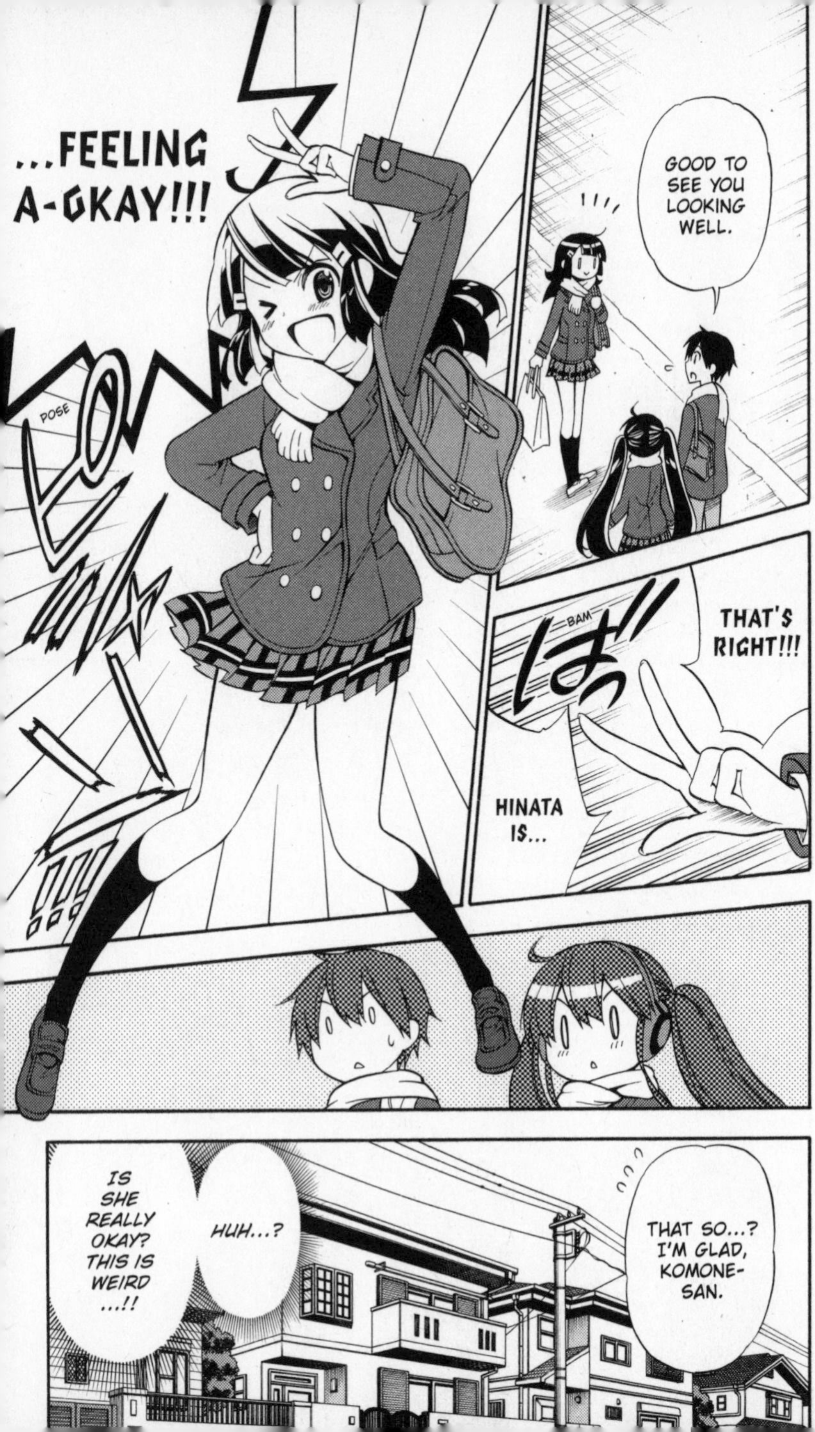
GOOD TO SEE YOU LOOKING WELL.
BAM
THAT'S RIGHT!!!
HINATA IS...
...FEELING A-OKAY!!!
POSE
THAT SO...? I'M GLAD, KOMONE-SAN.
HUH...?
IS SHE REALLY OKAY? THIS IS WEIRD ...!!

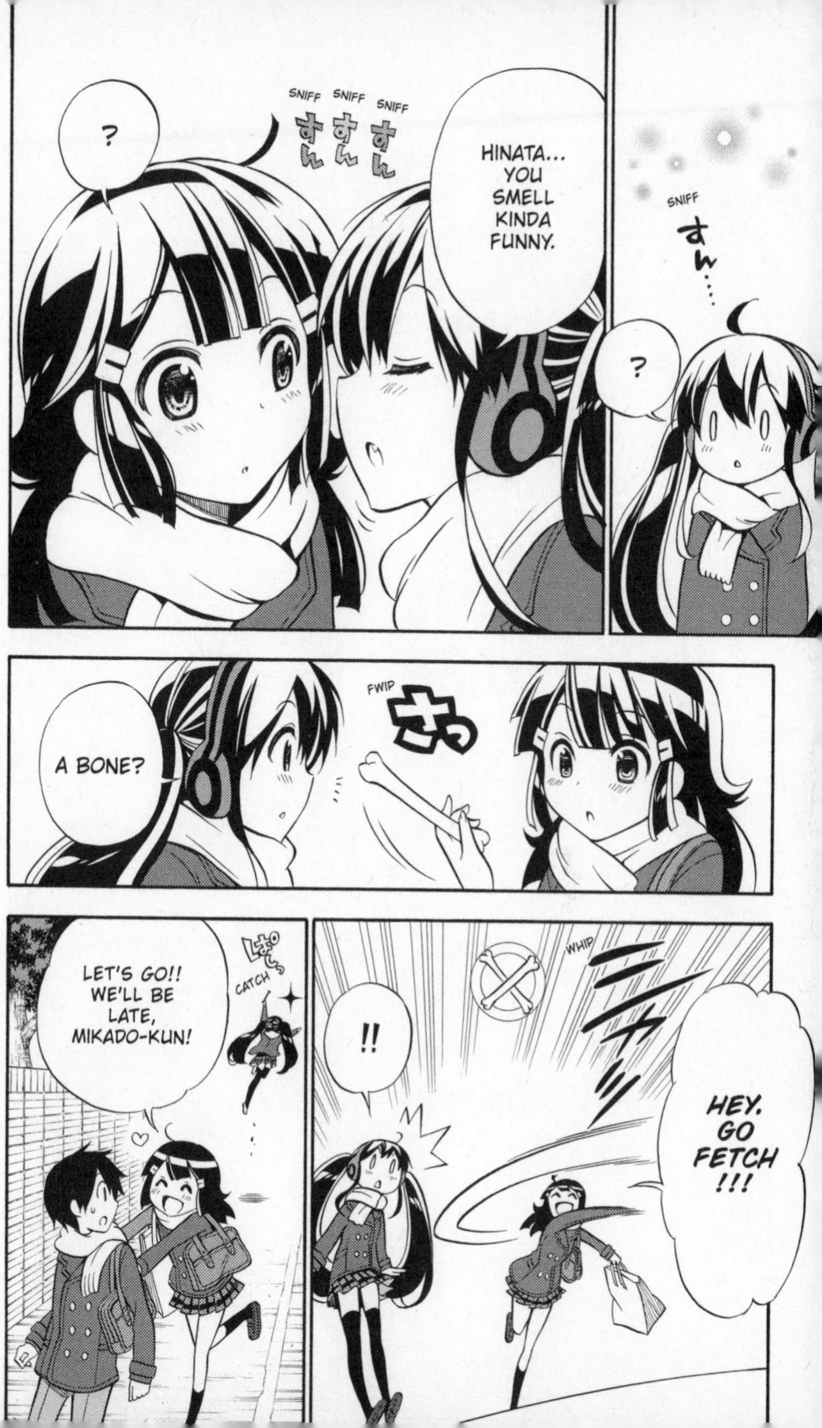
SNIFF
すん…
?
HINATA... YOU SMELL KINDA FUNNY.
SNIFF SNIFF SNIFF
すんすんすん
?
FWIP
さっ
A BONE?
HEY. GO FETCH!!!
WHIP
!!
CATCH
ぱしっ
LET'S GO!! WE'LL BE LATE, MIKADO-KUN!

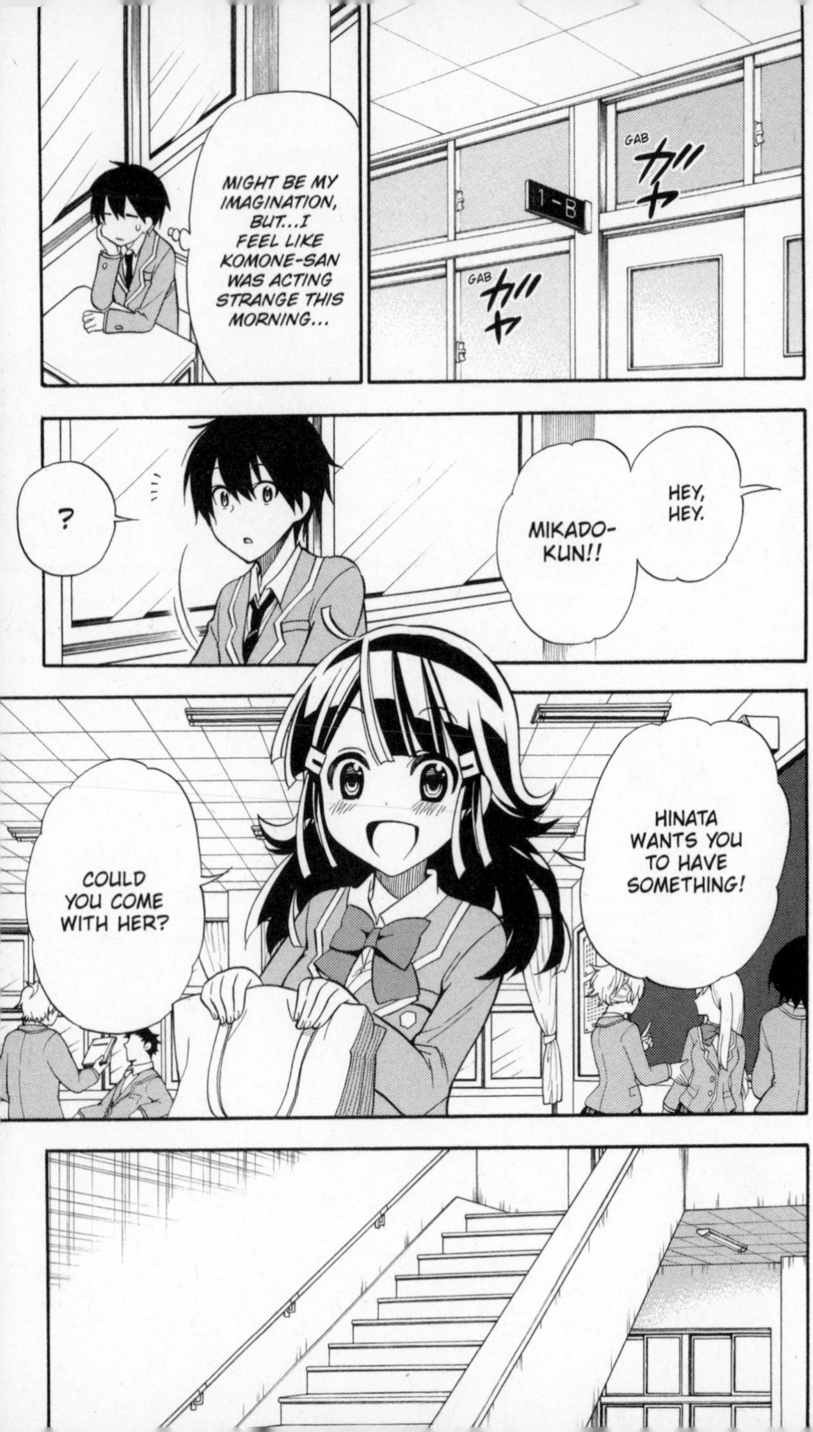
GAB
ガヤ
GAB
ガヤ
MIGHT BE MY IMAGINATION, BUT...I FEEL LIKE KOMONE-SAN WAS ACTING STRANGE THIS MORNING...
HEY, HEY.
MIKADO-KUN!!
?
HINATA WANTS YOU TO HAVE SOMETHING!
COULD YOU COME WITH HER?

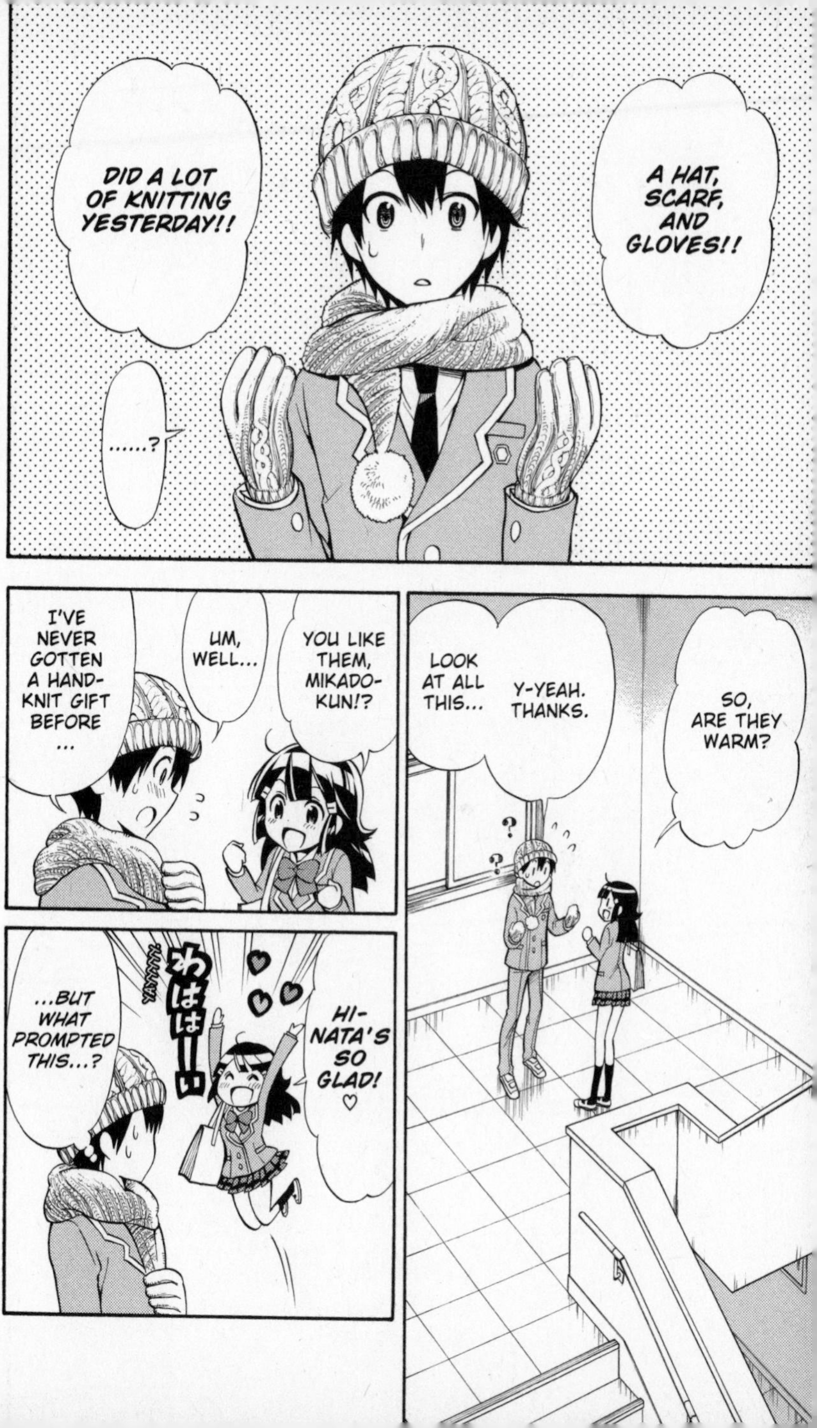
A HAT, SCARF, AND GLOVES!!
DID A LOT OF KNITTING YESTERDAY!!
......?
SO, ARE THEY WARM?
Y-YEAH. THANKS.
LOOK AT ALL THIS...
YOU LIKE THEM, MIKADO-KUN!?
UM, WELL...
I'VE NEVER GOTTEN A HAND-KNIT GIFT BEFORE ...
HI-NATA'S SO GLAD! ♡
わはは―い
YAYYYY.
...BUT WHAT PROMPTED THIS...?

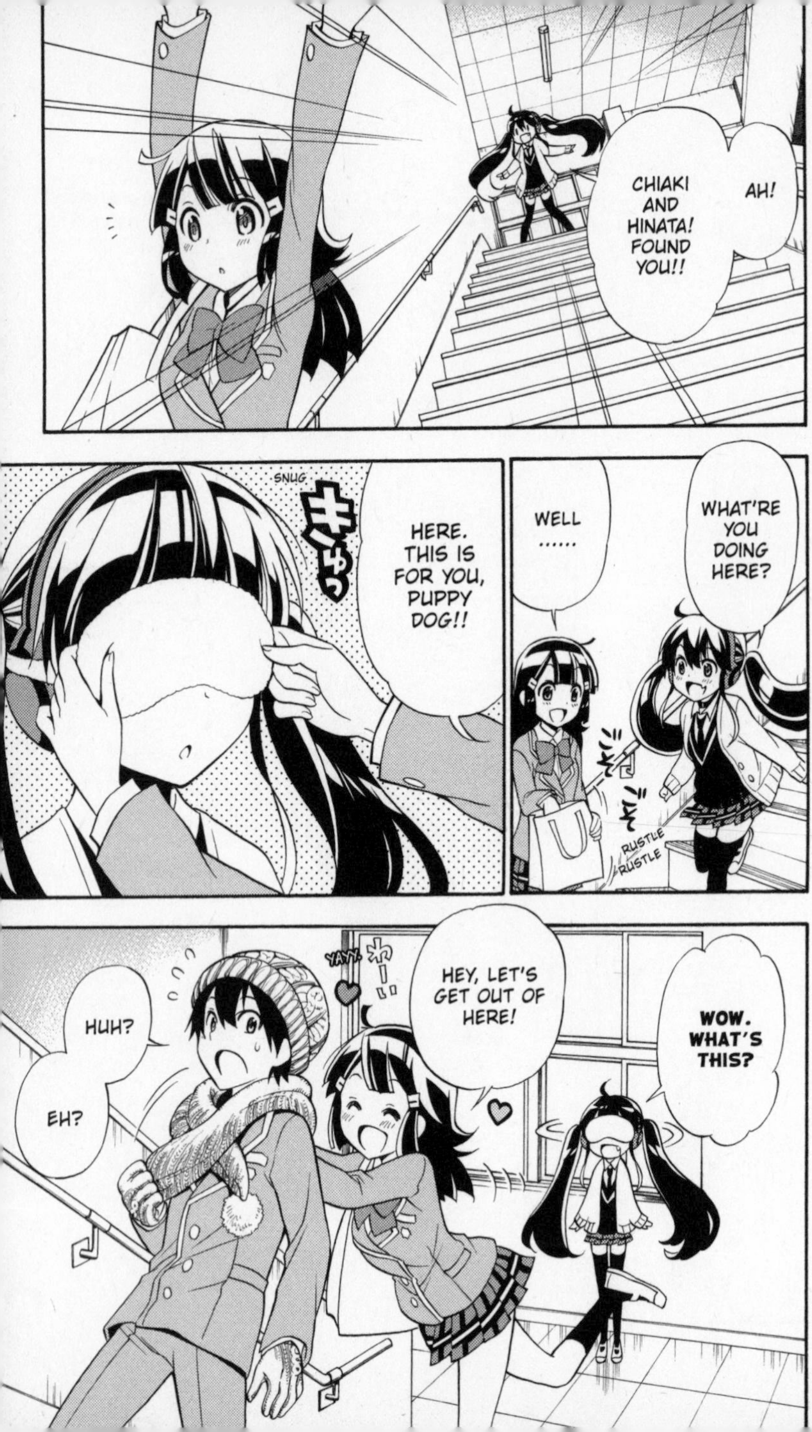
AH!
CHIAKI AND HINATA! FOUND YOU!!
WHAT'RE YOU DOING HERE?
WELL ......
RUSTLE RUSTLE
HERE. THIS IS FOR YOU, PUPPY DOG!!
SNUG
きゅっ
WOW. WHAT'S THIS?
HEY, LET'S GET OUT OF HERE!
YAY!
わー!!
HUH?
EH?

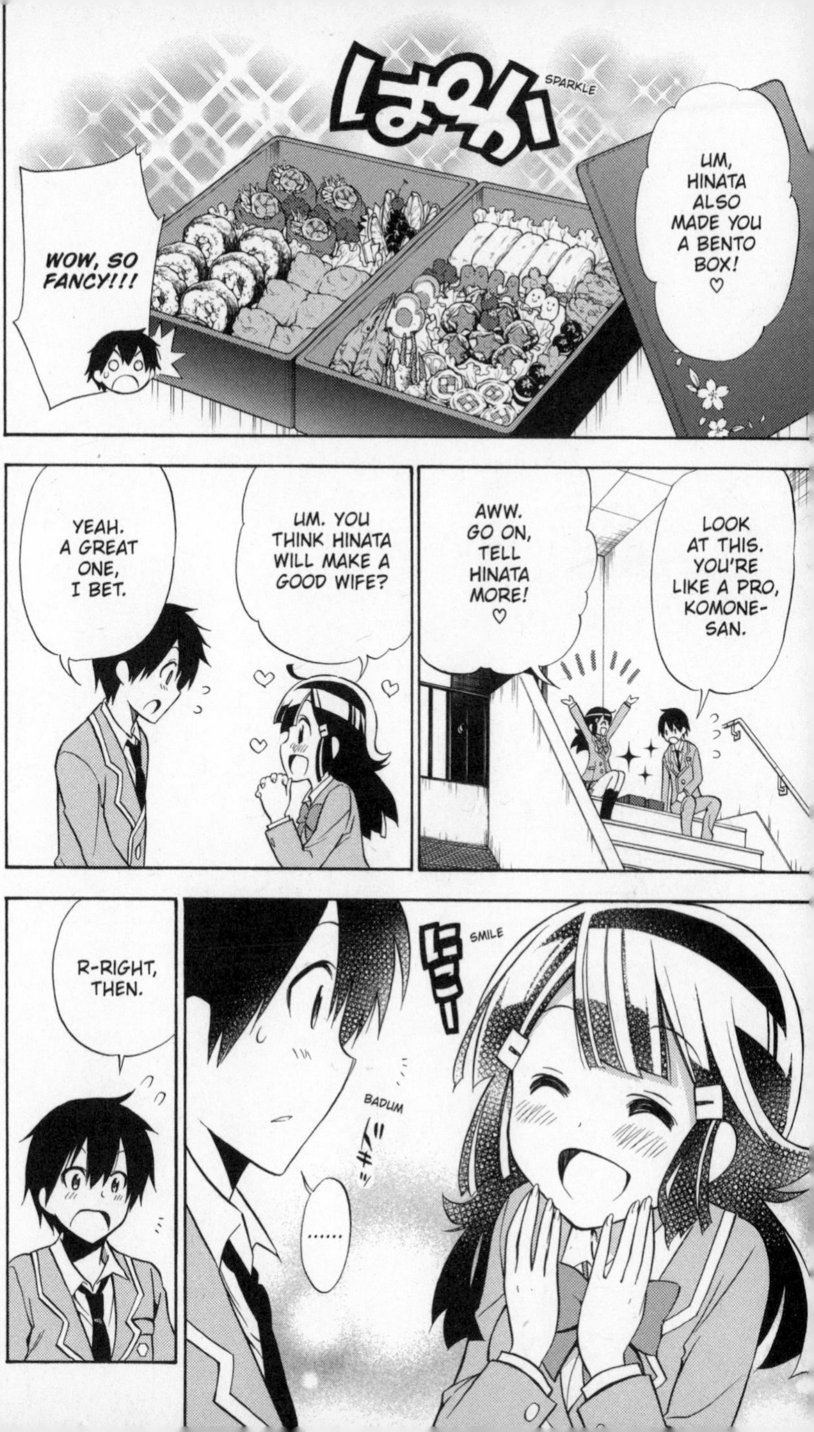
UM, HINATA ALSO MADE YOU A BENTO BOX! ♡
SPARKLE
WOW, SO FANCY!!!
LOOK AT THIS. YOU'RE LIKE A PRO, KOMONE-SAN.
AWW. GO ON, TELL HINATA MORE! ♡
UM. YOU THINK HINATA WILL MAKE A GOOD WIFE?
YEAH. A GREAT ONE, I BET.
SMILE
BADUM
......
R-RIGHT, THEN.

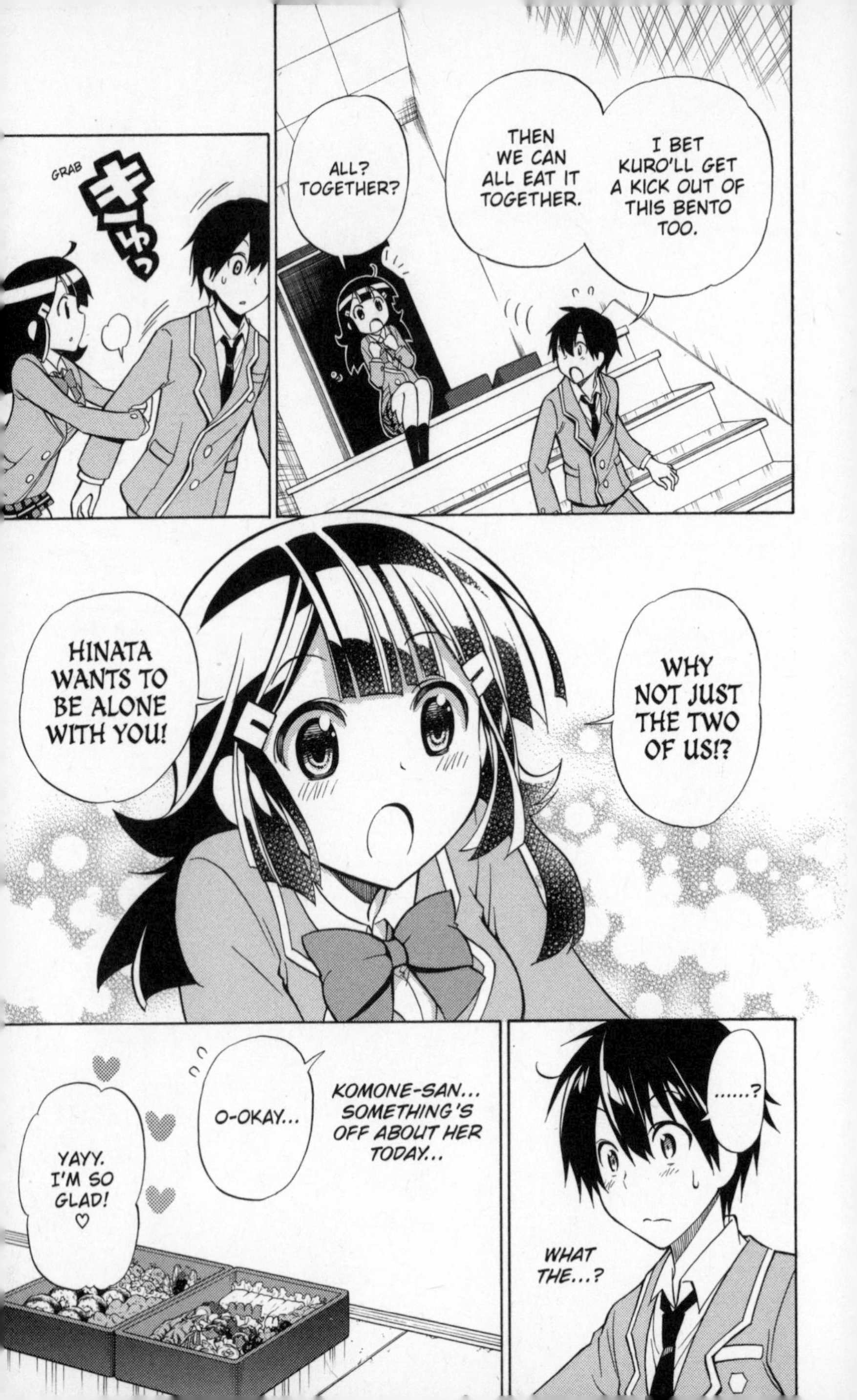
I BET KURO'LL GET A KICK OUT OF THIS BENTO TOO.
THEN WE CAN ALL EAT IT TOGETHER.
ALL? TOGETHER?
GRAB
WHY NOT JUST THE TWO OF US!?
HINATA WANTS TO BE ALONE WITH YOU!
......?
WHAT THE...?
KOMONE-SAN... SOMETHING'S OFF ABOUT HER TODAY...
O-OKAY...
YAYY. I'M SO GLAD! ♡

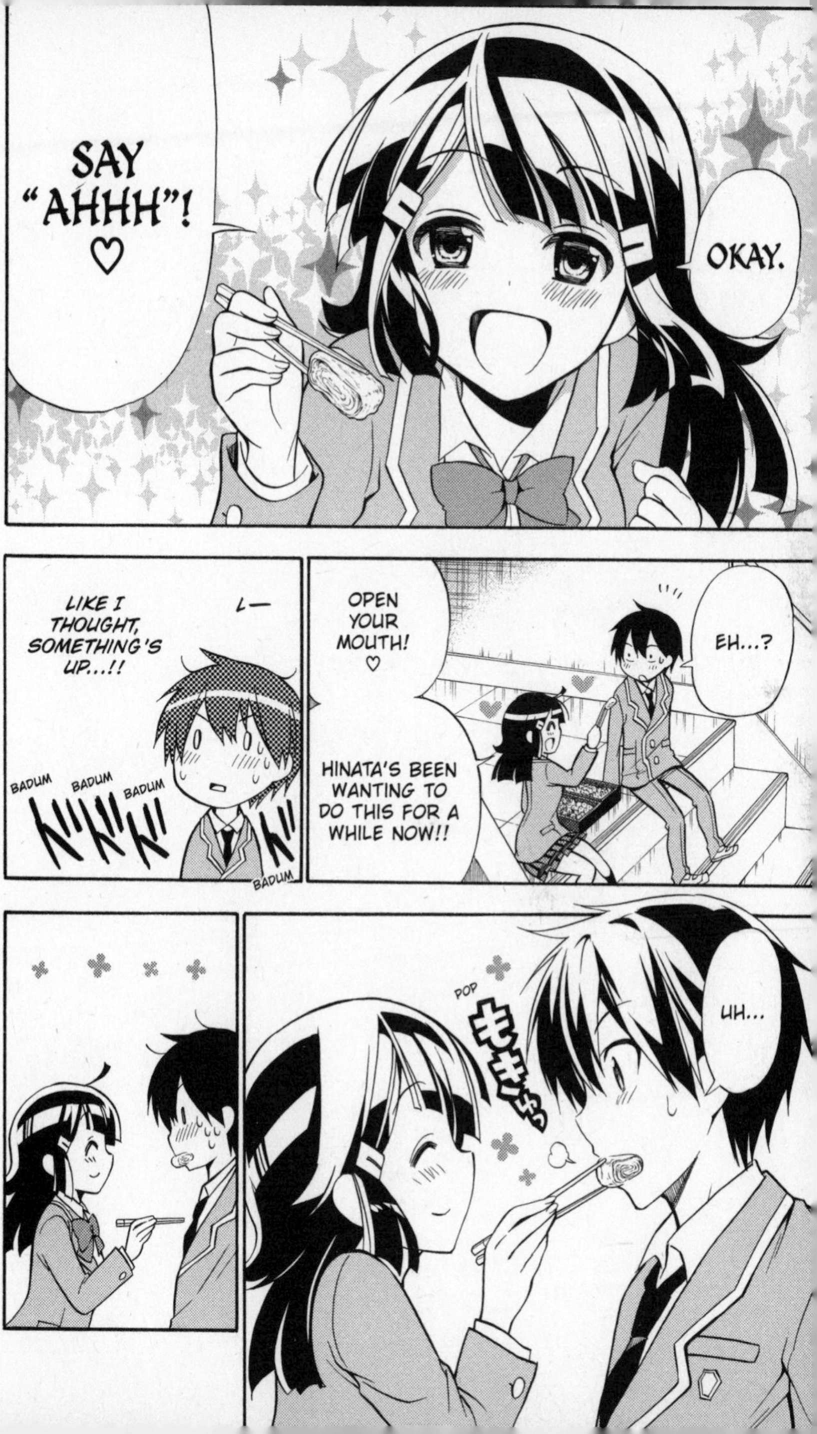
OKAY.
SAY "AHHH"! ♡
EH...?
OPEN YOUR MOUTH! ♡
HINATA'S BEEN WANTING TO DO THIS FOR A WHILE NOW!!
LIKE I THOUGHT, SOMETHING'S UP...!!
BADUM BADUM BADUM
BADUM
UH...
POP

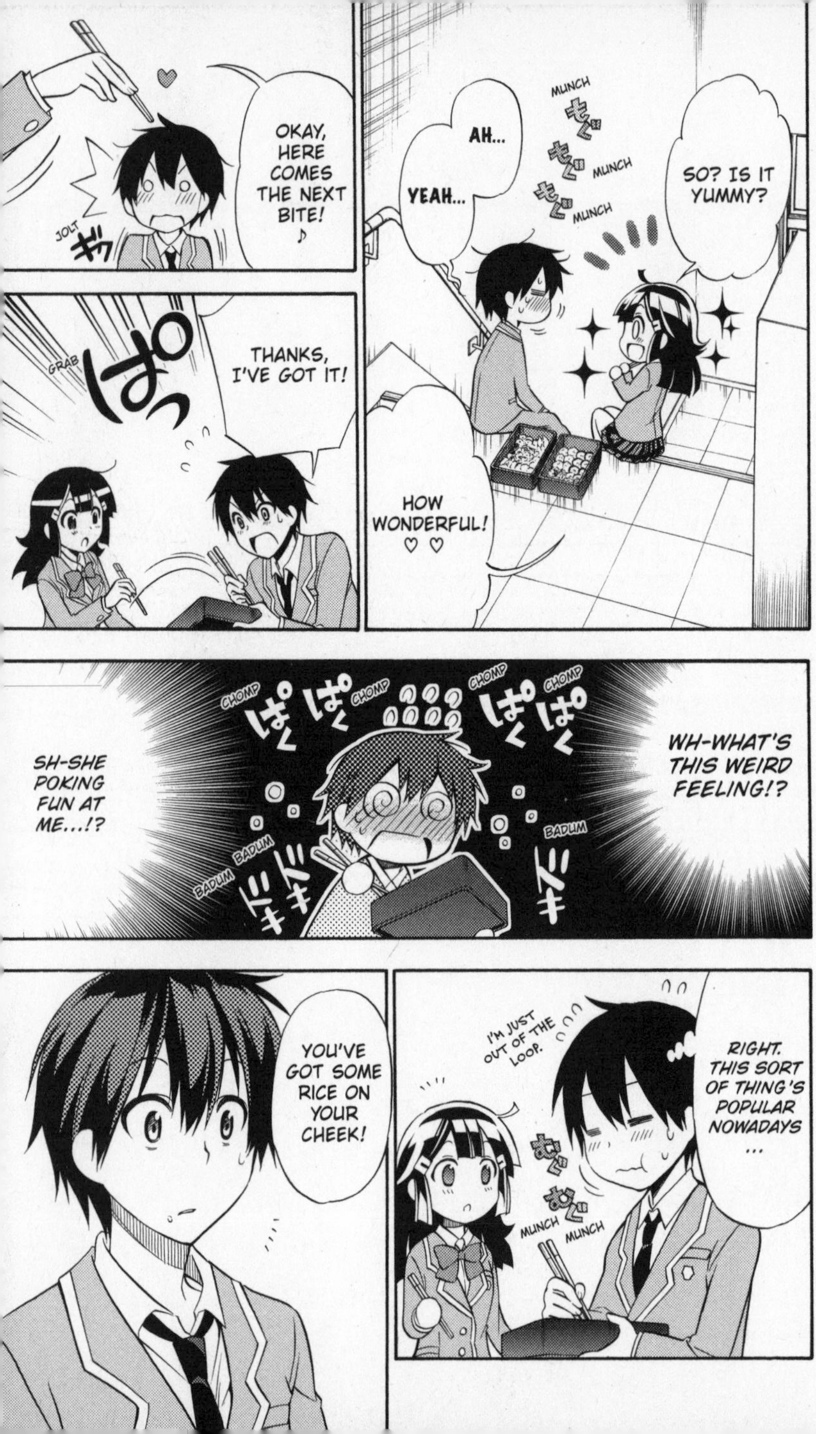
SO? IS IT YUMMY?
MUNCH もぐ MUNCH もぐ MUNCH もぐ
AH... YEAH...
HOW WONDERFUL! ♡ ♡
OKAY, HERE COMES THE NEXT BITE! ♪
JOLT ギク
THANKS, I'VE GOT IT!
GRAB ぱっ
WH-WHAT'S THIS WEIRD FEELING!?
CHOMP ぱく CHOMP ぱく CHOMP ぱく CHOMP ぱく
BADUM ドキ
BADUM BADUM ドキドキ
SH-SHE POKING FUN AT ME...!?
RIGHT. THIS SORT OF THING'S POPULAR NOWADAYS ...
I'M JUST OUT OF THE LOOP.
MUNCH むぐ MUNCH むぐ
YOU'VE GOT SOME RICE ON YOUR CHEEK!

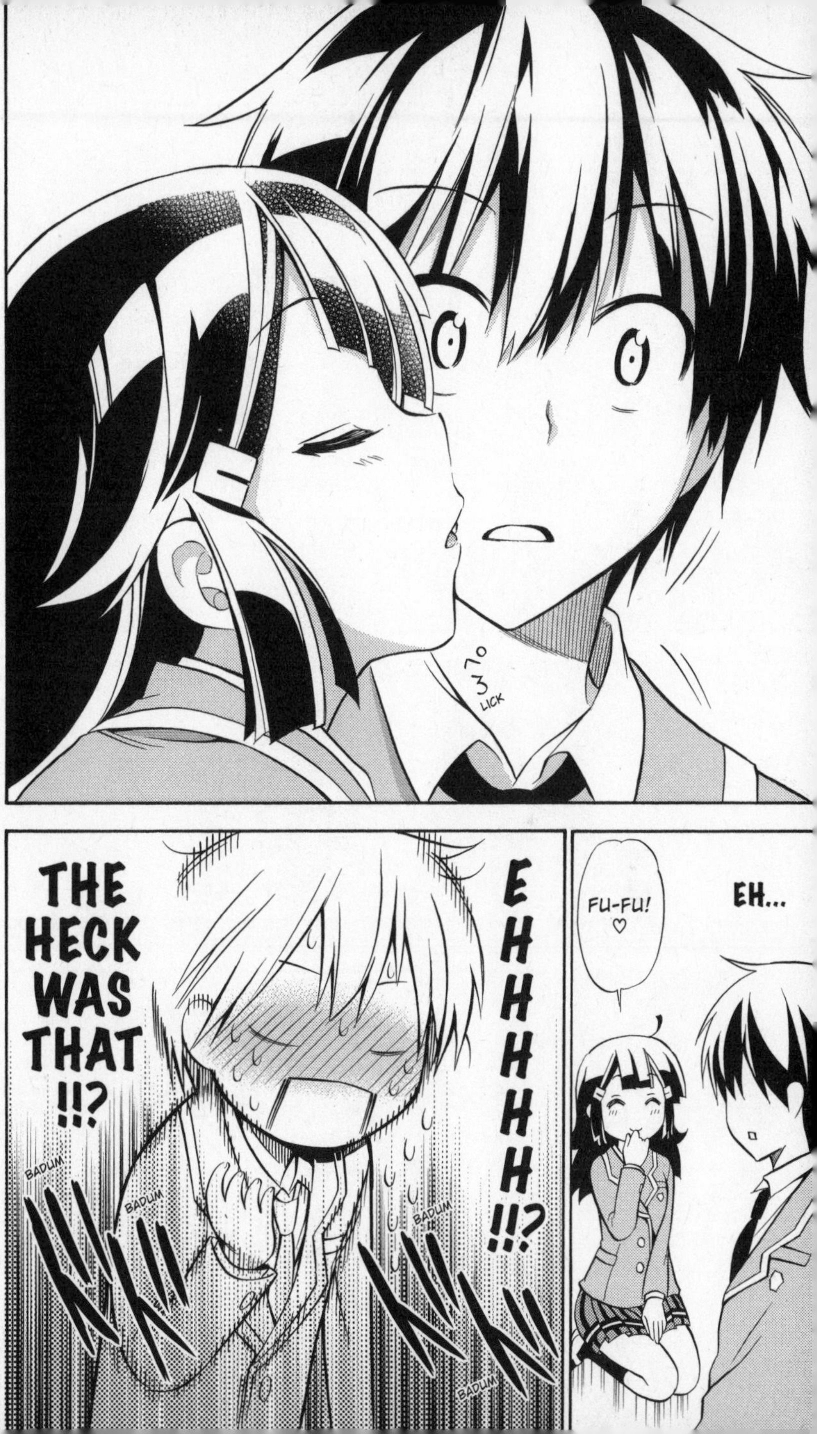
LICK
EH...
FU-FU! ♡
EHHHHHH!!?
THE HECK WAS THAT!!?
BADUM
BADUM
BADUM
BADUM

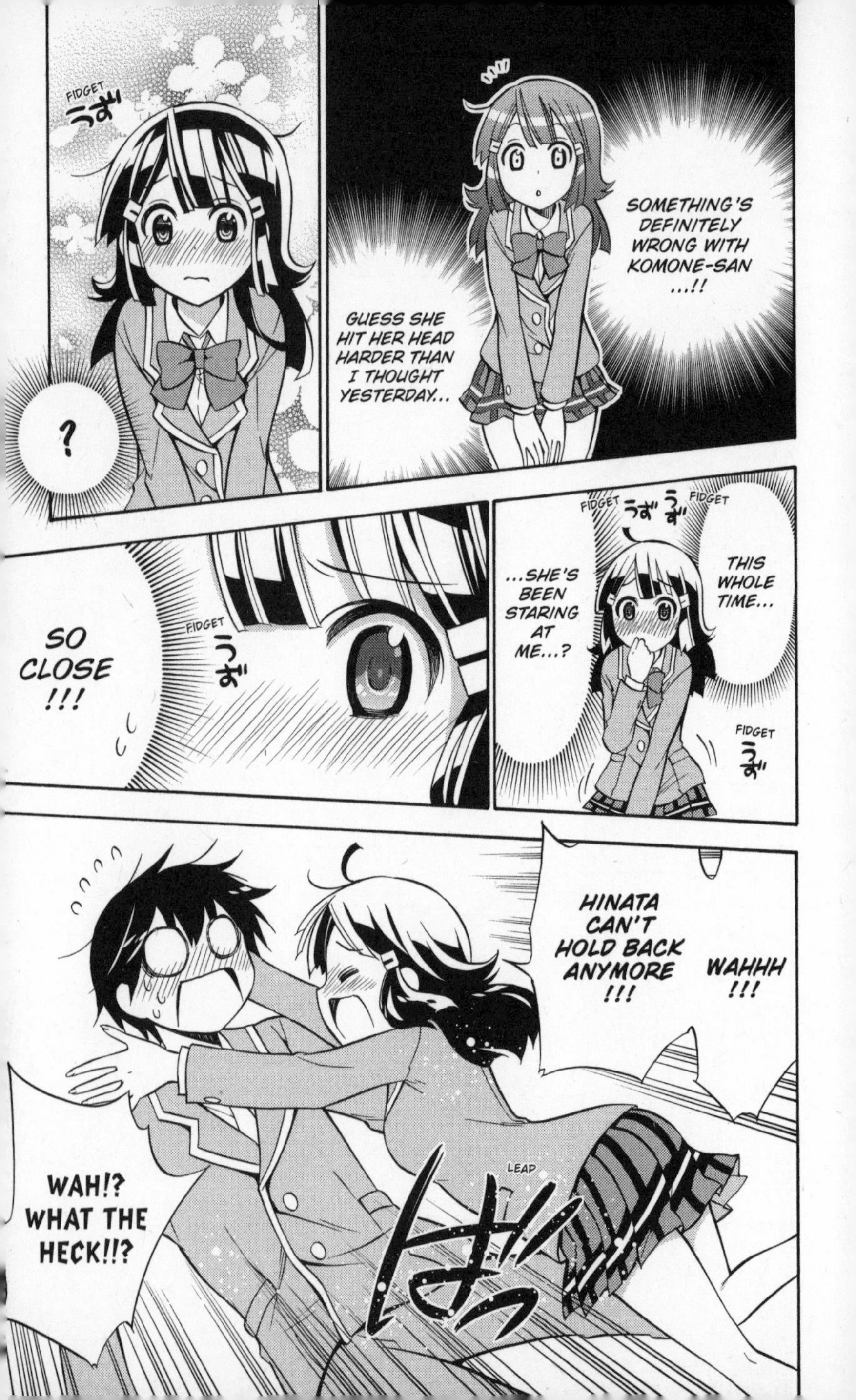
SOMETHING'S DEFINITELY WRONG WITH KOMONE-SAN ...!!
GUESS SHE HIT HER HEAD HARDER THAN I THOUGHT YESTERDAY...
FIDGET
うず
?
FIDGET
うず
うず
FIDGET
THIS WHOLE TIME...
...SHE'S BEEN STARING AT ME...?
FIDGET
うず
FIDGET
うず
SO CLOSE !!!
WAHHH !!!
HINATA CAN'T HOLD BACK ANYMORE !!!
LEAP
ばっ
WAH!? WHAT THE HECK!!?

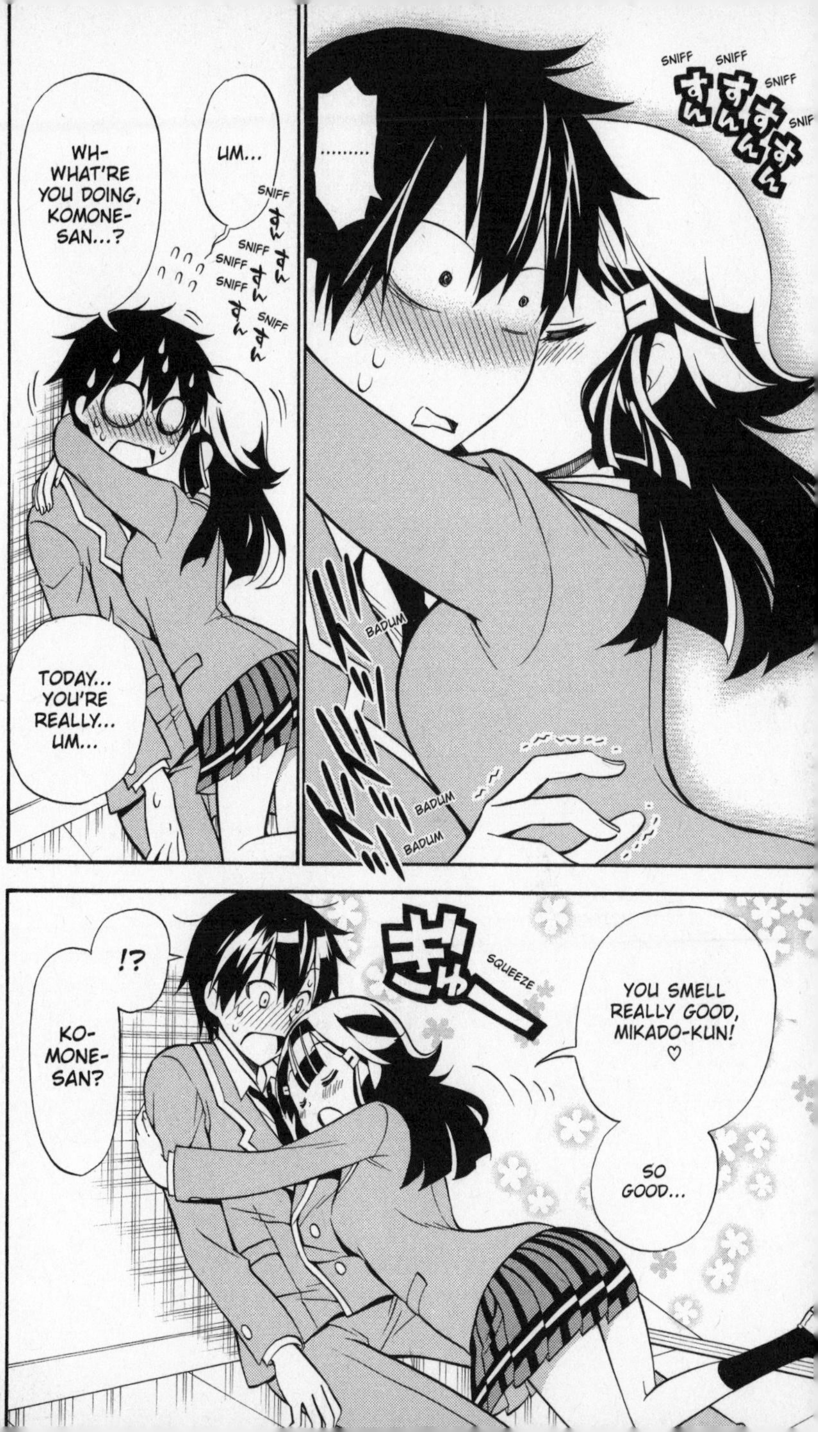
すんすんすんすん
SNIFF SNIFF SNIFF SNIF
....
BADUM
BADUM
BADUM
UM...
WH- WHAT'RE YOU DOING, KOMONE-SAN...?
すんすんすんすんすん
SNIFF SNIFF SNIFF SNIFF
TODAY... YOU'RE REALLY... UM...
YOU SMELL REALLY GOOD, MIKADO-KUN! ♡
SO GOOD...
ぎゅー
SQUEEZE
!?
KO-MONE-SAN?

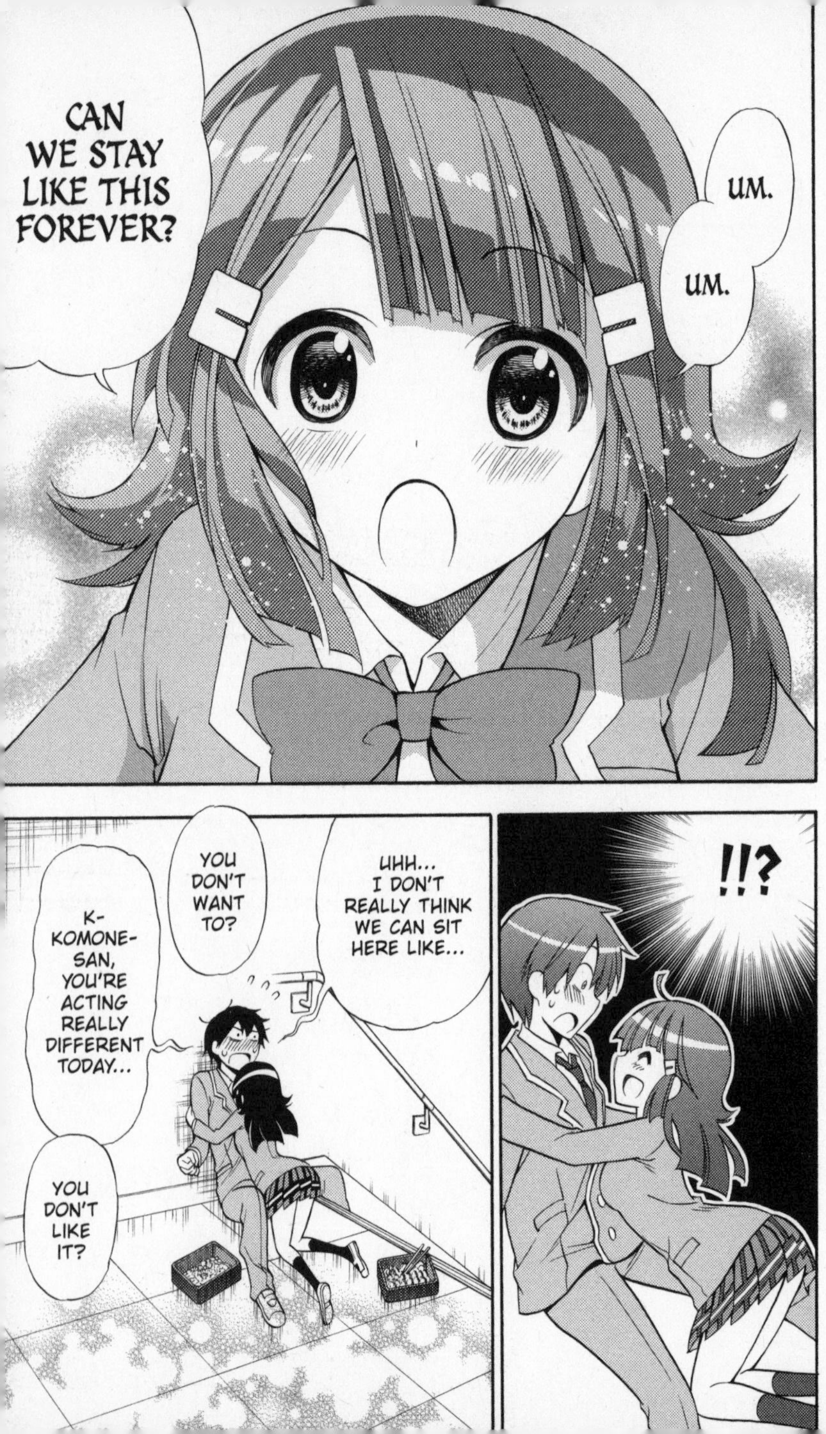
UM.
UM.
CAN WE STAY LIKE THIS FOREVER?
!!?
UHH... I DON'T REALLY THINK WE CAN SIT HERE LIKE...
YOU DON'T WANT TO?
K-KOMONE-SAN, YOU'RE ACTING REALLY DIFFERENT TODAY...
YOU DON'T LIKE IT?

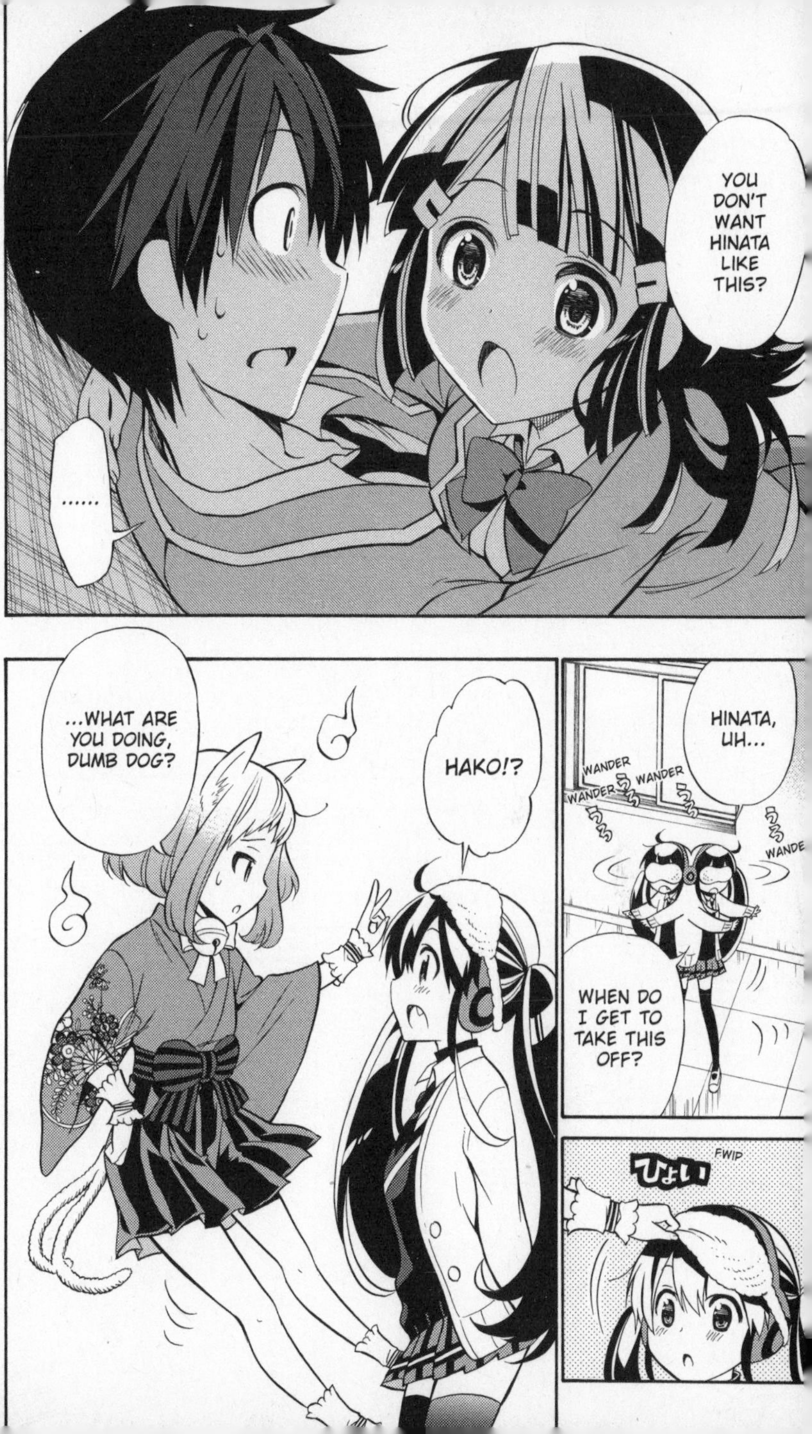
YOU DON'T WANT HINATA LIKE THIS?
......
HINATA, UH...
WANDER WANDER WANDER WANDE
WHEN DO I GET TO TAKE THIS OFF?
ひょい
FWIP
...WHAT ARE YOU DOING, DUMB DOG?
HAKO!?

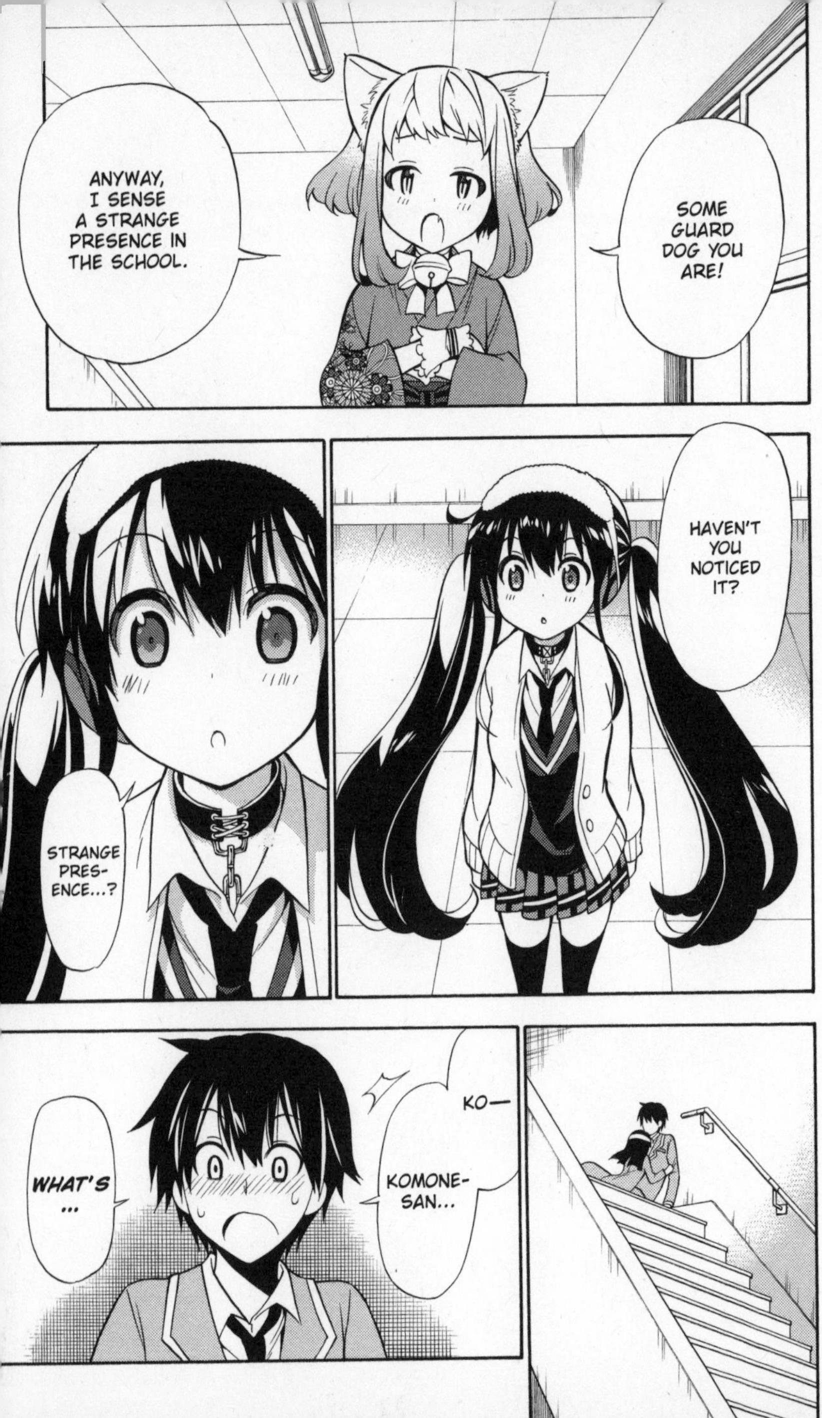
SOME GUARD DOG YOU ARE!
ANYWAY, I SENSE A STRANGE PRESENCE IN THE SCHOOL.
HAVEN'T YOU NOTICED IT?
STRANGE PRES-ENCE...?
KO—
KOMONE-SAN...
WHAT'S ...

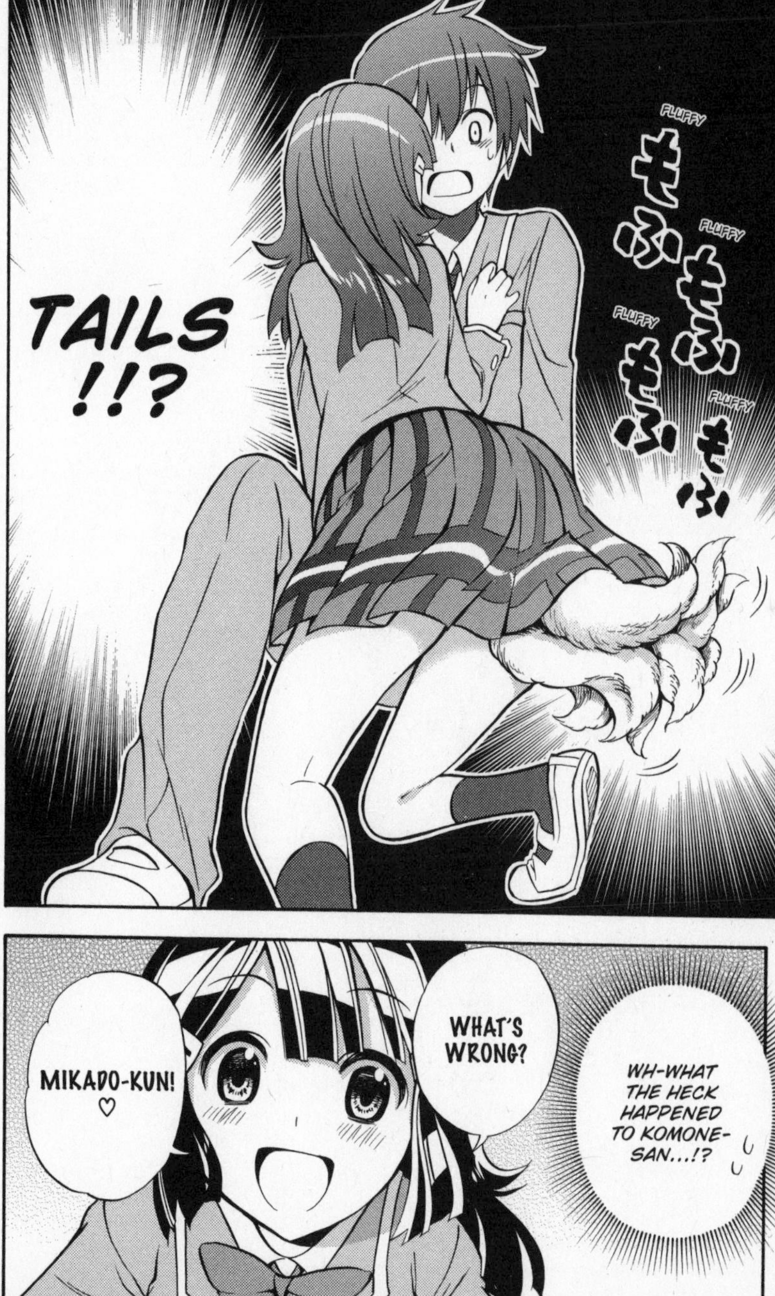
もふもふもふもふ
FLUFFY FLUFFY FLUFFY FLUFFY
TAILS !!?
WH-WHAT THE HECK HAPPENED TO KOMONE-SAN...!?
WHAT'S WRONG?
MIKADO-KUN! ♡

NOTES

PAGE 53
One line in the traditional Japanese nursery rhyme, "Snow," claims that when it snows, "...The dog runs about the yard and the cat curls under the *kotatsu*." This also explains Hako's later fondness for the *kotatsu*...

PAGE 61
Kamakura are igloo-like snow huts made for kamakura festivals in Japan. Visitors are served food and drink inside the structures.

PAGE 82
The *kotatsu* is a ubiquitous piece of furniture found in many Japanese homes—especially ones that experience cold winters. They're typically square tables, about two feet off the ground, with a built-in blanket that drapes from each side. While the earliest *kotatsu* were warmed by burning coals under a grate in the floor, modern ones include electric heaters mounted underneath the tabletop so chilly family members can warm their lower halves under the blanket. Although Idora doesn't have a *kotatsu* available to him in the chapter itself, readers can see an example of one in the bonus comic on page 193.

TODAY'S CERBERUS

※CERBERUS' ROOM
......
IDIOT! TAKE OFF THE BLIND-FOLD!!
おろおろ
FRET FRET
KURO, YOU DUMMY. WE CAN'T SEE!!
COME ONNNN.

NOTES

PAGE 90
The Ueno area in Tokyo is home to the real-life Ueno Zoo. The zoo in this chapter is modeled after that one, as Chiaki and Kuro meet at Ueno Station, but at the zoo, the first kanji in "Ueno" has been changed from "above" to "rabbit."

PAGE 99
In the West, we tend to think of the cat as the dog's traditional enemy, but in East Asia, it's dogs and monkeys who are said to be prone to squabbles. So much so that the idiom Chiaki mentions is used more generally to refer to incompatible people or things.

TODAY'S CERBERUS

UNDER MY SKIRT?
THAT'S A SECRET! ♡

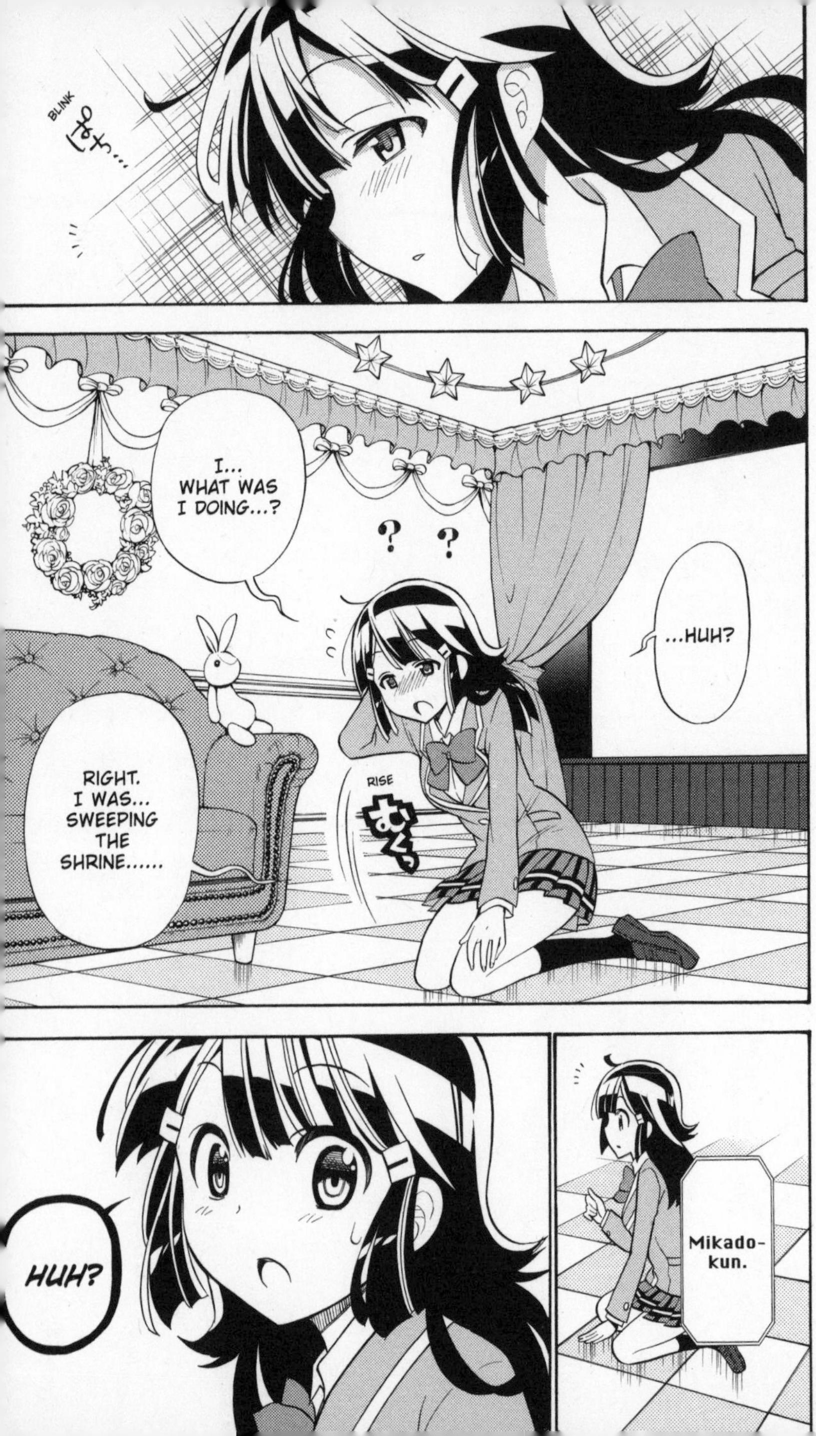
BLINK
...HUH?
I... WHAT WAS I DOING...?
RISE
RIGHT. I WAS... SWEEPING THE SHRINE......
Mikado-kun.
HUH?

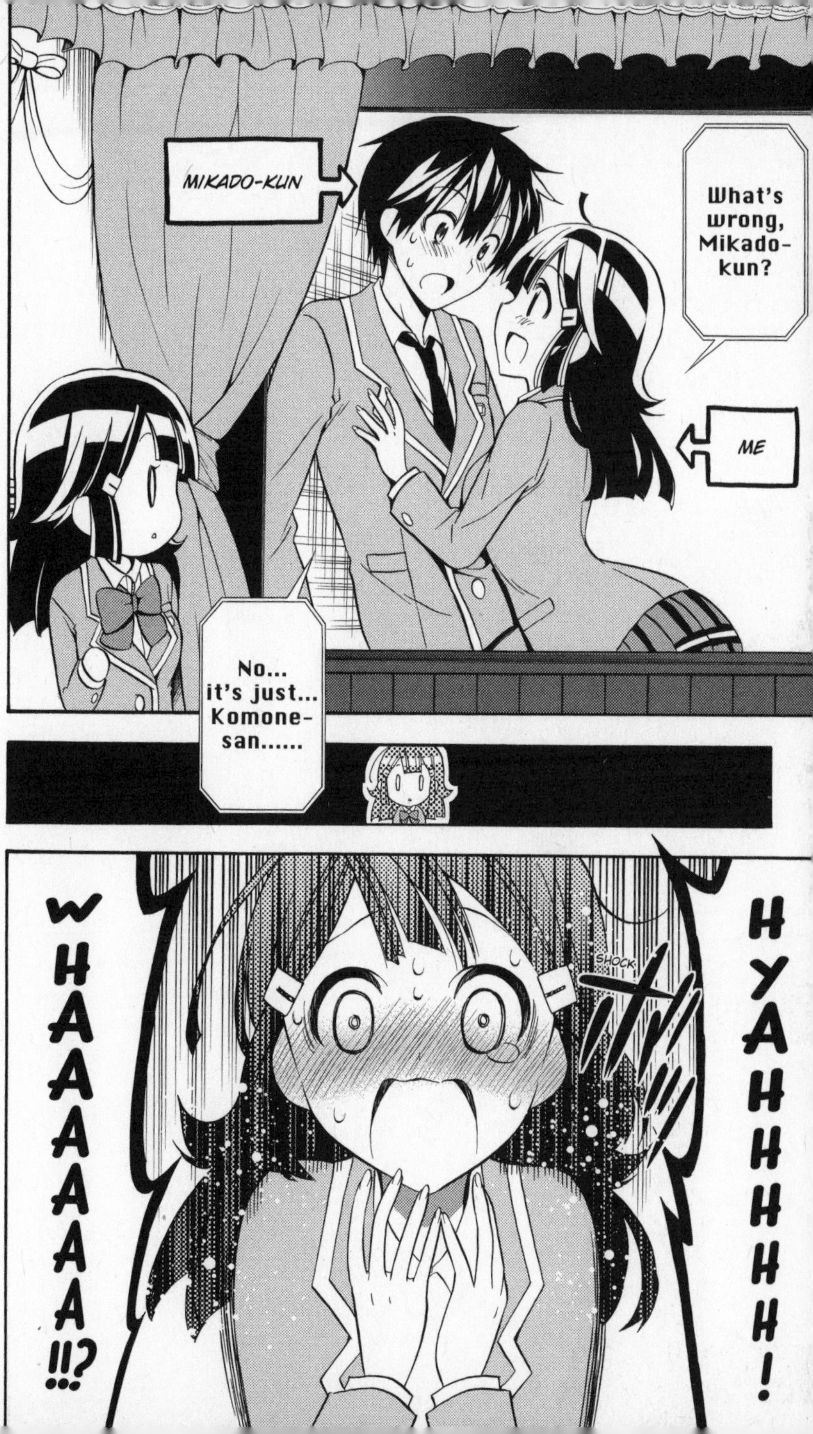
What's wrong, Mikado-kun?
ME
MIKADO-KUN
No... it's just... Komone-san......
HYAHHHHHH!
SHOCK
WHAAAAAAAA!!?

CHAPTER 19
HINATA'S HEART

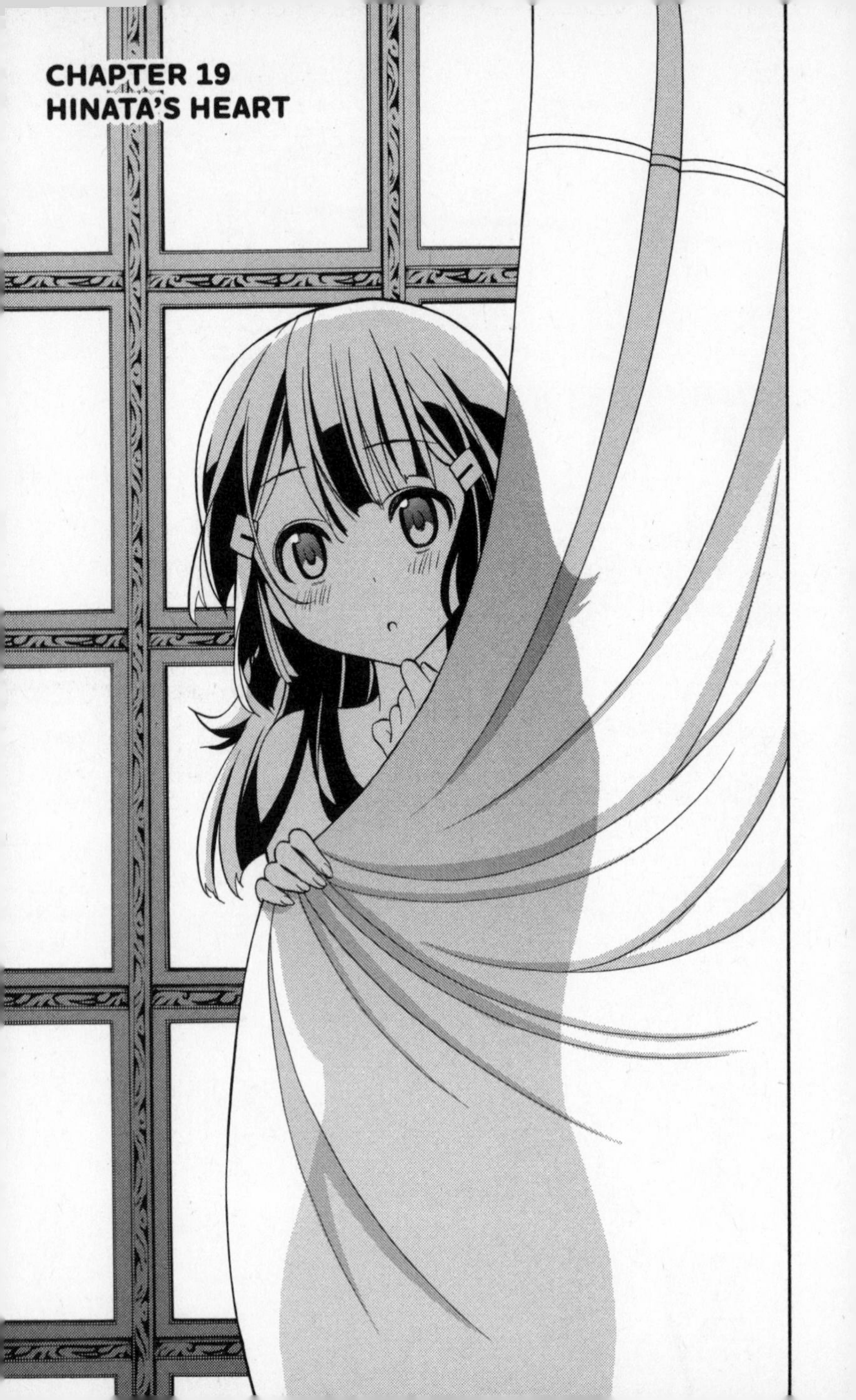

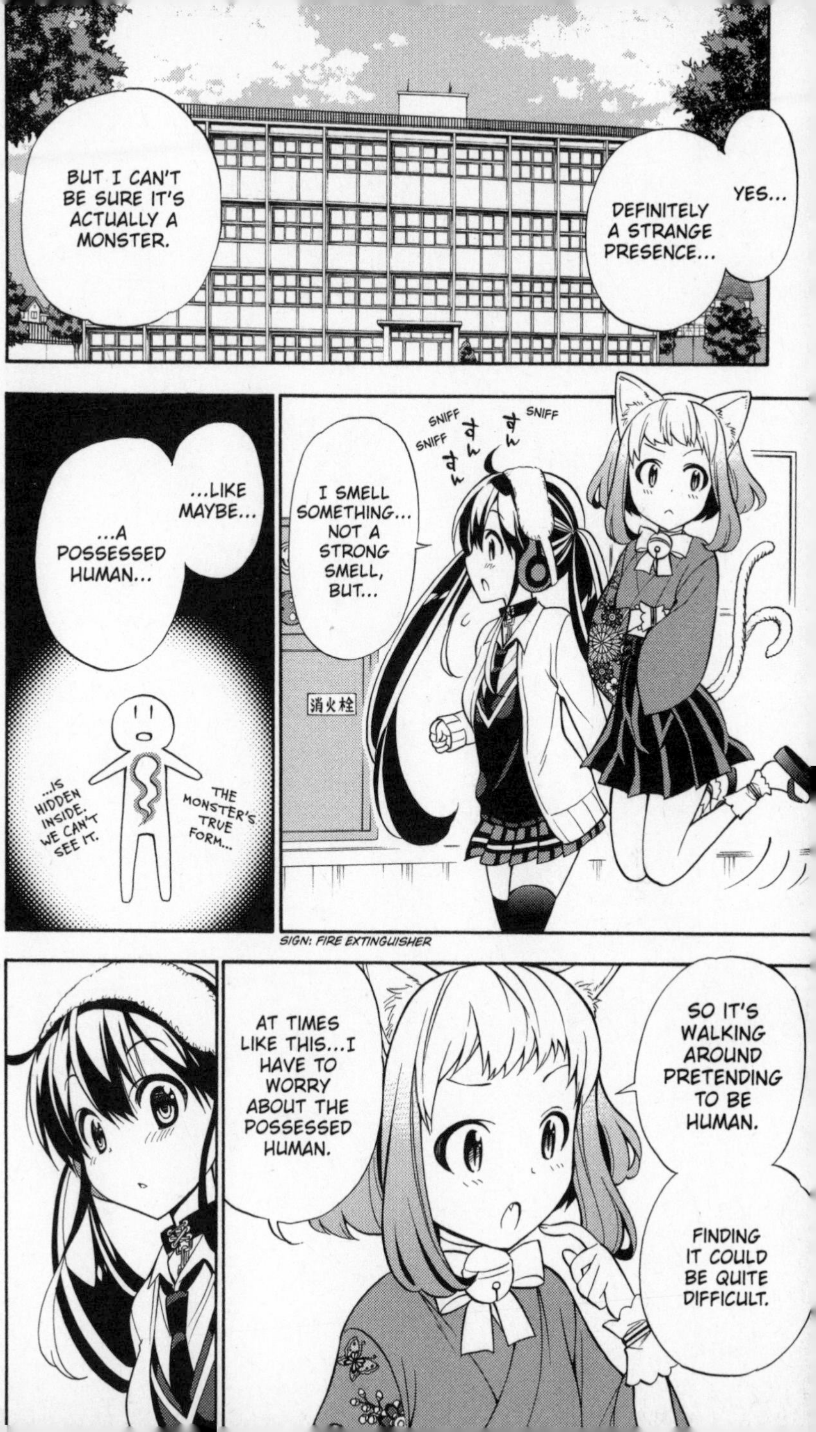
YES...
DEFINITELY A STRANGE PRESENCE...
BUT I CAN'T BE SURE IT'S ACTUALLY A MONSTER.
SNIFF
すん
SNIFF
すん
SNIFF
すん
I SMELL SOMETHING... NOT A STRONG SMELL, BUT...
消火栓
...LIKE MAYBE...
...A POSSESSED HUMAN...
THE MONSTER'S TRUE FORM...
...IS HIDDEN INSIDE. WE CAN'T SEE IT.
SIGN: FIRE EXTINGUISHER
SO IT'S WALKING AROUND PRETENDING TO BE HUMAN.
FINDING IT COULD BE QUITE DIFFICULT.
AT TIMES LIKE THIS...I HAVE TO WORRY ABOUT THE POSSESSED HUMAN.

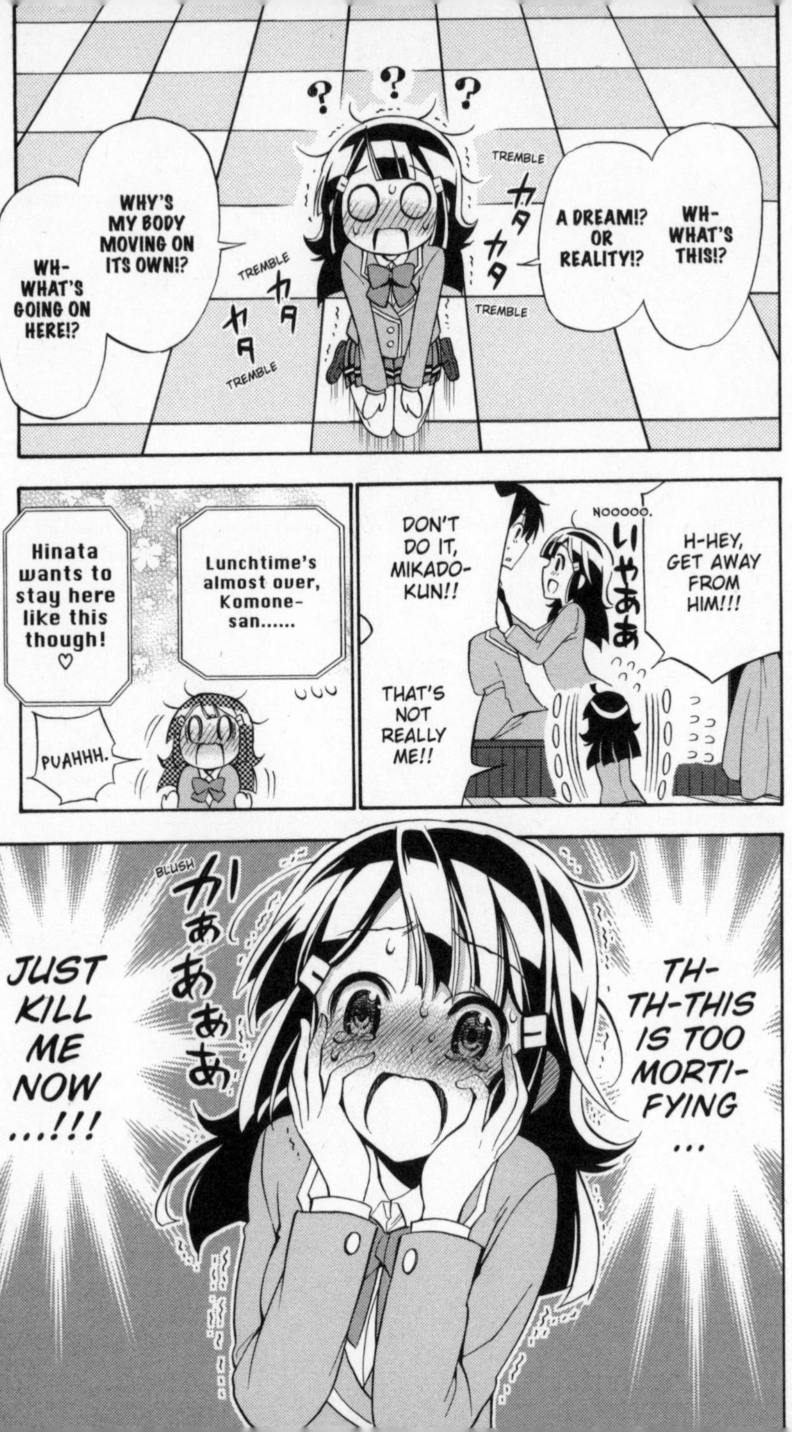
WH-WHAT'S THIS!?
A DREAM!? OR REALITY!?
TREMBLE
カタカタ
TREMBLE
WHY'S MY BODY MOVING ON ITS OWN!?
WH-WHAT'S GOING ON HERE!?
TREMBLE
カタカタ
TREMBLE
H-HEY, GET AWAY FROM HIM!!!
NOOOOO.
いやぁぁ
DON'T DO IT, MIKADO-KUN!!
THAT'S NOT REALLY ME!!
Lunchtime's almost over, Komone-san......
Hinata wants to stay here like this though! ♡
PUAHHH.
TH-TH-THIS IS TOO MORTI-FYING ...
BLUSH
かぁぁぁぁ
JUST KILL ME NOW ...!!!

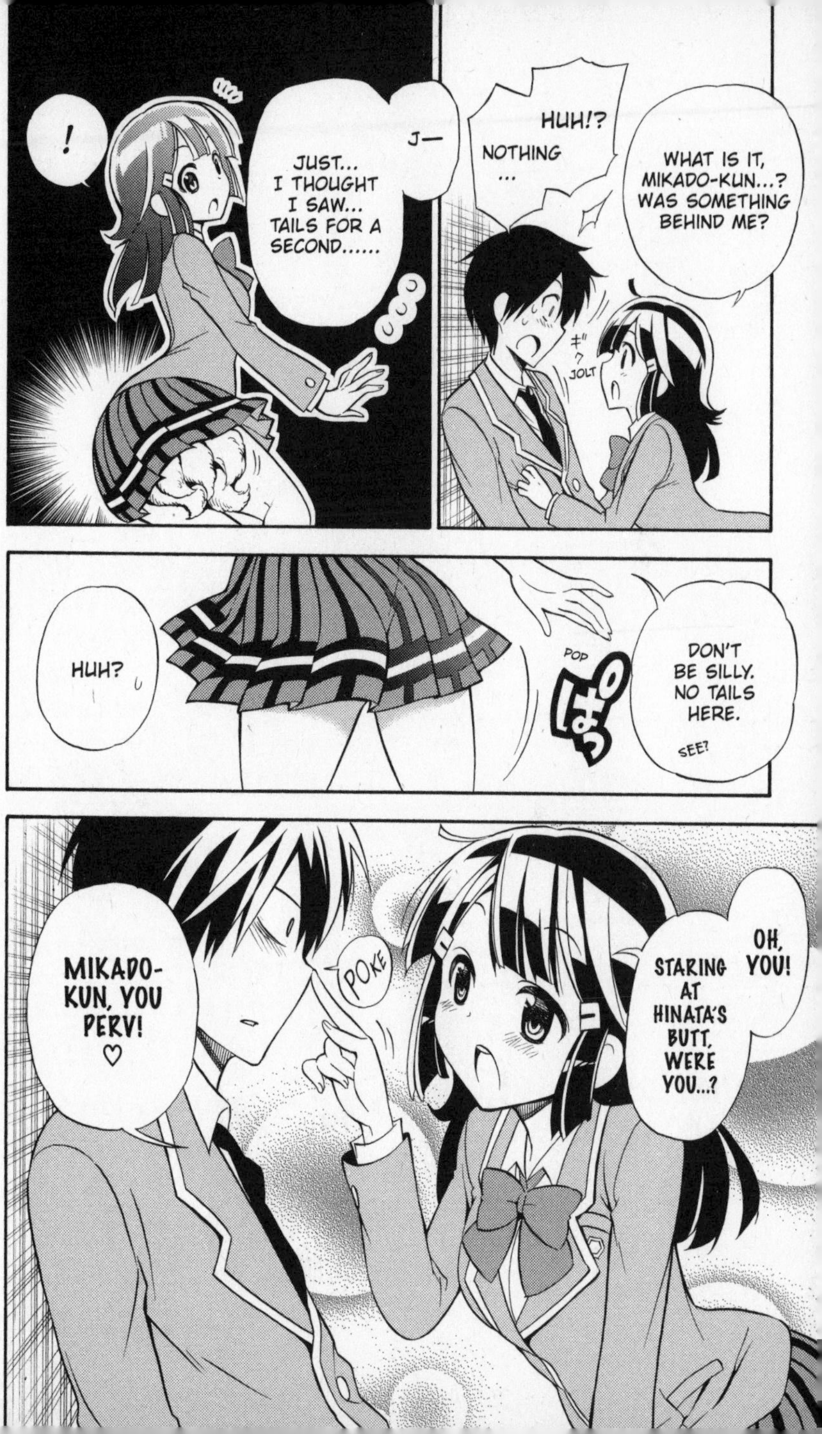
WHAT IS IT, MIKADO-KUN...? WAS SOMETHING BEHIND ME?
HUH!?
NOTHING ...
ギク
JOLT
J—
JUST... I THOUGHT I SAW... TAILS FOR A SECOND......
!
DON'T BE SILLY. NO TAILS HERE.
SEE?
POP
ぱっ
HUH?
OH, YOU!
STARING AT HINATA'S BUTT, WERE YOU...?
POKE
MIKADO-KUN, YOU PERV! ♡

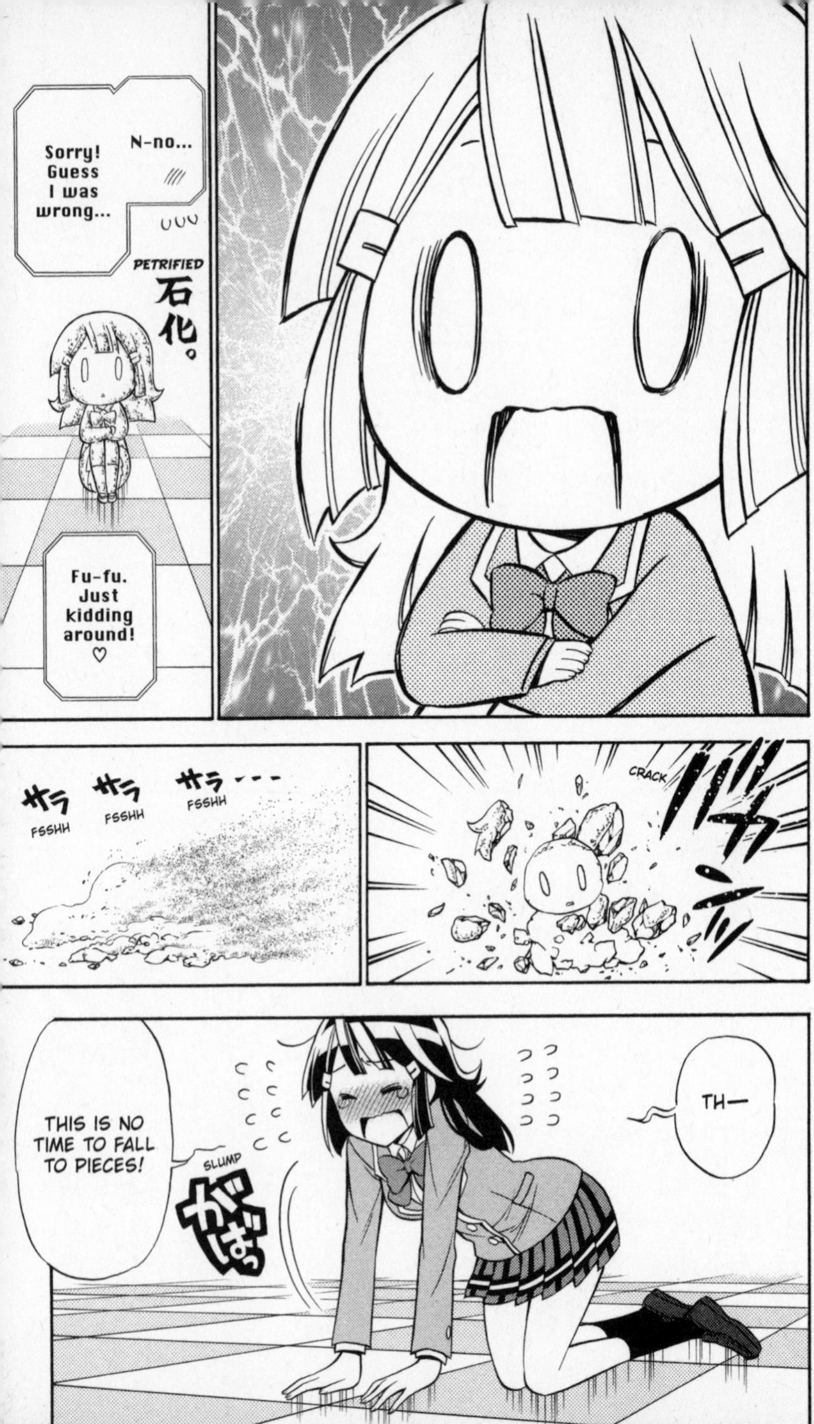
N-no...
Sorry! Guess I was wrong...
石化。
PETRIFIED
Fu-fu. Just kidding around! ♡
CRACK
サラ
FSSHH
サラ
FSSHH
サラ---
FSSHH
TH—
がばっ
SLUMP
THIS IS NO TIME TO FALL TO PIECES!

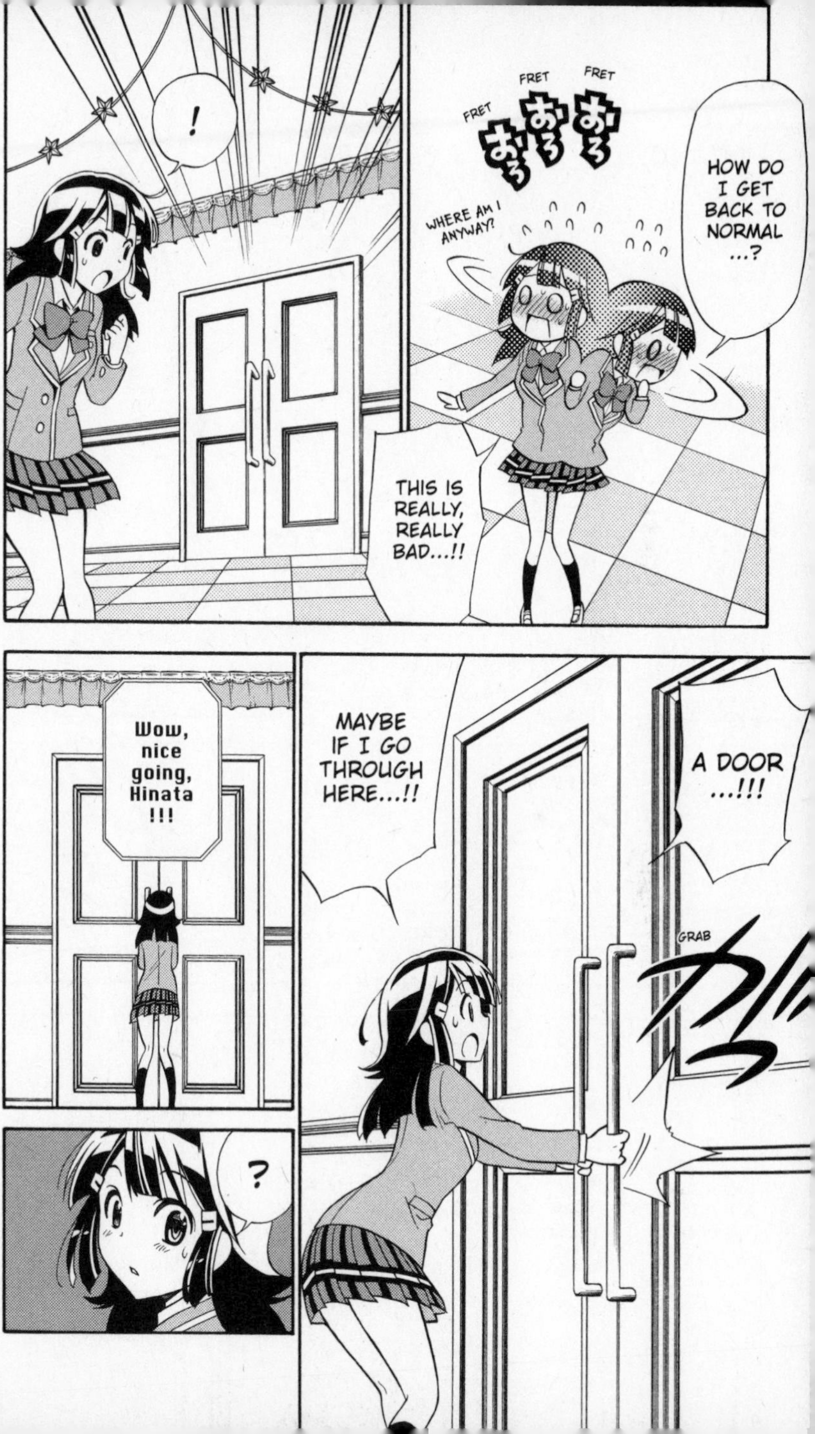
FRET FRET FRET
おろおろおろ
HOW DO I GET BACK TO NORMAL ...?
WHERE AM I ANYWAY?
THIS IS REALLY, REALLY BAD...!!
!
A DOOR ...!!!
MAYBE IF I GO THROUGH HERE...!!
GRAB
Wow, nice going, Hinata !!!
?

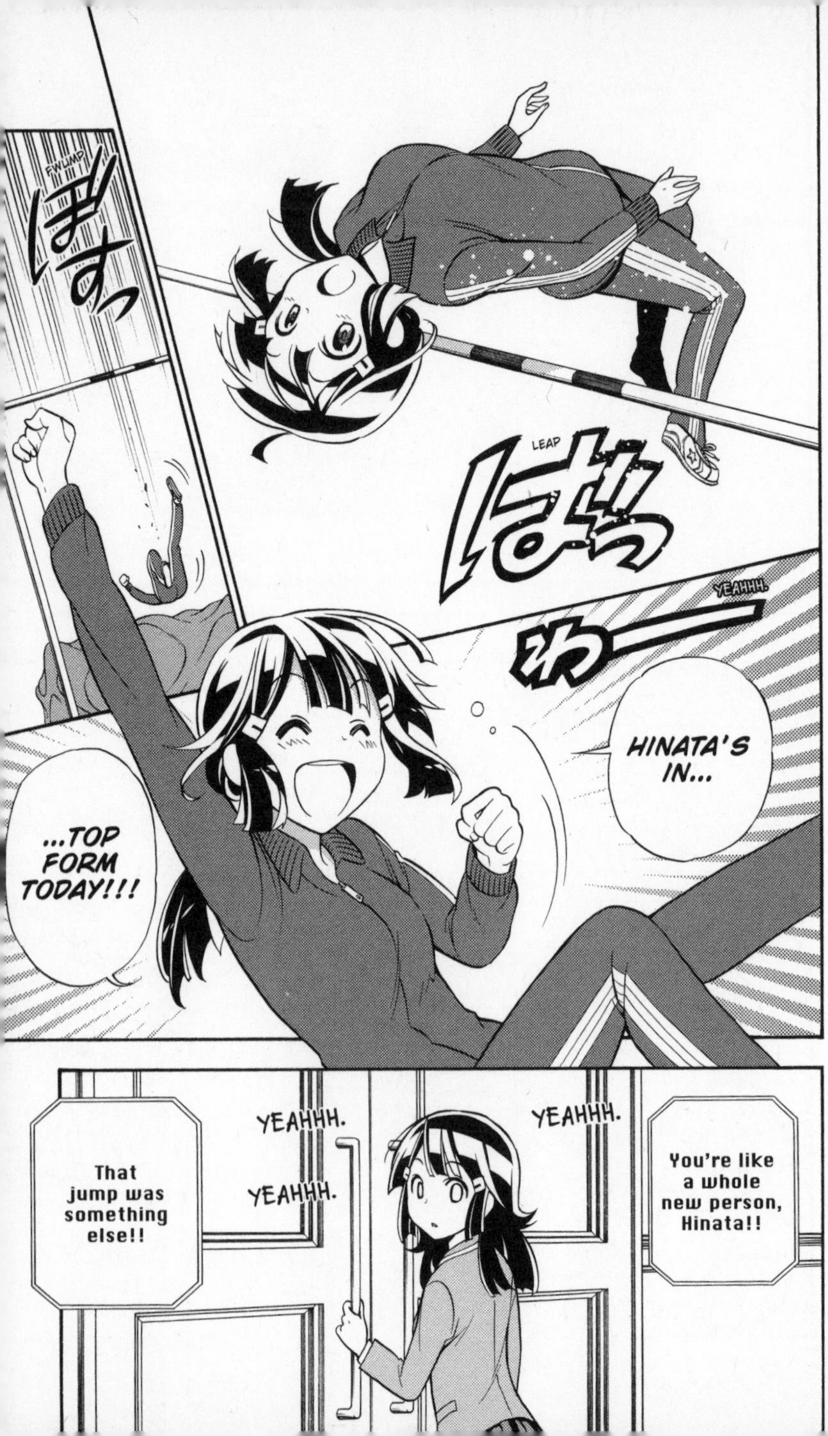
LEAP
はっ
FWLUMP
ぽすっ
YEAHHH.
わー
HINATA'S IN...
...TOP FORM TODAY!!!
You're like a whole new person, Hinata!!
YEAHHH.
YEAHHH.
YEAHHH.
That jump was something else!!

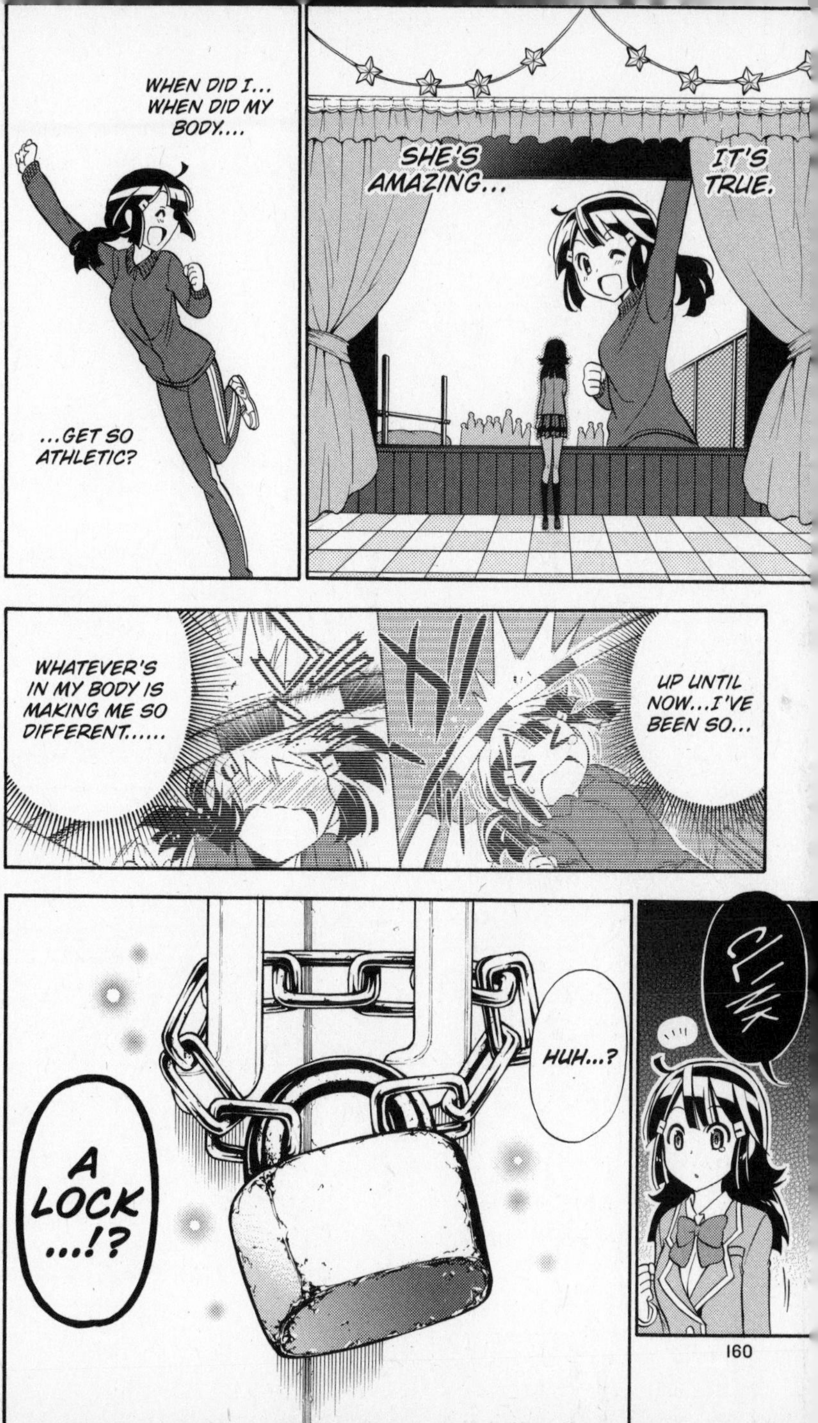
SHE'S AMAZING...
IT'S TRUE.
WHEN DID I... WHEN DID MY BODY....
...GET SO ATHLETIC?
UP UNTIL NOW...I'VE BEEN SO...
WHATEVER'S IN MY BODY IS MAKING ME SO DIFFERENT......
CLINK
HUH...?
A LOCK ...!?

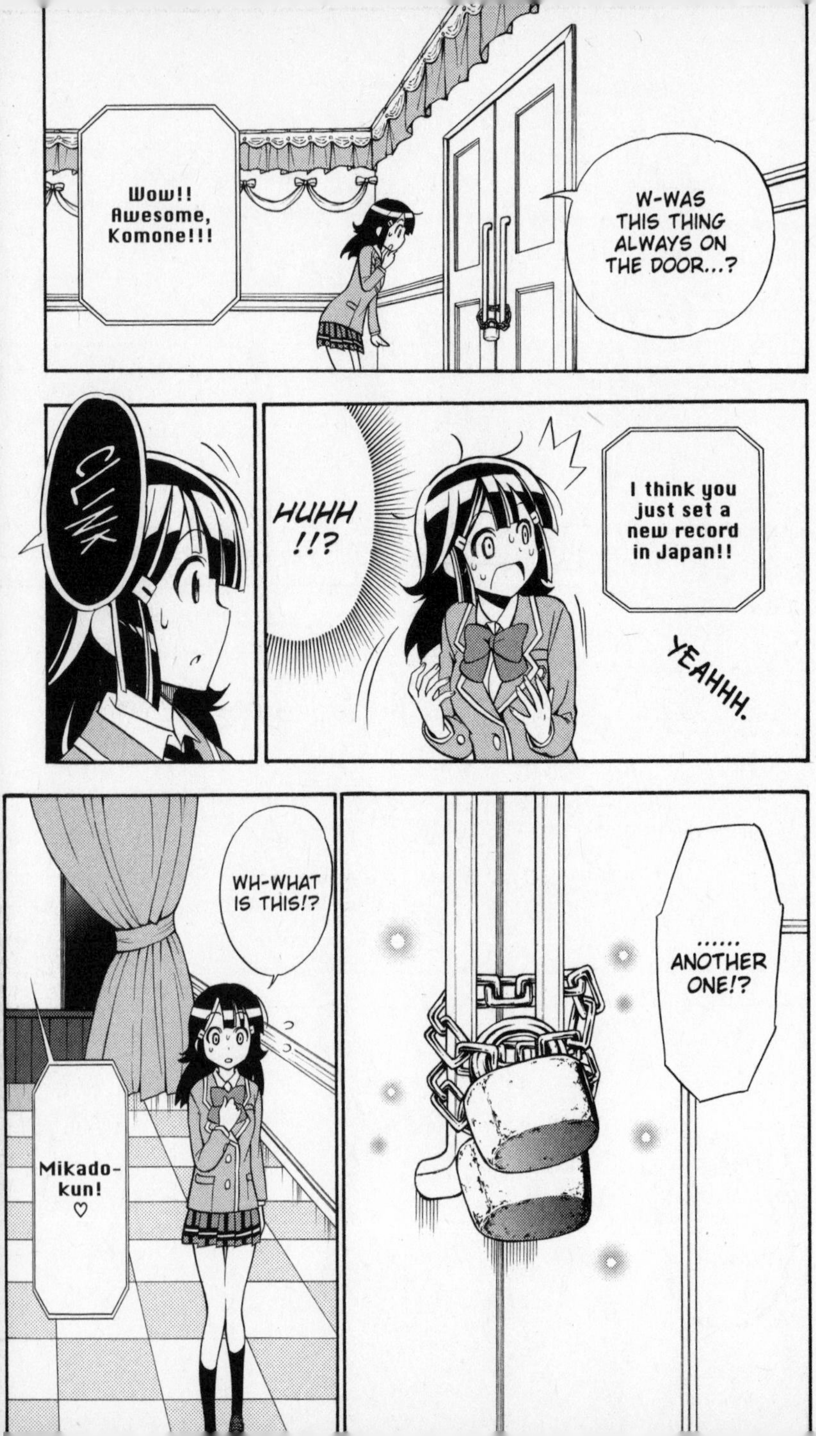
W-WAS THIS THING ALWAYS ON THE DOOR...?
Wow!! Awesome, Komone!!!
I think you just set a new record in Japan!!
YEAHHH.
HUHH !!?
CLINK
...... ANOTHER ONE!?
WH-WHAT IS THIS!?
Mikado-kun! ♡

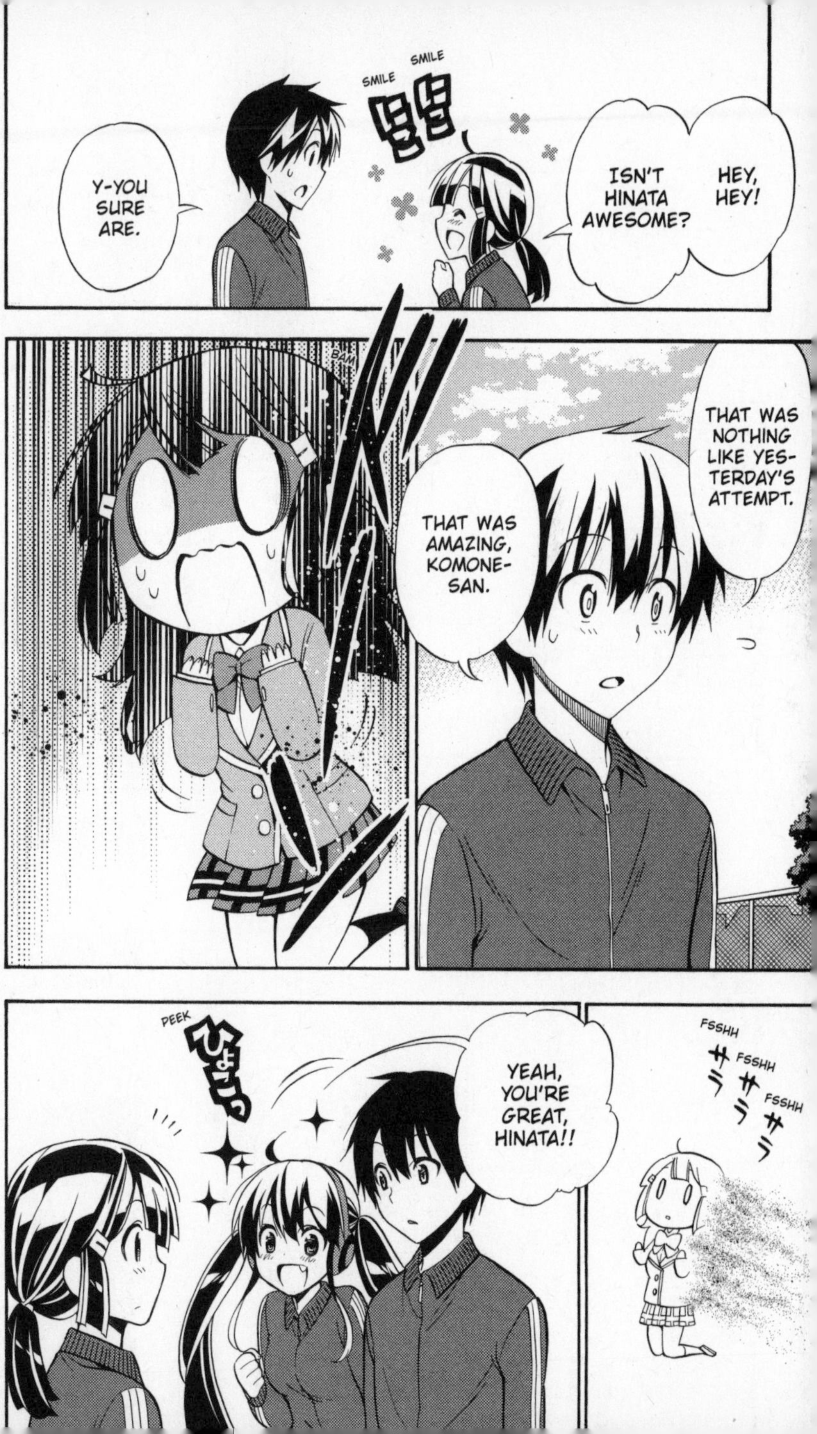
HEY, HEY!
ISN'T HINATA AWESOME?
SMILE SMILE
Y-YOU SURE ARE.
THAT WAS NOTHING LIKE YES-TERDAY'S ATTEMPT.
THAT WAS AMAZING, KOMONE-SAN.
BAM
FSSHH
サラ
FSSHH
サラ
FSSHH
サラ
YEAH, YOU'RE GREAT, HINATA!!
PEEK
ひょこっ

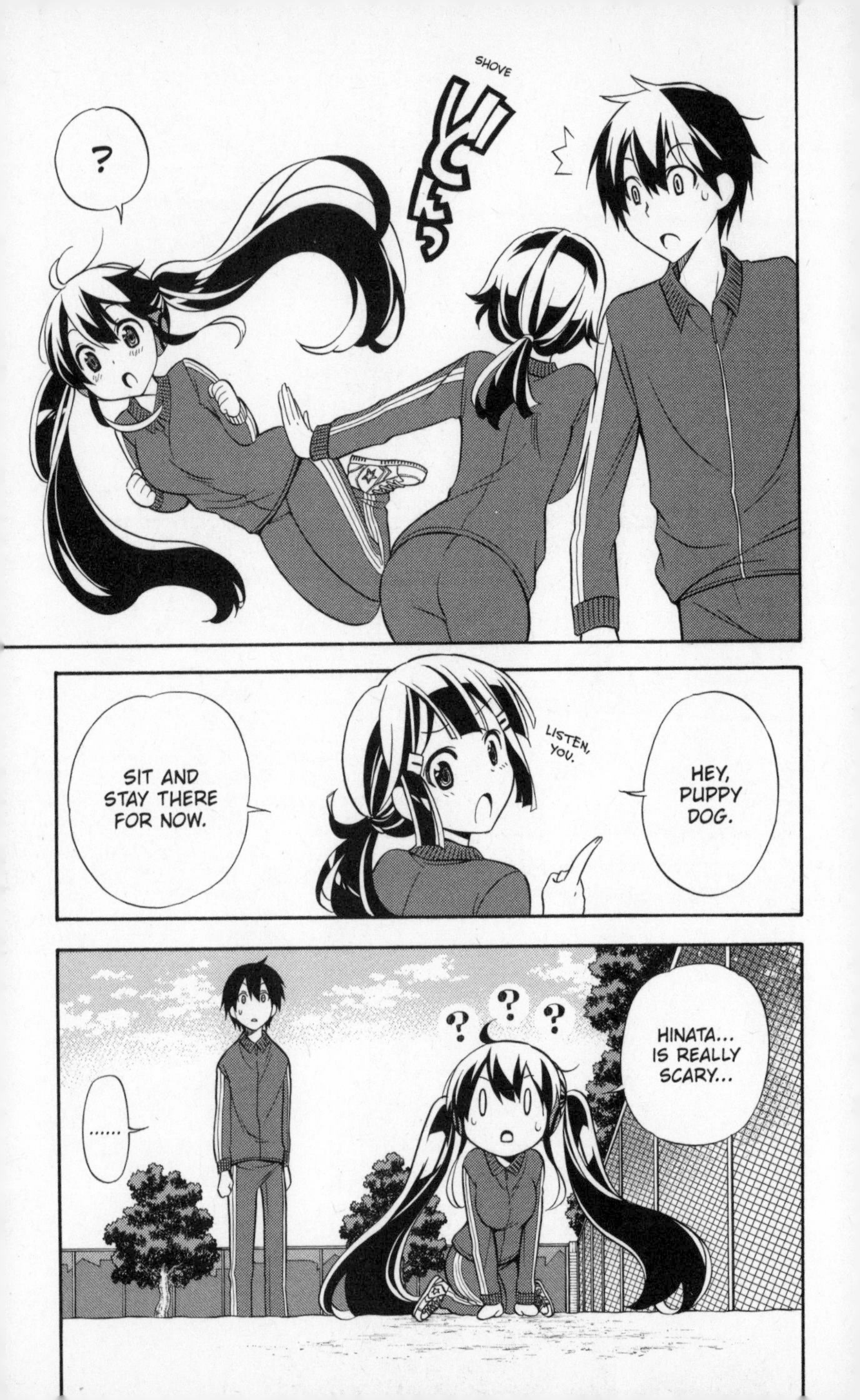
SHOVE
?
HEY, PUPPY DOG.
LISTEN, YOU.
SIT AND STAY THERE FOR NOW.
HINATA... IS REALLY SCARY...
? ? ?
......

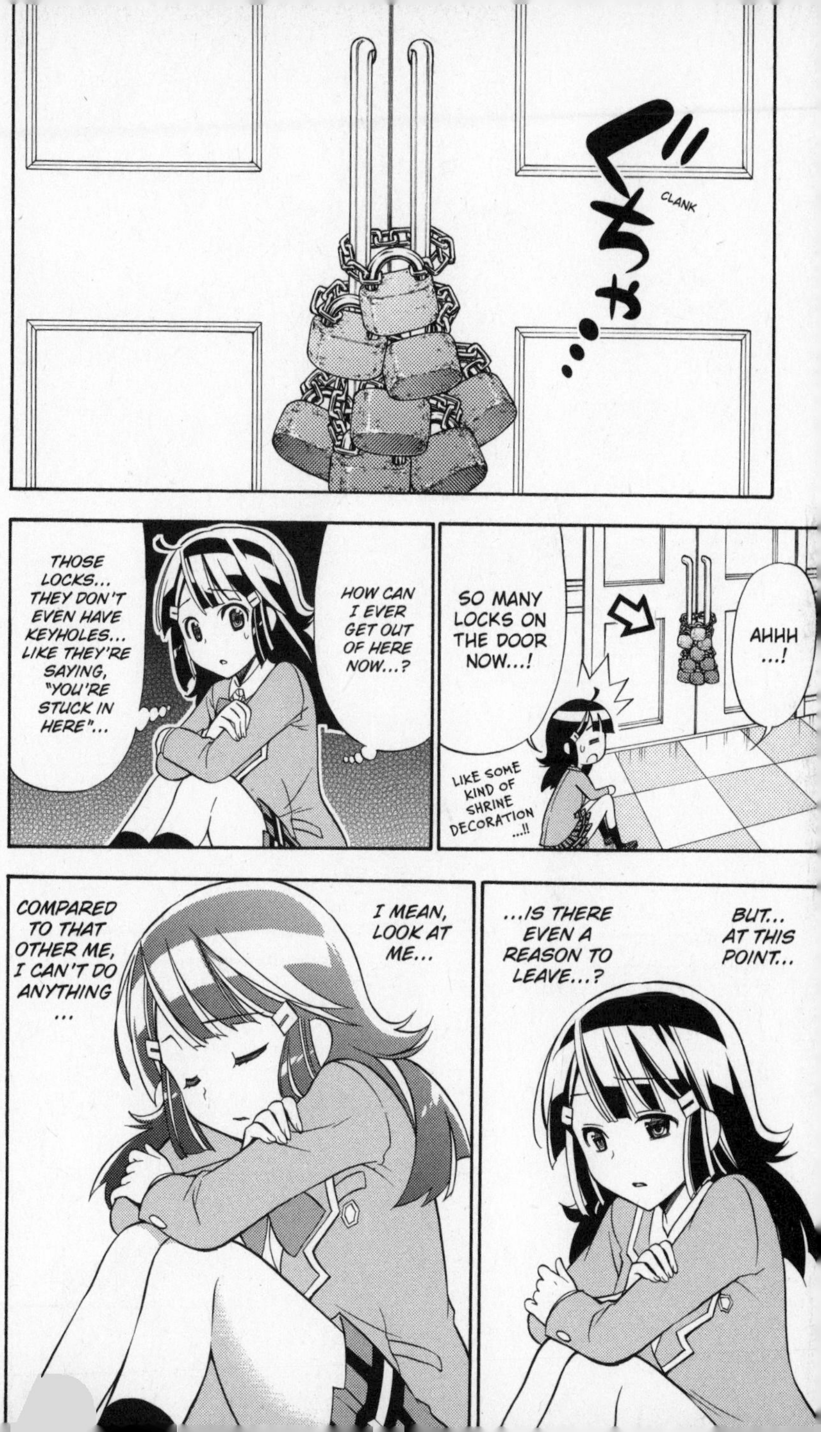
ぐちゃ…
CLANK
AHHH ...!
SO MANY LOCKS ON THE DOOR NOW...!
LIKE SOME KIND OF SHRINE DECORATION ...!!
HOW CAN I EVER GET OUT OF HERE NOW...?
THOSE LOCKS... THEY DON'T EVEN HAVE KEYHOLES... LIKE THEY'RE SAYING, "YOU'RE STUCK IN HERE"...
BUT... AT THIS POINT...
...IS THERE EVEN A REASON TO LEAVE...?
I MEAN, LOOK AT ME...
COMPARED TO THAT OTHER ME, I CAN'T DO ANYTHING ...

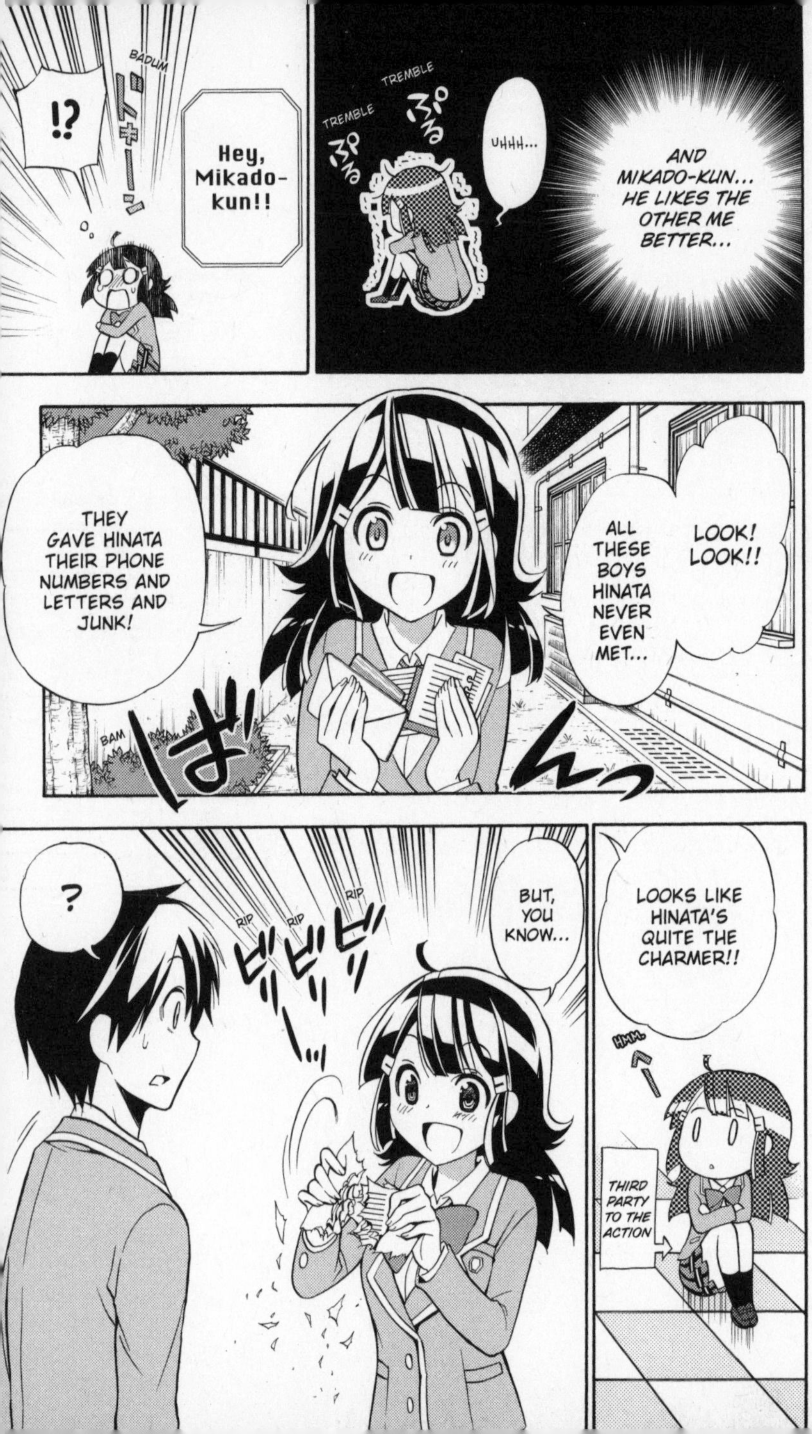
AND MIKADO-KUN... HE LIKES THE OTHER ME BETTER...
UHHH...
TREMBLE
ぷる
TREMBLE
ぷる
Hey, Mikado-kun!!
BADUM
!?
LOOK! LOOK!!
ALL THESE BOYS HINATA NEVER EVEN MET...
THEY GAVE HINATA THEIR PHONE NUMBERS AND LETTERS AND JUNK!
BAM
LOOKS LIKE HINATA'S QUITE THE CHARMER!!
HMM.
THIRD PARTY TO THE ACTION
BUT, YOU KNOW...
RIP
RIP
RIP
?

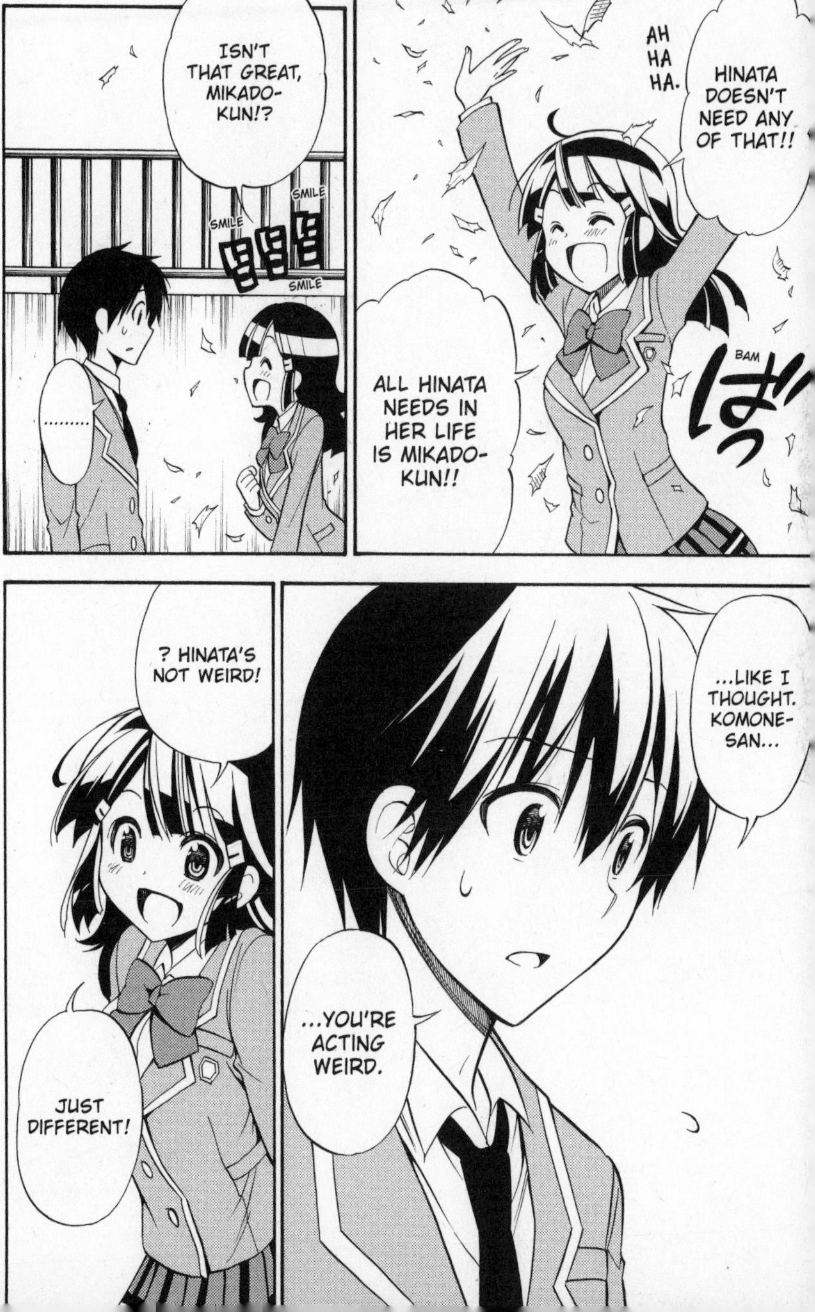
HINATA DOESN'T NEED ANY OF THAT!!
AH HA HA.
BAM
ALL HINATA NEEDS IN HER LIFE IS MIKADO-KUN!!
ISN'T THAT GREAT, MIKADO-KUN!?
SMILE
SMILE
SMILE
....
...LIKE I THOUGHT. KOMONE-SAN...
...YOU'RE ACTING WEIRD.
? HINATA'S NOT WEIRD!
JUST DIFFERENT!

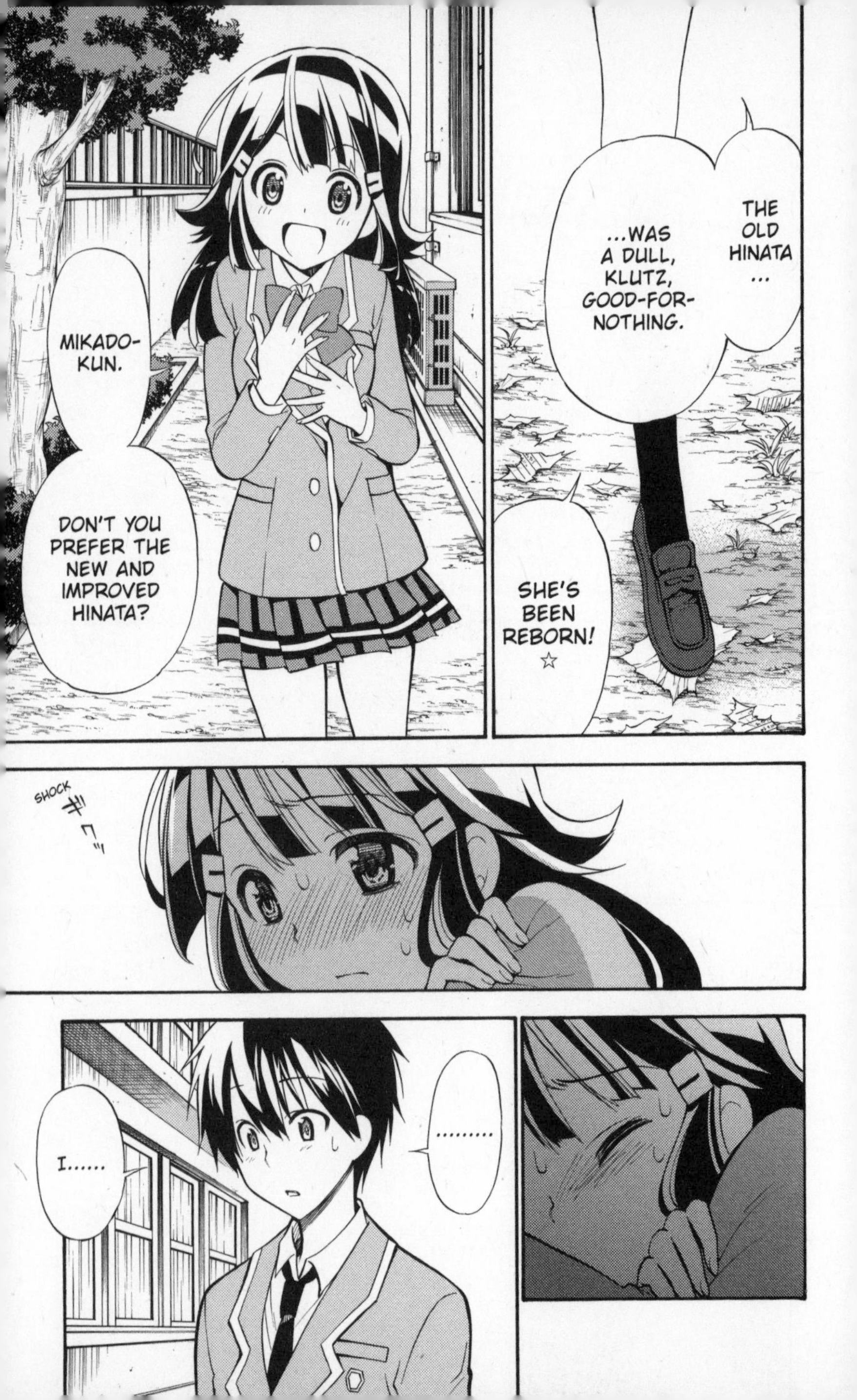
THE OLD HINATA ...
...WAS A DULL, KLUTZ, GOOD-FOR-NOTHING.
SHE'S BEEN REBORN! ☆
MIKADO-KUN.
DON'T YOU PREFER THE NEW AND IMPROVED HINATA?
SHOCK
....
I......

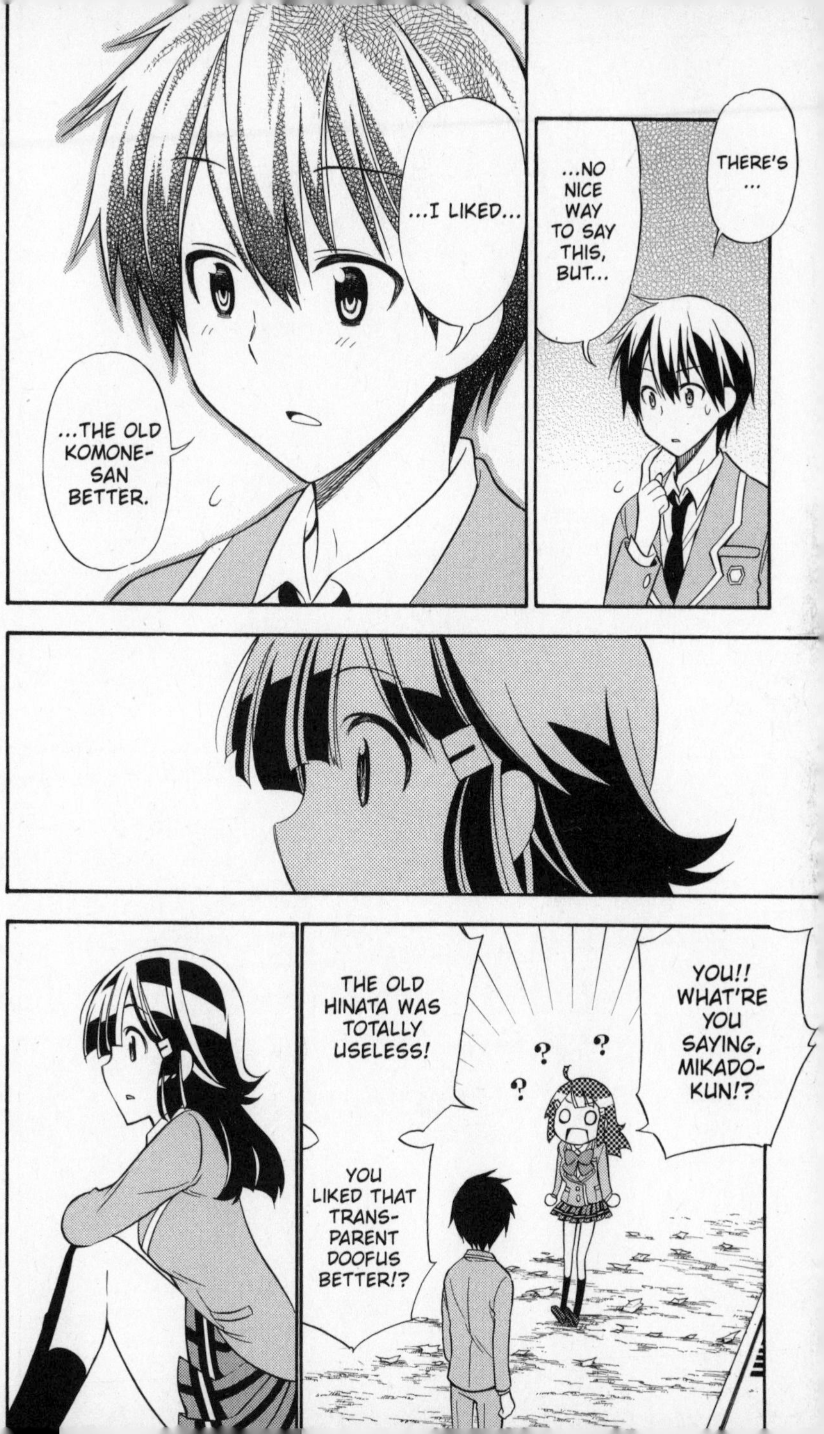
THERE'S ...
...NO NICE WAY TO SAY THIS, BUT...
...I LIKED...
...THE OLD KOMONE-SAN BETTER.
YOU!! WHAT'RE YOU SAYING, MIKADO-KUN!?
THE OLD HINATA WAS TOTALLY USELESS!
YOU LIKED THAT TRANS-PARENT DOOFUS BETTER!?

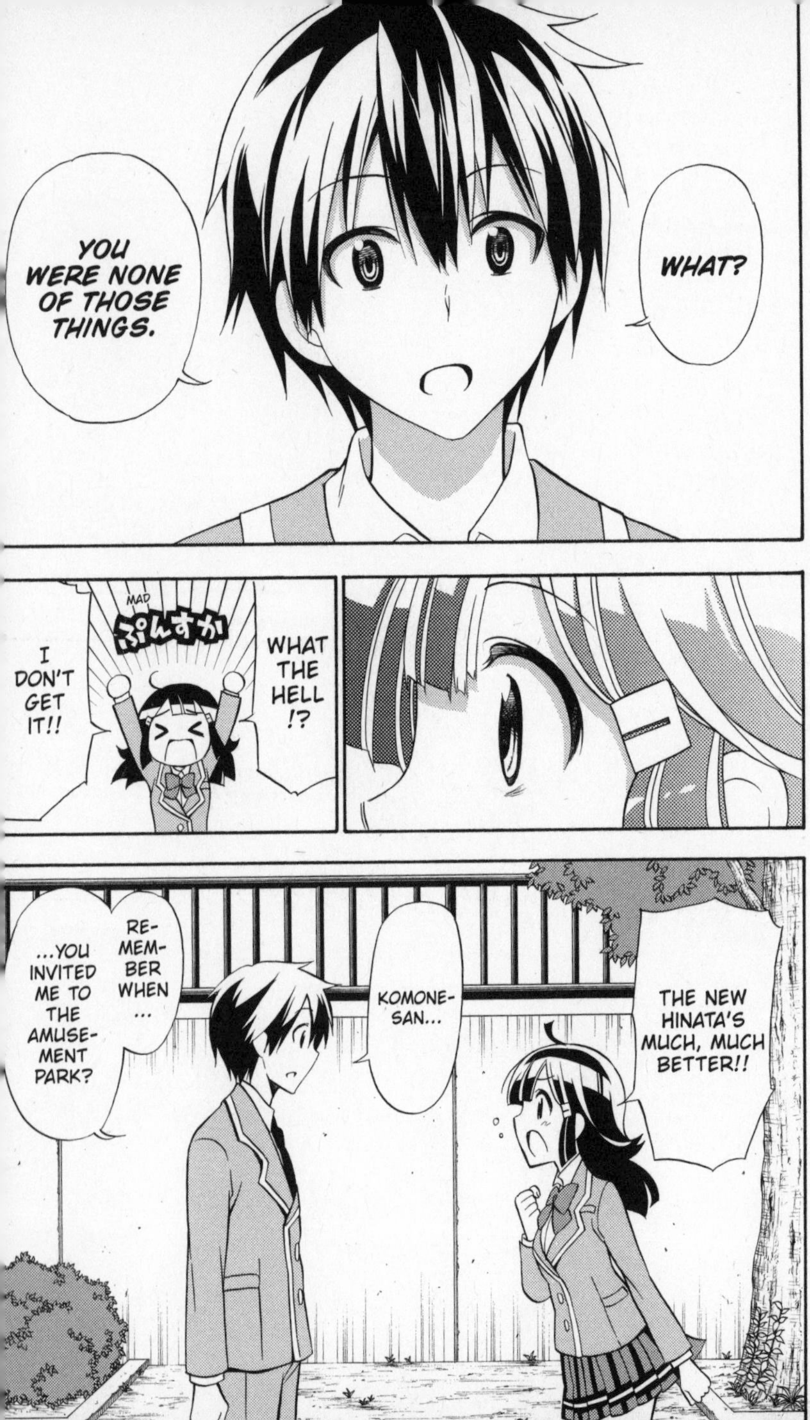
WHAT?
YOU WERE NONE OF THOSE THINGS.
WHAT THE HELL!?
MAD
ぷんすか
I DON'T GET IT!!
THE NEW HINATA'S MUCH, MUCH BETTER!!
KOMONE-SAN...
RE-MEM-BER WHEN...
...YOU INVITED ME TO THE AMUSE-MENT PARK?

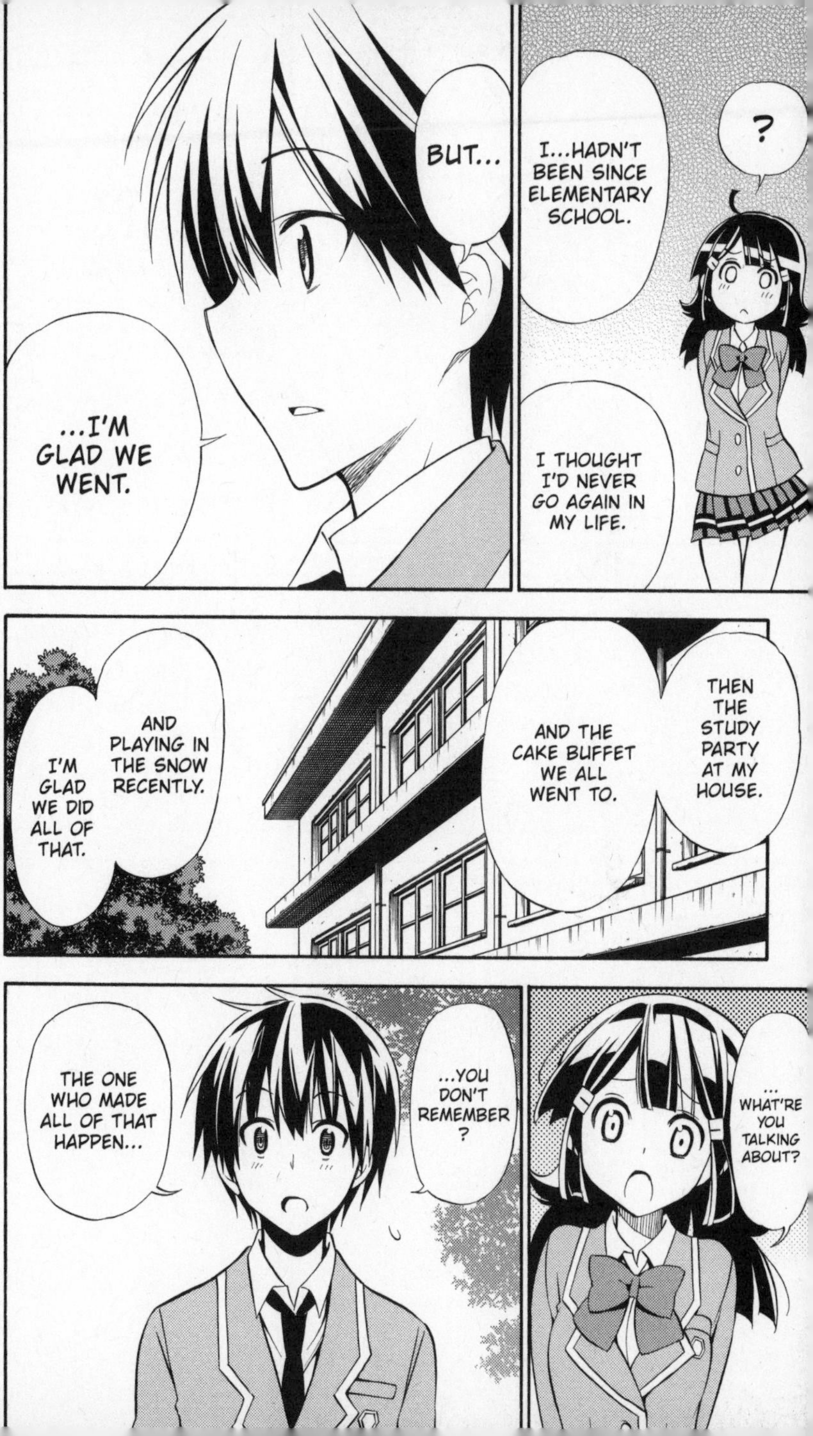
?
I...HADN'T BEEN SINCE ELEMENTARY SCHOOL.
I THOUGHT I'D NEVER GO AGAIN IN MY LIFE.
BUT...
...I'M GLAD WE WENT.
THEN THE STUDY PARTY AT MY HOUSE.
AND THE CAKE BUFFET WE ALL WENT TO.
AND PLAYING IN THE SNOW RECENTLY.
I'M GLAD WE DID ALL OF THAT.
...WHAT'RE YOU TALKING ABOUT?
...YOU DON'T REMEMBER?
THE ONE WHO MADE ALL OF THAT HAPPEN...

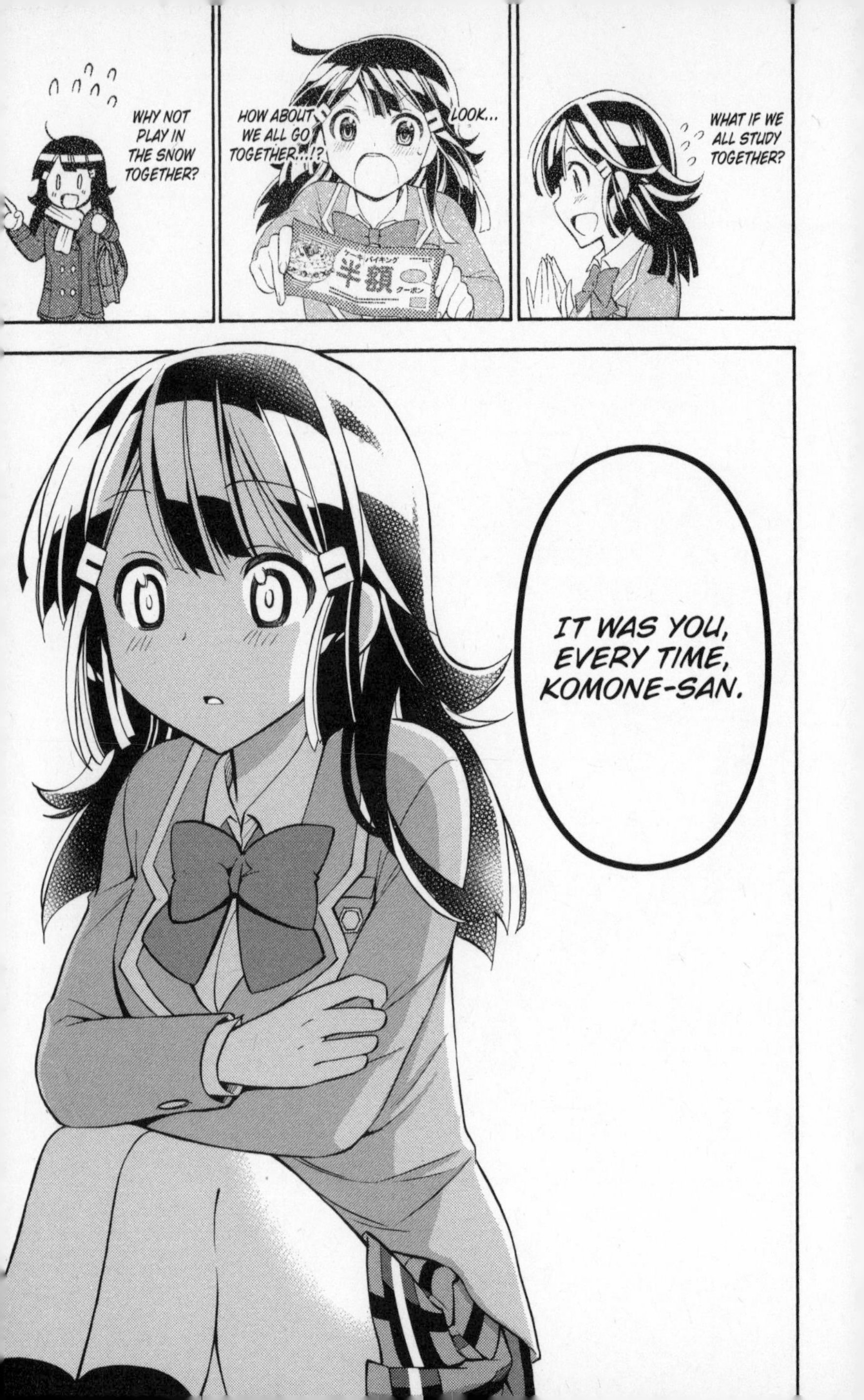
WHAT IF WE ALL STUDY TOGETHER?
LOOK...
HOW ABOUT WE ALL GO TOGETHER...!?
半額
クーポン
WHY NOT PLAY IN THE SNOW TOGETHER?
IT WAS YOU, EVERY TIME, KOMONE-SAN.

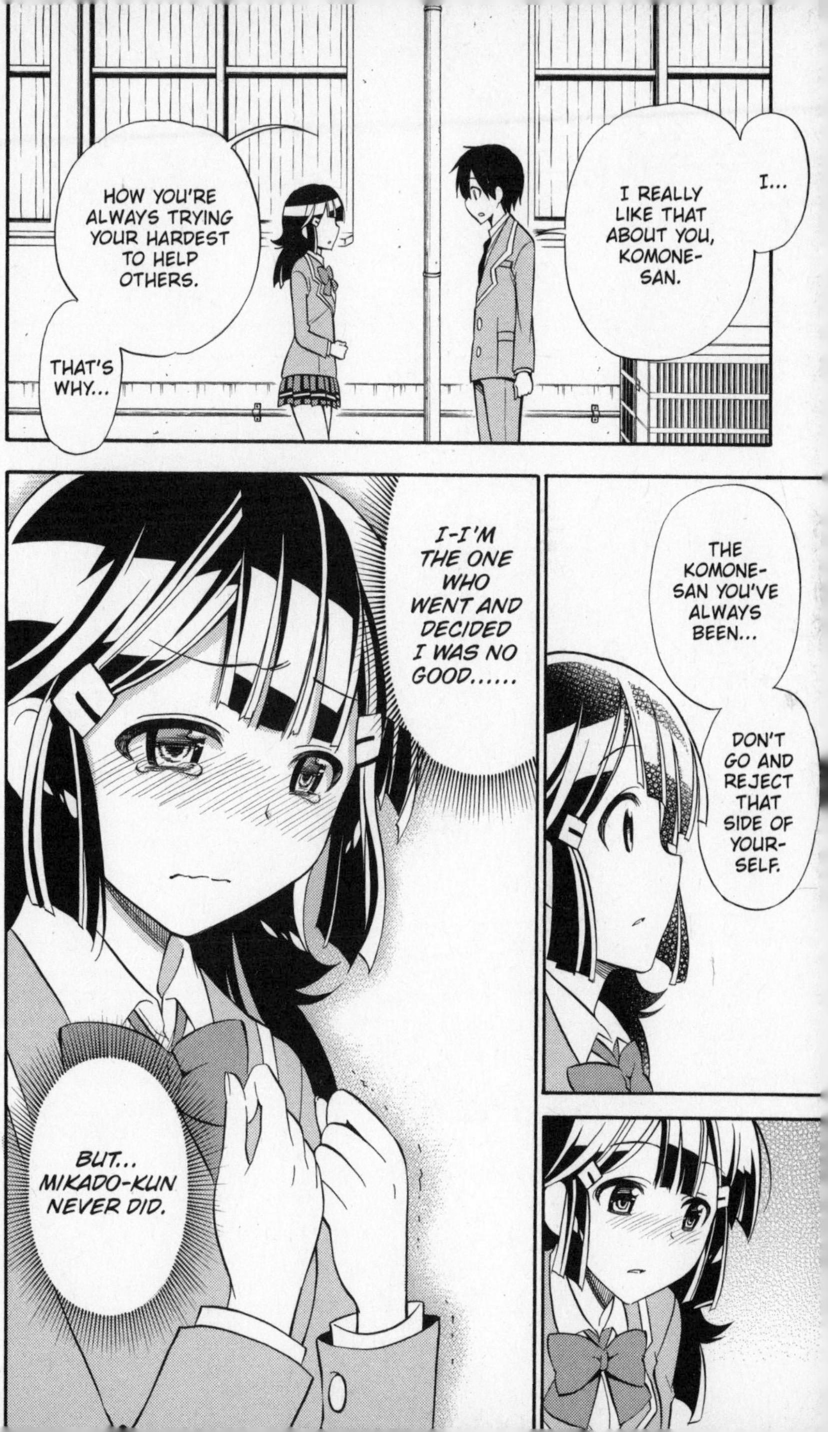
I...
I REALLY LIKE THAT ABOUT YOU, KOMONE-SAN.
HOW YOU'RE ALWAYS TRYING YOUR HARDEST TO HELP OTHERS.
THAT'S WHY...
THE KOMONE-SAN YOU'VE ALWAYS BEEN...
DON'T GO AND REJECT THAT SIDE OF YOUR-SELF.
I-I'M THE ONE WHO WENT AND DECIDED I WAS NO GOOD......
BUT... MIKADO-KUN NEVER DID.

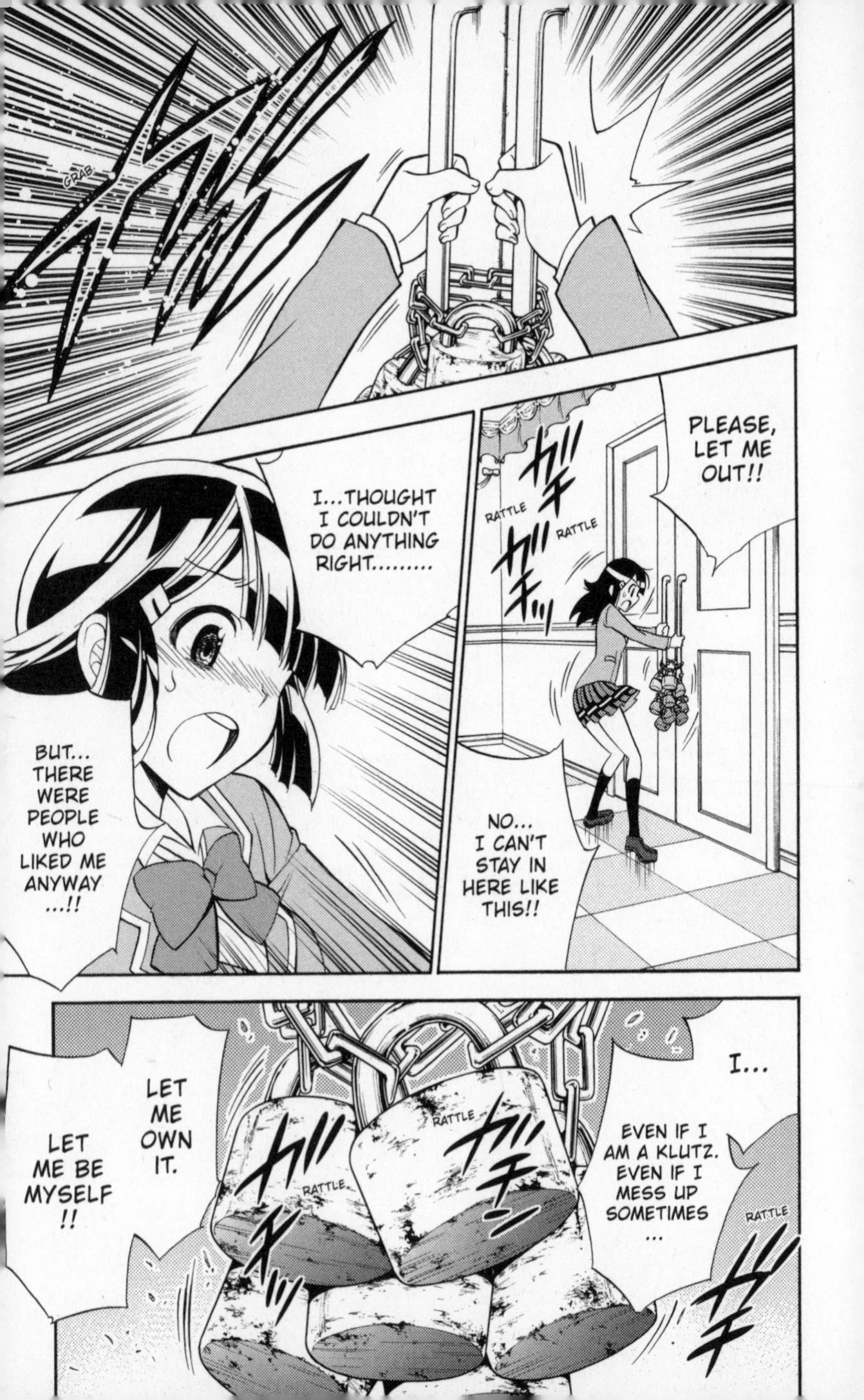
GRAB
PLEASE, LET ME OUT!!
RATTLE
RATTLE
NO... I CAN'T STAY IN HERE LIKE THIS!!
I...THOUGHT I COULDN'T DO ANYTHING RIGHT.........
BUT... THERE WERE PEOPLE WHO LIKED ME ANYWAY ...!!
I...
EVEN IF I AM A KLUTZ. EVEN IF I MESS UP SOMETIMES ...
RATTLE
RATTLE
RATTLE
LET ME OWN IT.
LET ME BE MYSELF !!

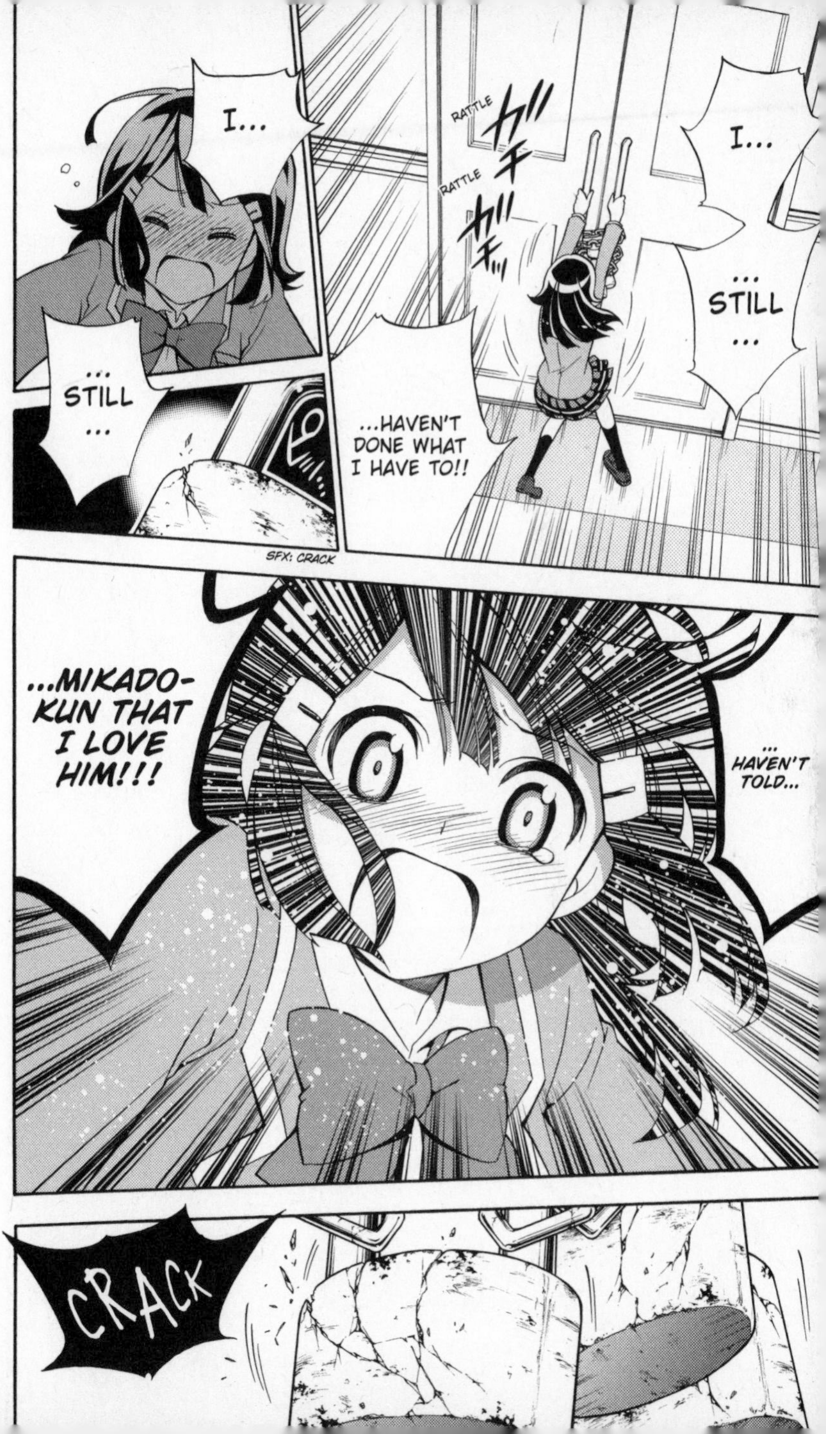
I...
... STILL ...
RATTLE
RATTLE
...HAVEN'T DONE WHAT I HAVE TO!!
I...
... STILL ...
SFX: CRACK
... HAVEN'T TOLD...
...MIKADO-KUN THAT I LOVE HIM!!!
CRACK

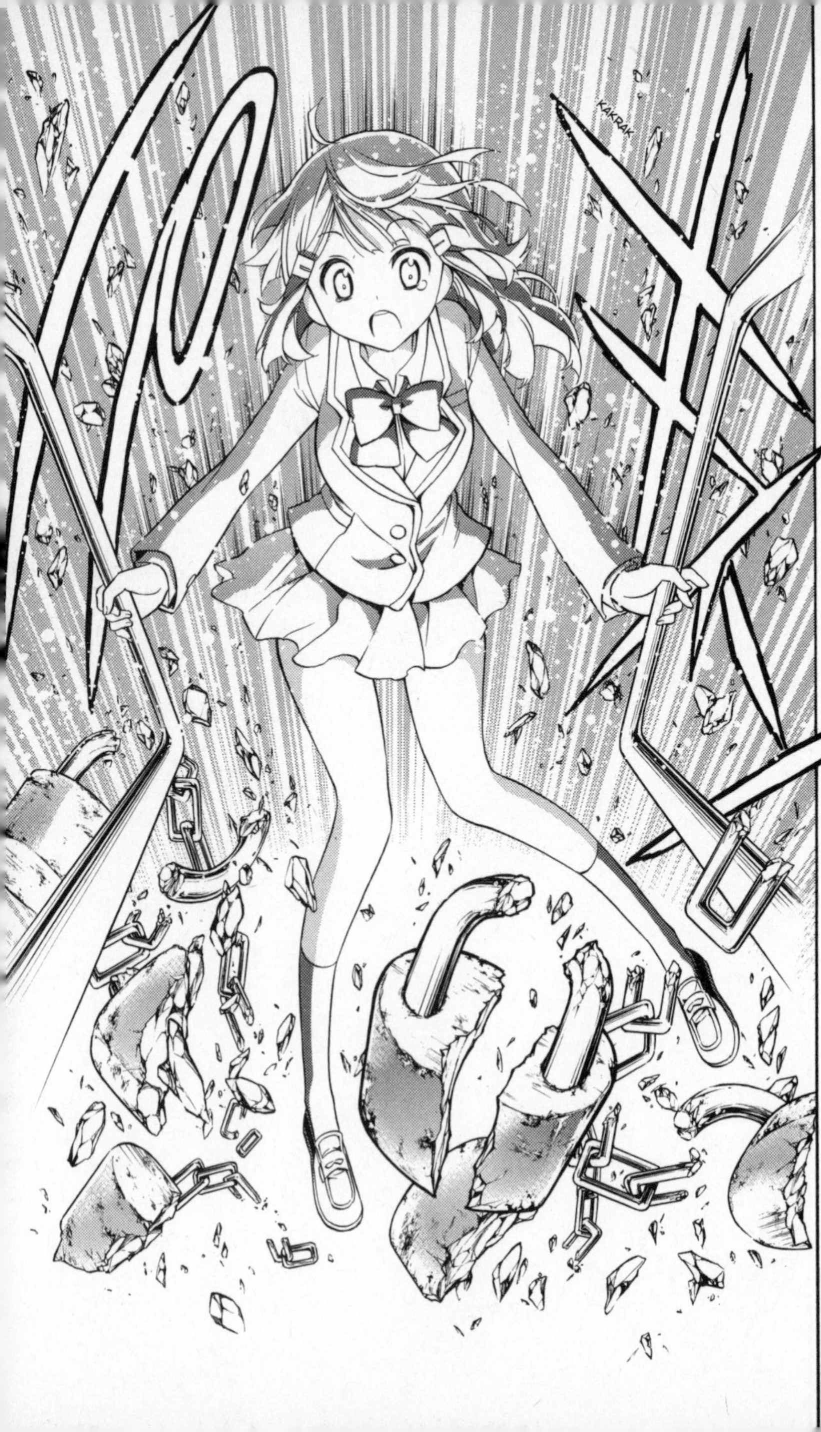
KAKRAK

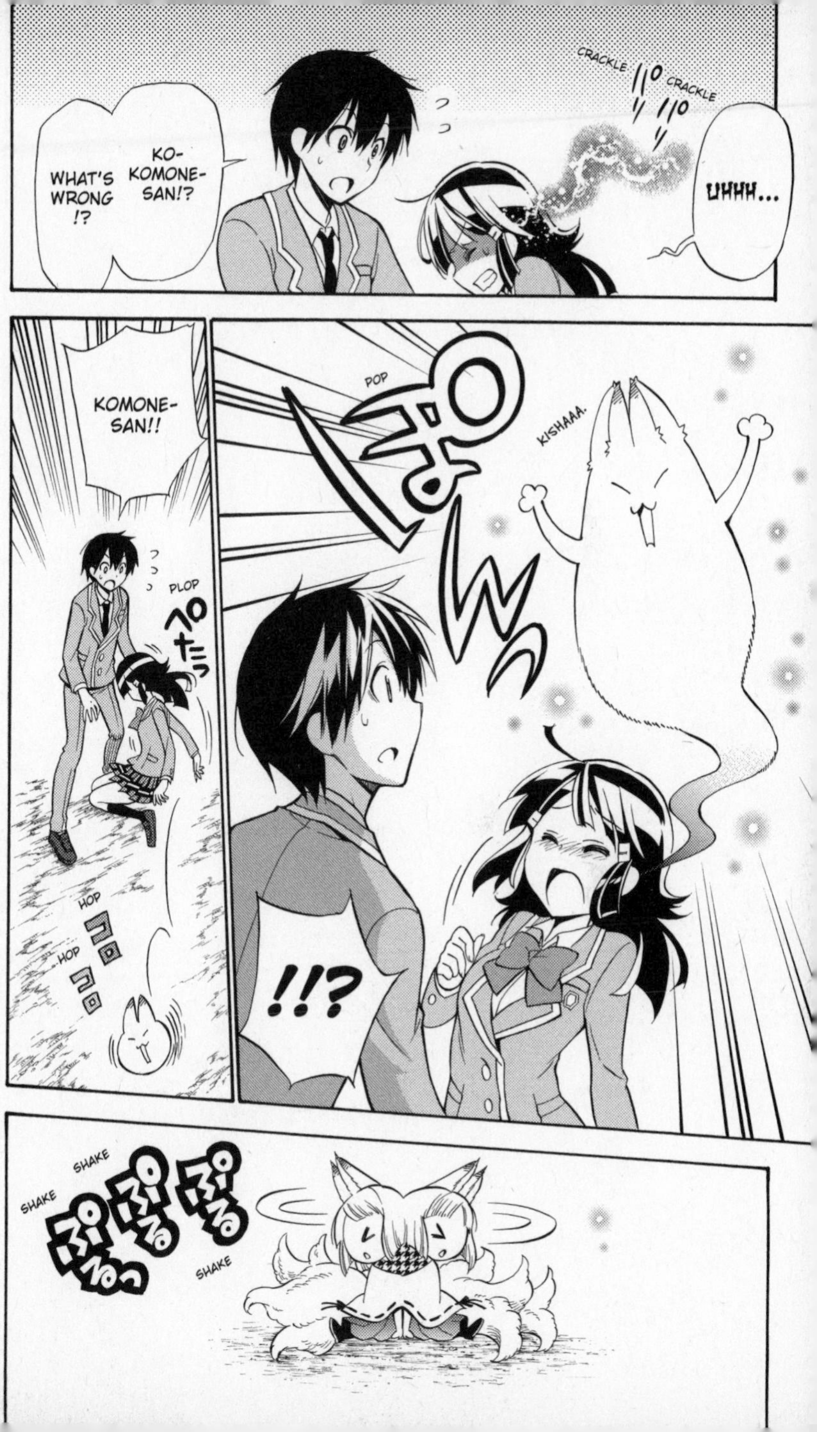
CRACKLE
CRACKLE
UHHH...
KO-KOMONE-SAN!?
WHAT'S WRONG!?
POP
KISHAAA.
!!?
KOMONE-SAN!!
PLOP
HOP
HOP
SHAKE
SHAKE
SHAKE

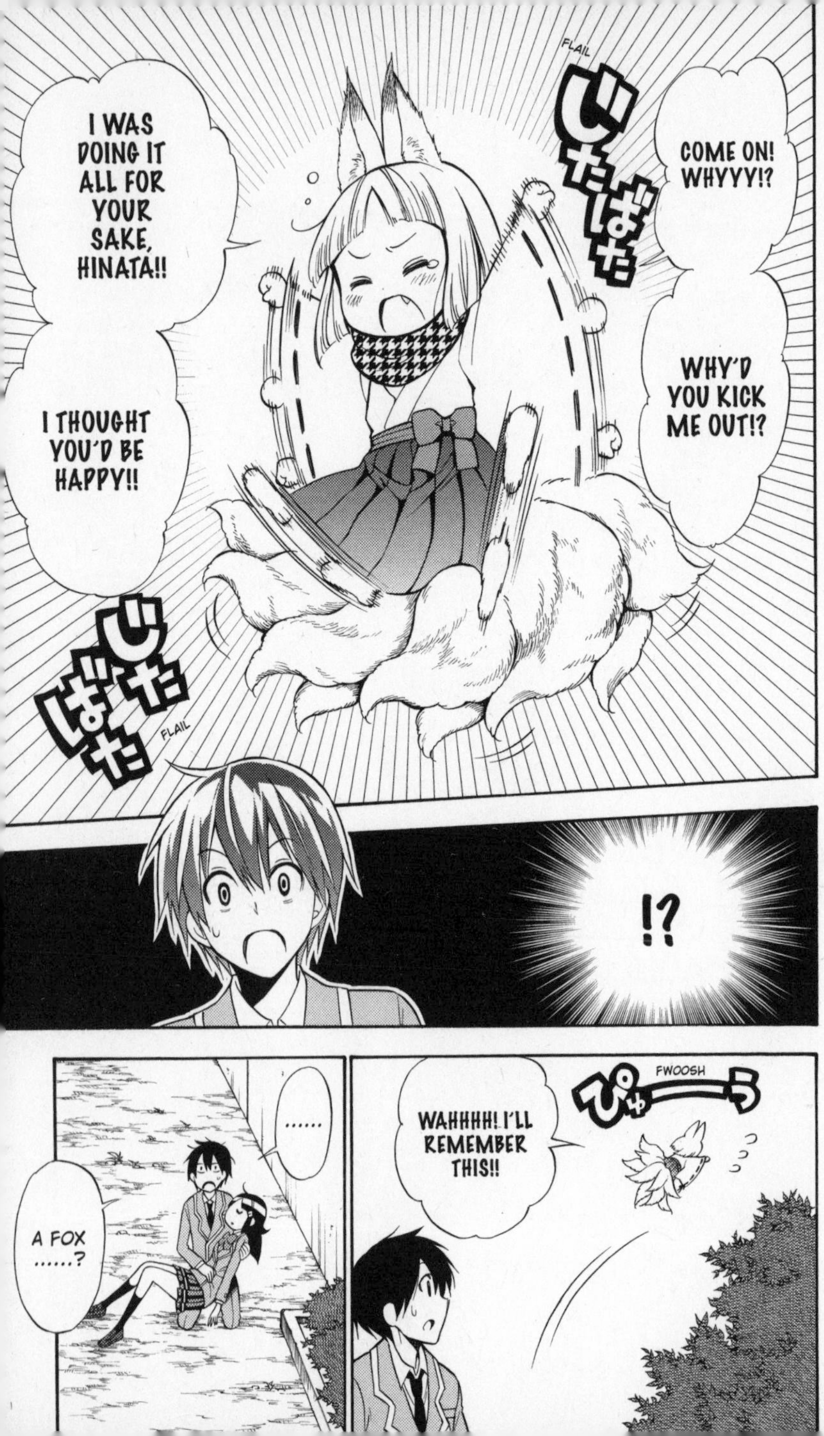
FLAIL
じたばた
COME ON! WHYYY!?
WHY'D YOU KICK ME OUT!?
I WAS DOING IT ALL FOR YOUR SAKE, HINATA!!
I THOUGHT YOU'D BE HAPPY!!
じたばた
FLAIL
!?
ぴゅ〜〜う
FWOOSH
WAHHHH! I'LL REMEMBER THIS!!
......
A FOX ......?

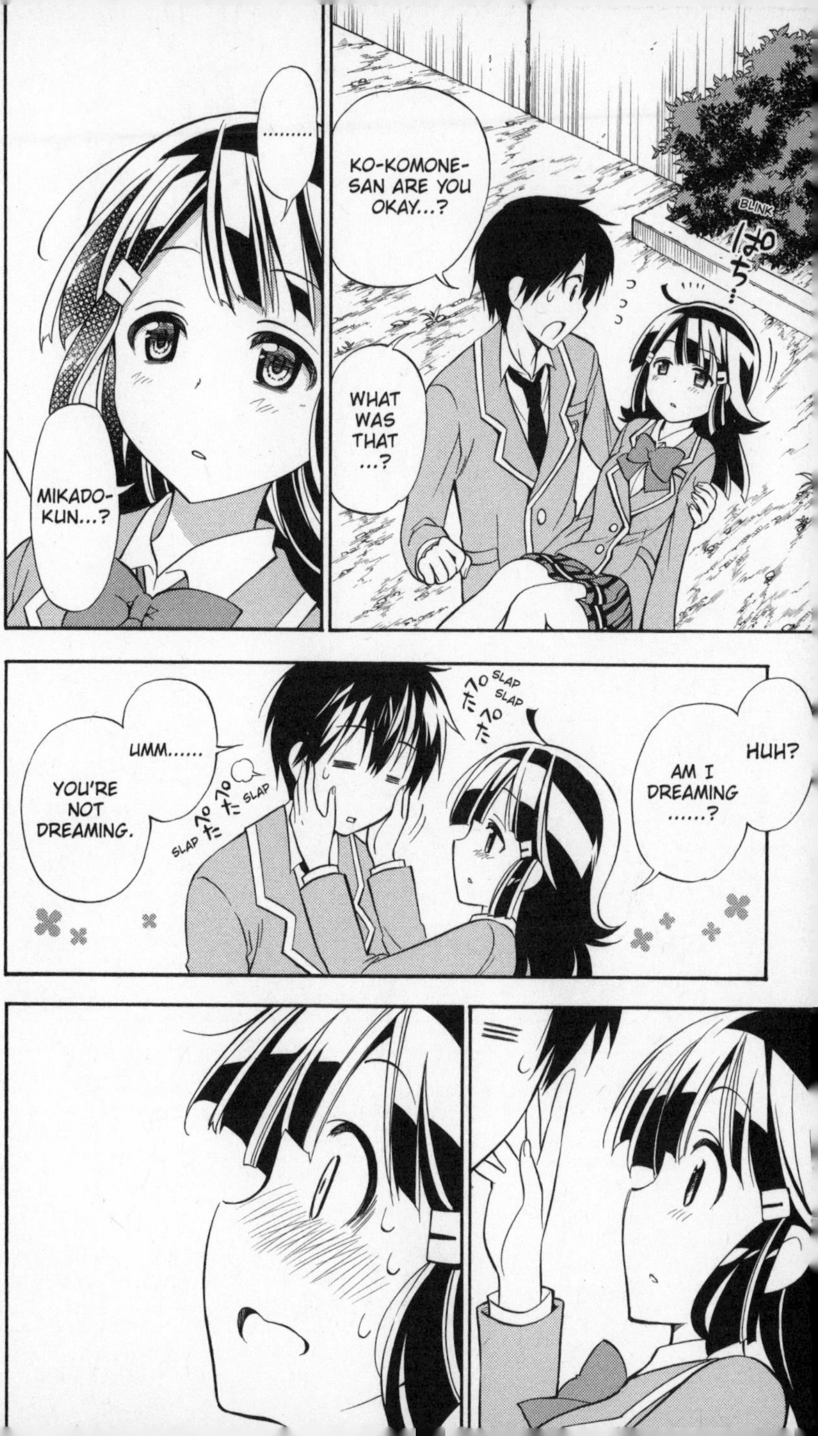
BLINK
ぱち…
KO-KOMONE-SAN ARE YOU OKAY...?
WHAT WAS THAT ...?
....
MIKADO-KUN...?
HUH? AM I DREAMING ......?
ぺたぺた SLAP SLAP
UMM...... YOU'RE NOT DREAMING.
ぺたぺた SLAP SLAP

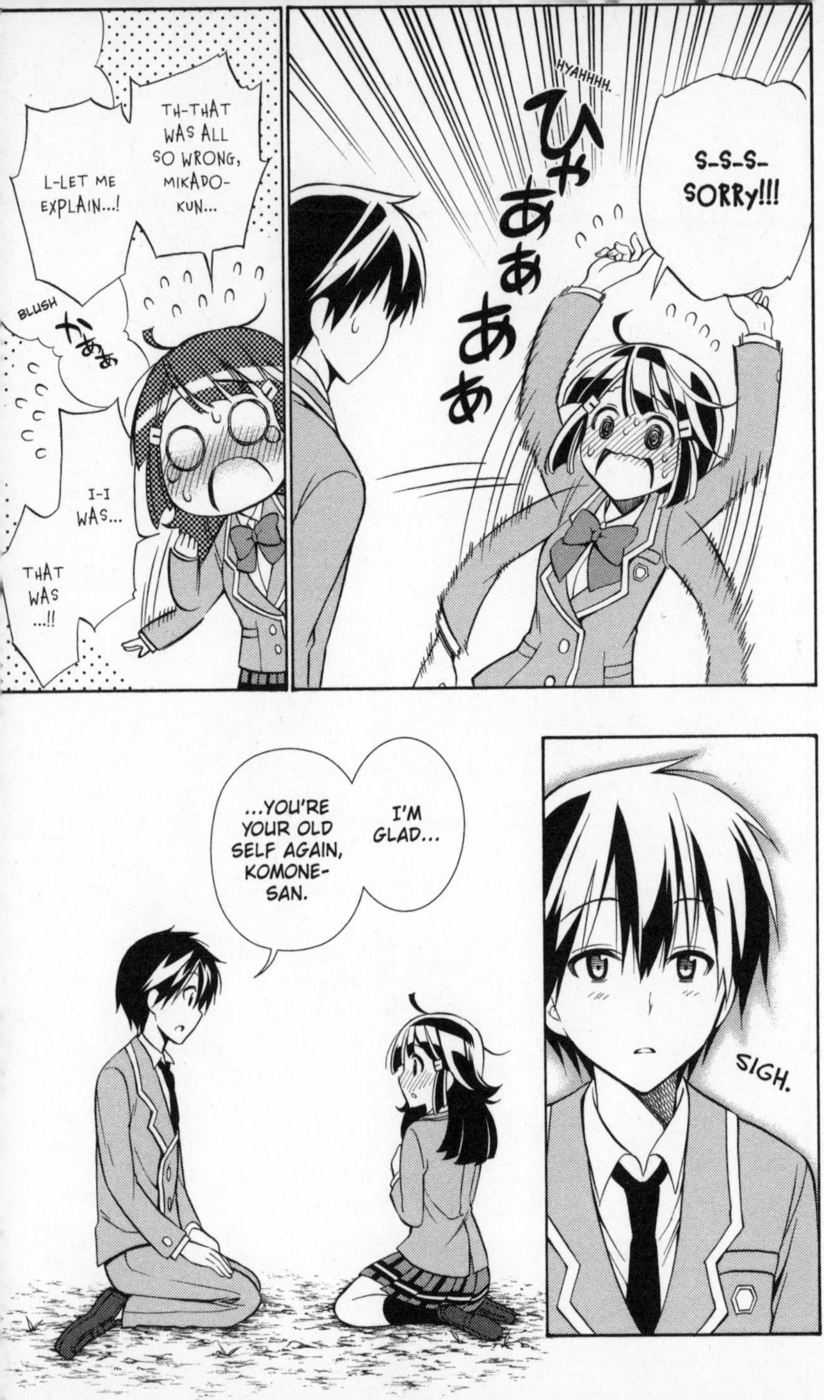
HYAHHHH.
ひゃああああ
S-S-S-SORRY!!!
TH-THAT WAS ALL SO WRONG, MIKADO-KUN...
L-LET ME EXPLAIN...!
BLUSH
かああ
I-I WAS...
THAT WAS ...!!
SIGH.
I'M GLAD...
...YOU'RE YOUR OLD SELF AGAIN, KOMONE-SAN.

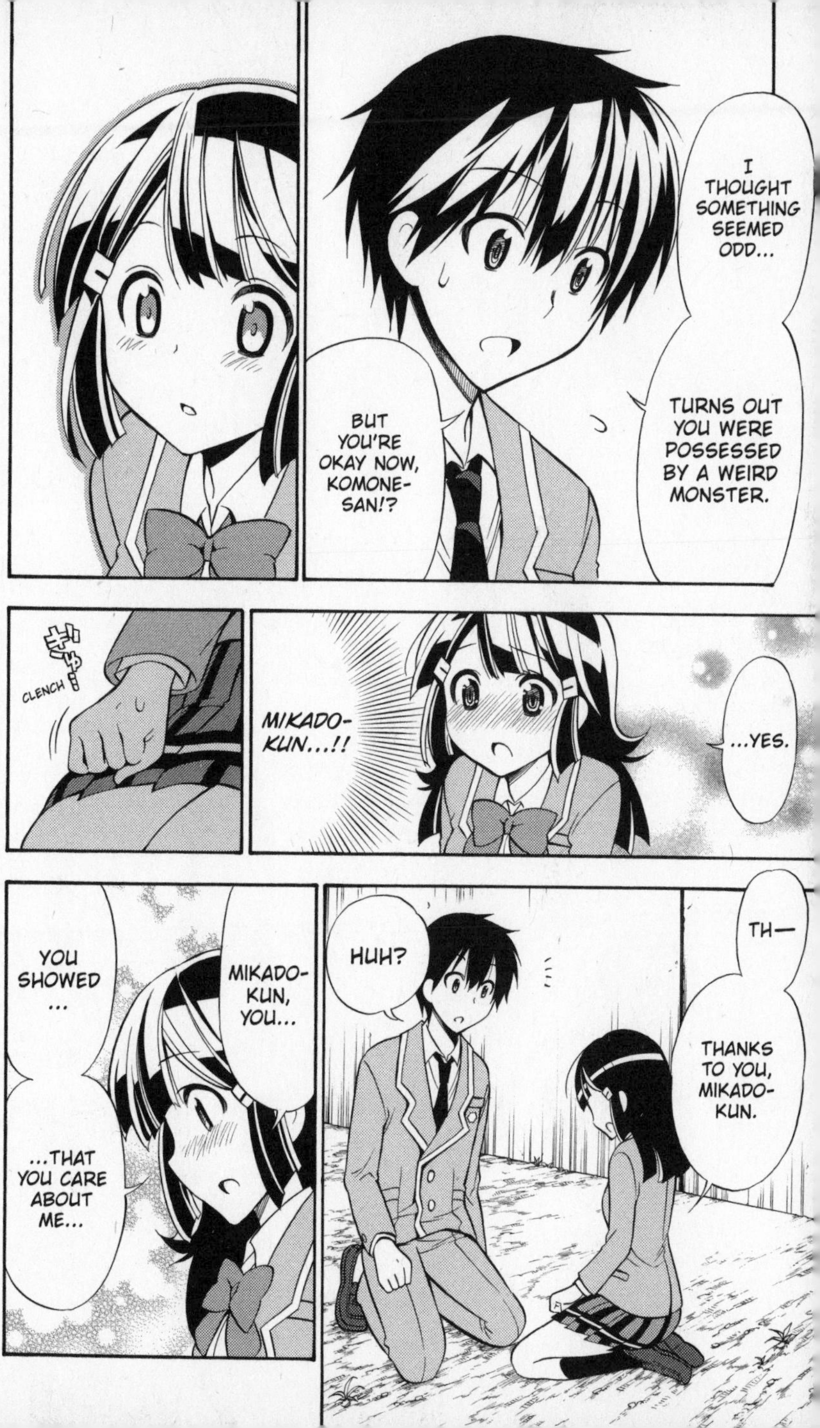
I THOUGHT SOMETHING SEEMED ODD...
TURNS OUT YOU WERE POSSESSED BY A WEIRD MONSTER.
BUT YOU'RE OKAY NOW, KOMONE-SAN!?
...YES.
MIKADO-KUN...!!
CLENCH
TH—
THANKS TO YOU, MIKADO-KUN.
HUH?
MIKADO-KUN, YOU...
YOU SHOWED...
...THAT YOU CARE ABOUT ME...

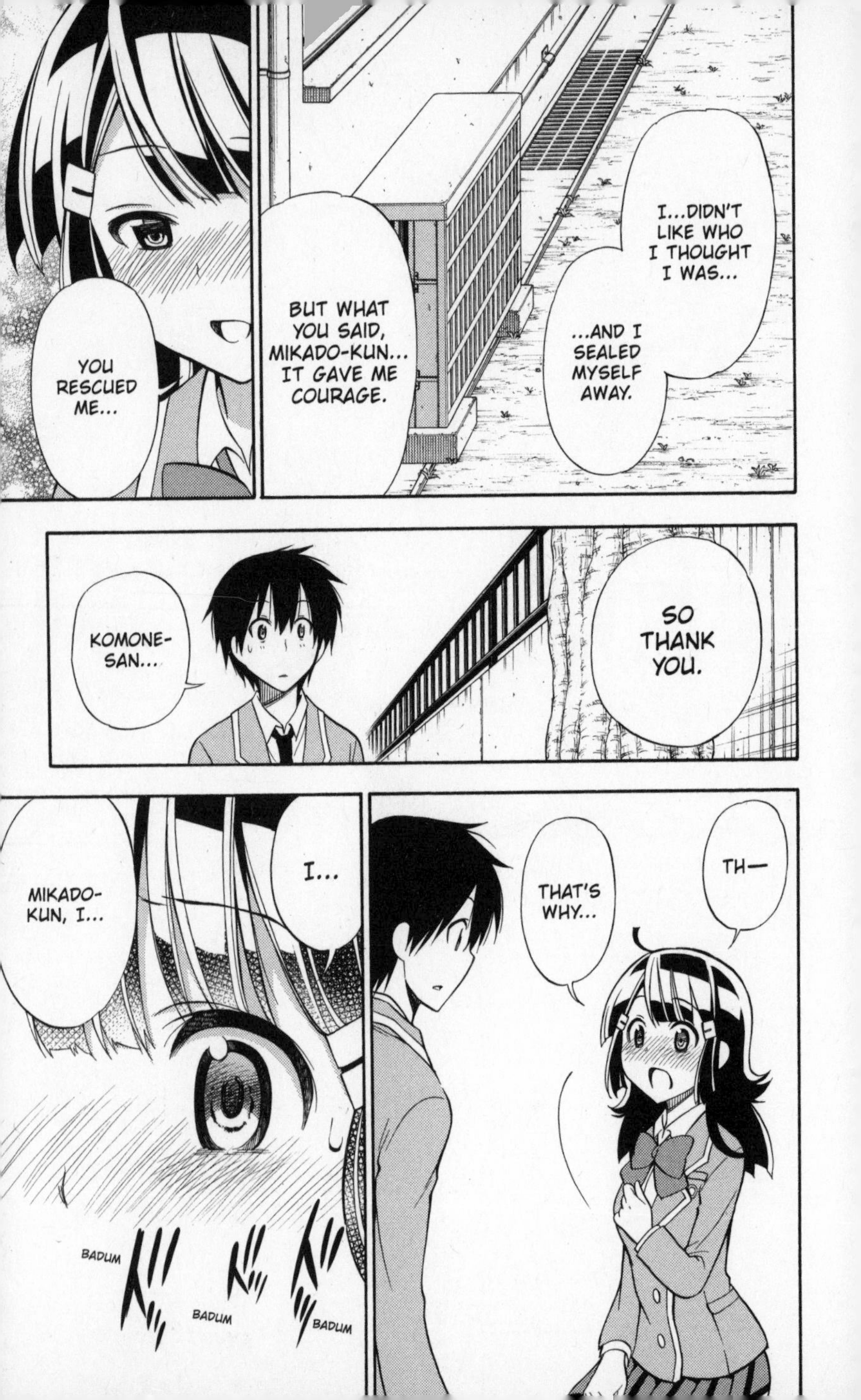
I...DIDN'T LIKE WHO I THOUGHT I WAS...
...AND I SEALED MYSELF AWAY.
BUT WHAT YOU SAID, MIKADO-KUN... IT GAVE ME COURAGE.
YOU RESCUED ME...
SO THANK YOU.
KOMONE-SAN...
TH—
THAT'S WHY...
I...
MIKADO-KUN, I...
BADUM
BADUM
BADUM

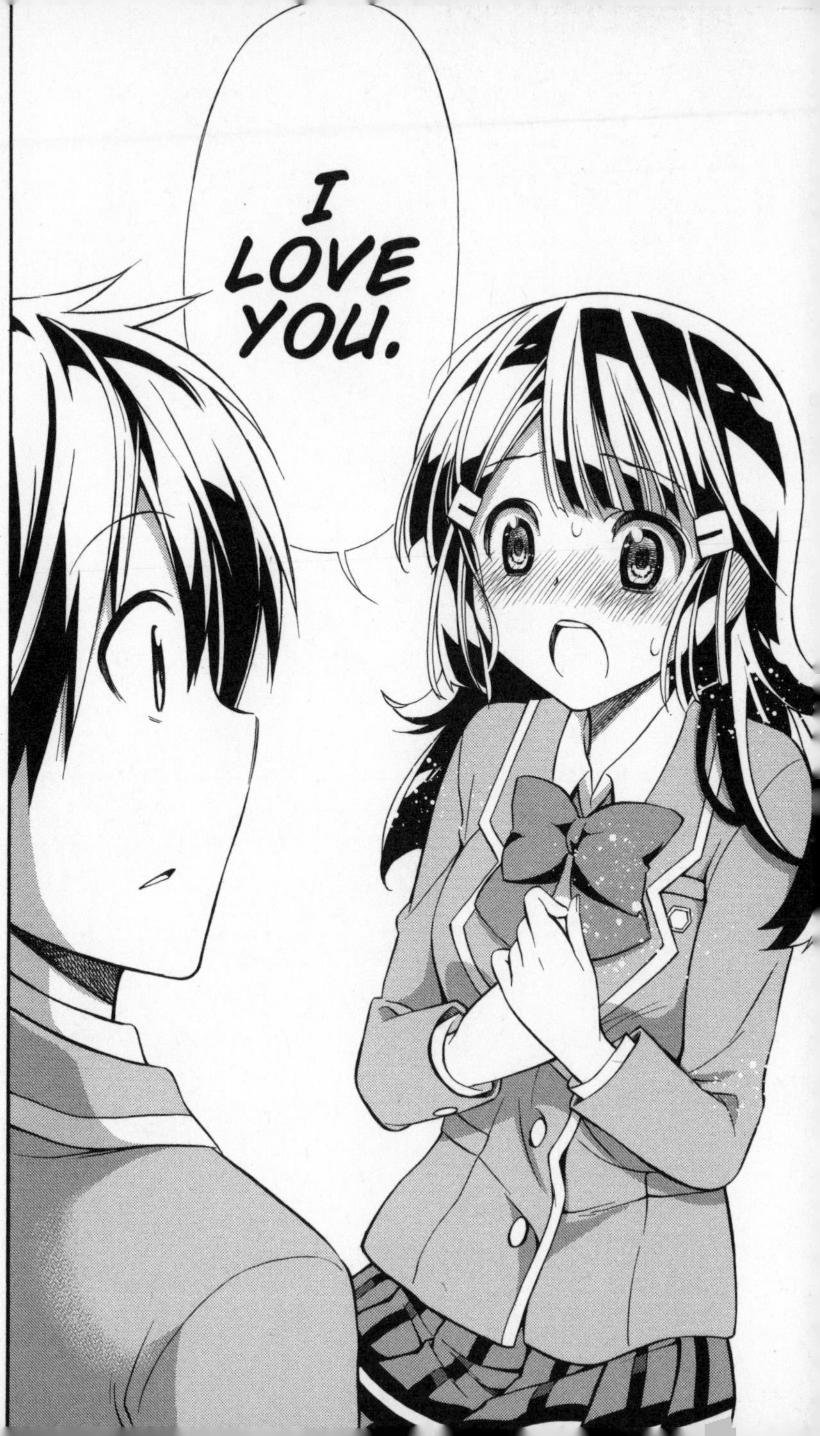
I LOVE YOU.

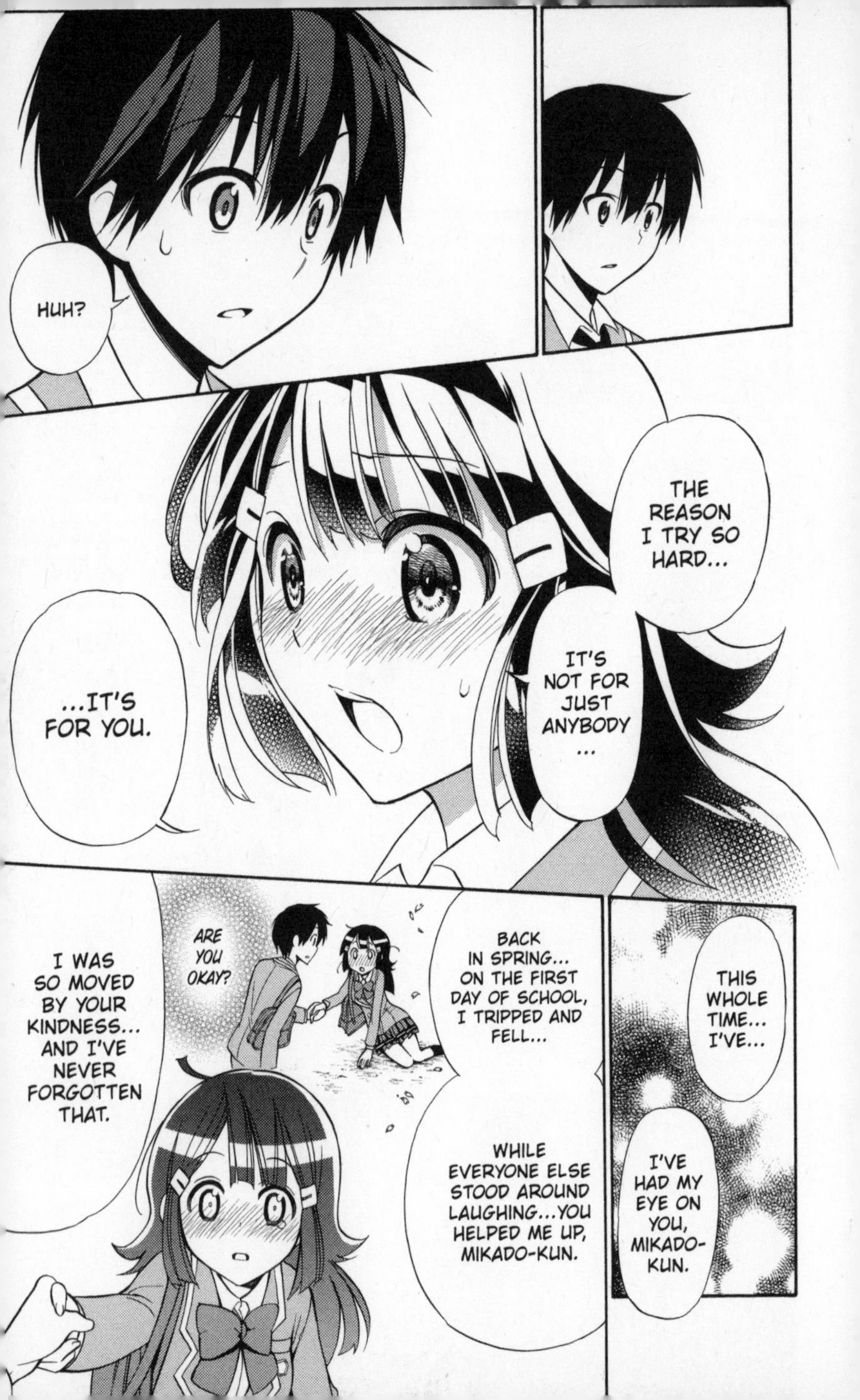
HUH?
THE REASON I TRY SO HARD...
IT'S NOT FOR JUST ANYBODY...
...IT'S FOR YOU.
THIS WHOLE TIME... I'VE...
I'VE HAD MY EYE ON YOU, MIKADO-KUN.
BACK IN SPRING... ON THE FIRST DAY OF SCHOOL, I TRIPPED AND FELL...
ARE YOU OKAY?
WHILE EVERYONE ELSE STOOD AROUND LAUGHING...YOU HELPED ME UP, MIKADO-KUN.
I WAS SO MOVED BY YOUR KINDNESS... AND I'VE NEVER FORGOTTEN THAT.

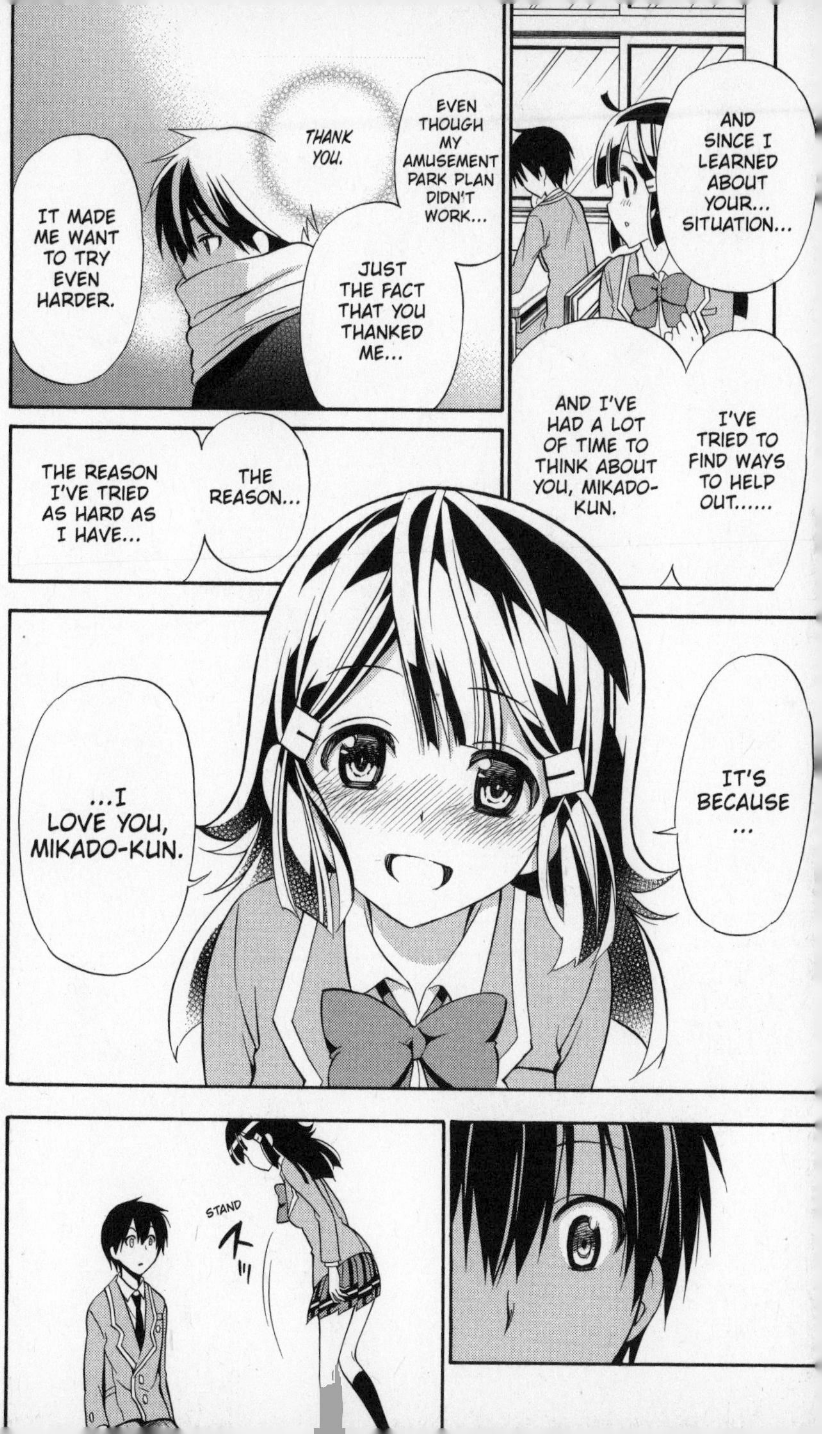
AND SINCE I LEARNED ABOUT YOUR... SITUATION...
I'VE TRIED TO FIND WAYS TO HELP OUT......
AND I'VE HAD A LOT OF TIME TO THINK ABOUT YOU, MIKADO-KUN.
EVEN THOUGH MY AMUSEMENT PARK PLAN DIDN'T WORK...
JUST THE FACT THAT YOU THANKED ME...
THANK YOU.
IT MADE ME WANT TO TRY EVEN HARDER.
THE REASON...
THE REASON I'VE TRIED AS HARD AS I HAVE...
IT'S BECAUSE...
...I LOVE YOU, MIKADO-KUN.
STAND

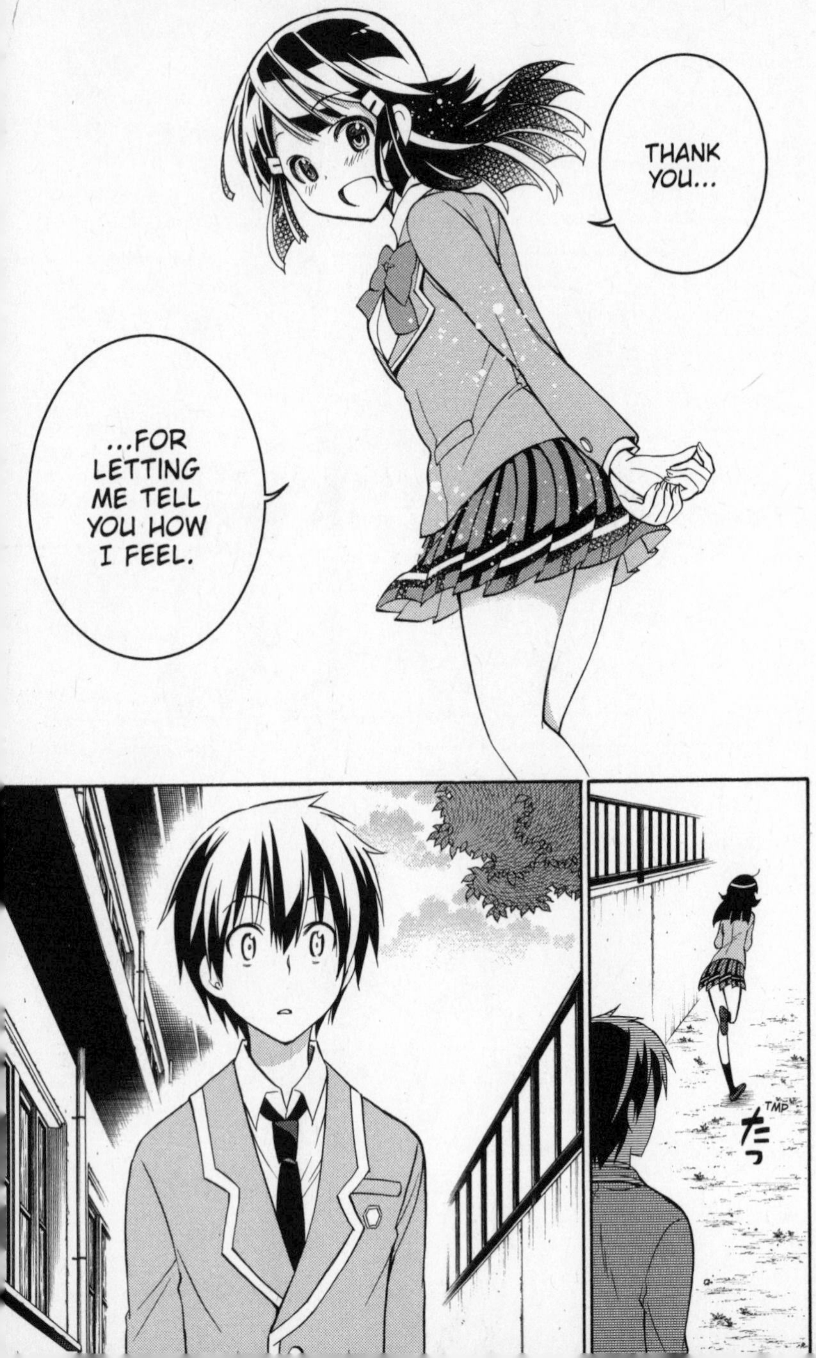
THANK YOU...
...FOR LETTING ME TELL YOU HOW I FEEL.
TMP
たっ

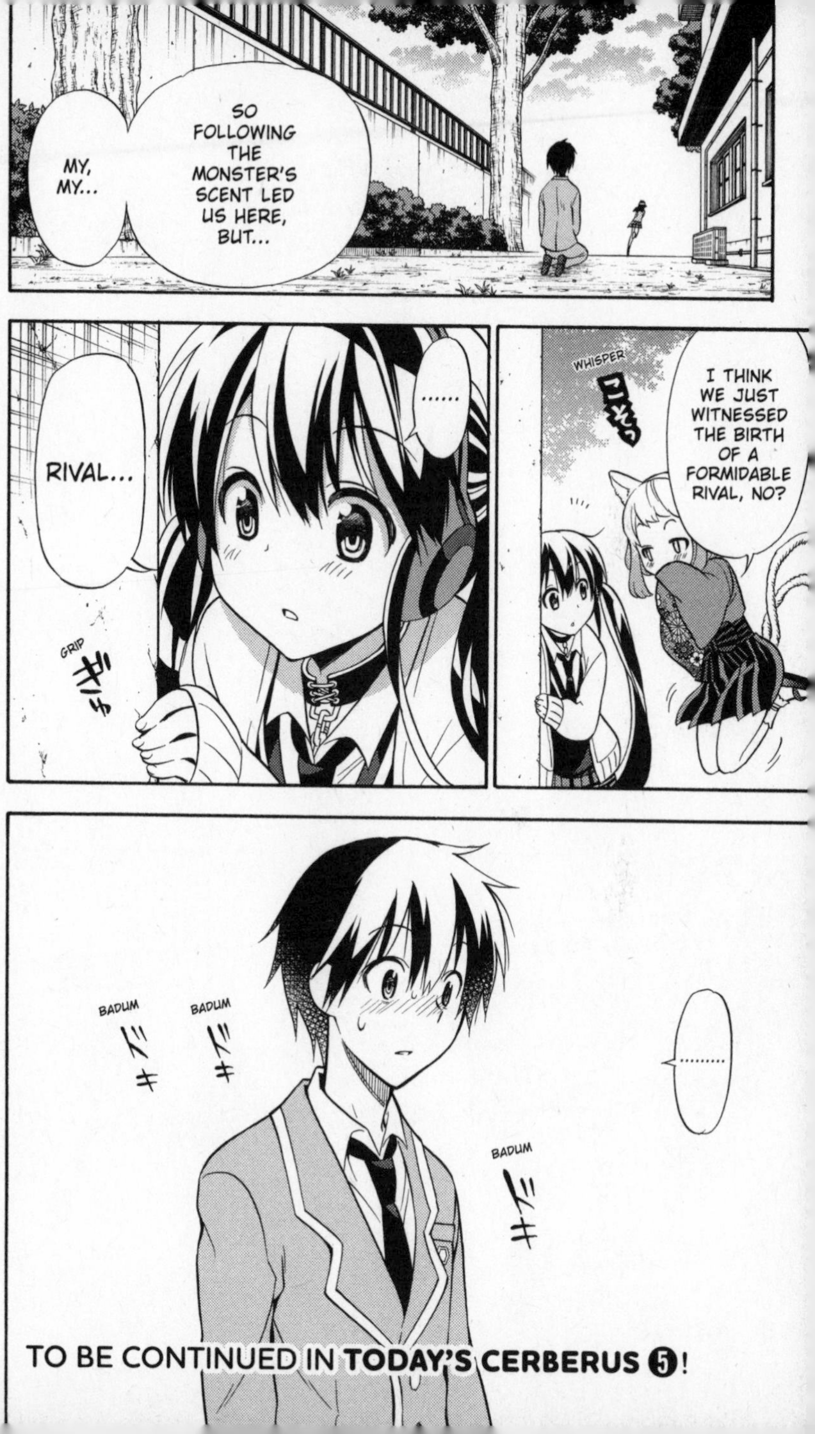
SO FOLLOWING THE MONSTER'S SCENT LED US HERE, BUT...
MY, MY...
WHISPER
I THINK WE JUST WITNESSED THE BIRTH OF A FORMIDABLE RIVAL, NO?
......
RIVAL...
GRIP
....
BADUM
BADUM
BADUM
TO BE CONTINUED IN TODAY'S CERBERUS 5!

TODAY'S CERBERUS -SAN

CHAPTER 15

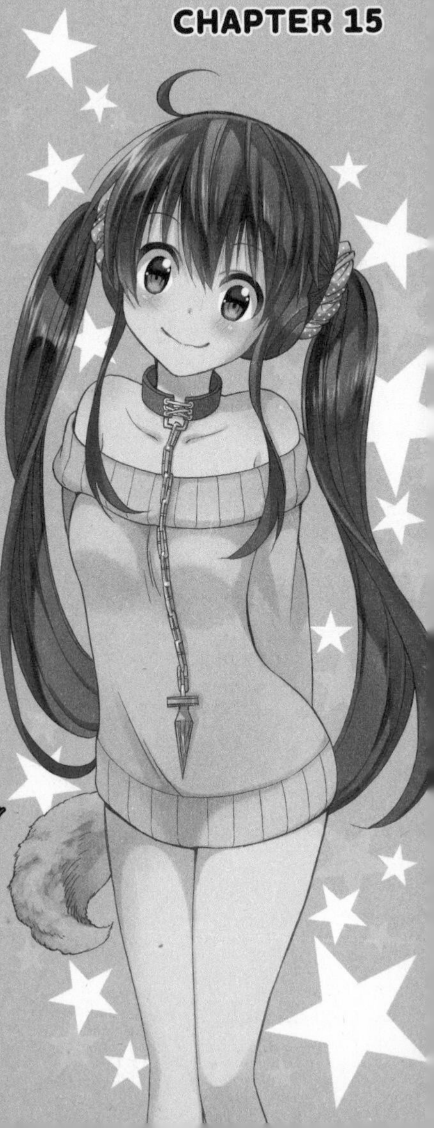

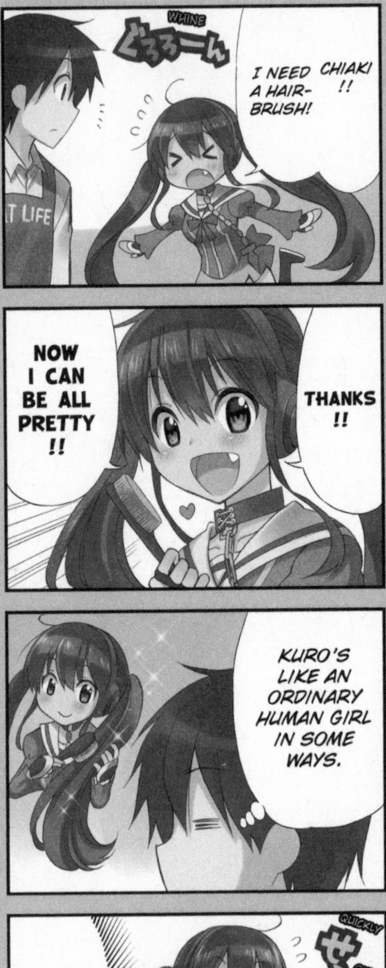

CHIAKI !!
I NEED A HAIR-BRUSH!
WHINE
ぐろろーん
THANKS !!
NOW I CAN BE ALL PRETTY !!
KURO'S LIKE AN ORDINARY HUMAN GIRL IN SOME WAYS.
QUICKLY
せっせっ
QUICKLY
BRUSH
もさもさ
BRUSH
BRUSH-ING HER TAIL!!?

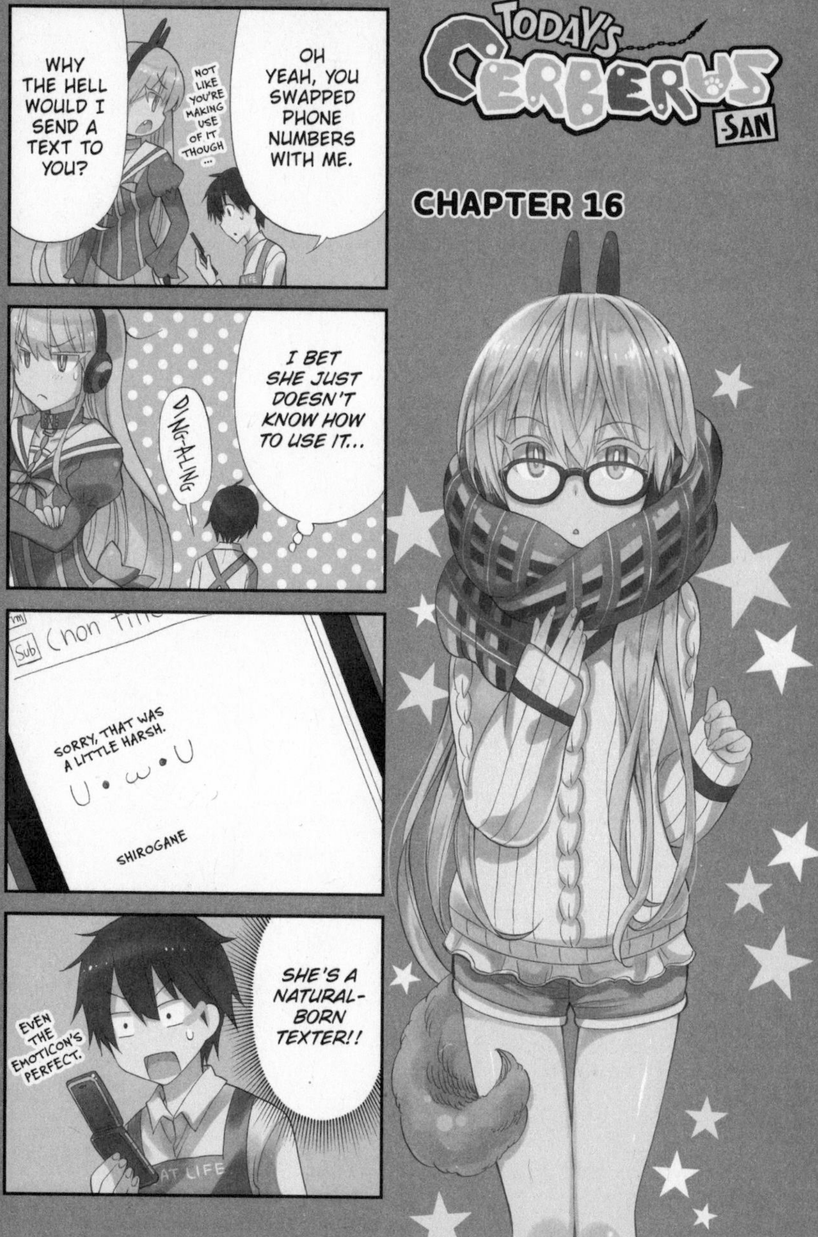
TODAY'S CERBERUS -SAN
CHAPTER 16
OH YEAH, YOU SWAPPED PHONE NUMBERS WITH ME.
NOT LIKE YOU'RE MAKING USE OF IT THOUGH...
WHY THE HELL WOULD I SEND A TEXT TO YOU?
I BET SHE JUST DOESN'T KNOW HOW TO USE IT...
DING-A-LING
SORRY, THAT WAS A LITTLE HARSH.
U•ω•U
SHIROGANE
SHE'S A NATURAL-BORN TEXTER!!
EVEN THE EMOTICON'S PERFECT.

TODAY'S CERBERUS-SAN

CHAPTER 17

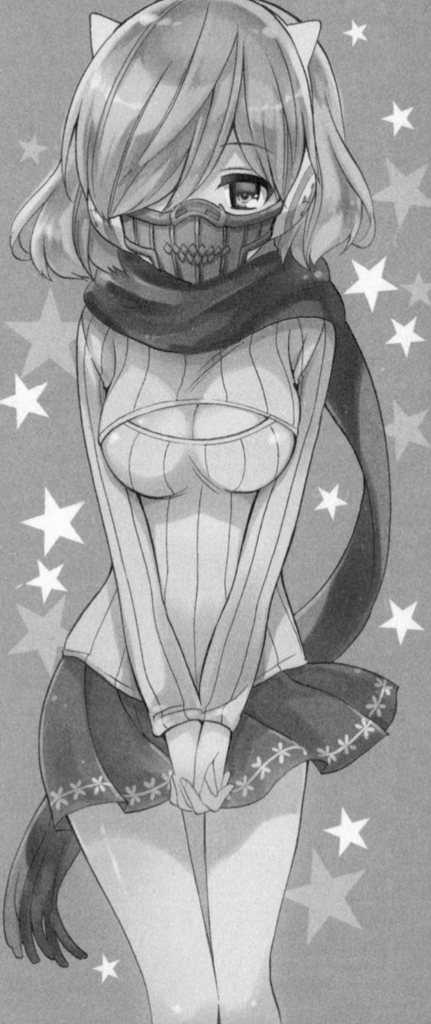

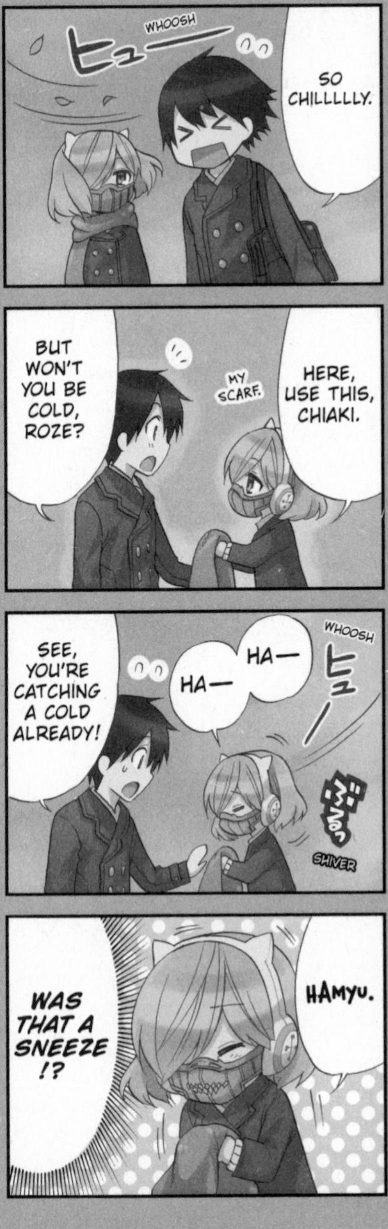
SO CHILLLLLY.
ヒュー
WHOOSH
HERE, USE THIS, CHIAKI.
MY SCARF.
BUT WON'T YOU BE COLD, ROZE?
ヒュー
WHOOSH
HA—
HA—
SHIVER
SEE, YOU'RE CATCHING A COLD ALREADY!
HAMYU.
WAS THAT A SNEEZE!?

TODAY'S CERBERUS-SAN

CHAPTER 18

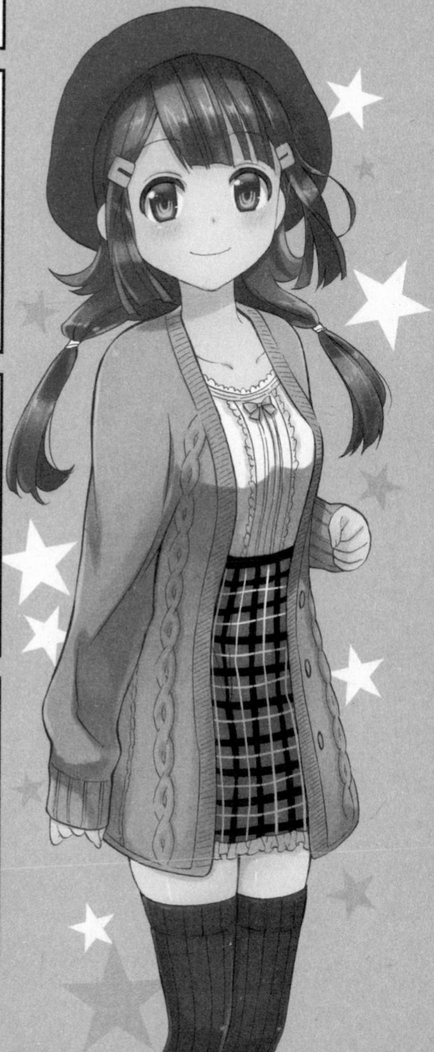

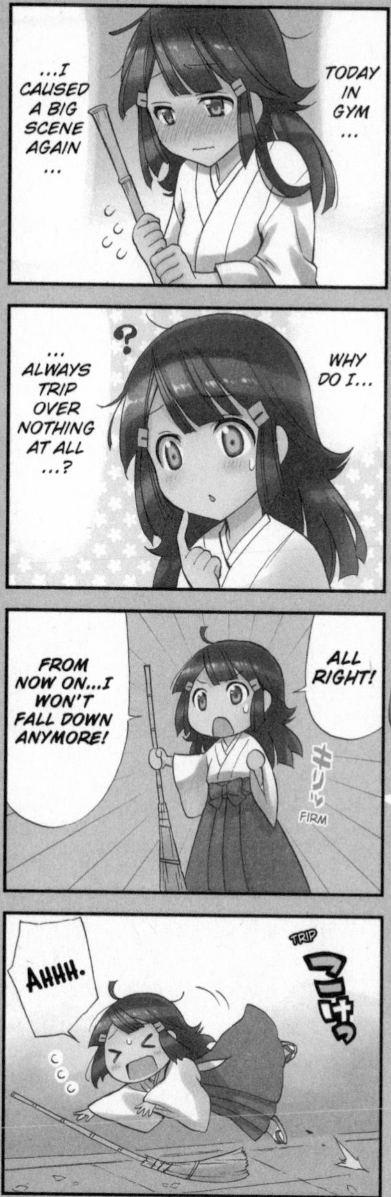
TODAY IN GYM ...
...I CAUSED A BIG SCENE AGAIN ...
WHY DO I...
... ALWAYS TRIP OVER NOTHING AT ALL ...?
ALL RIGHT!
キリッ
FIRM
FROM NOW ON...I WON'T FALL DOWN ANYMORE!
TRIP
AHHH.

TODAY'S CERBERUS -SAN

CHAPTER 19

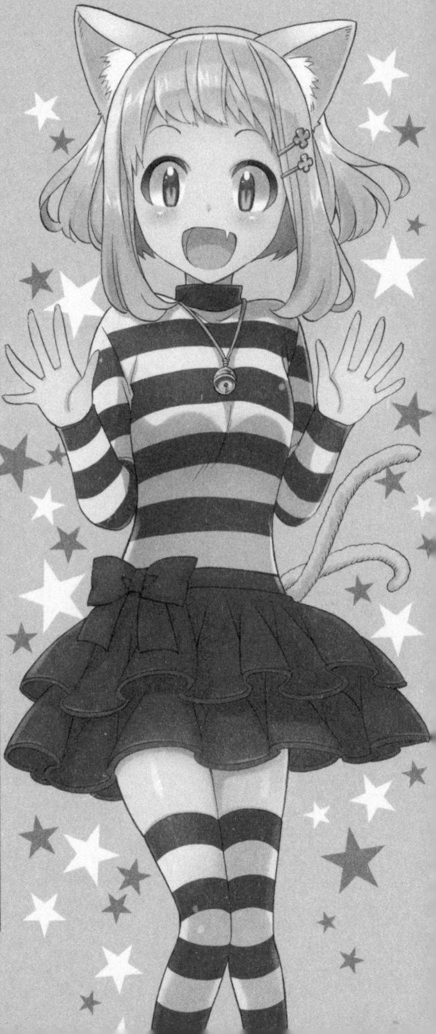

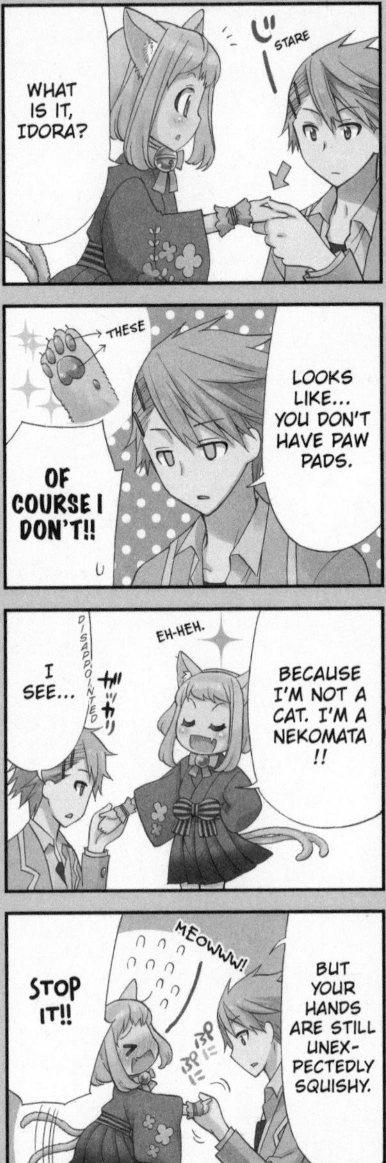
STARE
WHAT IS IT, IDORA?
LOOKS LIKE... YOU DON'T HAVE PAW PADS.
THESE
OF COURSE I DON'T!!
BECAUSE I'M NOT A CAT. I'M A NEKOMATA!!
EH-HEH.
DISAPPOINTED
I SEE...
BUT YOUR HANDS ARE STILL UNEX-PECTEDLY SQUISHY.
MEOWWW!
STOP IT!!

SFX: SQUISH SQUISH

FOOTPRINTS

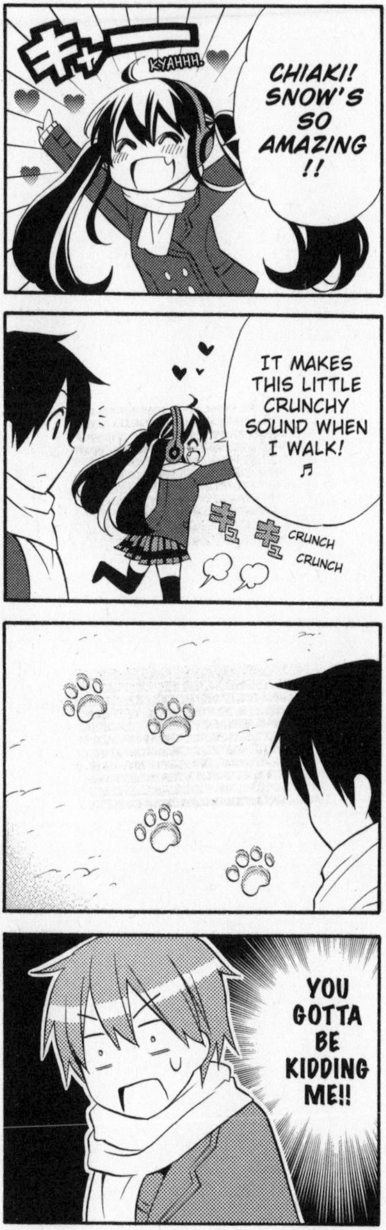
キャー
KYAHHH
CHIAKI! SNOW'S SO AMAZING!!
IT MAKES THIS LITTLE CRUNCHY SOUND WHEN I WALK! ♪
キュ キュ
CRUNCH CRUNCH
YOU GOTTA BE KIDDING ME!!

TABOO

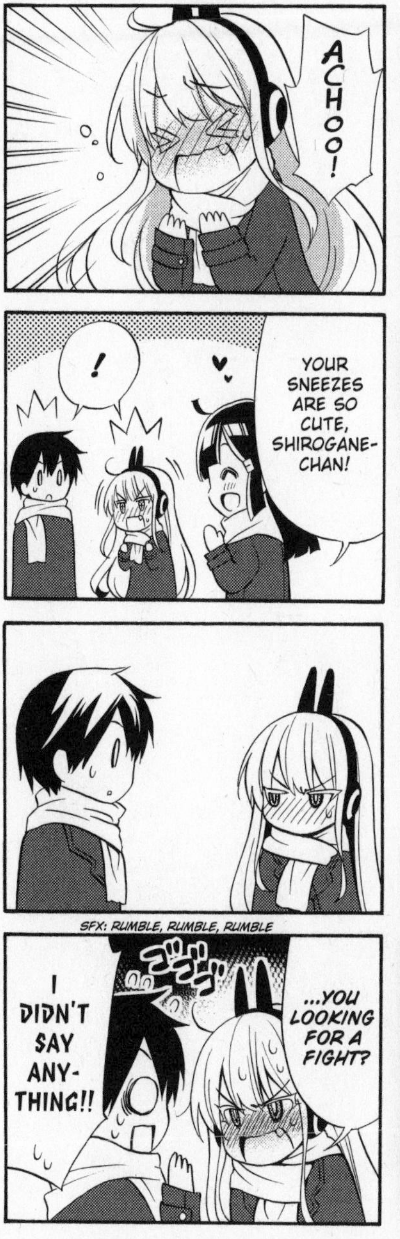
ACHOO!
!
YOUR SNEEZES ARE SO CUTE, SHIROGANE-CHAN!
SFX: RUMBLE, RUMBLE, RUMBLE
ゴゴゴ
...YOU LOOKING FOR A FIGHT?
I DIDN'T SAY ANY-THING!!

WITH ALL MY LOVE

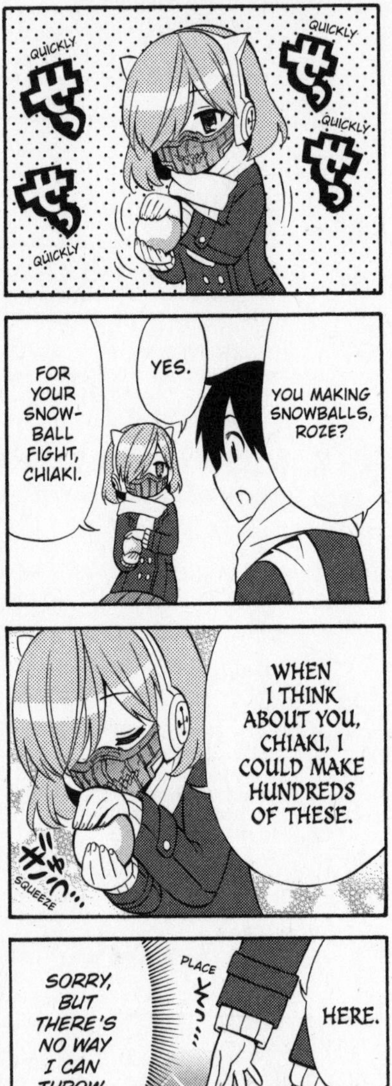

せっ QUICKLY
せっ QUICKLY
せっ QUICKLY
せっ QUICKLY
YOU MAKING SNOWBALLS, ROZE?
YES.
FOR YOUR SNOW-BALL FIGHT, CHIAKI.
WHEN I THINK ABOUT YOU, CHIAKI, I COULD MAKE HUNDREDS OF THESE.
ぎゅっ… SQUEEZE
HERE.
PLACE
SORRY, BUT THERE'S NO WAY I CAN THROW THAT.

FINALLY, A KOTATSU

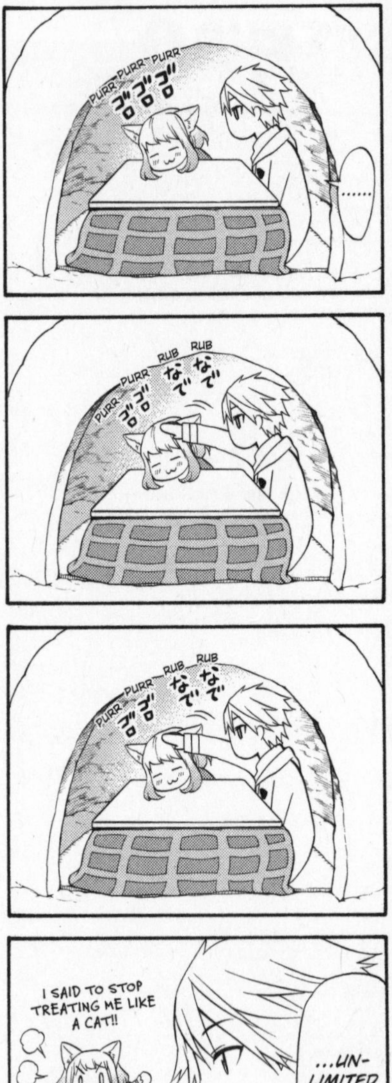

ゴロゴロ PURR PURR PURR
......
ゴロゴロ PURR PURR
なでなで RUB RUB
ゴロゴロ PURR PURR
なでなで RUB RUB
...UN-LIMITED PETTING FOR ME.
I SAID TO STOP TREATING ME LIKE A CAT!!
いつも↑ USUALLY

★STAFF-> MORI · GARAKUTA IMAYAMA · YUU JUNA · YONEDA ★DIGITAL-> WATARI NI FUNE ★COLOR/LAYER SPLIT-> TSUBASA FUKUCHI

TODAY'S CERBEROS 4

Ato Sakurai

Translation: Caleb Cook • **Lettering: Bianca Pistillo**

TODAY'S KERBEROS Vol. 4 ©2015 Ato Sakurai/SQUARE ENIX CO., LTD. First published in Japan in 2015 by SQUARE ENIX CO., LTD. English translation rights arranged with SQUARE ENIX CO., LTD. and Yen Press, LLC through Tuttle-Mori Agency, Inc.

English translation ©2015 by SQUARE ENIX CO., LTD.

Yen Press
1290 Avenue of the Americas
New York, NY 10104

Visit us at yenpress.com
facebook.com/yenpress
twitter.com/yenpress
yenpress.tumblr.com
instagram.com/yenpress

First Yen Press Print Edition: June 2017
Originally published as an ebook in August 2015 by Yen Press.

Yen Press is an imprint of Yen Press, LLC.
The Yen Press name and logo are trademarks of Yen Press, LLC.

The publisher is not responsible for websites (or their content) that are not owned by the publisher.

Library of Congress Control Number: 2016946072

ISBN: 978-0-316-43573-4 (paperback)

10 9 8 7 6 5 4 3

WOR

Printed in the United States of America